Voices and Viols in England, 1600-1650
The Sources and the Music

Studies in Musicology, No. 55

George Buelow, Series Editor

Professor of Musicology
Indiana University

Other Titles in This Series

Voices and Viols in England, 1600-1650
The Sources and the Music

by
Craig Monson

UMI RESEARCH PRESS
Ann Arbor, Michigan.

Produced and distributed by
UMI Research Press
an imprint of
University Microfilms International
Ann Arbor, Michigan 48106

Library of Congress Cataloging in Publication Data

Monson, Craig (Craig A.)
Voices and viols in England, 1600-1650.

(Studies in musicology ; no. 55)
"A revision of the author's thesis, University of
California, Berkeley, 1974."–T.p. verso.
Bibliography: p.
Includes index.
1. Music–England–History and criticism. 2. Music–
History and criticism–17th century. 3. Music–Manu-
scripts. I. Title. II. Series.

ML286.2.M65 1982   784.3'00942   82-1857
ISBN 0-8357-1302-4   AACR2

Contents

List of Plates

List of Manuscript Inventories

List of Abbreviations

Byrd *CW*   *The Collected Works of William Byrd*

Byrd *Ed*   *The Byrd Edition*

CN1560   John Day, *Certaine Notes* (1560)

CS1575   William Byrd and Thomas Tallis, *Cantiones Sacrae* (1575)

CS1589   William Byrd, *Cantiones Sacrae* (1589)

CS1591   William Byrd, *Cantiones Sacrae* (1591)

DNB   *The Dictionary of National Biography*

EECM   *Early English Church Music*

EM   *The English Madrigalists*

EMS   *The English Madrigal School*

EMu   *Early Music*

*Gr*1607   William Byrd, *Gradualia* (1607)

Grove 5   *Grove's Dictionary of Music and Musicians,* fifth edition

Grove 6   *The New Grove Dictionary of Music and Musicians,* sixth edition

*IM*1590   *Italian Madrigals Englished*

JAMS	*The Journal of the American Musicological Society*
MB	*Musica Britannica*
MD	*Musica Disciplina*
MGG	*Die Musik in Geschichte und Gegenwart*
ML	*Music and Letters*
MQ	*Musical Quarterly*
MT	*Musical Times*
MT1588	*Musica Transalpina* (1588)
MT1597	*Musica Transalpina* (1597)
NOHM	*New Oxford History of Music*
PRMA	*The Proceedings of the Royal Musical Association*
SIMG	*Sammelbände der Internationalen Musikgesellschaft*
TCM	*Tudor Church Music*
cs	consort song
cd	consort duet
ct	consort trio
f	full
v	verse
44	Christ Church MS 44
56	Christ Church MSS 56-60
61	Christ Church MSS 61-66

67	Christ Church MS 67
684	Royal College of Music MS 684
807	Tenbury MSS 807-811
1162	Tenbury MSS 1162-1167
4109	Brussels MS 11. 4109
4180	Drexel MSS 4180-4185
17786	B.L. Add. MSS 17786-17791
17792	B.L. Add. MSS 17792-17796
17797	B.L. Add. MS 17797
29366	B.L. Add. MSS 29366-29368
29372	B.L. Add. MSS 29372-29377
29427	B.L. Add. MS 29427
37402	B.L. Add. MSS 37402-37406
D212	Bodleian MSS Mus. Sch. D 212-216
F1	Bodleian MSS Mus. F1-6
F7	Bodleian MSS Mus. F7-10
F11	Bodleian MSS Mus. F11-15
F16	Bodleian MSS Mus. F16-19
F20	Bodleian MSS Mus. F20-24
F25	Bodleian MSS Mus. F25-28

Preface

Seven years have passed since the original version of this study was completed. Subsequent scholarly work, particularly in matters of scribal concordances, has added significantly to our knowledge of the sources. This information has been incorporated into the present text, necessitating a reassessment of the probable date and provenance of some manuscripts, and of their interrelationships. During these years, scholars have generally been more inclined to study the manuscripts than to confront the music they contain. The musical discussion in the present volume is therefore largely unchanged, except insofar as it incorporates my own subsequent re-examination of the music.

The greater portion of this study is given over to a discussion of the genesis of some two dozen sets of manuscripts. Hence, their inventories are central to the argument, whether for what they reveal about the process of compilation or for what they may suggest about the musical taste of the time. Since the reader must refer to them constantly, the catalogues of these sources have been made an integral part of the discussion, rather than grouped together in an appendix. Where possible, original pagination, foliation, and numbering of individual pieces have been retained in the inventories, since they reflect more closely the intentions of the seventeenth-century scribe than do the annotations of nineteenth- and twentieth-century librarians.

Because this is primarily a study of the verse idiom, titles of works for voices and viols are printed in italics in the manuscript catalogues, to make them more easily recognizable. In addition, the idiom of all vocal works, whether full, verse, consort song, consort duet, or consort trio, is indicated in the inventories. But no such indication is provided for vocal works left textless in a source, probably for instrumental performance.

As a rule, the first and second parts of longer works such as madrigals or anthems are considered as individual pieces, since seventeenth-century copyists and scribes frequently copy only the first or second half in isolation.[1] Where possible, the original printed source for pieces in the inventories has been indicated by the date of publication. Most of these dates correspond to the listings in the third edition of E.H. Fellowes's *English Madrigal Verse*.[2] Any others are explained in the list of abbreviations or in footnotes to the inventories.

Portions of chapters 2, 3, and 4 previously have appeared in the following articles: "George Kirbye and the English Madrigal," *ML,* LIX (1978), 290-315; "Richard Nicolson: madrigals from Jacobean Oxford," *EMu,* VI (1978), 429-435; "Thomas Myriell's Manuscript Collection: One View of Musical Taste in Jacobean London," *JAMS,* XXX (1977), 419-465. The material is reproduced here by kind permission of these journals.

Any study as bibliographical in character as the present one obviously owes a great deal to libraries and their staffs. My own work would have been impossible without the cooperation of the staffs of the British Library; the Bodleian Library; the Bibliothèque Royale de Belgique; the Library of Christ Church, Oxford; the Library of St. Michael's College, Tenbury; the Library of the Royal College of Music; and the New York Public Library, which showed great patience and courtesy in answering my many queries. In addition, I am indebted to them for permission to reproduce in facsimile numerous pages from the manuscripts, which are vital to the arguments contained herein. And special thanks must go to the staff of the Music Library of the University of California at Berkeley, not only for its willing and enthusiastic response to all manner of requests, but also for taking a personal interest in the progress of my research and for helping to create such a congenial atmosphere in which to work.

I should also like to thank Oliver Neighbour and Pamela Willetts of the British Library, John Wing of Christ Church Library, and Susan Sommer of the Music Division of New York Public Library, who all provided valuable help with several musical or paleographic questions. I am very grateful to Jane Bernstein, Richard Crocker, Mary Cyr, Robert Ford, Robert Harlan, Joseph Kerman, Walter Kreyszig, James Ladewig, Murray Lefkowitz, and Jeff Perrone for advice and assistance of various kinds. Above all, I wish to thank Philip Brett, who first sparked my interest in the verse idiom, pointed out the need for a study of the consort song and verse anthem, and has guided the project through all stages of its development.

1

Introduction

As first conceived, this study was intended to trace the history of the "verse" idiom, that is, the English musical style combining voices and viols in verse anthem and consort song, from its inception to the Commonwealth. Unlike madrigals and lute ayres, pieces for voices and viols are known primarily from manuscript sources: even though verse anthems and consort songs had appeared in print as early as Byrd's two secular song publications of 1588 and 1589, and after 1610 began increasingly to invade the contents of the later "madrigal" prints, our knowledge of the verse idiom would be exceedingly limited if based simply upon the printed works.

A clear understanding of the pre-Restoration manuscript sources was therefore essential to a study of the development of the verse idiom. All the pre-Restoration liturgical sources have been sorted out, dated, and catalogued in John Morehen's excellent study, "The Sources of English Cathedral Music, 1617-1644,"[1] and the sources of English consort music have more recently received similar treatment in Warwick Edwards's equally admirable "The Sources of Elizabethan Consort Music."[2] But the secular manuscripts for voices and viols have never been so carefully scrutinized. Indeed, the necessity for a close study of them had eluded some of the leading scholars in the field, for in 1960 Peter le Huray wrote:

> The secular sources are all centred in the major English and American Libraries and are in the main well indexed and described in printed library catalogues. I have listed these sources therefore with very little comment.[3]

Le Huray's primary intention was to make the point that secular sources are generally more accessible than the sacred manuscripts, which often remain tucked away in the libraries of British cathedrals. To describe the secular sources as "in the main well indexed and described in printed library catalogues" was highly misleading, however. In fact, only the catalogues of the collections of the British Library[4] and St. Michael's College, Tenbury,[5] provide anything like a detailed description and inventory of the manuscripts in question. And the compiler of the former made it well nigh impossible to obtain an impression of a manuscript as a whole owing to his system of categorizing the entries. For the manuscripts at the other important libraries (e.g., the Bodleian Library, Christ Church Library, the Royal College of Music Library, the New York Public Library), one can find only cursory descriptions or catalogues in print.[6] For all the sources, in whatever library, the published descriptions and indices inevitably need revision.

The secular manuscripts, which until now have never been the object of a thorough study, are central to a full understanding of the verse idiom for several reasons. During the reigns of James I and Charles I, verse anthems appeared as frequently in the secular as in the sacred sources. In fact, the number of extant pre-Restoration secular sets of partbooks relevant to the issue is as large as the number of sacred ones. The importance of these secular manuscripts is enhanced by the fact that all the extant liturgical sources are relatively late: none can be dated before 1617 (the date of Tenbury MS 1382), the majority dating from the 1630s and 1640s. Of the secular manuscript sources, on the other hand, the majority were compiled before the death of James I in 1625, and a few even before 1617. Thus, the extant secular sources date from precisely the time when the verse anthem was in its ascendancy. It is the secular, rather than the sacred, sources that represent our contemporary witness to the emergence and growth in popularity of the verse idiom.

Furthermore, the secular sources preserve verse anthems and consort songs in what we may consider their original form, for voices and viols.[7] Ecclesiastics, and even such High-Church musical enthusiasts as Charles Butler,[8] did not welcome stringed instruments in church, where the organ took their place. Among the many anthems that survive both in their consort and organ versions, there are virtually none to my knowledge originally composed for the organ and later adapted to strings.[9] Though there can still be room for doubt about the origins of the verse anthem and the point at which it first entered the service of the church, the main line of development from secular through extraliturgical and finally to liturgical use seems fairly clear. William Byrd is the key figure in the early history of the genre.[10] Most of his verse anthems probably began life as consort anthems and were transferred to the sanctuary somewhat later, with their viol accompaniments arranged for organ. His work has been closely studied by Philip Brett in "The Songs of William Byrd," which includes an admirable discussion of both the music and the sources, particularly those from the collection of Edward Paston.[11] Because of their thorough treatment in Brett's work, the Paston manuscripts do not figure prominently in the following discussion. The next step, then, is to examine the secular sources which preserve verse anthems of the next generation of composers not only at a stage nearer the time of composition, but also, perhaps more importantly, in a state closer to the composers' original conception than the versions in the liturgical sources.[12] Therefore, before one can understand the consort song and verse anthem, it is necessary to have a thorough knowledge of their secular sources; the present volume is primarily devoted to an examination of the Jacobean and Caroline manuscripts containing verse anthems.

Although the sacred pre-Restoration manuscripts remain relatively inaccessible in cathedral libraries, they have in some ways been protected by that very inaccessibility. There can be little doubt that the sampling of sacred manuscripts which remains represents but a fraction of the number burned, worn out, or stolen over the years. But, as John Morehen's dissertation has shown, a fair number of the survivors still rest in the libraries of the cathedrals which they served in the seventeenth century (e.g., the Durham manuscripts). As a result, the musical paleographer has a reasonable chance of unraveling the knotty problems of their date and provenance. A search through the records of the cathedrals has often yielded, for example, records of payments to scribes for copying. And in some cases, samples of handwriting have come to light in the cathedral records which can be matched with the hands in the partbooks themselves, thereby establishing the identity of their copyists beyond any doubt. Thus, the fact that these sources were retired from service and left to gather dust on a library shelf in the building where they were once in use frequently simplifies the historian's attempts to establish their date and provenance.

The secular sources, on the other hand, lack these advantages for the musical scholar. Not infrequently they had passed from owner to owner over the years until what was left of them finally found its way to the security of the shelves of the major British or American libraries. But even a place on such library shelves was no guarantee that their wanderings were over.[13] By that time any links with their original owners had long been severed. Unless the scribe or original owner had obligingly entered his name on the flyleaf, later scholars frequently have had little in the way of external evidence to guide them in their attempts to establish the date and provenance of the secular sources. Furthermore, even when a name and date is provided, as in Thomas Myriell's *Tristitiae Remedium,* it may take decades to establish beyond a doubt a scribe's true identity.[14] In many cases the presence of a name in the partbooks remains only a tantalizing clue, yielding no ready solutions.

In dealing with any sources, then, it is necessary not merely to rely upon whatever paleographic evidence they may provide, but also to scrutinize the music closely, for the repertories and the composers present in the sources often yield the primary clues to their possible provenance and date. The various repertories may be compared with those of manuscripts whose date and place of origin can be pinpointed quite closely, such as those of Thomas Myriell or Thomas Hamond. On this basis one may suggest, however tentatively, where and when these more enigmatic sources may have been compiled, but with the knowledge that such hypotheses will very probably be subject to revision in the light of future discoveries.

This sort of comparison has made it possible to group the various sources by locality—London, the eastern counties (showing strong links with the capital), the west country, and Oxford. The following discussion has been organized into chapters along these lines. One intractable source, Add. MSS 37402-6, which fails to fall into any of these categories, has been treated in a separate chapter. Finally, Tenbury MSS 1162-7, though falling geographically into the chapter on London, is considered at the very end of the book, since it appears to have been compiled somewhat later than previously believed, and therefore represents the state of the verse idiom nearer mid-century.

Equally important, the comparison of the various sources has revealed several basic aesthetic attitudes of the manuscript compilers. These may be either characteristic of one particular sector of Britain or common to all the scribes who betray an interest in music for voices and viols. Therefore, while the object behind this present study may be primarily bibliographical, the discussion of the music contained in the manuscripts begins to suggest the essential guidelines for a broader consideration of the history of the verse idiom, which are summarized in chapter 8, the conclusion.

2

London

The Myriell Sources

For several generations musical scholars have been aware of an elusive
Jacobean figure by the name of Thomas Myriell, who left behind him an
imposing monument in the form of a set of manuscript partbooks entitled
Tristitiae Remedium...1616, now housed in the British Library under the
signature Additional MSS 29372-7. Although this set of manuscripts, containing more than 225 pieces, has served as a prime source for scholars of Jacobean
music, the identity of its copyist long remained a mystery. Until quite recently
the primary contender had been a busy cleric who, among his many
ecclesiastical appointments, had held the post of archdeacon of Norfolk and
precentor of Chichester Cathedral.[1] In an article published in 1968, however,
Pamela Willetts not only called this tentative identification into question, but
also brought to light the close connections between Add. 29372-7 and other
manuscripts in the British Library and at Christ Church, Oxford.[2] More
recently, Miss Willetts has identified this assiduous music collector and scribe
beyond any doubt as the Thomas Myriell who from 19 September 1616 until
his death late in 1625 served as rector of St. Stephen's Walbrook.[3]

Thus, over several years, Pamela Willetts has succeeded not only in
establishing Myriell's true identity, but has also given some idea of the range of
his contacts with musical circles of Jacobean England. With this background,
the time seems ripe for a closer, more detailed examination of Myriell's
manuscripts themselves and of their contents, which can provide one of the
most revealing guides to the taste of the time and an illustration of the manner
in which one avid musical amateur reacted to changing musical styles during
the second decade of the seventeenth century. To this end we must discuss each
set of manuscripts individually, beginning with the two that apparently
antedate the monumental *Tristitiae Remedium* and help to enlarge upon our
knowledge of Myriell's musical activity (Add. 29427 and Brussels MS II. 4109).
After a consideration of Add. MSS 29372-7, we shall proceed to the later,
peripheral sets.

Additional MS 29427

The physical condition of this single altus partbook makes it one of the most problematic of the Myriell books. In its present state (the individual leaves have been strengthened and the whole collection re-bound with each leaf separate rather than in gatherings), the partbook gives only a limited idea of what its original format may have been. Clearly, however, it must have grown rather haphazardly, for it contains several hands, many sizes and varieties of paper, and a greater diversity of pieces than appears in either 29372 or 4109.[4] The presence of canceled numbers indicates that the leaves have already undergone at least two different arrangements. Willetts's statement that "it contains first copies of many of the items subsequently fairly transcribed for that work[29372]"[5] is correct; but perhaps more intriguing is the fact that 29427 apparently became the final resting place for certain pages originally copied into 29372 itself. Thus, its final form does not necessarily antedate the compilation of 29372.

The basic corpus of the partbook originally included only items [1] to 99 in the latest numbering (i.e., fols 1-64v). This section can be further subdivided into three kinds of pieces: instrumental fantasias and In Nomines; vocal works; and instrumental versions of Italian madrigals or fantasias with Italian titles. To judge by the canceled numberings, the entire corpus of vocal pieces (fols. 13-44v) may have been inserted between folios 12 and 45. Thus, the four-part instrumental pieces resume on folio 45, and the canceled numberings correspond more or less to the sequence of the opening section. The opening group of three-part fantasias all occur without attribution, but can be ascribed to Thomas Lupo on the basis of Christ Church MSS 423-28, where they appear in exactly the same order. The version of the hand which copies the Lupo fantasias does not recur in the other Myriell sources identified by Pamela Willetts. It can be identified in another, previously unrecognized scribal concordance, however, British Library, Royal Appendix MS 63. This neatly copied manuscript is likewise related to the Myriell sources in its repertory, for it contains works from Sir William Leighton's *Tears or Lamentations* (1614), a print which figures prominently in both 29427 and 29372.

Of the remaining instrumental works, most are complete with the names of their composers; fantasias no. 74-76 can be attributed to Ferrabosco on the basis of B.L. Add. 17792-6. The large group of Italian madrigals without words reflects a practice that recurs in other manuscripts where verse anthems and consort songs play a prominent role (e.g., Add. 37402-6, Drexel 4180-5).

As Pamela Willetts's most recent article has shown,[6] Myriell's ecclesiastical career apparently began in Cambridge, whence he gradually moved southward to London; it may best be summarized:

Matriculated at Corpus Christi College, Cambridge—ca. 1596
Received B.A. degree—1600-1601
Ordained deacon—5 April 1601
Ordained priest—17 May 1601
Rector of Cold Norton, Essex—1609
"Preacher of the word of God, at Barnet"—1610
Rector of St. Stephen's Walbrook—1616
Chaplain to the Archbishop of Canterbury—1616/18
Rector of Shellow Bowells, Essex (held by license together with St. Stephen's Walbrook)—
  1620

The contents of 29427 may likewise reflect this progression from the Cambridge area to London, with its more cosmopolitan, up-to-date musical life. Thus, in the midst of the opening instrumental section of the manuscript appears a group of three fantasias by the easterner, John Wilbye, of Hengrave Hall, Suffolk—the only surviving instrumental works by this outstanding madrigalist, aside from an isolated six-part fantasia in Dublin, Marsh's Library MSS Z 3.4.7-12. The first section of vocal pieces (fols. 13 to 18) includes a consort song, *O thrice blessed earthbed,* by John Tomkins, organist of King's College, Cambridge, from 1606 until 1619, who (like Myriell) subsequently made his way to London where he served as organist of St. Paul's Cathedral.[7] In the later group of vocal works on folios 25-34, there occurs not only a setting of *When David heard* by Robert Ramsey, whose musical activities were largely limited to Cambridge, but also a setting of the same text by the singularly obscure William Bearsley, a composer otherwise known only from sources from the Cambridge area (Bodleian MSS Mus. F 1-28; perhaps Add. MSS 29366-8).[8] Furthermore, as we shall see, the *I am the resurrection* on folio 30[v], anonymous here but ascribed to Orlando Gibbons in Add. 29366-8, might be an early work dating from Gibbons's days at King's College, Cambridge. It is significant that, with the exception of *O thrice blessed earthbed,* none of these works found its way into the later *Tristitiae Remedium.*

Myriell's move to St. Stephen's Walbrook (pl. 1 [a]) was most auspicious from a musical standpoint, for the church was situated in what must have been a highly musical neighborhood. Among the streets radiating outward from St. Mary Woolchurch Haw (pl. 1 [b]), a stone's throw from St. Stephen's, was Cornhill (pl. 1 [c]), in which Nicholas Yonge, a lay clerk of nearby St. Paul's Cathedral (p. 1 [d]), resided until his death in 1619. Yonge is best known for his anthologies of Italian madrigals published in 1588 and 1597 under the title *Musica Transalpina.* The foreward to Yonge's publication attests to the active musical life of the district:

Since I first began to keepe house in this Citie, it hath been no small comfort unto me, that a great number of Gentlemen and Merchants of good accompt (as well of this realme as of forreine nations) have taken in good part such entertainment of pleasure, as my poore abilitie was able to afford them, both by the exercise of Musicke daily used in my house, and by furnishing them with Bookes of that kind yeerely sent me out of Italy and other places.

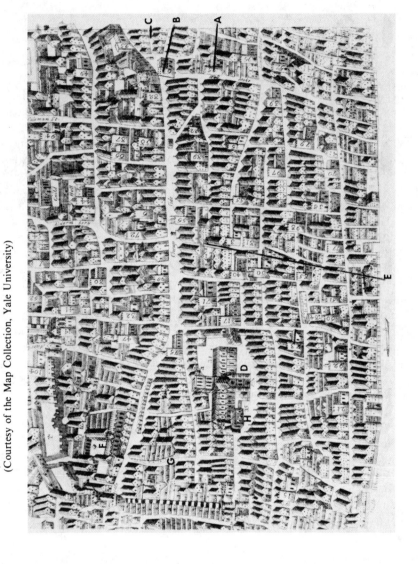

Pl. 1.   Richard Newcourt, *An Exact Delineation of the Cities of London and Westminster* (London, 1658). (Courtesy of the Map Collection, Yale University)

It seems quite plausible that Myriell would have come into contact with Yonge, whose landlords, the Merchant Taylors' Company, were patrons of St. Stephen's.[9] The rector very likely encountered the other lay clerks of St. Paul's who owned a property by St. Mary Woolchurch Haw during Myriell's tenure at St. Stephen's.[10]

The impact of London and the St. Paul's musical circle becomes immediately apparent after the opening section of vocal pieces in 29427. Beginning on folio 19, a different group of composers appears, representing the musical circle that Myriell must have joined about the time of his appointment at St. Stephen's. John Milton the Elder, whose residence and scrivener's shop at the sign of the Spread-Eagle in Bread Street (pl. 1 [e]), was only some 400 yards from St. Stephen's and whom Myriell must have known personally,[11] provides a half dozen pieces, several of them unique to Myriell's collection. Martin Peerson, who, after having made his way from the Cambridge area to London as early as 1604, later became master of the choristers at St. Paul's, contributes several others.[12] Peerson rubs shoulders in 29427 with his friend Thomas Ravenscroft, who had been a chorister under Edward Pearce at St. Paul's, apparently had received his B. Mus. at Cambridge in 1605,[13] had included several songs from plays performed by the St. Paul's boys in his *Pammelia* (1609), *Deuteromelia* (1609), *Melismata* (1611), and *A Brief Discourse* (1614),[14] and who would become music master at nearby Christ's Hospital (pl. 1 [f]) in 1618. Of the next twenty-seven works in 29427, more than half are by these three composers, who must represent the central figures of a musical enclave around the cathedral. Giles Farnaby, recently returned to London,[15] provides another two pieces unique to this source. To judge by 29427, and by *Tristitiae Remedium* as well, the rector of St. Stephen's must have become an important member of this St. Paul's group after moving to St. Stephen's from Barnet, ten miles to the north.

Myriell's extensive contacts with this London musical circle may have tempered his musical taste, but they did not drastically alter the clergyman's preferences in vocal music. Viewed as a whole, the corpus of vocal works reveals a somewhat traditional and highly serious bias. The madrigal is noticeably absent. The only genuine madrigals are by Italian composers and appear later in the manuscript, among the four- and five-part instrumental fantasias and In Nomines. As was so frequently the case with Italian madrigals in Jacobean manuscripts, these are left textless for instrumental performance. It seems that seventeenth-century Englishmen found this the best solution to the problem of pieces in the Italian tongue, aptly summed up by Nicholas Yonge in *Musica Transalpina* some twenty-five years earlier:

> Italian songs, are for sweetness of Aire, verie well liked of all, but most in account with them that understand the language. As for the rest, they do either not sing them at all, or at the least with little delight.

It would appear that Myriell considered them appropriate for viols and organ in combination, for seven of the examples in 29427 reappear in Myriell's organ book, Christ Church MS 67.

Examples of the Elizabethan madrigal are virtually nonexistent in this source. The only exception, No. 23, Weelkes's *Cease now delight,* hardly proves the rule since it falls into the Elizabethan tradition of the elegy, inaugurated by William Byrd with his lament on the death of Tallis and his published pieces in memory of Sir Philip Sidney (1588). Weelkes's lament for Lord Borough is, in fact, just the sort of traditional, serious work the scribe might be expected to choose if he were to turn to the madrigal vein recently in vogue.

Weelkes's *Cease now delight* is, however, only one of an unusually large number of works probably intended as elegies that find their way into 29427. Virtually all the others appear to have had as their object the youthful Prince Henry, eldest son of James I, to whom men of war, arts, and religion had looked for a restoration of England's former glory. Little wonder, then, that the prince's untimely death in 1612 should have provoked an unusual outpouring of stylized grief, not only literary, but musical as well. For the texts of their elegies musicians seem frequently to have turned to II Samuel 1:25 and 18:33, David's lamentations for the deaths of Jonathan and Absalom[16]—it seems that James I, the promulgator of the divine right of kings, was not averse to lofty comparisons with King David. Such Henrician laments turn up frequently in the later Jacobean manuscripts, such as Christ Church MSS 56-60 and British Library, Add. MSS 29366-8, for example. Nowhere, however, are they so numerous as in the Myriell sources. Add. 29427 alone preserves as many as ten settings of the Absalom and Jonathan texts, including, aside from the ever-popular Weelkes settings, much more obscure ones by William Bearsley and John Milton. Furthermore, the inclusion of the burial sentence, "I am the resurrection," in settings by Milton and Gibbons, and of Thomas Tomkins's *O Lord let me know mine end,* may have been prompted by the same sentiment. Myriell was not quick to forget the prince, for several other elegies for Henry turn up in the later Myriell sources as well.

The strength of the bond with the Elizabethan native tradition is further emphasized by works such as No. 20, *Come tread the paths,* and No. 25, *Abradad* (both in the initial vocal section), which represent the old consort song of the 1570s, and which would have sounded decidedly archaic to a Jacobean audience at the time 29427 was put together. Indeed, Myriell himself finally must have concluded that they had become simply too out-dated, for, as we shall see, he refrained from including them in *Tristitiae Remedium.*

These Elizabethan songs appear in 29427 together with their more up-to-date Jacobean counterparts, Nos. 21-22, *When Israel came out of Egypt/What aileth thee,* and No. 26, *Turn thy face,* all by Michael East. These three verse anthems, the only works which the scribe chose to copy from East's *Third Set of Books* of 1610, not only attest to his keen interest in works for voices and viols, but also reflect a serious turn of mind. For while he initially chooses to include three of the four verse anthems from *The Third Set,*[17] he ignores the three "verse pastorals" for voices and viols, perhaps because of their lighter character. Only in the later collection, 29372, do the "verse pastorals" also find a place.

One is struck by the scarcity of pieces by the best known composers of the age: Weelkes is represented by his laments, Tallis by the old favorite *I call and cry,* Byrd and Gibbons provide only *In resurrectione* and *I am the resurrection,* respectively. The most common names include John Milton, John Ward, Martin Peerson, Michael East, and Thomas Ravenscroft. These last three, Peerson and East in particular, were among the favorites of copyists showing an interest in the verse idiom, especially its more up-to-date manifestations. In addition, the manscript contains works by a number of lesser lights: Bearsley, Farnaby, Ramsey, and the puzzling William Simms, who enjoyed a popularity with devotees of the secular verse idiom far out of proportion to his musical capabilities. Were it not for the compiler's passion for laments for Prince Henry and his early links with the Cambridge area, some of these works would undoubtedly have been omitted. Myriell himself obviously employed a certain amount of musical judgment by rejecting several of them from his major anthologies.

The last fourteen folios form an appendix to the main body of 29427, acting as a catchall for various loose manuscript leaves from which Myriell made fair copies for *Tristitiae Remedium.* As will be shown later, folios 65-70, all in Myriell's own hand, actually orginated in 29372, and only found their way into this collection when it proved necessary to re-copy a section of 29372. This also helps explain why Ward's *Down caitif wretch/Prayer is an endless chain, How long wilt thou forget,* and Milton's *If that a sinner's sighs* and *O woe is me* should make second appearances in the manuscript. The last few folios consist of various odds and ends probably acquired by Myriell after he had exhausted the repertory of the original corpus. Rather than discard these later acquisitions after recopying them into *Tristitiae Remedium,* Myriell simply appended them to this older collection. Folio 71 is a single, badly soiled leaf of music paper printed by Thomas East. The hand which copied the four penitential works on folios 72-73 (see pl. 2a) was also responsible for Egerton MS 995 and Egerton MS 3512, and reappears in some Christ Church books. Pamela Willetts has shown that this copyist must have been close to the court, and she has tentatively suggested that he might even have been John Ward.[18] To judge by 29427 and 61, this scribe's usual practice was to send pieces to Myriell, which the clergyman then recopied, while the originals found their way into the peripheral collections.

Pl. 2a. Add. MS 29427, fol. 72v. The "Courtly Scribe," possibly John Ward.
(Reproduced by permission of the British Library)

The actual compilation of 29427 must have stretched over several years. The presence of pieces from East's *Third Set* (1610), the large number of Absalom and Jonathan pieces, and the description of Martin Peerson as "Ba: Mu:" (a distinction which he achieved only in 1613), indicate that the collection was not begun until at least 1612-1613. The fact that the appendix seems to be concurrent with 29372 must place the terminal date a year or two after 1616. But although it may be the earliest manuscript from Myriell's collection, 29427 already reveals several of the aesthetic preferences that receive further emphasis in the later sources.

Brussels MS II.4109

By contrast with Add. 29427, Brussels II.4109 was both carefully planned and meticulously copied. Like *Tristitiae Remedium*, it is entirely in Myriell's own hand. The most lavish of the Myriell sources, 4109 not only emulates the characteristic G-clefs from the publications of Thomas East, the music printer, but even goes so far as to duplicate the elaborate historiated initials from his prints. Myriell's adoption of square notation may also have resulted from his emulation of these printed sources (see pl. 3). For the format of this manuscript Myriell imitated not the madrigal books but the prints of the lutenist song writers, or possibly *The Tears or Lamentations of a Sorrowful Soul*, published in 1614 by the courtly figure, Sir William Leighton (a print which would provide some sixteen pieces for *Tristitiae Remedium* and which served as the source for Royal Appendix 63, the previously unrecognized Myriell source). The parts for each piece are arranged on one opening of the manuscript so that a group sitting around a table could perform from the single volume. The various scribal affectations, particularly the elegant capitals, suggest that 4109 might possibly have been conceived as a presentation copy. The abandonment of some of these mannerisms in 29372 suggests a slightly later date for *Tristitiae Remedium*. Brussels II. 4109, then, seems to date from before 1616, but probably not earlier than 1612 (as indicated by the presence of a single Absalom piece on p. 52).

In terms of repertory, 4109 and 29372 differ markedly, for with the exception of seven pieces, 4109 consists entirely of published works, methodically copied into the manuscript in large blocks. If the collection originally were conceived as a presentation copy, such a format would be readily understandable: prints could provide an easily accessible source of pieces and free the scribe from the uncertainties and delays resulting from a reliance upon manuscript sources.

A look at the prints best represented not only confirms our view of the scribe's discrimination and elevated musical taste, as evident from 29427, but also reflects some popular trends of the time. The prominence afforded

Pl. 3. Brussels, Bibliothèque Royale Albert 1er, MS II.4109, p. 21. A sample of Thomas Myriell's attempts to reproduce the historiated initials from Thomas East's printed collections.
(Copyright Bibliothèque Royale Albert 1er, Brussels)

William Byrd's 1588 *Psalms* (twenty-two pieces—more than twice the number of the nearest competitor) shows that even in a repository for published works Myriell gives pride of place to the leading exponent of the native song style. This leaning toward the consort song is confirmed by Myriell's treatment of the fifteen songs from Dowland's 1597 and 1600 collections, which he transforms into consort songs by eliminating the text from all but one part for the pieces from the 1597 set and by "scoring" the pieces from the 1600 print for solo and three instruments. In both instances the lute part is entirely absent. It is perhaps telling that all of the most important prints in 4109 except Michael East's *First Set* achieved sufficient popularity with the Elizabethans and Jacobeans to require new editions. Thus, Myriell's choices of printed music would seem a fairly accurate reflection of contemporary taste in this realm. The inevitable and perhaps more important question arises: could not his strong interest in the less published and, therefore, more elusive music for voices and viols be equally representative of musical taste early in the seventeenth century?

Additional MSS 29372-7

This, the primary set of manuscripts associated with Thomas Myriell, repeatedly has come under investigation by musical scholars. A typical point of view is put forward by Denis Stevens in his biography of Thomas Tomkins:

> Thomas Myriell invited contributions to *Tristitiae Remedium,* an anthology compiled during the years immediately preceding 1616, when it was apparently completed . . . The idea of Myriell's collection, a *mélange* of serious anthems, delightful madrigals, and novelties such as the *London Cries* of Orlando Gibbons, may have inspired Tomkins to compile his own anthology [the 1622 *Songs*] as well as to plan it with variety in mind.[19]

A closer look at 29372, especially in conjunction with the related sources, reveals that this view, particularly with regard to dating the source, must be revised slightly. It may also be possible to define more precisely the guiding principles behind Myriell's *mélange.*

Tristitiae Remedium represents another, and complementary side of Thomas Myriell's musical interests when viewed in conjunction with 4109. For *Tristitiae Remedium,* Myriell abstained from inserting the elaborate historiated initials present in the Brussels source, but he achieved an effect equally imposing by including at the beginning of each volume an elaborate, engraved title page. The plate from which Myriell's title page was pulled was not entirely new, however. It had, in fact, been engraved some three years earlier by William Hole (the engraver of *Parthenia*) for the *Prime musiche nuove* of the Italian emigré Angelo Notari. The elaborate architectural frame was retained for Myriell's title page, but the original text (including the attribution to William Hole) was replaced (see pl. 4).[20]

Each of the two collections which Myriell undertook to copy entirely in his own hand fulfills different requirements. While the Brussels source served almost entirely as a repository for works from prints, 29372 relied primarily upon unpublished materials, the works that circulated in manuscript and came to the scribe's attention through his extensive musical contacts. In accordance with the motto at the top of the engraved title page, "Peritus non ignorat ordines," Myriell must have settled upon a guiding principle before he began to copy the collection. Some categories of pieces he rejected outright, although they may still appear in other of his collections: purely instrumental pieces (e.g., fantasias, In Nomines), madrigals in Italian, lute ayres. Myriell only turns to the madrigal prints when he has nothing else suitable to hand, and he totally ignores unpublished madrigals. What remains of primary importance are the less madrigalian genres: consort songs, verse anthems, motets, and full anthems.

The madrigals by Italian composers which Myriell allows come exclusively from the Elizabethan prints of English translations such as Yonge's *Musica Transalpina,* and show the usual English preference for Marenzio (ten pieces) and Ferrabosco (seven pieces), who far outnumber their nearest Italian competitors, Vecchi, Croce, and Pallavicino (two pieces each). In his choice of madrigals by English composers, Myriell reveals both musical discrimination and a marked gravity, just what one might have anticipated on the basis of 29427. Thus, of approximately fifty pieces from "madrigalian" prints, more than one-third are by Wilbye (two from 1598 and seventeen from 1609), by common consent the finest madrigalist of them all. John Ward, noted for the seriousness of his contributions to the genre,[21] is the next most prominent (thirteen works from 1613), while Weelkes, usually considered second only to Wilbye, ranks a rather distant third (two from 1597 and six from 1598). It is also striking that of the remaining composers whose "madrigal" prints provide pieces for 29372—Kirbye (one from 1597), Byrd (five from 1588 and two from 1589), Morley (three from *Balletts,* 1595), Bateson (four from 1604), Tomkins (three published in 1622), and East (five from 1610 and two from 1618)—Byrd, East, and Tomkins contribute works that fall largely, if not entirely, outside the secular madrigal style. So when the scribe turned to the madrigal, his choice fell upon the best or most conservative Italians, or the best or most serious Englishmen. In a collection so rich in compositions for voices and viols, there was little room for the lighter vocal confections of the Morleian variety. What remains a puzzle, given Myriell's aesthetic preferences, is the total absence of works from Gibbons's *First Set* of 1612.

Observations about Myriell's musical taste, however, need to be tested against whatever evidence we can glean about the sequence in which additions were made in the partbooks. The character of the scribe's musical hand provides the primary clue in this context, for during the course of the compilation of *Tristitiae Remedium,* Myriell's hand evolved from a square, more formal character employing lozenge-shaped notes which had first appeared in the Brussels source (see pl. 5a) to a freer, more flowing style in which the note forms are more rounded (see pl. 5b). These changes help to clarify the layers in the partbooks and can strengthen our hypotheses with regard to their date.

The vicissitudes of time, years of perusal, and the repairs of modern binders have somewhat obscured the original state of the partbooks. But it seems that the gatherings were put together before copying, although the leather bindings could not have been added until later (a fact confirmed by the severe cropping of page 73 in the tenor book). It would appear that the engraved title page was added at the beginning of the compilation, which, contrary to accepted opinion, was not completed in 1616 but stretched over at least two years and perhaps even into the 1620s, as we shall see.

When Myriell began the collection, his first step was to organize the books systematically into sections for four, five, and six voices, which were probably all begun simultaneously. It seems quite probable, however, that the scribe encountered some difficulty in the compilation of the four-voice section, as suggested by the thinness of this layer and by the speed with which Myriell apparently abandoned it. He would, after all, have had greater difficulty finding verse anthems or consort songs for this combination of instrumental parts. Add. 29427 could offer him nothing suitable, and he was forced to fall back upon other sources, chiefly prints. He did manage to come up with a few Latin motets and several works from Sir William Leighton's *Tears or Lamentations* (1614) after the initial group of Wilbye madrigals. But when sometime later he could only amplify this section by returning to madrigalian works such as *Adieu, sweet Amaryllis,* his last entry (in the later, rounded hand), Myriell seems to have given up.[22]

Add. 29427 obviously acted as the primary source for the opening leaves of the five-part section. With the exception of Wilbye's only surviving consort song, *Ne reminiscaris* (perhaps a last witness to Myriell's old links with the Cambridge area), all the compositions in the block from pages 25 to 39 occur in 29427, often in the same order (e.g., pp. 27-32). Of the next eighteen pieces, only two appear in 29427; it is interesting to note that *O thrice blessed earthbed* is correctly attributed here to John Tomkins, a correction of the misattribution to his better-known elder brother in 29427. The second group of five-part pieces draws primarily upon two recent prints, East's *Third Set* (1610) and Leighton's *Tears or Lamentations* (1614), and it seems reasonable to assume that the eight compositions from the latter were copied concurrently with pages 20-23 of the four-part section.

After the distraction of Leighton's collection, Myriell returned to 29427 for a few more pieces (pp. 61-66), but by now he was apparently exhausting the potential of the older collection and coming to rely more upon other sources. These must have included one particularly rich in the works of Martin Peerson from St. Paul's, for pages 72-94 consist entirely of his works and include six of the thirteen extant verse anthems by the composer, in addition to an interesting lament, *Wake sorrow,* on the death of Lady Arbella Stuart (d. 1615).

After a few more works from 29427 (pages 96-101), Myriell had apparently exhausted his supply of manuscript sources temporarily, and he turned for the first time to madrigalian prints, which he had previously avoided in the five-part section. Perhaps while waiting for more pieces of the preferred varieties to come to hand, he filled pages 102-26 with madrigals from various printed collections. Pages 127-47, in their original form, represented the last section of the older layer of the manuscript. Originally they must have contained:

127	*See the word is incarnate,* Gibbons
130	*Down caitif wretch,* Ward
132	*Prayer is an endless chain,* Ward
134	*How long wilt thou forget,* Ward
136	*Long have I lifted up,* Hanford
137	*If that a sinner's sighs,* Milton
138	*O woe is me,* Milton
140	*Almighty god who by the leading of a star,* Bull
142	*Hear me, O God,* Ferrabosco
143	*So far dear life,* Eremita
144	*If silent then grief,* Ferrabosco
145	*I languish to complain,* Ferrabosco
146	*Ne irascaris,* Byrd
147	*Civitas sancti tui,* Byrd
148	*I lift my heart to thee,* Tallis

But at some later date, at least as late as the addition of the page numbers, Myriell became dissatisfied with pages 132-42. Perhaps he realized that the two Milton works had already been copied a fourth higher on pages 34 and 36 above. So he detached pages 131-42 midway through *Down caitif wretch* (not too difficult a task since the partbooks were still without hard covers). He then inserted new leaves and recopied them, keeping the Ward pieces in the same sequence and retaining the Ferrabosco *Hear me, O God* at the end of the section. Having omitted the Hanford and Milton pieces, however, he moved the Bull *Star Anthem* from page 140 to page 136, and to fill the gap before *Hear me O God* he again fell back upon the most immediate thing to hand, Wilbye's *Second Set.*

It is a witness to the value placed upon manuscript music that Myriell did not simply discard the leaves he had removed from 29372 but instead appended them to the original corpus of 29427, despite the fact that Ward's *Down caitif wretch* thereby began in midstream and, in any event, could already be found

Pl. 5a.   Add. MS 29372, p. 25. The first entry in the five-part
section of the manuscript.
(Reproduced by permission of the British Library)

complete on folio 35ᵛ, together with the other Ward anthems. The Milton pieces had also made earlier appearances on folios 22ᵛ and 33 of 29427. This explanation accounts for the change to Myriell's more flowing hand with rounded noteheads and fatter penstrokes on pages 131-42 of *Tristitiae Remedium,* in contrast to the more formal hand with square notes of the pages on either side of this section (see pl. 6a and 6b). As one might already anticipate, a look at the first appendix to 29427 reveals the thinner penstrokes and square noteheads which match perfectly with the original hand of 29372 (see pl. 6c).

By the time Myriell had reached page 150 of *Tristitiae Remedium,* Add. 29427 had been quite exhausted. Perhaps this led him to put the partbooks aside for a while. Some time may have passed before he took them up again, to judge by the musical hand of subsequent entries, for from this point to the end of the five-part section the more flowing hand with rounded noteheads, often including a more flamboyant time-signature as well, is omnipresent. The more haphazard organization of the remainder of the five-part section could indicate that Myriell had to wait longer for new pieces to come his way and would enter them on a first-come, first-served basis. The last folios of 29427 attest to this scheme. Thus, *Blessed art thou,* which, despite the battered state of the manuscript leaf, became folio 71 of 29427, was copied on page 159 of 29372, while the pieces numbered 112-15 in 29427 were scattered over pages 181-97, and the original manuscript leaves inserted in 29427. As one might expect, Myriell frequently had to fall back upon the printed sources to occupy himself until new manuscript sources of suitable music came to hand. Printed works, therefore, are liberally sprinkled among the full anthems, consort songs, and verse anthems, but never from large blocks. It is interesting to note that Myriell's preference for the verse idiom was strong enough for him to convert the two parts of William Byrd's famous *Lullaby* (1588), which appear here together with the unpublished consort song, *Delight is dead,* back into its original medium of the consort song, simply by eliminating the words from the lower parts.[23]

Michael East's *O clap your hands/God is gone up* (pp. 182-85) may provide a clue to the time when Myriell was at work on this later section of the partbooks. This verse anthem was published in East's *Fourth Set* in 1618. The version in *Tristitiae Remedium* corresponds so closely to the printed text, even incorporating the oversights from the original printed version,[24] that there can be little doubt that Myriell was working from the print. This he must have done sometime after late March 1618, when East's *Fourth Set* first appeared. Thus, some two years must have passed before the scribe reached this point in the partbooks.

This later portion of the five-part section introduces another obscure composer who further attests to Myriell's connection with the musical circle around St. Paul's: Simon Stubbs. This minor figure, who provides two works,

Pl. 6c. Add. Ms 29427, fol. 65. The concluding fragment of John Ward's *Down caitif wretch* in Myriell's "square" hand.
(Reproduced by permission of the British Library)

Have mercy upon me and *Father of love,* for *Tristitiae Remedium,* occupied the ninth minor canonry of St. Paul's from 4 December 1613 until his death in 1621/22. He also served as rector of St. Gregory's by St. Paul's, which stood at the south side of the cathedral near the west end (see pl. 1 [h]), from 1616 until his death.[25] The parish register of St. Gregory's (London, Guildhall MS 10231) records that on 24 January 1621/22 "Mr Simon Stubbes one of the Petticannons & curate of this church was (buried) in the Petticanons cloister."[26]

It is puzzling to come upon Tomkins's *When David heard,* the work actually dedicated to Myriell in Tomkins's *Songs* of 1622, so late in the collection. Given what must have been a close connection between the two men (Tomkins's hand actually appears in the peripheral Myriell source, Christ Church MS 67), and given the scribe's obvious interest in laments for Prince Henry as revealed by 29427, it is surprising to find the Tomkins piece in a part of the manuscript apparently copied after 1618. This might indicate that Tomkins's setting of the popular text was not composed until a considerable time after Henry's death. Had it been written any earlier, surely it would have found its way into 29427, which contains so many Absalom and Jonathan pieces.

The six-part section of the partbooks confirms the pattern which emerged in the previous sections. Add. 29427 had little to offer in the way of six-part works, and Myriell lost no time in getting them down on pages 232-35. Suitable six-part pieces were apparently difficult to come by, and the scribe constantly had recourse to the madrigal prints. The usual pattern in scribal entries consists of an anthem or two followed by several madrigals, a few more anthems and then more madrigals. Occasional pages have also been left blank, a practice which was very rare in the five-part section. The first appearances of names such as Matthew Jeffreys (vicar-choral of Wells Cathedral) could indicate that Myriell was coming into contact with musicians from further afield in his search for manuscript music.

In addition to the entire closing section of Ward's *First Set,* which Myriell copied as one large block on pages 314-31, he added another elegy for Prince Henry, Ward's *No object dearer,* on page 336. This work may have been acquired concurrently with Ward's *Let God arise,* which concludes the five-part section. These two pieces reappear in each of the Christ Church sets from Myriell's collection, 61-66 and 67. The badly tattered copies of *No object dearer* glued into 61 may represent the original parts transmitted to Myriell, which again he could not quite bring himself to throw away, and the same might apply to the organ parts for the two anthems glued into 67. The late acquisition of these two pieces could explain the mix-up in pagination for *Let God arise* (numbered "232-235," though the six-part section begins with p. 230).

If the last Ward entries were made concurrently, then the two Tomkins pieces at the end of the six-part section must be the final additions to the manuscripts. *Oft did I marl*, like *It is my well-beloved's voice* and *When David heard*, also appears in Tomkins's print of 1622. Myriell's manuscript source for *It is my well-beloved's voice* (transposed down a tone from the printed text) apparently came to rest in 29427 (p. 116). But no manuscript source for *Oft did I marl* has survived in the peripheral Myriell sources. A comparison of Myriell's text with the printed version reveals a very close correspondence, incorporating some of the anomalies from the original: the omission of two notes from the sextus part (p. 166),[27] the repetition of the word "dwell"(p. 172), the use of brackets for "love" in the tenor (p. 173). There are, however, some inconsistencies, particularly in the addition or omission of accidentals, so that the correspondence to the printed source is not so close as it was in the case of East's *O clap your hands*. It remains a distinct possibility—although not a certainty—that Myriell was in this instance copying from the printed source. If this were true, it would mean that the last entry in the partbooks was made in 1622 or later.

Christ Church MSS 61-66

Although large sections of Christ Church 61-66 are the work of Myriell himself, a number of other scribes had a hand in the compilation of these partbooks. The overall character of the manuscripts resembles that of 29427, and one may hypothesize that in its original form, before the ravages of three centuries, 29427 must have been similar to 61. The resemblance also extends to a similarity of repertory, though that of 61 seems about a decade later.

The partbooks might best be described as a hodgepodge—incorporating several kinds of pieces, several different papers, and the work of at least five different scribes—given some sort of order on the basis of the number of parts and the kinds of pieces. The opening three-part section, devoted entirely to fantasias by Orlando Gibbons, forms a distinct layer in that the pages making up the gatherings are slightly smaller than those of the other gatherings. This section also reintroduces the hand that appeared in the appendix of 29427 on folios 72-73. Just as Myriell himself subsequently recopied those folios into a collection devoted entirely to vocal music (29372), he likewise recopied some of the Gibbons fantasias into another small set of books devoted entirely to instrumental pieces (Christ Church MSS 459-62). With the exception of a single cantus part, the same scribe was also responsible for the second section (fols. 13-17), devoted entirely to three-part anthems by John Ward, with verses for cantus and altus, joined by the bassus for the "chorus" (see pl. 2b). Items 1-5 seem to form a single piece based upon Psalm 103, while 6-9 all draw upon Psalm 51.[28]

In the next section (fols. 34-9) Myriell turns to instrumental pieces with Italian titles, as he had done in a large section of 29427. With the exception of a single part of *Cresce in voi,* the section is entirely the work of Myriell himself. Skipping to the end of the partbooks, we find a large group of six-part fantasias and In Nomines. The copying of these was divided between Myriell, who entered the altus, tenor, sextus, and bassus parts, and an as yet unidentified scribe who makes his sole appearance in any of the Myriell sets here, where he copies the six-part instrumental pieces into the cantus and quintus books.

The section of five- and six-part vocal works which intrudes between the five- and six-part instrumental pieces is best compared to the appendix of 29427. Here, as in 29427, we find strange hands and loose sheets added to the main corpus of the partbooks. The basic hand is still Myriell's, but pieces in foreign hands have been inserted amongst the works which he copied. The already familiar "courtly scribe" returns to enter a transposed version of *Let God arise* a fourth lower than that on folio 49. A hand not previously encountered (pl. 7a) provides *Mount up my soul, Vota per solvam,* and *No object dearer,* all three of which are on paper that contrasts with the surrounding folios. Another unknown hand, which also appears in Christ Church 67 (pl. 9), occurs here in a solitary example, the quintus part of Tomkins's *Dear Lord of life.*

The vocal section of 61 contains the partbooks' only concordances with *Tristitiae Remedium*:

> *Let God arise,* Ward   29372:232
> *It is my well-beloved's voice,* Tomkins   29372:308
> *Lord bend thy righteous ears,* (Anon.)   29372:335
> *No object dearer,* Ward   29372:336

It is striking that all these works were among the last to be copied into 29372: *Let God arise* ends the five-part section, and *Lord bend thy righteous ears* and *No object dearer* appear consecutively as the last works but two in the six-part section, while *It is my well-beloved's voice* occurs only slightly earlier. The Tomkins piece is, significantly, 61's only concordance with 29427. Perhaps Myriell had changed his mind about entering it from 29427 into 61 and copied it into 29372 instead, after inscribing only a fragment of the quintus part in 62. Judging by the position of the other three pieces in 29372, we may assume that the vocal section of 61 must be contemporary with the very end of *Tristitiae Remedium,* and therefore must date from sometime shortly after 1618.[29]

Thus, like 29427, 61 served as one of Myriell's catchalls, upon which he could draw in making up his more specialized collections. It is very unlikely that the manuscripts could have been bound before copying. The gathering containing the Gibbons fantasias has been bound in with the rest, which would have proved a difficult undertaking after binding. The same is true of *Mount up my soul* and the sextus part of *Vota per solvam.* In addition, what was apparently a note to the binder, "sprinkled [?] with red . . . th____"(referring to the red spatterings on the cropped edges?) appears on the outside folio of 63, which later was pasted to the vellum cover during the binding process.

The list of composers present in 61 does not add a great deal to that from 29372. William Pysing, here given credit for the verse anthem, *The Lord hear thee,* makes his only appearance in any Myriell source. Both William Pysing Senior and William Pysing Junior served as lay clerks at Canterbury Cathedral over a period of more than seventy years.[30] Myriell was, of course, chaplain to the Archbishop of Canterbury. Perhaps Myriell acquired the anthem through this indirect connection with Canterbury. He could just as easily have obtained it through the St. Paul's circle, however, for Pysing's only other sacred piece, *I will magnify thee,* is limited to St. Paul's sources (RCM MSS 1045-51 and Tenbury MS 791).[31]

One or two names for the instrumental section deserve mention. William White provides two six-part fantasias; he was also the composer of a verse anthem in two sections occuring (predictably) in the latest layer of 29372. Charles Coleman, on the other hand, appears in no other Myriell source. He and Simon Ives, who makes his one and only appearance at the very end of the partbooks, must represent the youngest generation of Myriell's connections. Ives hailed from Ware in Hertfordshire, site of the Fanshawe estate; he became a vicar choral at St. Paul's in the years shortly after Myriell's death.[32]

Christ Church MS 67

This organ book is one of the unifying features among the Myriell sets, closely connected to 29427 and 61 through concordances, and to 29372 because of the note in Myriell's hand on the final leaf. The link with 29427 and 61 depends as much on their similar character as on concordances, however. Again we find a wide variety of hands, and several papers. Indeed, the closeness of the connections makes it difficult to consider the organ book in isolation, rather than to refer to it frequently in the discussions of 29427 and 61.

Christ Church 67 must have been intended to serve as the organ book for both 61 and 29427. The organ accompaniments for several pieces from both sets were systematically copied here, or pasted into the primary corpus of the manuscript. Thus, 67 opens with the organ parts for the three-voice Ward anthems that followed the Gibbons fantasias in 61. What we find is in fact a truncated version, for the last two sections of Psalm 51, *Turn thy face* and *Deliver me from bloodguiltiness,* have been omitted. In 67, however, the text is not in the hand of the "courtly scribe" as it was in 61. The actual hand (see pl. 8) may be Myriell's own, though it shows some inconsistency with his practice elsewhere in the partbooks (e.g., contrasting treble and bass clefs).[33] After an

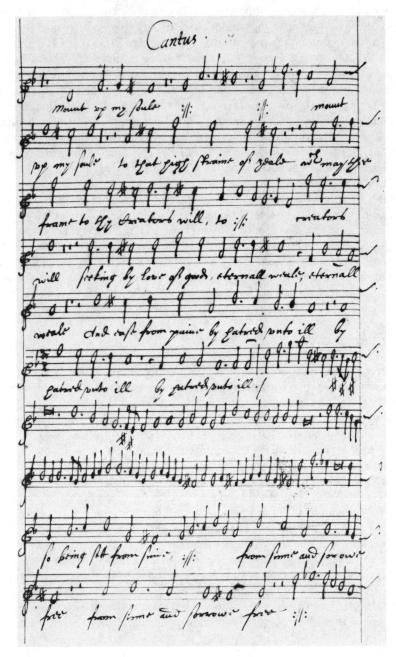

Pl. 7b.   Christ Church MS 67, fol. 55ᵛ.
(By kind permission of the Governing Body of Christ
Church, Oxford)

incomplete fantasia by Ferrabosco (a fragment of the bass parts only) in Myriell's hand, we encounter another scribe, (pl. 9), who made a very fleeting appearance in 61. Here he plays a much more prominent role, second only to that of Myriell himself. This scribe's prominent position in the organ book alone suggests that perhaps he acted as organist in Myriell's musical gatherings. The hand has also been identified in another, more important organ book, Bodleian MS Mus. Sch. D. 229, William Lawes's autograph organ score, where it copies pages 20-21 (reversed).[34] The entries in the Lawes organ book must date from considerably after the scribe worked on Myriell's organ book, however (Pinto suggests that D 229 must date from after 1640).[35] The identity of the copyist has yet to be established.

After two fantasias the scribe skips a few folios before entering the three anonymous full anthems which also formed a group on folios 55-57 of 61. For the latter half of *O sweet Jesus* he received the assistance of none other than Thomas Tomkins, who also went on to copy Marenzio's *I must depart* on folio 20^V.[36] This little bit of evidence confirms the close connection between Myriell and the illustrious composer, who reaffirmed it by dedicating *When David heard* to Myriell in his 1622 *Songs*.

The next large section, including folios 23^V-39^V, emphasizes the relationship of 67 and 29427, for it incorporates the organ parts for seven of the "instrumentalized" Italian madrigals from folios 87-97 of 29427, plus another ten absent from that source. For this section the hand is largely Myriell's (pl. 10), though he receives occasional assistance from the scribe of the previous section. This layer ends with three more fantasias, the last of which is incomplete, but recognizable as Coperario's. The other two, ascribed to William Simms, show another compositional side to this mysterious composer otherwise known only for his few inferior, but remarkably popular, verse anthems.

The remainder of the organ book is very much a patchwork, comparable to the final section of 29427 and the middle section of 61, with which it shares several concordances. The by now familiar "courtly scribe" returns for the Gibbons *Cry of London* (fols. 52-53^V—see pl. 2c), here an incomplete version providing only the lower parts on a single bass staff. Myriell obviously received the piece as a folio from the scribe. There was no satisfactory way to include the folio in the manuscript short of recopying it. But instead Myriell chose to glue it at the fold directly into the organ book—hence the unsatisfactory sequence of sides: "4-1-2-3." The confusion apparently extended to 29427, which may have been copied from the "courtly scribe's" text (both agree in their variants; see especially bars 20-23). Perhaps it was not apparent which side of the folio came first, and as a result we find parts 1 and 2 entered into 29427 in the reverse order. But before transcribing the *Cry* into *Tristitiae Remedium,* Myriell must have learned of the alternative order for the two halves, for they appear there in the order, *God give you good morrow/ A good sausage.* The annotations "first pt" and "2. pt" might have been added to the folio in 29427 at that time to sort out the confusion.

A similar mix-up in pagination resulted for John Bennet's *O God of gods* (fol. 55); once again Myriell chose to glue a folio directly into the manuscript. The scribe is recognizable as the same person who provided three of the pieces inserted into 61 (see pl. 7b). This hand also reappears on folio 72^v of 67 for the organ part of Ward's *No object dearer,* which has been inserted at the center of a gathering. In this case the connection with 61 could scarcely be closer, for the same scribe was also responsible for the separate parts inserted there. This is the only instance in which we apparently possess the complete set of parts as acquired by Myriell from a member of his musical circle.

The last of the insertions appears on folio 58, where Ward's popular *Let God arise* is glued into the organ book. The hand is ambiguous, but bears some resemblance to the one which copied the Ward three-part anthems at the opening of 67. As with 61, the conclusion of 67 reflects the final sequence of 29372. After *Let God arise,* which ends the five-part section of *Tristitiae Remedium,* the scribe adds four pieces from Croce's *Musica Sacra* (1608) to 67. Two of these are among the very last entries in 29372 (the other two, however, occur much earlier there), and in 67 they are followed by Ward's *No object dearer,* the last entry in the organ book and the last but two in 29372. This once again confirms the impression that the final sections of these catchalls, Christ Church 61-66 and Christ Church 67, are contemporary with the conclusion of *Tristitiae Remedium.*

The table on the concluding folio of 67 offers a very tangible link with 29372, as Pamela Willetts first observed.[37] It provides a list of those pieces in the "great bookes" (i.e., Add. 29372-7) "fit for vials and organ." Miss Willetts points out that the list confirms Denis Stevens's suggestion (*Thomas Tomkins,* pp. 35-36) that both viols and organ were meant to play along with the voices.[38] But the most striking feature of the list is that it contains no verse music at all, but madrigals (both native and "Englished" Italian) and Latin motets. Therefore the title seems to mean "those pieces normally sung by voices alone which can also be satisfactorily performed with instrumental accompaniment," or "which can be performed by viols and organ *without* voices." One intriguing omission from the list, especially in the light of Denis Stevens's quotation from Charles Butler,[39] is Tomkins's *When David heard.* It is possible, of course, that Myriell had not yet proceeded as far as page 212 of 29372 when he entered the list in 67. But we do know that he had progressed at least as far as page 197, by which time he was using his later, rounded hand. He had also recopied the section on pages 131-42 and presumably added the rejected pages to 29427. Given the amount that Myriell had copied by this time, the list of works suitable for viols and organ seems a very short one indeed.

Pl. 9.   Christ Church MS 67, fol. 17ᵛ. Myriell's primary
            assistant for the organ book.
            (By kind permission of the Governing Body of Christ
            Church, Oxford)

Pl. 10.   Christ Church MS 67, fol. 23ᵛ. Myriell's hand.
              (By kind permission of the Governing Body of Christ
              Church, Oxford)

Christ Church MS 44

For the sake of completeness one should make some mention of Christ Church 44, a manuscript in score whose primary layer is entirely in Myriell's own hand. It does not, however, contain any of the pieces from Myriell's other collections. The layer of the manuscript in Myriell's hand consists entirely of fantasias and a pavan, except for folios 45^V-52, onto which Myriell has entered three Italian madrigals and John Milton's *If ye love me (4 a),* which seems decidedly out of place in this context. All four are textless save for their titles. In addition, the Italian works retain the numbers of their original order in the foreign prints (and for *Luci serene* even the designation "lib.4"), which would seem to indicate that Myriell had copies of the Italian publications to hand.

Of all the pieces in Myriell's hand, only these Italian works lack a curious superscript: a number plus "Leat^9 boo^k" or "le^9 boo:," which must refer to the source from which Myriell was copying. We seem to have another "ghost," like the organ book meant to accompany *Tristitiae Remedium,* which has yet to come to light. In addition to the eighteen works which it provides for 44, this "ghost" must also have been the source for the two instrumental pieces by Lupo on folios 11^V and 36^V of 67, where the same annotation occurs. From the clues in 67 and 44 we may at least conclude that it must have been another very large collection, comparable in size to *Tristitiae Remedium,* divided into five-part and six-part sections, and with some attempt to separate the works by individual composers into large blocks. Perhaps it was Myriell's final repository for the fair copies of instrumental pieces, in the same way that 29372 became the source for fair copies of strictly vocal music.

In addition to Myriell's own hand, we find the work of another scribe on folios 1 and 123^V-33^V. Again, it was Pamela Willetts who first recognized this to be the hand of Benjamin Cosyn, whose signature also occurs on folios 125^V.[40] Judging by the manner in which the pieces are entered and by the character of the repertory, it seems unlikely that Myriell supervised their copying. The most reasonable explanation for the presence of Cosyn's hand would be that the manuscript passed from Myriell's possession (perhaps at his death in 1625) to Cosyn, who subsequently made the additions.

Another previously unidentified Cosyn manuscript, Washington, Folger Library MS V.a.412, may also attest to Cosyn's link with Myriell's circle. This single partbook, devoted primarily to madrigals, includes numerous concordances with Myriell's collection and several Absalom laments. Of these, Dering's *And the king was moved* is otherwise known only from Myriell sources, and occurs in a reading identical to Myriell's except for one of two ambiguous accidentals. The Folger partbook suggests a closer link between Cosyn and Myriell's circle, and may help to explain why Christ Church 44 subsequently found its way into Cosyn's hands.

One possible connection with 44 remains to be explored. Among the more recent acquisitions of the British Library there is a set of partbooks of fantasias and In Nomines, Add. MSS 39550-4, partly in the hand of Sir Nicholas Le Strange of Hunstanton, Norfolk, which contains, as part of its very large repertory, eleven of the eighteen fantasias in 44.[41] This set of manuscripts is most unusual in that it contains contemporary listings of variants in other sources. Over a dozen other sources are listed, some of which are of special interest in terms of Myriell and what we know of his musical connections: "Rampley," "Mr Fanshaw Score B," "Barnard Score B," "Couzens," "Ives," "Mr Coleman." The mention of "Couzens" is especially intriguing. A comparison of 44 and the annotations in Add. 39550-4 could reveal if it is among those named by Le Strange and, if so, would provide more concrete evidence of Myriell's musical connections. Or the comparison might throw further light upon subsequent ownership of the score.[42]

Tristitiae Remedium and Thomas Myriell's other major manuscripts, whose compilation we have studied so closely, represent one of the most important witnesses to musical taste in the British capital during the last dozen years of the reign of James I. The evidence of the manuscripts suggests, more specifically, that Myriell's musical circle centered around nearby St. Paul's Cathedral. But Myriell's contacts may have expanded into courtly circles as well. Pamela Willetts has already raised the possibility of such a courtly link— the presence in several Myriell manuscripts of the hand that copied the important seventeenth-century score of Tallis's forty-part motet (Egerton MS 3512).[43] This version, with an alternative text beginning "Sing and glorify heaven's Majesty," was performed at the investiture of Henry as Prince of Wales in 1610 and again at the investiture of his brother six years later. Miss Willetts suggests that this scribe might have been John Ward, who, as we have seen, was among the most prominent composers in the Myriell sources. Ward's patron, Sir Henry Fanshawe, the remembrancer of the exchequer, had been an intimate of the young Prince Henry, and Ward surely would have encountered the musicians in the prince's retinue, perhaps at Fanshawe's London house in Warwick Lane.

There is much to support Willetts's suggested link between Myriell, the court, and John Ward. Warwick Lane is quite close to St. Paul's (see pl. 1 [g]), and there can be little doubt that John Ward came into contact with the St. Paul's circle. The fact that the petty canon of St. Paul's, John Barnard, chose to include two anthems and a service by Ward in his *First Book of Selected Church Musick* (1641) probably testifies to such a connection. Indeed, Ward's few pieces of extant service music only survive in manuscripts associated with Barnard or Adrian Batten, organist of the cathedral after 1626.[44]

Myriell, as a member of the St. Paul's enclave, could easily have encountered Ward and courtly musical circles. The remarkable profusion of laments for Prince Henry in the Myriell collection represents one of the most striking witnesses to such a courtly connection and may indicate that *Tristitiae Remedium* was perhaps originally intended as a musical memorial to the dead prince. Several of the musicians in Henry's service—Alfonso Ferrabosco II (Henry's music teacher), John Bull, and Thomas Lupo—appear prominently in the Myriell collection. Furthermore, Angelo Notari, whose *Prime musiche nuove* provided the engraved title page for *Tristitiae Remedium,* had also been in the service of the prince. One additional piece of evidence may strengthen the suggested link between Myriell and the musician from the Fanshawe household. A note on the flyleaf of Brussels II.4109 reveals that in 1784 Isaac Reed, the bibliophile and Shakespearean editor, bought the manuscript at Ware—the seat of Henry Fanshawe's country estate in Hertfordshire. This could, of course, be an unusual coincidence; given the other evidence, however, it more reasonably suggests that at least one of Myriell's manuscripts may have found its way into the collection of John Ward or the Fanshawes, perhaps at Myriell's death in 1625.

We know that Thomas Myriell was something of a pluralist and, in his ecclesiastical capacity, was not averse to strengthening any possible courtly ties. His sermon, *The Devout Soul's Search,* published in 1610, for example, had been dedicated to James Montague, dean of the Chapel Royal, and bishop of Bath and Wells. In 1613, while still at Barnet, the cleric dedicated his *Christ's Suite to his Church* to the Lord Mayor of London, in appreciation of past favors, lest he "should justly ever after be held unworthy of any favour, for the time to come." Shortly before his death, Myriell again ventured into print with an edition of a sermon by Robert Wilkinson, chaplain in ordinary to the king, which he dedicated to Maurice Abbot, brother of the Archbishop of Canterbury, whom Myriell had in fact served as chaplain since ca. 1616. It is plausible that Myriell may have decided to use his musical interests as another possible means of advancement as well. As mentioned earlier, the Brussels source possessed some of the earmarks of a presentation copy. Add. 29372-7 might also have been intended to fulfill such a purpose. The imposing scale of the partbooks, their lavish, engraved title page, and even perhaps the title itself, suggest this possibility. The year 1616, which witnessed Charles's creation as Prince of Wales (and also the death of Sir Henry Fanshawe), was an important one for Myriell, marking his appointment as rector of St. Stephen's and also perhaps as chaplain to the Archbishop of Canterbury. At this highpoint of his career, Myriell might have undertaken the copying of *Tristitiae Remedium* in anticipation of some future benefaction. But if this hypothesis were in fact true, the scheme apparently came to naught. The notation, "Tho: Myriell me tenet," on the flyleaf of Brussels II.4109 and the presence of Myriell's own initials on the leather bindings of *Tristitiae Remedium,* probably indicate that both sources remained in the clergyman's possession.

In any event, Myriell chose the more than 200 pieces for 29372-7 with great care and discrimination, and one may reasonably surmise that his choices provide an accurate index of his own musical taste and that in the St. Paul's circle about 1616. Myriell's taste was by no means narrow—the contents of his manuscripts range from instrumental fantasias to madrigals (both English and Italian), lute ayres, motets, consort songs, full anthems, and verse anthems—but it was surely discriminating. Although there can be no doubt about his serious turn of mind, it would be a mistake to view it as old-fashioned. Myriell's neglect of the old Tudor motets of Taverner, Tallis, and Tye, for example, attests to quite the opposite. These older works continue to reappear in profusion in more retrospective Jacobean sources, most notably those of the provincial lay clerk of Gloucester Cathedral, John Merro (New York Public Library, Drexel MSS 4180-5), but also in others such as British Library Add. MSS 37402-6 and St. Michael's College, Tenbury MSS 807-11. The two dozen motets that do appear in *Tristitiae Remedium* include nothing earlier than three from Byrd's *Cantiones sacrae* of 1589: *In resurrectione, Ne irascaris,* and *Civitas sancti tui.* But these were, and in fact still remain, among the most popular pieces Byrd ever composed. Aside from a few late Elizabethan motets by Thomas Morley, which Myriell perhaps copied from sources at St. Paul's where Morley had been organist in the early 1590s, virtually all the other motets are of the more up-to-date variety by Alfonso Ferrabosco II, Thomas Lupo, and Thomas Ravenscroft. Given Myriell's serious, discriminating musical outlook, he would quite naturally turn to this time-honored genre, though obviously not from any underlying crypto-Catholic leanings. The Jacobeans' continued cultivation of the motet does not imply any special liturgical intent, but rather an abiding interest in what was traditionally regarded as the most elevated musical form. It would certainly be wrong, for example, to attribute high church or popish motives to the staunch Puritan, John Milton, because he chose to set *Precamur sancte Domine,* which survives in the Myriell partbooks.

The clergyman's secondary interest in the madrigal, rather than indicating a retrospective turn of mind, may likewise testify to what was considered up-to-date among London's serious-minded musicians by the middle of James I's reign. The lighter madrigalian pieces of Thomas Morley, so prominent at the height of the madrigalian vogue of the 1590s, are strikingly absent from all Myriell's manuscripts. The glamorous flurry of the madrigal was passing. This apparent change in taste had in fact been anticipated by one of the cleric's preferred young composers, Michael East, who, after publishing two relatively orthodox collections of madrigals in 1604 and 1606, had turned to a more diversified content by his *Third Set* of 1610, where madrigals mix freely with "Pastorals, Anthems, Neopolitanes, Fancies... Apt both for Viols and Voyces." Many of the later "madrigal" publications, such as Byrd's *Psalms* (1611), East's *Fourth Set* (1618), or Vautor's *Songs of Diverse Airs and Natures* (1619), would likewise continue to reflect this trend. Indeed, in some prints such as John Amner's *Sacred Hymns* (1615) or Michael East's *Sixth Set* (1624), madrigals disappear entirely.

Above all, the London clergyman was interested in excellence in every genre, together with a seriousness that reflects the melancholy turn of mind in Jacobean England observed by Jean Jacquot and Wilfred Mellers.[45] Hence, Myriell's choice of madrigals gives pride of place to the Italian anthologies, Wilbye, Ward, and Weelkes, while his selections from the Elizabethan anthem repertory include only the best and most popular pieces. It is surely significant that virtually all Myriell's older anthem choices were also picked for inclusion in John Barnard's monumental *First Book of Selected Church Musick* some twenty-five years later.[46]

Myriell's interest in music for voices and viols, already perceptible in his earliest manuscript collections, attains greater prominence in *Tristitiae Remedium*. Once again, it would be wrong to interpret this interest as old-fashioned, for the verse anthems and consort songs of *Tristitiae Remedium*, in fact, reveal a preference for the most up-to-date works in these genres. Of the pieces from 29427 eligible for inclusion in 29372, No. 20, *Come tread the paths*, and No. 25, *Abradad*, are notably absent. As mentioned above, Myriell may have concluded that they were simply too old-fashioned, lacking on the one hand, the incessant false relations so beloved by the Jacobeans (cf. the incredibly popular *Behold it is Christ* by Hooper), and on the other, the more madrigalian gestures in harmony, declamation, and word painting which had begun to creep into the verse anthems of East and Peerson by 1610.[47]

In this light, it seems less surprising that William Byrd, without doubt the finest practitioner of the consort song, should be so meagerly represented in *Tristitiae Remedium*. Of some sixty works in the verse idiom contained in 29372, Byrd accounts for only five: *Lullaby/Be still my blessed babe, Delight is dead,* and *Christ rising/Christ is risen. Lullaby,* one of the most celebrated pieces of the period, had been popular even before it had appeared in print in 1588, and its popularity waned very slowly. *Christ rising* of 1589 may have retained its popularity because its scoring (with two sopranos in every verse and no fewer than eight choral interjections) had anticipated the more variegated timbres of the Jacobean age. The scarcity of Byrd's works in *Tristitiae Remedium* may in part be explained by the prominence of the 1588 set in the earlier manuscript, Brussels II.4109. But it more probably reflects a change in taste which judged Byrd too old-fashioned in outlook to compete with the Easts, Peersons, and Wards, whose musical innovations Byrd must have found indecorous and therefore to be avoided. So, while *Lullaby* and *Christ rising* were too popular to be ignored, Byrd's other pieces and all the riches of his *Psalms* of 1611 were left untouched.

To judge by Myriell's manuscripts for the musicians around St. Paul's, it was the verse anthems by East, Peerson, Ravenscroft, Simms, and Ward that, in fact, represented the "modern music" of the day. In them, the older native tradition of secular song enjoys a resurgence, but made more "fashionable" by an infusion of elements of harmony and word setting borrowed from the madrigal. This revitalized version of the older consort song, to whose revival Myriell bears witness, would continue to flourish in some secular circles throughout the Jacobean and Caroline periods, as later chapters will show.

folio[1] no.		Title	idiom	Composer	Concordances	Prints
1		"Altus" (otherwise blank)				

(fol. 1^V blank)

(three-part pieces)

folio[1] no.		Title	idiom	Composer	Concordances	Prints
2		[Fantasia]		[T. Lupo]		
2^V		["]		[" "]		
3^V	3	["]		[" "]		
4^V	4	["]		[" "]		
5	5	["]		[" "]		
5^V	6	["]		[" "]		
6	7	["]		[" "]		
6^V	8	["]		[" "]		
7	9	["]		[" "]		
7^V		["]		[" "]		

(fol. 8^V blank)

(four-part pieces)

folio[1] no.		Title	idiom	Composer	Concordances	Prints
9	11	Fantasia		J. Wilbye		
9^V	12	"		" "		
10	13	"		" "		

(fol. 10^V blank)

| 11 | 14 | La Chromatica | | G. Guami | | 1601[2]:11 |

(fol. 11^V blank)

| 12 | 15 | La Tedeschina | | " " | | " :5 |

(fol. 12^V blank)

(five-part pieces)

folio[1] no.		Title	idiom	Composer	Concordances	Prints
13	16	*Cease now vain thoughts*	cs	N. Giles	29372:97	
13^V	17	*O thrice-blessed[earth-bed]*	cs	[J. Tomkins][3]	" :51	
14	19	Out of the deep	f	[T. Lupo]	" :66	
14^V	20	*Come tread the path*	cs	[Anon.]		
15	21	When Israel came out (i)	v	[M. East]	" :38	1610:4
15^V	22	*What aileth thee (ii)*	v	[" "]	" :39	" :5
16	23	O my son Absalom (a 6)	f	[T. Weelkes]	" :234	
16		O Jonathen (a 6)	f	[" "]	" :235	
16^V	23	Cease now delight (a 6)	f	[" "]	" :232 4109:66	1598:24
17	24	I call and cry[4]	f	T. Tallis	29372:150	
17^V	25	Abradad	cs	[Anon.]		
18	26	*Turn thy face (i)*[5]	v	[M. East]		1610:16

(fol. 18^V blank)

| 19 | 27 | O Lord behold my miseries | f | J. Milton | 29372:33 | 1614[6]:34 |

(fols. 19^V-20 blank)

20^V	28	By Euphrates flowery side	f	M. Peerson		
21^V	29	I am the resurrection	f	J. Milton	" :37	
22	30	O had I wings	f	" "		1614:46
22^V	31	If that a sinner's sighs	f	" "	" :34	" :51
23	32	*O Jesu sweet [meek]*	v	T. Ravenscroft	" :27	

(fol. 23^V blank)

| 24 | 33 | *Plead thou my cause* | v | M. Peerson | " :28 | |

(fol. 24^V blank)

25	34	*Ah helpless wretch*	v	T. Ravenscroft	" :29	
25^V	35	*O that my ways (i)*	v	M. Peerson	" :30 and 286	
26	36	*I will thank thee (ii)*	v	" "	" :31 and 287	

---

1 Modern foliation.

2 *Partidura per sonare della Canzonette alla Francese, del Sig. Giuseppe Guami*, 1601.

3 Ascribed to "Thomas Tomkins" in 29427, but corrected in 29372.

4 Adaptation of the motet, *O sacrum convivium*, from CS1575.

5 Part 1 only.

6 Leighton's *Tears or Lamentations*, 1614.

folio	no.	Title	idiom	Composer	Concordances	Prints
26^V	37	*All laud and praise*	v	[T. Ravenscroft][1]	29372:32	
27	38	And the king was moved	f	[R. Dering]	" :25	
					4109:52	
27^V	39	*O Lord let me know*				
		mine end	v	[T. Tomkins]		
28^V	40	Sing joyfully	f	[R. Jones]		
29	41	When David heard	f	W. Bearsley		
29^V	42	*O Lord, in thee*	v	T. Ravenscroft		
30^V	43	I am the resurrection	f	[O. Gibbons]		
31	44	In resurrectione	f	W. Byrd	29372:96	CS1589:17
					4109:98	
31^V	45	O my son Absalom (a 6)	f	[T. Weelkes]	29372:234	
31^V	46	O Jonathen (" ")	f	[" "]	" :235	
32	47	O my son Absalom (i)	f	Giles Farnaby		
32		Saul and Jonathen (ii)	f	" "		
32^V	48	When David heard (a 6)	f	R. Ramsey		
32^V	49	When David heard	f	J. Milton	29372:35	
33	50	O woe is me	f	[" "]	" :36	
33^V	51	*Arise [Rise O my soul](i)*	v	W. Simms	" :40	
33^V		*And thou my soul (ii)*	v	" "	" :41	
34		*To thee, O Jesu (iii)*	v	" "	" :42	
34^V	52	Hear my prayer...and con-				
		sider	f	[T. Lupo]		

(fol. 35 blank)

folio	no.	Title	idiom	Composer	Concordances	Prints
35^V	53	*Down [caitif wretch] (i)*	v	J. Ward	29372:130	
36^V	54	*Prayer is an endless chain*	v	" "	" :132	
37^V	55	*How long [wilt thou forget]*	v	" "	" :134	
38	56	O vos omnes	f	T. Lupo	" :50 &	
					152	
					67: table	

(fol. 38^V blank)

folio	no.	Title	idiom	Composer	Concordances	Prints
39	57	*The Cries of London*	cs	T. Weelkes		

(fols. 40^V-41 blank)

folio	no.	Title	idiom	Composer	Concordances	Prints
41^V	58	*The Country Cries*	v	R. Dering	29372:98	
43	59	*The Cries of London*	v	O. Gibbons	" :61	
					67:52	

44^V (an untidy canonic exercise)

(four-part pieces)

folio	no.	Title	idiom	Composer	Concordances	Prints
45	61	Fantasia		W. Byrd		
45^V	62	"		" "		
46	63	So fa lo pensoso[2]		G.B. Moscaglia		
46	64	Se d'altro [mai]		G. de Macque		
46^V	65	Fantasia		A. Ferrabosco [II]		
47	66	"		" " ["]		
47^V	67	"		" " ["]		
48	68	"		" " ["]		
48^V	69	"		" " ["]		
49	70	"		" " ["]		
49^V	71	"		" " ["]		
50	72	"		" " ["]		
50^V	73	"		" " ["]		
51	74	"		[" " "]		
51^V	75	"		[" " "]		
52	76	"		[" " "]		
52^V	77	"		" " ["]		
53		"5 pts./ Altus" (otherwise blank)				

(fol. 53^V blank)

folio	no.	Title	idiom	Composer	Concordances	Prints
54	78	In Nomine a5		A. Ferrabosco II		
54^V	79	" "		" " II		
55	80	" "		" " I		
55^V	81	" "		" " I		
56	82	Morrir[3] [non puo'l mio core]		G.M. Nanino		
56^V	83	Vince labianio		R. Giovanelli		
57	84	Tutte le stelle		G. Feretti		
57^V	85	Donna mi fuggi [ogn' hora]		" "		

---

1 Attributed to M. Peerson in the source.

2 The following two pieces are madrigals, left textless for instrumental performance.

3 Numbers 82-99 are madrigals, left textless for instrumental performance.

folio	no.	Title	idiom	Composer	Concordances	Prints
58	86	Deh resta		[Anon.]		
58^V	87	Cor mio		[B. Pallavicino]	67:30^V	
59	88	Ohime		[Anon.]		
59^V	89	Ond'ei di morte		C. Monteverdi	67:23^V	
60	90	Latra'l sangue		" "	" :24^V	
60^V	91	Al suon d'amata		L. Quintiani		
61	92	Clorinda [hai vinto]		H. Vecchi	67:31^V	
61^V	93	O com' gran martire		C. Monteverdi	" :25^V	
62	94	Sovra tenera		" "	" :26^V	
62^V	95	Ond' all' hor		H. Vecchi		
63	96	Non vi bastava		P. Masneli		
63		[no title]				
63^V	97	Ond'ei di morte		L. Marenzio	67:32	
64	98	Tu dolce anima		A. Ferrabosco [I]		
64	99	Pastorella [graziosella]		H. Vecchi		
64^V		"a 5 Fancies of 3.4. and 5. Altus" (otherwise blank)				
65	100	[Down caitif wretch (i)]	v	J. Ward	29372:131	
65^V	101	Prayer is an endless chain (ii)	v	" "	" :132	
66^V	103	How long	v	" "	" :134	
67^V	104	Long have I lifted	f	G. Hanford	" :171	
68	105	If that a sinner's sighs	f	J. Milton	" :34	1614^1:51
68^V	106	O woe is me	f	" "	" :36	
69^V	108	Almighty God, who by the leading of a star	v	J. Bull	" :136 270	
70^V	110	Hear me O God^2	cs	A. Ferrabosco [II]	" :142	
71	111	Blessed art thou that fearest God	f	[P. Van Wilder]	" :159	

(fol. 71^V blank)

folio	no.	Title	idiom	Composer	Concordances	Prints
72	112	O Lord turn thy wrath (i)^3	f	W. Byrd	" :192	
72^V	113	Bow thine ear (ii)	f	" "	" :194	
73	114	Salva nos Domine	f	T. Lupo	" :181,	67: table
73^V	115	Heu mihi Domine	f	" "	" :197	67: table
74	116	It is my well-beloved's voice	f	[T. Tomkins]	" :308 62:21^V	1622:27

(fols. 74^V-75 blank)

folio	no.	Title	idiom	Composer	Concordances	Prints
75^V		Frail man despise (a4)	f	J. Bull	29372:16	
76^V	117	Blow out the trumpet	v	[M. Peerson]	" :74	
77^V	118	How doth the holy city (i)	f	[J. Milton]	" :266	
78	119	She weepeth continually (ii)	f	[" "]	" :268	

(fol. 78^V blank. Followed by another unnumbered, blank, ruled folio)

---

1 Leighton's *Tears or Lamentations*, 1614.

2 Adaptation of the "Four-Note Pavan".

3 Adaptation of the motet, *Ne irascaris/Civitas sancti tui*, from CS1589.

page	Title	idiom Composer	Concordances	Prints

(four-part pieces)

page	Title	idiom	Composer	Concordances	Prints
2	*If my complaints*	cs	[J. Dowland]		1597:4
4	*Can she excuse my wrongs*	cs	[" "]		" :5
6	*Now O now I needs must part*	cs	[" "]		" :6
8	*Away with these self-loving lads*	cs	[" "]		" :21
10	*Burst forth, my tears*	cs	[" "]		" :8
12	*Sleep wayward thoughts*	cs	[" "]		" :13
14	*Come again sweet love*	cs	[" "]		" :17
16	*His golden locks*	cs	[" "]		" :18
18	*Dear if you change*	cs	[" "]		" :7
20	*Humor say*	v	[" "]		1600:22
22	*A shepherd in a shade*	cs	[" "]		" :17
24	*If floods of tears*	cs	[" "]		" :11
26	*Toss not my soul*	cs	[" "]		" :20
28	*Praise blindness eyes*	cs	[" "]		" :9
30	*Shall I sue*	cs	[" "]		" :19

(three-part pieces)

page	Title	idiom	Composer	Concordances	Prints
32	*Do you not know*	f	T. Morley		1593:16
34	*Thirsis, O let pity*	f	" "		" :12
36	*Now must I die*	f	[" "]		" :13
38	*Lady if I through grief*	f	[" "]		" :14
40	*Cease mine eyes*	f	[" "]		" :15
42	*Arise, get up my dear*	f	[" "]		" :20
44	*Spring time mantleth*	f	[" "]		" :24
46	*Eheu sustulerunt* (*a 4*)	f	" "	29372:13	

(five-part pieces)

page	Title	idiom	Composer	Concordances	Prints
48	*Dentes tui*	f	[T. Morley]	" :69	
50	*O amica mea*	f	" "	" :68	
52	*And the king was moved*	f	[R. Dering]	" :25 / 29427:38	
54	*All at once well met*	f	T. Weelkes		1598:1
56	*Give me my heart*	f	" "	29372:106	" :7
58	*Come clap thy hands* (i)	f	" "	" :108	" :19
60	*Phillis hath sworn* (ii)	f	" "	" :109	" :20
62	*Unto our flocks*	f	" "	" :216	" :23
64	*Now is my Cloris fresh*	f	" "	" :214	" :22
66	*Cease now delight* (*a 6*)	f	" "	" :232 / 29427:23	" :24
68	*Farewell my joy* (*a 5*)	f	" "		" :21

(four-part pieces)

page	Title	idiom	Composer	Concordances	Prints
70	*Now that each creature*	f	G. Bassano		MT1597:1
72	*Lady, let me behold*	f	G. Croce		" :3
74	*Since that the time*	f	" "		" :2
76	*Flora fair love*	f	F. Anerio		" :7
78	*My heart why hast thou*	f	T. Morley		" :8
80	*Daphne the bright*	f	G. Croce		" :20
82	*Pearl, crystal, gold*	f	F. Anerio		" :18
84	*Cock-a-do-dell-do*	f	R. Jones		1607:9
86	*Sing merry birds*	f	" "		" :7
88	*I come sweet birds*	f	" "		" :8
90	*Shrill sounding bird*	f	" "		" :10

(five-part pieces)

page	Title	idiom	Composer	Concordances	Prints
92	*Come doleful owl*	f	R. Jones		" :13
94	*Sweet, when thou sing'st*	f	" "		" :14
96	*Your presence breeds* (*a 6*)	f	" "		" :22
98	*In resurrectione*	f	[W. Byrd]	29372:96 / 29427:44	CS1589:17
100	*Noblesse gift au coeur*[1]	f	O. Lassus		
102	*Susann*	f	" "		
104	*Mine eyes with fervency*	f	[W. Byrd]	29372:70	1588:2
106	*How shall a young man*	f	[" "]		" :4
108	*Constant Penelope*	f	[" "]		" :23
110	*Farewell false love*	f	[" "]		" :25
112	*Care for thy soul*	f	[" "]		" :31
114	*The match that's made*	f	[" "]		" :26
116	*Why do I use*	f	[" "]		" :33
118	*Come to me grief*	f	[" "]		" :34

1 The tenor of the two Lassus chansons is textless in the source.

page	Title	idiom	Composer	Concordances	Prints
120	*Complain with tears*	cs	[Anon.]		
122	O sacrum convivium[1]	f	T. Tallis		CS1575:9
124	In manus tuas	f	[" "]		" :3
126	Emendemus in melius	f	W. Byrd		" :4
128	O nata lux	f	[T. Tallis]		" :8
130	Salvator mundi	f	" "		" :1
132	**Libera me Domine (i)**	f	W. Byrd		" :5
134	Dies mei (ii)	f	" "		" :5

(four-part pieces)

136	You pretty flowers	f	J. Farmer		1599:1
138	Now each creature joys	f	[" "]		" :2
140	I thought my love	f	" "		" :8
142	Who would have thought	f	" "		" :10

(five-part pieces)

144	Dainty fine sweet nymph	f	[T. Morley]		1595:1
146	Shoot false love	f	[" "]		" :2
148	No, no Nigella	f	[" "]		" :6
150	Singing alone	f	[" "]		" :5
152	You that wont	f	[" "]		" :13
154	Lo, she flies	f	[" "]		" :18
156	**Why weeps, alas**	f	[" "]	29372:105	" :20
158	O God give ear	f	[W. Byrd]		1588:1
160	My soul oppressed	f	[" "]	" :71	" :3
162	I joy not	f	[" "]		" :11
164	Though Amaryllis	f	[" "]		" :12
166	**Who likes to love**	f	[" "]		" :13
168	My mind to me	f	[" "]		" :14
170	La virginella	f	[" "]		" :24
172	**All as a sea**	f	[" "]		" :28
174	In fields abroad	f	[" "]		" :22
176	Lullaby (i)	f	[" "]	" :208	" :32
178	Be still (ii)	f	[" "]	" :209	" :32
180	Susanna fair	f	[" "]		" :29
182	O that most rare breast	f	[" "]		" :35
134	The doleful debt	f	[" "]		" :35
186	Ne irascaris (i)	f	[" "]	" :146	CS1589:20
188	Civitas sancti tui (ii)	f	[" "]	" :147	" :21
190	Deus venerunt gentes	f	[" "]		" :11
192	Posuerunt morticina	f	[" "]		" :12

(four-part pieces)

194	Sweet love, I err	f	M. East		1604:13
196	Joy of my life	f	[" "]		" :16
198	Pity dear love	f	[" "]		" :11
200	My hope a counsel	f	[" "]		" :10
202	All ye that joy	f	[" "]		" :17
204	My prime of youth	f	[" "]		" :18
206	The spring is past	f	[" "]		" :19
208	Fair is my love	f	[" "]		" :20
210	Sly thief	f	[" "]		" :21
212	What thing more cruel[2]	f	[" "]		" :22

(The remainder of the manuscript is missing)

---

1 For the next seven entries, only four parts have been copied.

2 Only three parts survive.

folio[1]	page	Title	idiom	Composer	Concordances	Prints
i		(blank, unruled)				
1		Peritus non ignorat ordines./TRISTITIAE/REMEDIUM./CANTIONES/ selectissimae, diversorū tū/authorum, tum argumentorū;/labore & manu exaratae/THOMAE MYRIELL./A.D. 1616.				

(four-part pieces)

folio[1]	page	Title	idiom	Composer	Concordances	Prints
2	1	When Cloris heard	f	J. Wilbye		1609:9
2ᵛ	2	Happy streams	f	[" "]		" :10
3ᵛ	4	Change me O heavens	f	[" "]		" :11
4ᵛ	6	Love me not for comely grace	f	[" "]		" :12
5ᵛ	8	I love alas	f	[" "]		" :14
6ᵛ	10	Lo! here my heart	f	G. Kirbye		1597:1
7ᵛ	12	Fuerunt mihi lachrymae	f	A. Ferrabosco [II]		
8	13	Eheu, sustulerunt	f	T. Morley	4109:46	
8ᵛ	14	Nolo mortem peccatoris	f	" "		
9ᵛ	16	Frail man despise	f	J. Bull	29427:116	
10ᵛ	18	Quare dereliquerunt me	f	A. Ferrabosco [II]		
11ᵛ	20	In the departure of the Lord	f[3]	J. Bull		1614[2]: unnumbered
11ᵛ	20	Thou God of might	f	J. Milton		" :10
12	21	O let me tread	f	J. Ward		" :26
12	21	Attend unto my tears	f	J. Bull		" :17
12ᵛ	22	O Lord give ear	f	T. Lupo		" :21
13	23	I am quite tired	f	J. Wilbye		" :27
13ᵛ	24	Adieu, sweet Amarillis	f	" "		1598:12

(from 15 to 28 blank, ruled folios in the various partbooks)

(five-part pieces)

folio[1]	page	Title	idiom	Composer	Concordances	Prints
14	25	And the king was moved	f	R. Dering	29427:38 4109:52	
14ᵛ	26	*Ne reminiscaris*	cs	J. Wilbye		
15	27	*O Jesu meek*	v	T. Ravenscroft	29427:32	
15ᵛ	28	*Plead thou my cause*	v	M. Peerson	" :33	

(2 blank, ruled folios)

folio[1]	page	Title	idiom	Composer	Concordances	Prints
16	29	*Ah, helpless wretch*	v	T. Ravenscroft	29427:34	
16ᵛ	30	*Oh that my ways (i)*	v	M. Peerson	" :35	
17	31	*I will thank thee (ii)*	v	" "	" :36	
17ᵛ	32	*All laud and praise*	v	T. Ravenscroft	" :37	
18	33	O Lord behold my miseries	f[3]	J. Milton	" :27	1614[2]:34
18ᵛ	34	If that a sinner's sighs	f	" "	" :31 & 105	" :51
19	35	When David heard	f	" "	" :49	
19ᵛ	36	O woe is me for thee	f	" "	" :50 & 106	
20	37	I am the resurrection	f	" "	" :29	
20ᵛ	38	*When Israel came out (i)*	v	M. East	" :21	1610:4
21	39	*What aileth thee (ii)*	v	" "	" :22	" :5
21ᵛ	40	*Rise O my soul (i)*	v	W. Simms	" :51	
22	41	*And thou, my soul (ii)*	v	" "		
22ᵛ	42	*To thee, O Jesu (iii)*	v	" "		
23	43	O heavenly God	f	W. Daman		
23ᵛ	44	*Sweet Muses (i)*	v	[M. East]		1610:1
24	45	*Aye me, wherefore sighs(ii)*	v	[" "]		" :2
24ᵛ	46	*My peace & my pleasure(iii)*	v	[" "]		" :3
25	47	Ne laeteris inimica mea	f	T. Ravenscroft		
25ᵛ	48	O sacred & holy banquet[4]	f	T. Tallis		
26ᵛ	50	O vos omnes	f	T. Lupo	29427:56 67:table	
27	51	*O thrice blessed earth-bed*	cs	J. Tomkins	29427:17	
27ᵛ	52	Come help, O God	f[3]	W. Byrd		1614[2]:53
28	53	Not unto us	f	T. Ford		" :44
28ᵛ	53	O happy he	f	T. Weelkes		" :41
29	55	O let me at thy footstool	f	M. Peerson		" :39
29ᵛ	56	Judge them, O Lord	f	R. Kindersly		" :52
30	57	O Lord consider my great groan	f	J. Wilbye		" :48
30ᵛ	58	I laid me down to rest	f	W. Byrd		" :31
31	59	O Lord, how do my woes	f	J. Coperario		" :40
31ᵛ	60	Miserere nostri, Domine	f	W. Daman	67:table	

---

1 Modern foliation, from 29372

2 Leighton's *Tears or Lamentations,* 1614

3 These pieces, as published, include instrumental parts for broken consort. In *Tristitiae Remedium* only the vocal parts are included.

4 Adaptation of the motet, *O sacrum convivium,* from CS1575

folio	page	Title	idiom	Composer	Concordances	Prints
32	61	*God give you good morrow (i)*	v	O. Gibbons	29427:59 67:52ᵛ	
33ᵛ	64	*A good sausage (ii)*	v	" "	29427:60 67:53ᵛ	
34ᵛ	66	Out of the deep	f	T. Lupo	29427:19	
35ᵛ	68	O amica mea (i)	f	T. Morley	4109:50	
36	69	Dentes tui (ii)	f	" "	" :48	
36ᵛ	70	Mine eyes with fervency	f	W. Byrd	" :104	1588:2
37	71	My soul oppressed	f	" "	" :160	" :3
37ᵛ	72	*O go not from me*	v	[M. Peerson]		
38ᵛ	74	*Blow out the trumpet*	v	" "	29427:117	
39ᵛ	76	*Who will rise up (i)*	v	[" "]		
40	77	*But when I said (ii)*	v	" "		
40ᵛ	78	*Rain eyes*[1]	v	" "		
41ᵛ	80	*Fly ravished soul (i)*	v	[" "]		
42	81	*Rest there awhile (ii)*	v	" "		
42ᵛ	82	*Muse still thereon (iii)*	v	[" "]		
43ᵛ	84	*I am brought (i)*	v	" "		
44ᵛ	86	*My heart panteth (ii)*	v	" "		
45ᵛ	88	*Wake sorrow (i)*	v	[" "]		
46ᵛ	90	*Arbella, sole paragon (ii)*	v	" "		
47	91	*O Lord thou hast searched me out (i)*	v	" "		
47ᵛ	92	*Thou art about (ii)*	v	" "		
48	93	*Thou hast fashioned (iii)*	v	[" "]		
48ᵛ	94	*Whither then shall (iv)*	v	" "		
49	95	Miserere mei Domine	f	T. Lupo	67:table	
49ᵛ	96	In resurrectione	f	W. Byrd	29427:44 4109:98	CS1589:17
50	97	*Cease now vain thoughts*	cs	N. Giles	29427:16	
50ᵛ	98	*Country Cries*	v	R. Dering	" :58	
52ᵛ	102	My lovely wanton jewel	f	T. Morley		1595:12
53ᵛ	104	Leave alas this tormenting	f	" "		" :19
54	105	Why weeps alas my lady	f	" "	4109:156	" :20
54ᵛ	106	Give me my heart	f	T. Weelkes	" :56	1598:7
55ᵛ	108	Come clap thy hands (i)	f	" "	" :58	" :19
56	109	Phillis hath sworn (ii)	f	" "	" :60	" :20
56ᵛ	110	Sound out my voice	f	G. Palestrina		MT1588:30
57	111	I must depart	f	L. Marenzio		" :22
57ᵛ	112	Life tell me	f	H. Vecchi		Mol598:11
58	113	Flora fair nymph	f	J. ward		1613:15
58ᵛ	114	Sweet honey-sucking bees	f	J. Wilbye		1609:17
59ᵛ	116	Yet sweet take heed (ii)	f	[" "]		" :18
60	117	Weep weep mine eyes	f	[" "]		" :23
60ᵛ	118	Down in a valley (i)	f	" "		]609:21
61ᵛ	120	Hard destinies (ii)	f	" "		" :22
62ᵛ	122	Alas, where is my love	f	T. Bateson		1604:18
63ᵛ	124	Hark, hear ye not	f	" "		" :22
64ᵛ	126	Dolorous mournful cares	f	L. Marenzio		MT1597:9
65	127	*See the word is incarnate*	v	O. Gibbons		
66ᵛ	130	*Down caitif wretch (i)*	v	J. Ward	29427:53 & 100	
67ᵛ	132	*Prayer is an endless chain (ii)*	v	" "	" :54 & 101	
68ᵛ	134	*How long wilt thou forget*	v	" "	" :55 & 103	
69ᵛ	136	*Almighty God, who by the leading of a star*	v	J. Bull	" :108	
70ᵛ	138	There where I saw he	f	J. Wilbye		1609:24
71ᵛ	140	All pleasure is of this	f	" "		" :19
72ᵛ	142	*Hear me, O God*[2]	cs	A. Ferrabosco [II]	" :110	
73	143	So far dear life	f	G. Eremita		MT1597:3
73ᵛ	144	If silent then grief	f	A. Ferrabosco [I]	67:table	Mol598:13
74	145	I languish to complain me	f	" "	["] " "	" :15
74ᵛ	146	Ne irascaris (i)	f	W. Byrd	4109:186	CS1589:20
75	147	Civitas sancti tui (ii)	f	" "	" :188	" :21
75ᵛ	148	I lift my heart to thee	f	C. Tye		
76ᵛ	150	I call and cry[3]	f	T. Tallis	29427:24	
77ᵛ	152	O vos omnes	f	T. Lupo	" :56 67:table	
78	153	Miserere	f	" "	67:table	
78ᵛ	154	Save me C God	f	M. Coste[4]		
79ᵛ	156	O give thanks unto the Lord	f	[J. Mundy]		

---

1 Other MSS include this piece as part 4 of the following anthem.

2 Adaptation of the "Four-Note Pavan."

3 Adaptation of the motet, *O sacrum convivium*, from CS1575.

4 Attributed to Byrd in other sources.

folio	page	Title	idiom	Composer	Concordances	Prints
80[V]	158	Deliver me from mine enemies	f	[R. Parsons]		
81	159	Blessed art thou that fearest God	f	[P. Van Wilder][1]	29427:111	
81[V]	160	O Jesu, look	f	G. Kirbye		
82	161	Peccantem quotidie	f	A. Ferrabosco [I]	67:table	
82[V]	162	*Hear my prayer O Lord*	v	T. Wilkinson		
83[V]	164	It is a good thing	f	J. Lugge		
84[V]	166	*The City Cries*	v	R. Dering		
87	171	Long have I lifted up	f	G. Hanford	29427:104	
87[V]	172	*O God of Gods (i)*	v	J. Bennet	67:55	
88[V]	174	*To the almighty Trinity (ii)*	v	" "	" :55[V]	
89	175	The white delightful swan	f	H. Vecchi		MT1597:1
89v	176	Zephyrus brings the time	f	A. Ferrabosco [I]		" :2
90[V]	178	O nomen Jesu	f	" "	[II]	
91	179	Ego dixi Domine	f	" "	["]	
91[V]	180	*Give ear, O God*	v	T. Weelkes		
92	181	Salva nos Domine	f	T. Lupo	29427:114 67:table	
92[V]	182	*O clap your hands (i)*	v	M. East		1618:10
93[V]	184	*God is gone up (ii)*	v	" "		" :11
94[V]	186	I saw my lady weeping (i)	f	A. Ferrabosco [I]		MT1588:23
95[V]	188	Like as from heaven (ii)	f	" "	["]	" :24
96[V]	190	When shall I cease	f	N. Faignient		" :21
97[V]	192	O Lord turn thy wrath (i)[1]f		W. Byrd	29427:112	
98[V]	194	Bow thine ear (ii)	f	" "	" :113	
99[V]	196	Prevent us, O Lord	f	" "		
100	197	Heu mihi Domine	f	T. Lupo	" :115 67:table	
100[V]	198	*Have mercy upon me*	v	S. Stubbs		
101[V]	200	*Sing joyfully*	v	J. Mundy		
103	203	O my loving sweetheart	f	L. Marenzio		Mo1598:14
103[V]	204	*Preserve me O Lord*	v	T. Wilkinson		
104[V]	206	*Put me not to rebuke*	v	" "		
105[V]	208	*Lullaby (i)*	cs	W. Byrd	4109:176	1588:32
106	209	*Be still (ii)*	cs	" "	4109:178	" :32
106[V]	210	*Delight is dead*	cs	" "		
107[V]	212	When David heard	f	T. Tomkins		1622:19
108[V]	214	Now is my Cloris	f	T. Weelkes	4109:64	1598:22
109[V]	216	Unto our flocks	f	" "	" :62	" :23
110[V]	218	Father of love	f	S. Stubbs		
111[V]	220	Alleluia, I heard a voice	f	T. Weelkes		
112[V]	222	The nightingale that sweetly	f	P. Philips		Mo1598:19
113[V]	224	Hope of my heart	f	J. Ward		1613:17
114[V]	226	Upon a bank with roses	f	" "		" :18
115[V]	228	Behold, it is Christ	f	E. Hooper		
116[V]	230	With all our heart[2]	f	T. Tallis		
117[V]	232	*Let God arise*	v	J. Ward	61:49 & 51 67:58	

(fol. 119[V], plus from 8 to 36 folios blank in the various partbooks)

(six-part pieces)

(fol. 120 blank)

folio	page	Title	idiom	Composer	Concordances	Prints
120[V]	230	De profundis	f	T. Morley		
121[V]	232	Cease now delight	f	T. Weelkes	29427:23 4109:66	1598:24
122[V]	234	O my son **Absalom**	f	" "	29427:23, 45	
123	235	O Jonathen	f	" "	" :23, 46	
123[V]	236	O wretched man	f	J. Wilbye		1609:27
124	237	Where most my thoughts	f	" "		" :28
124[V]	238	Draw on sweet night	f	" "		" :31
125[V]	240	Softly drop mine eyes	f	" "		" :33
126[V]	242	Long have I made	f	" "		" :34
127[V]	244	O gracious & worthiest	f	G. Croce		MT1597:19
128[V]	246	Shall I live so far	f	L. Marenzio		" :20
129	247	Dainty white pearl	f	A. Bicci		" :23
129[V]	248	Hard by a chrystal fountain	f	G. Croce		" :24
130[V]	250	Lord in thy wrath (i)	f	" "		1608[3]:1
131	251	Long have I languished (ii)f		" "		" :2
131[V]	252	Show mercy (i)	f	[" "]	67:64[V]	" :7
132	253	Give me a clean heart (ii)f		" "	" :65[V]	" :8

---

1 Adaptation of *Ne irascaris/Civitas sancti tui* from CS1589.

2 Adaptation of *Salvator mundi* from CS1575.

3 *Musica Sacra*, 1608

folio	page	Title	idiom	Composer	Concordances	Prints
132^V	254	Fair Hebe when Dame Flora	f	T. Bateson		1604:24
133^V	256	Thirsis on his fair Phillis	f	" "		" :26
134^V	258	Fair Orion in the morn	f	J. Milton		1601:18
135^V	260	Precamur Sancte Domine	f	" "		
136	261	Those spots	f	T. Weelkes		1597:21
136^V	262	Retire my thoughts	f	" "		" :19
137	263	*Christ rising (i)*	v	W. Byrd		1589:46
137^V	264	*Christ is risen (ii)*	v	" "		" :47
138^V	266	How doth the holy city	f	J. Milton	29427:118	
139^V	268	She weepeth continually	f	" "	" :119	
140^V	270	*Almighty God, who by the leading of a star*	v	J. Bull	" : 108	
141^V	272	**Lord remember David**	f	M. Jeffreys		
142^V	274	In thee, O Lord do I trust	f	" "		
143	275	When David heard	f	T. Weelkes		
143^V	276	*If the Lord himself*	v	M. Jeffreys		
144^V	278	*Thou art my king*	v	T. Tomkins		
145^V	280	Stay, Coridon thou swain	f	J. Wilbye		1609:32
146^V	282	Love, quench this heart	f	B. Palavicino		MT1597:17
147^V	284	Cruel, why dost thou fly me	f	" "		" :18
148^V	286	*O that my ways (i)*	v	M. Peerson	29427:35	
149	287	*I will thank thee (ii)*	v	" "	" :36	
149^V	288	So far from my delight (i)	f	A. Ferrabosco [I]		MT1588:48
150^V	290	She only doth not feel (ii)	f	" "	"	" :49
151^V	292	Now must I part	f	L. Marenzio		" :51
152	293	I sung sometimes (i)	f	" "		" :56
152^V	294	Because my life (ii)	f	" "		" :57

(fol. 153 blank)

folio	page	Title	idiom	Composer	Concordances	Prints
153^V	296	Laboravi in gemitu	f	T. Morley		
154^V	298	O hear me heavenly powers	f	L. Marenzio		IM1590:21
155	299	In chains of hope	f	" "		" :22
155^V	300	Unkind oh stay	f	" "		" :25

(fol. 156 blank)

folio	page	Title	idiom	Composer	Concordances	Prints
156^V	302	Sing joyfully	f	W. Byrd		
157^V	304	*Almighty God whose love (i)*	v	W. White		
158^V	306	*Bend down (ii)*	v	" "		
159^V	308	It is my well-beloved's voice	f	T. Tomkins	29427:116 61:21^V	1622:27
160^V	310	*Sing unto God*	v	" "		

(pp. 310, 313, 312, [leaf cut], "313": all blank)

folio	page	Title	idiom	Composer	Concordances	Prints
162^V	314	**Retire my troubled soul**	f	J. Ward		1613:19
163	315	Out from the vale	f	" "		" :21
163^V	316	Oft have I tendered	f	" "		" :20
164^V	318	O divine Love	f	" "		" :22
165^V	320	If the deep sighs	f	" "		" :23
166^V	322	There's not a grove	f	" "		" :24
167^V	324	Weep forth your tears	f	" "		" :28
168^V	326	Die not, fond man	f	" "		" :25
169^V	328	Come sable night	f	" "		" :27
170^V	330	I have entreated	f	" "		" :26
171^V	332	Lord in thine anger	f	G. Croce	67:66^V	1608^1:5
172^V	334	My strength even fails	f	" "	" :67^V	" :6
173	335	Lord bend thy righteous ears	f	[Anon.]	61:70	
173^V	336	No object dearer	f	J. Ward	61:71 67:72^V	
174^V	338	From deepest horror	f	T. Tomkins		
175^V	340	Oft did I mar'l	f	" "		1622:25

(fol. 176^V blank, plus from 5 to 37 blank, ruled folios in the various partbooks.)

---

1 *Musica Sacra*, 1608

folio[1] no.		Title	idiom	Composer	Concordances	Prints
1	1	Fantasia		[O. Gibbons]	459:2	
1ᵛ	2	"		[" "]	" :3	
2	3	"		[" "]		
2ᵛ	4	"		[" "]	" :6	
3	5	"		[" "]		
3ᵛ	6	"		[" "]	" :7	
4	7	"		[" "]		
4ᵛ	8	"		[" "]		

(8 blank, ruled folios)

13		*Praise the Lord*	v	J. Ward	67:ivᵛ	
13ᵛ	2	*The Lord executeth righteousness*	v	" "	":1ᵛ	
14	3	*For look how high*	v	" "	":2ᵛ	
14ᵛ	4	*The days of man*	v	" "	":3ᵛ	
15	5	*The Lord hath prepared*	v	" "	":4ᵛ	
15ᵛ	6	*Have mercy upon me*	v	" "	":5ᵛ	
16	7	*Behold I was shapen*	v	" "	":6ᵛ	
16ᵛ	8	*Turn thy face*	v	" "		
17	9	*Deliver me from blood-guiltiness*	v	" "		
21ᵛ		It is my well-beloved's voice[2]	f	[T. Tomkins]	29372:303 29427:116	

(16 blank, ruled folios)

34	1	Leno[3]		G. Coperario		
34ᵛ	2	Luce beata e care		" "		
35	3	Lucretia mia		" "		
35ᵛ	4	[Fantasia]		" "		
36	5	Cresce in voi		" "		
36ᵛ	6	Crudel perche		" "		
37	7	Io son ferrito		" "		
37ᵛ	8	Voi caro il mio contento		" "		
38	9	Fuga dunque la luce		" "		
38ᵛ	10	O sonno della mio morte		" "		
39	11	Dolce ben mio		" "		

(9-10 blank, ruled folios)

48ᵛ		*I will magnify thee*[4]	v	[M. Peerson]		
49		*Let God arise*	v	J. Ward	29372:232 67:58	
51ᵛ		*Let God arise*[5]	v	" "	29372:232 67:58	
53		My heart with grief doth languish	f			
53ᵛ		*The Lord hear thee*	v	W. Pising		

(fol. 54ᵛ blank)

55		**When wilt thou, O Lord**	f			
55ᵛ		O sweet Jesus, save	f		67:18ᵛ	

(fol. 56ᵛ blank)

57ᵛ		Hear my prayer O Lord	f		67:19ᵛ	

(4 blank folios)

62ᵛ		*Mount up, my soul*	v			

(5 blank folios)

69		Vota per solvam	f			
70		Lord, bend thy righteous ears	f		29372:335	
71ᵛ		Fond love thou play'st	f			

---

1 Modern foliation, from 61.

2 This piece appears in 62 only.

3 This group of pieces consists of fantasias with Italian titles.

4 This piece appears in 63 and 66 only.

5 A fourth lower than the previous version.

folio no.	Title	idiom	Composer	Concordances	Prints
72	No object dearer[1]	f	[J. Ward]	29372:336 67:72^V	
73	Dear Lord of life	f	T. Tomkins		

(fols. 73^V-14 blank)

74^V	*Know ye not*[2]	v	" "		

(fol. 75^V blank)

76	[Fantasia]		A. Ferrabosco [II]		
76^V	"		W. White		
77	"		" "		
77^V	"		G. Coperario		
78	"		C. Coleman		
78^V	"		" "		
79	"		" "		
80	"		" "		
80^V	"		A. Ferrabosco [II]		
81	In Nomine		" " "		
81^V	" "		S. Ives		

(13 blank folios)

---

1 "Passions on the death of Prince Henry."

2 "Prince Henry his funeral" (The piece occurs only in 61).

folio[1]	Title	idiom	Composer	Concordances	Prints
iv	"103 Psalme." (title only; crossed out)				
iv[v]	*Praise the Lord*	v	[J. Ward]	61:13	
1[v]	*The Lord executeth righteousness*	v	[" "]	" :13[v]	
2[v]	*For look how high*	v	[" "]	" :14	
3[v]	*The days of man*	v	[" "]	" :14[v]	
4[v]	*The Lord [hath prepared]*	v	[" "]	" :15	
5[v]	*Have mercy*	v	[" "]	" :15[v]	
6[v]	*Behold I was shapen*	v	[" "]	" :16	
7[v]	[Fantasia] (incomplete)		A. Ferrabosco [II]		

(fols. 8-11 blank)

| 11[v] | [Fantasia][2] *a 5* | | T. Lupo | | |

(fol. 12[v] blank)

| 13 | [Fantasia] | | [J. Ward] | | |

(fols. 14[v]-17 blank)

17[v]	When wilt thou O Lord	f		61:55	
18[v]	O sweet Jesus	f		" :55[v]	
19[v]	Hear my prayer	f		" :57[v]	
20[v]	I must depart	f	[L. Marenzio]	29372:111	MT1588:22

(fols. 21-23 blank)

23[v]	Ond' ei di morte[3]		C. Monteverdi	29427:89	
24[v]	Latra'l sangue		" "	" :90	
25[v]	O come gran martire		" "	" :93	
26[v]	tenere		" "	" :94	
27[v]	[Fantasia]		G. Coperario		
28[v]	"		W. White		
29[v]	Cor mio		J. Ward		
30[v]	Cor mio		B. Pallavicino	" :87	
31[v]	Clorinda		H. Vecchi	" :92	
32	di morte		L. Marenzio	" :97	
32[v]	Deh poi cn'ora		" "		
33	Udite lagrimosi spiriti		" "		
34	Che sei tu		" "		
34[v]	Come vivro		B. Pallavicino		
35[v]	O caro dolce		L. Marenzio		
36[v]	Alte parole[4]		J. Lupo[5]		
37[v]	Fantasia		W. Simms		
38	["]		" "		
39[v]	["] (incomplete)		[G. Coperario]		

(fols. 40-51[v] blank)

52	[end of Gibbons's *Cry*][6]				
52[v]	*The Cry (i)*	v	O. Gibbons	29372:61	
	A good sausage (ii)			29427:59	

(fols. 54-54[v] blank)

| 55 | [end of *O God of Gods*][6] | | | | |
| 55[v] | *O God of gods* | v | J. Bennet | 29372:172 | |

(fols. 57-57[v] blank)

| 58 | *Let God arise*[7] | v | J. Ward | 29372:232
61:49 & 51[v] | |

(fols. 60-64 blank)

| 64[v] | Show mercy (i) | f | G. Croce | 29372:252 | 1608[8]:7 |

---

1 Modern folation.

2 Bears annotation "36 Leat[9] boo"

3 The following madrigals, some of which appear in 29427, where they are textless, were probably intended for instrumental performance.

4 Bears annotation "38 Le[9] boo:".

5 "Thomas" crossed out.

6 The two leaves have been glued in so that the sides follow the order "4-1-2-3".

7 Glued into the manuscript.

8 *Musica Sacra*, 1608.

folio	Title	idiom	Composer	Concordances	Prints
65^V	Give me a clean heart (ii)	f	[G. Croce]	29372:253	1608:8
66^V	Lord in thine anger (i)	f	[" "]	" :332	" :5
67^V	My strength even fails (ii)	f	[" "]	" :334	" :6

(folios 68^V-72 blank)

| 72^V | No object [dearer] | f | [J. Ward] | 29372:336 | |
| | | | | 61:72 | |

(fols. 74-83^V blank)

(fols. i-ii blank, unruled)

iii^V Songs fit for vials and organ in the great bookes.[1]

Organ book.   Song bookes.

55.	If silent	144.
17.	I languish	145.
35.	O vos omnes	50.
34.	Miserere Lupo	95.
52.	There where I saw	138.
19.	Peccantem me	161.
10.	Dolorosa[2]	120
37.	Heu mihi Domine	197.
38.	Salva nos	181.
60.	Miserere Daman	60.

---

1 "the great bookes" are B.M. Add. MSS 29372-7.

2 There is no such entry in 29372. Could this be "Dolorous mournful cares" on
p. 126?

folio[1] no.		Title	Composer	Annotations
		Fantasia (fragment only)		
		[Untitled piece a 4] "35"	"R. Rom."	
1^V		Fantasia	[T. Lupo]	83:1e^9 boo:
4		["]	[" "]	84:1e^9 boo:
8	3	"	[" "]	85:1e^9 boo:
11	4	"	" "	86:1e^9 boo:

(two sides, containing music, glued together)

13^V		Fantasia	J. Ward	58:1e^9 boo:
17^V		"	" "	60:1e^9 boo:
21^V		Per far una[2]	J. Coperario	69:1e^9 boo:
24^V		Fuggi	" "	70:1e^9 boo:
27^V		[Untitled]	" "	110:1e^9 boo:
30^V		Io piango	" "	68:1e^9 boo:

(folio cut out between 30 and 31; stub remains)

34^V	11	[Fantasia]	W. White	26:1e^9 boo:
37^V		"	" "	27:1e^9 boo:
40^V		"	J. Ward	54:1e^9 boo:
43		"	" "	56:1e^9 boo:
45^V	15	O disaventurosa[3]	L. Marenzio	.Cant. 24
47^V	16	Luci serene	C. Monteverdi	.lib.4.cant.8.
49^V		Allume de stello	L. Marenzio	Cant 25
51^V		If ye love me	J. Milton	

(fols. 53^V-105 blank; 2 fols. torn out, stubs remain)

105^V	19	Pavan	W. White	156:1e^9 boo:
107^V	20	Fantasia	J. Ward	164:1e^9 boo:
110^V	21	"	" "	168:1e^9 boo:
113^V		"	[T. Lupo]	180:1e^9 boo:

(fols. 116^V-123 blank)

124^V	36	[Untitled]		
125	37	["]		
125		O praise God in his holiness	B. Cosyn	
130^V		A cry: O yes, if any man		
131^V		A maske		
132		The gypsies mask		

(fol. cut out between 132 and 133)

| 133^V | | Praise the Lord | | |
| 133^V | | [Untitled] | | |

(folio cut out)

---

1 Modern foliation.

2 The following four pieces are instrumental fantasias with Italian titles.

3 The following four pieces are textless in the source.

Christ Church MSS 56-60

Christ Church MSS 56-60, an incomplete set of partbooks lacking the bassus book, have on occasion been considered in conjunction with Thomas Myriell's sources because of their similar contents.[48] Indeed, Peter le Huray at one point suggested that 56-60 were in the same hand as Myriell's set, Christ Church 61-66.[49] Although the connection between 56-60 and Myriell's sources is not so close as le Huray suggests,[50] the Christ Church set must have stemmed from much the same musical atmosphere which gave rise to the collection of the vicar of St. Stephen's Walbrook.

A glance through the catalogue of the Christ Church source reveals some twenty-one concordances with Myriell's manuscripts, more than a quarter of the eighty items in 56-60. Although many of these works enjoyed considerable popularity, and crop up in numerous other partbooks as well, half of the concordances are rarely encountered outside 56-60 or Myriell's collection:

> *Sing joyfully,* R. Jones
> *Out of the deep,* T. Lupo
> *Hear my prayer O Lord,* T. Lupo
> *How long wilt thou forget,* J. Ward
> *Down caitif wretch* (i), J. Ward
> *Prayer is an endless chain* (ii), J. Ward
> *O heavenly God,* W. Daman
> *The City Cries,* R. Dering
> *Father of love,* S. Stubbs
> *See the word is incarnate,* O. Gibbons
> *No object dearer,* J. Ward
> *Lord remember David,* M. Jeffreys
> *If the Lord himself,* M. Jeffreys

In some cases, such as Ward's *Down caitif wretch/Prayer is an endless chain,* the readings in 29372 and 56-60 are so close that they might well have been copied from a common source. In other instances, such as Stubbs's *Father of love* (unique to 56-60 and Myriell's collection) the readings are clearly divergent, however. It is unlikely that *Tristitiae Remedium* actually served as the direct source for 56-60 since the concordances are scattered throughout the Christ Church manuscripts, rather than occuring in large blocks as one might expect if the scribes of 56-60 were working directly from 29372.[51] Furthermore, for Matthew Jeffreys's *If the Lord himself,* Myriell contains errors which do not reappear in 56-60; *Tristitiae Remedium* could not have been the copy text. For Jeffreys's *Lord remember David,* on the other hand, the opposite is true: 56-60 contain errors absent from 29372.

Aside from the many concordances with Myriell's manuscripts, additional evidence strongly points to the London area as the origin of 56-60. The majority of the composers present were active in the capital, and one group seems to center around St. Paul's Cathedral. The little-known William Cranford (a singing man at St. Paul's) provides three works for the source, at least one of which is unique to it *(My sinful soul)*. Simon Stubbs (minor canon of St. Paul's) offers *Father of Love. O Lord in thee is all my trust* by Martin Peerson (master of the choristers at St. Paul's) survives only in 56-60. Peerson's frequent companion in pre-Restoration sources, Thomas Ravenscroft (sometime chorister of St. Paul's), is represented by four works, including one *unicum.*[52] Another composer from 56-60, John Bennet, represented here by his only surviving anthem, *O God of gods,* must also have been an intimate of Ravenscroft, who not only praises him highly in the *Brief Discourse* (1614), but also includes some of his pieces in the musical section of that curious work. Ravenscroft must also have been connected with the singularly obscure composer from 56-60, Simon Stubbs, who contributed to *The Whole Book of Psalms* of 1622. All these composers, Ravenscroft, Peerson, Cranford, Bennet, Stubbs, and also Edmund Hooper, in fact reappear in Ravenscroft's 1622 print. They seem to form an enclave around St. Paul's, which may be linked to the Christ Church partbooks.

On the other hand, a substantial number of pieces connect these manuscripts with the musical circle around the court. Several of the composers who appear here were employed in the king's service:

Edmund Hooper (Chapel Royal)
Thomas Warwick (Chapel Royal)
Thomas Lupo (King's Musick)
John Bull (Chapel Royal)
Richard Dering (King's Musick)
Orlando Gibbons (Chapel Royal)
Thomas Ford (musician to Prince Henry: member of the lutes and voices to Prince Charles)

Although this list may not at first seem particularly unusual, some of the composers (e.g., Warwick, Lupo, Ford) are represented only rarely in manuscript sources by sacred works. The majority of the works they provide for 56-60 occur in no other secular sources; indeed, Lupo's *Have Mercy* and Bull's *How joyful and how glad* survive nowhere else. Furthermore, two other composers from the Christ Church partbooks reveal other, more tenuous, connections with the court. The lutenist songwriter, Robert Jones, whose one manuscript anthem, *Sing joyfully,* survives solely in 56-60 and Add. 29427,[53] had dedicated his *Ultimum Vale* to Prince Henry in 1605. After 1610 Jones was instructor of the Children of the Queen's Revels. On the other hand, John Ward, the most prominent composer in the manuscripts, very likely came into contact with Prince Henry through his very musical employer, Sir Henry Fanshawe, remembrancer of the exchequer to the prince.

A remarkable number of pieces in 56-60 are connected with court holidays:

How joyful and how glad a thing, Bull
O God of gods, Bennet
This is a joyful, happy holiday, Ward
Hearken ye nations, Hooper

Numerous others lament the death of Prince Henry:

No object dearer, Ward
'Tis now dead night, Ford
Weep, Britains, weep, Cranford
When David heard (i), Weelkes
O my son Absalom (ii), Weelkes
O Jonathan, Weelkes

The Weelkes works were, of course, tremendously popular, but the first three "Passions on the death of Prince Henry" are very rare. A few other "anthems" might in fact have served for courtly festivals:

Sing joyfully, R. Jones
Lord, remember David, M. Jeffreys
Hosanna to the son of David, T. Weelkes

The Jones piece gives special emphasis to its final phrase, "our feast day," accounting for roughly one-third of the anthem. Perhaps it was originally inspired by some court occasion. The mention of "the God of Jacob" in the text suggests James I; the last two pieces may also have been directed at the king himself, or at one of his sons, for James apparently did not object to being linked with Old Testament monarchs.[54]

Finally, one of the secondary scribes in the source reappears in Christ Church MSS 397-400, Cambridge, Fitzwilliam Museum MSS Mus. 24.E.13-17, Madrigal Society MSS G.37-42 (now housed in the British Library), and Los Angeles, William Andrews Clark Memorial Library, Music MSS FF 1995M4.[55] Some twenty-five years ago Thurston Dart suggested that the Fitzwilliam manuscripts were intended for the Royal Wind Music.[56] More recently Robert Ford, while questioning Dart's basic premise, has suggested that the sources emanate from courtly circles, and that the scribe might have been one of the Italian emigrés active at court.[57]

The links with the court are especially strong, perhaps stronger than those with the St. Paul's circle. In any case, the compilers were probably connected with one, or perhaps several, of the major choral foundations in London. They include nearly a dozen sacred works which otherwise survive only in cathedral partbooks, and another twelve of a markedly sacred character which are unique to the source (marked with asterisks)—though they may not actually have been intended for performance within the sanctuary:

> *The blessed lamb,* Hooper
> *I am for peace,* Amner
> *O God of my salvation,* Warwick
> **Have mercy upon me* (i), Lupo
> **For I knowledge* (ii), Lupo
> *O let me hear thy loving-kindness,* Ravenscroft
> **This is the day when first,* Ravenscroft
> **Praise the Lord,* Corkine
> **How joyful and how glad,* Bull
> **O Lord in thee is all my trust,* Peerson
> **O Lord deliver me,* R. White
> *Consider all ye passers-by,* Amner
> **My love is crucified,* M. Jeffreys
> *Lord to thee I make my moan,* Weelkes
> **To Father, Son, and Holy Ghost,* Tye
> *This is a joyful, happy holiday,* Ward
> **My sinful soul,* Cranford
> *Miserere my maker,* Ford
> *Hearken, ye nations,* Hooper
> *Praise the Lord,* Ward
> **Christ rising* (i), Tye
> **Christ is risen* (ii), Tye
> *Let us with loud and cheerful voice,* Ford

This group accounts for almost one-third of the pieces in the manuscripts.

Among the most distinctive, as well as the most problematic, aspects of this source is the number of hands which it reveals, and the apparent lack of order in the delegation of copying responsibilities. It is not at all uncommon for a single piece to be the work of several scribes,[58] and in some cases even text and music may be in different hands.[59] Nor does any single copyist show a preference for a particular partbook. One hand (see pl. 11) definitely predominates in the manuscripts, entering well over twice as many parts as the nearest competitor. Of all the scribes, he alone is responsible for large blocks of pieces, often devoted primarily to a single composer or type of piece, which give the impression of having been entered as a group. It seems reasonable to assume that he was in fact the owner or keeper of the manuscripts and would have had them readily to hand for the copying of such blocks. The next most common hand bears a remarkable similarity to the first (see pl. 12), and might be the first copyist in a different "scribal guise." This "scribe" may occasionally be responsible for all the parts in two consecutive pieces, but he never enters larger groups. The other hands are much less prominent, and with few exceptions only add the odd part here and there.

Pl. 12. Christ Church MS 56, p. 24. The second hand in the partbooks.
(By kind permission of the Governing Body of Christ Church, Oxford)

One is left with the overall impression, therefore, that the owner and chief scribe was frequently aided by one or more others, perhaps when they all gathered for group music making. The group of pieces stretching from Cranford's *Weep, Britains, weep* through Ward's *This is a joyful, happy holiday,* where we find all the hands haphazardly distributed within a small space, suggests three or four people working concurrently, finishing off one part and taking up whatever other book was lying free, or even copying only the music, while leaving the words to someone else.

The copyists, then, must have been in very close contact for this haphazard system not to result in much greater disorganization. The pieces, in fact, follow one after another with few of the half-empty pages or odd blank folios that are a regular feature of other manuscripts in which several scribes had a hand (e.g., Add. 29427, Christ Church 61-66, Christ Church 67, Add. 29366-8). Perhaps in this instance the compilers shared a common affiliation with one of the important London musical organizations. Much of the evidence, as outlined above, seems in fact to point to a musical establishment reasonably close to the king himself.

John Aplin has suggested that both 56-60 and 61-67 were intended for the household of Henry Fanshawe.[60] The work of Pamela Willetts and the present writer on Myriell's collection calls Aplin's hypothesis about 61-67 into question. The connection of 56-60 with the Fanshawe household, on the other hand, seems more plausible. Perhaps the rather haphazard distribution of scribal hands indicates that the partbooks were prepared on relatively short notice for presentation. The numerous copying mistakes, which were never corrected, further suggests that the manuscripts found their way to some library shelf and may not have been used for performance.

In any event, 56-60 clearly originated in a London musical circle, one reasonably close to that of Thomas Myriell and the court. The time of compilation can be narrowed down to a span of ten years, thanks to several clues in the source itself. To judge by the laments for Prince Henry, among the first entries in the six-part section, the compilation could not have begun before 1612. Ward's "Passions on the death of S[r] Hen: Fanshawe," on the other hand, must date from after 1616. The section for two basses opens with Michael East's *Sing we merrily,* which appeared in print in 1624. The piece in 56-60 is an earlier, prepublication version, however.[61] East was never one to withhold a work from the printers, so one may assume that this anthem was probably composed between 1618, the date of East's previous set, and 1624. Thus, the compilation of the earlier sections of the manuscripts could not have begun before 1612, and perhaps as late as 1616, while the section for two basses, at least, is probably later than 1618.

Bennet's *O God of gods,* appearing at the very end of the five-part section, provides the clue to the time of completion. This anthem, intended for the anniversary of the coronation of King James, if not in fact for the actual coronation,[62] specifically mentions "our sovereign king *James*" (italics added). It must therefore have been entered before the accession of Charles I, and 56-60 must have been completed before 1625.

This set of partbooks, then, must be roughly contemporary with Myriell's collection, and it confirms many of the aesthetic preferences in evidence there. Christ Church 56-60 is in fact among the most single-minded of the sources for voices and viols in terms of its underlying aesthetic principles. Like *Tristitiae Remedium,* it includes only vocal music, but it even goes so far as to exclude all printed music except Daman's *Oh heavenly God* and all non-English composers except the Anglicized Italians, Thomas Lupo and Alfonso Ferrabosco II. The few obvious madrigals (only ten) which creep into the collection were never printed, and are primarily by John Ward, the most prominent composer in the partbooks.

The scribes were concerned primarily with sacred music. This interest did not include either Tudor or Jacobean motets, however, which would still retain a place in some provincial sources well into the reign of Charles I. Even Myriell had included a number of Byrd's most popular motets, as well as a few by Morley or Lupo, in his collection. But for 56-60 only English sacred music would do, whether for full chorus or for voices and viols.

The full anthems are notably up-to-date, with greatest prominence going to Jacobeans such as Weelkes, Lupo, and Thomas Ford, and with isolated examples by Warwick, R. Jones, John Mundy, Corkine, Ravenscroft, and Stubbs. Some of these manuscripts were hardly renowned as sacred composers (e.g., Jones and Corkine), and their appearance here further emphasizes the nonliturgical character of many "sacred works" in the source. Philip Brett has already pointed out the possible secular origin of several of the Weelkes anthems found here,[63] but many other anthems in the source, whether because of their extravagant texts, madrigalian gestures, or chromatic experiments,[64] might have been rejected from seventeenth-century cathedrals, despite the new wave of High Churchmanship during the reigns of James I and Charles I.

Aside from these up-to-date full anthems, a number of others represent the Elizabethan age. Some, such as Parsons's *Deliver me from mine enemies, Save me O God,* usually attributed to Byrd,[65] and William Mundy's *O Lord I bow the knees of my heart,* were among the most popular anthems of the age, and found their way into many pre-Restoration sources, whether sacred or secular. Others, such as Tye's *To Father, Son, and Holy Ghost, Christ rising/Christ is risen,* or Robert White's *O Lord deliver me from mine enemies,* are unique to this source. Their presence here further strengthens the hypothesis that the scribes may have been intimately connected with some choral foundation, for Tye's sacred works—even the popular *I lift my heart to thee* (also present in 56-60)—are scarcely ever to be found in Jacobean secular sources.

Music for voices and viols plays as prominent a role in the Christ Church source as does the full anthem. The outlook concurs to a remarkable degree with that of Thomas Myriell. But while Myriell still retains some vestigial interest in the solo consort song, as represented by such old favorites as Byrd's *Lullaby* or more modern pieces such as John Tomkins's *O thrice-blessed earthbed,* the scribes of 56-60 totally neglect the solo song. They concentrate only upon those manifestations of the verse idiom that make allowance for chorus as well as soloists. Furthermore, the compilers virtually ignore those pieces with overtly secular texts which conform in all other respects to the verse anthem ideal. Such pieces had begun to appear in print around 1610 (e.g., the "verse pastorals" of East's *Third Set*), and Myriell included one or two in *Tristitiae Remedium.* The only secular piece for voices and viols which finds a place in 56-60 is Dering's relatively uncommon *City Cries,* which otherwise survives only in *Tristitiae Remedium* and in the considerably later Tenbury 1162-7.

Thus, 56-60 reveals perhaps the most single-minded attitude of any source in which music for voices and viols plays a prominent role. The scribes' interest in the verse idiom includes verse anthems and verse anthems alone. A few examples, such as Bull's very popular *Almighty God who by the leading of a star,* may hearken back to the reign of Elizabeth, but the majority, as in Myriell's sources, are by Jacobean composers. But although Myriell might still find a place for Byrd's ever-popular *Christ rising/Christ is risen* in *Tristitiae Remedium,* the same was not true for the scribes of 56-60. Indeed, their almost total neglect of William Byrd carries on the trend, already evident in Myriell's sources, away from the older composer, whose music apparently sounded increasingly archaic in secular musical circles toward the end of James's reign.

Rather, it is the more fashionable, younger generation of verse anthem composers which predominates in 56-60. The most prominent composers may vary slightly from those in Myriell's sources, but their styles are essentially similar. Thus, the Christ Church source serves as an additional witness to what was up-to-date in some London circles around 1620, and it confirms the essential patterns apparent in the collection of the London clergyman. Myriell's collection and Christ Church 56-60 may act as one basic standard with which to compare other sources. Indeed, were it not for their testimony, the origins of Tenbury 807-811, to which we must turn next, would remain a mystery.

page	Title	idiom	Composer	Prints
1	*The blessed lamb*	v	E. Hooper	
4	*Preserve me O Lord*	v	T. Wilkinson	
6	*I am for peace*	v	J. Amner	
8	Deliver me from mine enemies	f	[R. Parsons]	
9	O God of my salvation	f	T. Warwick	
10	Save me O God	f	[W. Byrd]	
12	Sing joyfully	f	R. Jones	
14	Alleluia, I heard a voice	f	T. Weelkes	
16	Oh give thanks unto the Lord	f	[J. Mundy]	
18	Have mercy upon me (i)	f	T. Lupo	
19	For I knowledge (ii)	f	" "	
20	Out of the deep	f	" "	
21	Hear my prayer	f	" "	
22	*How long wilt thou forget*	v	J. Ward	
24	*Down caitif wretch (i)*	v	" "	
26	*Prayer is an endless chain (ii)*	v	" "	
28	*Rise, O my soul (i)*	v	W. Simms	
29	*And thou, my soul (ii)*	v	" "	
30	*To thee, O Jesu (iii)*	v	" "	
31	*Oh let me hear thy lovingkind-ness*	v	T. Ravenscroft	
34	*This is the day when first our saviour*	v	" "	
36	*In thee, O Lord, have I put*	v	" "	
38	*I lift mine eyes up to the hills*	v	T. Warwick	
40	O woeful ruins[1]	f	T. Ravenscroft	
41	Praise the Lord	f	W. Corkine	
42	A sea nymph sat	f	[T. Wilkinson]	
43	Sweet violets	f		
44	Down in a dale	f	J. Ward	
46	My breast I'll set	f	" "	
47	Cruel, unkind, oh stay	f	" "	
48	*How joyful and how glad*	v	J. Bull	
51	Oh heavenly God, oh father dear	f	W. Daman	1591:46[6]
52	*The City Cries*	v	R. Dering	

(more than 30 blank, ruled folios)

| 86[2] | Father of love | f | S. Stubbs | |

(page 87 blank)

88	*O Lord in thee is all my trust*	v	M. Peerson	
90	Oh Lord I bow the knees of my heart	f	W. Mundy	
92	I lift my heart to thee	f	C. Tye	
94	Oh Lord, deliver me from mine enemies[3]	f	R. White	
95	*See the word is incarnate*	v	O. Gibbons	
98	*Consider all ye passers-by*	v	J. Amner	
100	My love is crucified	f	M. Jeffreys	
102	Lord to thee I make my moan	f	T. Weelkes	
103	To Father, Son, and Holy Ghost	f	C. Tye	
104	*Hear my prayer, O Lord*	v	T. Wilkinson	
106	*Put me not to rebuke*	v	" "	
108	Wounded with sin extremely[4]	f	[Palestrina]	
110	*Almighty God, who by the lead-ing of a star*	v	J. Bull	
113	*Oh God of gods (i)*	v	J. Bennet	
	To the almighty Trinity (ii)	v	" "	
116	*Let God arise*	v	J. Ward	

(six-part pieces)

1	Aye me, can love and beauty	f	T. Lupo	
2	Well-sounding pipes (i)	f	J. Ward	
3	As sharps and flats (ii)	f	" "	
4	No object dearer[5]	f	" "	
6	'Tis now dead night[5]	f	T. Ford	
8	Weep, Britains, weep[5]	f	W. Cranforth	

1 A second and third part (with verses) survive in the Hamond MSS.

2 The numbering of pp. 86-116 is modern.

3 Adaptation of the motet, *Manus tuae.*

4 Adaptation of the madrigal, *Io son ferrito.*

5 "Passions on the Death of Prince Henry"

6 *The Second Book of the Musicke of M. William Damon* (1591).

---

1 "Passions on the death of S[r] Hen: Fanshawe".

2 The numbering of pp. 209-227 is modern.

3 Not the version published in East's *Sixth Set* (1624).

4 Adaptation of the madrigal, *Cantai mentre*.

St. Michael's College, Tenbury MSS 807-811

Tenbury MSS 807-811 provide no external evidence to aid in establishing their date and provenance. At first glance their appearance and their contents might even prove misleading, for both the scribal hand and the nature of the first twenty entries, resembling those of sixteenth-century manuscripts (e.g., Oxford, Bodleian MS Mus Sch E423), might easily suggest a date in the 1590s. It is only when one arrives at the group of pieces to English texts toward the back of the manuscripts that this initial archaic impression is undermined. The English anthems in fact provide the most important clues to the date and probable origins of the partbooks.

Tenbury 807-11 open with twenty Latin motets, copied one after another without a break. There is nothing to suggest that all entries were not made within a relatively short span of time. The first twelve were taken directly from Byrd's *Cantiones Sacrae* of 1591, where they comprise the entire six-part section of the print. For the subsequent group of motets the scribe turned to a distinctly older repertory, whose appearance here is especially noteworthy. Old-fashioned motets occasionally occur in seventeenth-century manuscripts, especially those that exhibit an interest in voices and viols. But this dense concentration of very archaic Latin works by Taverner, Tallis, and their generations is without parallel in Jacobean sources, except perhaps in the much more extensive manuscript collection of the conservative Catholic recusant, Edward Paston,[66] a decidedly special case. In every instance it appears that these old Latin works, some of which had been in circulation before 1550, were copied for the very last time by the scribe of 807-11.

Many of the motets were comparatively well known, at least to judge by the number of Elizabethan manuscripts in which they have survived. The last motet of the group, a setting of the Easter antiphon, *Christus resurgens* by William Parsons, on the other hand, appears in no other source. Little is known of William Parsons's life except that he served as vical choral at Wells in 1555 and is listed in the *Communar's Paper Book* as a music copyist there between 1552 and 1560.[67] Aside from his numerous contributions to Day's *Certaine Notes,* Parson's works are relatively uncommon. His presence in 807-11 is therefore cause for comment, and offers the possibility of a link with Wells.

The presence of so many pre-Reformation Latin works in a seventeenth-century source may be remarkable, but aside from Parsons's motet they offer no help in establishing the date and provenance of 807. The block of English works provides the most useful evidence in this regard. The first five anthems which follow directly after Parsons's *Christus resurgens* include two ascribed to Matthew Jeffreys. *Sing we merrily,* sandwiched between the two attributed anthems, can also be ascribed to him on the basis of a concordance in Christ Church 56-60. Given the copyist's tendency to organize the collection by composer or type of piece, it is quite likely that *Behold how good and joyful a thing* and *Let God arise* may also be Jeffreys's work. In any event, 807 contains three of the five verse anthems definitely attributed to him.[68]

We know very little about Matthew Jeffreys except that he took his B. Mus. at Oxford in 1593; interestingly enough, like William Parsons, he, too, subsequently served as vicar choral of Wells Cathedral.[69] The Wells connection suggested by the Parsons unicum thus receives some confirmation from the Jeffreys anthem. Matthew Jeffreys was only slightly better known than his predecessor at Wells, and his anthems appear as frequently in secular as in sacred sources.[70] The most important manuscripts derive, not from the West Country,[71] but from London: *Tristitiae Remedium,* which contains three anthems, and Christ Church 56-60, which contains no less than five. The three attributable Jeffreys anthems in 807 in fact only reappear in these two London sources. A comparison of their readings reveals the following relationships:

1. Neither 807 nor 56 transmits errors present in Myriell's copy of *If the Lord himself;* 807 transmits additional errors absent from the other two.

2. For *Sing we merrily,* 807 contains errors not present in 56.

3. Variants for *Out of the deep* concern underlay and accidentals, and are inconclusive.

This information suggests that although neither *Tristitiae Remedium* nor 807 could have served as the source for 56, it is not impossible that 56 might have provided their copy text.

In the light of the Jeffreys concordances, it is especially intriguing that all three Weelkes pieces which form a block after the Jeffreys anthems reappear in 56 or 29372. *When David heard/ O my son Absalom* was a popular work, of course, but it is significant that both the prima and secunda partes only survive in 807, 56, and *Tristitiae Remedium;* 807 stands somewhat apart from the other two, however, in transmitting a unique variant at the closing repetition of *O my son Absalom.* Aside from 56 and 807, the sources for the other two Weelkes anthems derive from Oxford (Add. 17786-91 and Tenbury 1382—see chap. 5). In both cases the readings from 807 agree more closely with 56 than with the Oxford manuscripts. At one point in *Hosannah to the Son of David* the tenor parts of both 56 and 807 even transmit an identical *error,* which reappears nowhere else (see ex. 1). Such a mistake strengthens the possibility of an especially close connection between them.[72] For both works 807 includes additional errors absent from 56. The Weelkes anthems thus reinforce the possibility already apparent from the Jeffreys anthems that although 807 could not have served as the source for 56, the reverse situation would not be impossible.

Ex. 1.

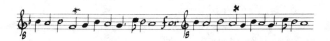

The group of English anthems concludes with John Bull's *In thee, O Lord.* This, one of Bull's most popular anthems, otherwise survives only in sacred sources. Its presence here further strengthens the link with *Tristitiae Remedium* and 56, for they are the most important—indeed, virtually the only—secular sources for Bull's anthems. To judge by surviving manuscripts, the primary secular audience for his anthems could be found in London.[73]

After the Bull anthem the relatively systematic organization of the source breaks down. Up to this point pieces had followed one after another with virtually no staves left blank. After the Bull anthem, however, one to three empty staves appear in all partbooks, a pattern which commonly recurs after subsequent pieces as well. The single-minded consistency of the previous sections gives way to a hodge-podge of different sorts of works: three more archaic motets, two late Elizabethan or Jacobean motets, a pair of Magnificats by Robert Parsons and Robert White, a textless madrigal entered after one or more completely blank pages, and finally a second, more accurate version of the earlier Parsons Magnificat, apparently added on the concluding flyleaves.

The two Jacobean motets are unique to the source. Weelkes's *Laboravi in gemitu* was inspired by the setting of the same text by Weelkes's teacher, Thomas Morley.[74] Morley's setting survives, interestingly enough, in Myriell's collection. The scribe of 807 might have acquired Weelkes's motet concurrently with the three Weelkes anthems. Perhaps he put it aside temporarily because it was inappropriate for the section of works to English texts. The presence of the Kirbye motet is more remarkable, because unpublished music by this Suffolk madrigalist is very rare, and settings of sacred texts by him are scarcer still. His only other motet, *Quare tristis es anima/Convertere anima mea,* survives in the collection of Kirbye's neighbor, Thomas Hamond (Bodl. MSS Mus. F 16-19—see chap. 3). His only setting of an English sacred text to survive in a contemporary manuscript can be found in *Tristitiae Remedium: O Jesu, look.* The Kirbye motet in 807 may provide another tenuous link to that London source.

The Paradiso textless madrigal was obviously considered inappropriate to the collection and hence, only found a place on the back of the very last regularly ruled folio of the partbooks. Virtually nothing is known of the composer, except that he had been a wind player in the service of Queen Elizabeth, and had died January 16, 1569.[75] Another textless piece with the title *In qual parte del ciel* survives in Hamond's collection, Bodl. MSS Mus. F 1-5.

All these works suggest a more direct connection with London than with Wells. The link with *Tristitiae Remedium* and particularly with 56 is especially noteworthy. A side-by-side comparison of the three sources makes this more apparent:

807		56		29372	
23	If the Lord himself	20	Lord remember David	272	Lord remember David
24	Sing we merrily	22	Sing we merrily	274	In thee O Lord
25	Out of the deep	24	Out of the deep	275	When David heard
		26	If the Lord himself	276	If the Lord himself
26	Gloria in excelsis	28	When David heard		
27	Hosannah to the son		O my son Absalom		
28	When David heard		O Jonathan		
	O my son Absalom		Miserere my maker		
			Music divine		
			If heaven's just wrath		
			Gloria in excelsis		
			Hosannah (2 basses)		

Both 807 and 56 group the six-part Jeffreys and Weelkes works in close proximity, and in one instance in the same order. Because it contained a special section for pieces with two basses, 56 had to present *Hosannah to the Son of David* in a later portion of the partbooks, rather than with the earlier works. Myriell, on the other hand, not only groups the six-part Jeffreys anthems together, but also sandwiches the first half of *When David heard* among them.[76] As the comparison of their readings has shown, 807 could not have provided the copy text for 56. The relationship between their readings does not entirely rule out the opposite possibility, however. It is perhaps unlikely because one might otherwise expect to find other works from this portion of 56 (e.g., Jeffreys's *Lord remember David*) in 807. Very probably both were copied from common sources.

Tenbury 807-11 serve most importantly as a witness to one man's conservative interests, which find no equivalent in the other London sources considered earlier. These contain no Latin music at all, or primarily motets by the more madrigalian Jacobean stylists. Indeed, were it not for the scribe's later inclusion of works by Jeffreys and Weelkes, one would never think to associate the manuscripts with the capital. It is only because of these concordances that one may propose that 807-11 derive from the same musical surroundings as *Tristitiae Remedium* and 56 in particular. Weelkes's *When David heard* suggests a copying date after the death of Prince Henry in 1612. The close connections with the London sources imply a date a few years later, when they likewise were copied. Sometime around the end of the decade is most plausible. The general appearance of the partbooks suggests that the scribe carried out the project in a relatively short timespan. Once they were completed, however, 807-11 may scarcely have been taken up again. Their numerous uncorrected errors suggest that they were not used in performance, but left on the library shelf.

807	808	809	810	811	Title	idiom	Composer	print
1	1	1	1	1	Descendit de coelis (i)	f	[W. Byrd]	CS1591:21
1^v	1^v	1^v	1	1^v	Et exivit (ii)	f	[" "]	" :22
1^v	1	1^v	1^v	1^v	Domine non sum dignus	f	[" "]	" :23
2^v	2	2^v	1^v	2	Infelix ego (i)	f	[" "]	" :24
2^v	2^v	2^v	2	2	Quid igitur (ii)	f	[" "]	" :25
2^v	2^v	3^v	2^v	2^v	Ad te igitur (iii)	f	[" "]	" :26
3^v	3^v	3^v	3	3^v	Afflicti pro peccatis (i)	f	[" "]	" :27
4	3^v	4	3^v	3^v	Ut eruas nos (ii)	f	[" "]	" :28
4^v	3^v	4^v	3^v	3	Cantate domino	f	[" "]	" :29
4^v	4	4^v	4	4	Cunctis diebus	f	[" "]	" :30
5^v	4^v	5^v	4^v	4^v	Domine salva nos	f	[" "]	" :31
5^v	5	5^v	5	5	Haec dies	f	" "	" :32
6^v	5^v	6^v	5^v	5^v	Manus tuae fecerunt (i)	f	[R. White]	
6^v	6	6^v	5^v	6	Veniant mihi (ii)	f	" "	
7^v	6^v	7^v	6	6^v	Gaude gloriosa (i)	f	[T. Tallis]	
8^v	7^v	7^v	7	7^v	Gaude virgo (ii)	f	" "	
10^v	8^v	9	8^v	8	Salve intemerata	f	" "	
11^v	10	11	9^v	9^v	Magnificat	f	J. Taverner	
12^v	11^v	12^v	10^v	10^v	[Christus resurgens] ex mortuis (i)	f	[W. Parsons]	
13^v	12^v	12^v	10^v	11	Dicant nunc Judei (ii)	f	" "	
13^v	12^v	13	11^v	11^v	*Behold how good and joyful*	v	[Anon.]	
14^v	13^v	14	11^v	12	Let God arise	f	["]	
15^v	14	14^v	12^v	13^v	*If the Lord himself*	v	[M. Jeffries]	
15^v	15^v	15	13	13^v	*Sing we merrily*	f	[" "]	
16^v	15^v	16^v	14	14^v	*Out of the deep*	v	" "	
17^v	16^v	16^v	14^v	15^v	Gloria in excelsis deo, sing my soul	f	T. Weelkes	
17^v	17^v	17^v	15^v	15^v	Hosanna to the son of David	f	" "	
18^v	17	18	15^v	16	When David heard (i)	f	[" "]	
18^v	17^v	18^v	16	16^v	O my son Absalom (ii)	f	" "	
18^v	18^v	18^v	16^v	16^v	*In thee, O Lord*	v	J. Bull	
20	19^v	20	17^v	17^v	Gaude virgo	f	J. Shepherd	
21^v	21	21	18^v	18^v	Peccavimus cum patribus nostris	f	C. Tye	
22^v	22	--	21^v	19^v	Ave dei patris	f	R. Johnson	
24	23^v	22^v	22^v	21	Laboravi in gemitu	f	T. Weelkes	
24^v	24^v	23	23	21^v	Vox in Rama	f	G. Kirbye	
25^v	25	23^v	23^v	22	Magnificat	f	R. Parsons	
26^v	26	25^v	25^v	23^v	Magnificat	f	R. White	
28	28	26^v- 27	26^v- 27	25	(blank, pre-ruled)			
28^v	28^v	27^v	27^v	25^v	Laura gentil[1]	f[1]	R. Paradiso	
29	29	28	28	26	Magnificat[2]	f	R. Parsons	

1 Only the incipit of the text appears in the partbooks.

2 A corrected version of the previous Magnificat by R. Parsons

3

The Eastern Counties

The Hamond Sources

The eastern counties of England (Cambridgeshire, Norfolk, Suffolk) had their own equivalent of Thomas Myriell: a Mr. Thomas Hamond of Hawkedon, Suffolk. But as we shall see, Hamond himself provides many of the answers about his musical collection that Myriell had left to the resourcefulness of later musical historians. Hamond serves as the primary witness to the state of secular vocal music in the eastern counties during the reign of Charles I. His collection, together with a few other isolated manuscripts of known provenance,[1] prove an invaluable guide in the attempts to assign more ambiguous sources to the eastern counties later in this chapter.

Thomas Hamond, whose music manuscripts have formed part of the Bodleian music collection since 1800, was the sort of person who makes lighter the work of later historians. His copious notations and scribblings on flyleaves and on individual compositions in his partbooks provide much of the basic material necessary for ascertaining how and when his manuscripts were copied. Several years ago Margaret Crum pieced together this information into one of the more thorough and least problematic portraits of a seventeenth-century musical enthusiast.[2] From her article we know that Hamond owned at least eight sets of manuscripts. Six of them he copied personally, largely between 1631 and 1656 (Bodl. MSS Mus. F 1-28). Although F 7-10, 11-15, and 25-28 are undated, and difficult to pin down more precisely, F 1-6 bear the date "1631," with further notes dating from the 1640s and as late as 1661, while F 16-19 were finished in 1655-1656, though probably begun much earlier. F 20-24 are dated "1630" and "1633," with a note that the six-part section was added in 1650.

Another set that Hamond had acquired by 1615 dates back to the reign of Elizabeth I (British Library Add. MSS 30480-4); and it may be surmised that he owned a further set (of purely instrumental pieces) from a note on folio 2 of Bodl. MS Mus. F 7: "The rest of the ditty is in my viole book." In addition, as Miss Crum has shown, Hamond very often reveals his own sources, whether printed (e.g., "John Amner's set of bookes, Bachelor of Musique, Master of the

Choristers & organist of the Cathedrall church of Ely, Cum Privilegio Regali. 1615" [F 20, fol. 7]) or manuscript ("Most ~~or all~~ [*sic*] of these latten & Etalian songs ware taken out of Mr Kirbies blacke books"[F 1, fol. 2]). So even a hasty glance through the six sets that constitute Bodl. MSS Mus. F 1-28 provides a relatively clear picture of how the manuscript collection grew, especially by comparison with many other sources discussed elsewhere in this study. Since Miss Crum has outlined this material about Hamond's manuscripts so lucidly, one can move further afield to try to discover what more can be gleaned about the nature of Hamond's musical taste as it relates to that of his time.

Hamond held the manor of Cressners in the parish of Hawkedon, ten miles from Bury-St.-Edmunds. As Miss Crum points out,[3] this very musical neighborhood included close at hand both George Kirbye at Rushbrooke Hall and John Wilbye at Hengrave Hall, and a bit further afield William Byrd, Thomas Ravenscroft, Martin Peerson, John Jenkins, John Tomkins, and Robert Ramsey, all of whom lived in, or had connections with, the eastern counties of England. But a look beyond Hamond's own manuscript collection makes it possible to elaborate more fully upon the character of the musical milieu of which Hamond was a part, and especially upon George Kirbye's place in it. As mentioned above, the notation to F 1-6, "Italian and Latin Songs. to 5. and 6. voc.", indicates that George Kirbye's own manuscripts were available to Hamond. A further witness to the connection between Hamond and Kirbye appears in F 20-24, which contain some eight vocal works by Kirbye that never found their way into print. A wider search for unpublished Kirbye madrigals leads to another set of partbooks (London, Royal College of Music MS 684) that provides ten more unpublished madrigals by Kirbye. RCM 684 has never been connected with Hamond's collection; but a closer look at its contents reveals other links with Hamond's books besides this common interest in unpublished Kirbye. The Royal College partbooks contain more than 250 madrigals, some by native English composers, others by Italians but with English texts,[4] and also some Italian madrigals and a few chansons in the original tongue. The similarities to Hamond's set, F 1-6, are striking: of the forty-two Italian or French pieces in F 1-6, fourteen also occur among the seventy-three in RCM 684. Some of the composers who appear in both sets, such as André Pevernage, for example, very rarely occur in English sources. Other such coincidences also link the two sources. All of the madrigals by Valerio Bona, whether in F 1-6 or RCM 684, seem to derive from a single publication, *Madrigali et Canzoni a cinque Voci di Valerio Bona. Libro Primo... Venetia... 1601*.[5] Furthermore, a comparison of the versions of the Italian and French concordances in F 1-6 and RCM 684 reveals very few discrepancies, usually not more than the omission of an accidental or two, frequently where the omitted sharp could be redundant. Thus, it is tempting to surmise that these "blacke bookes" of George Kirbye's served as a common source for both sets.

Finally, the most striking link between the Hamond sources and RCM 684 involves the hand of the copyist, which seems to be the same in both cases. As the facsimiles show (pls. 13a, 13b, 14a, and 14b), the layout of the pages is identical, with the part designation at the top in the center, flanked on the right by the composer's name and on the left by the indication of the number of voices, with a space below for the time signature. The clefs are similar in both sources, even down to such small details as the different formation of the first c-clef in each piece and the insertion of the flat in some key signatures between the two segments of the g-clef (" $g^{\flat}_{\rho}$ "). Other details common to both sources include the use of "ij" instead of ":// :" for text repetitions, the "/____" sign under the first word of a new line of text, and the asymmetrical fermatas. Finally, the same ":-" ornament concluding both music and text appears in both sources. The shapes of the notes, with unusually long stems, elongated, thin noteheads, curving beams with flourishes at both ends, and breves which are fatter on the left end than on the right, all point to the work of a single scribe. The italic text offers the only real differences, and here, too, several underlying similarities emerge. The differences could be the result of a time lag between the copying of RCM 684 and the Bodleian MSS, or simply a matter of the difference in calligraphic styles that any accomplished scribe of the time could be assumed to have at his command.

We know from Hamond's own testimony that the Bodleian sources were copied primarily between 1631 and 1656. The Royal College manuscripts, on the other hand, must date from at least a decade earlier. Their covers bear the name of one William Firmage, who matriculated at Emanuel College, Cambridge in 1602, and who died in 1622.[6] His will, dated 1 November 1621, is of particular interest since the bequests include one "To Mr Robert Drury of Rougham my Sett of English and Italian Madrigalls manuscript to 3, 4, 5, and 6 voices,"[7] which very probably refers to the set of partbooks now in the Royal College, since the flyleaves of the bass book bear the names of George Drury, John Drury, Charles Drury, and Thomas Drury. The will also proves that Firmage, like Hamond, must have been an intimate of George Kirbye, who also figures in the bequests: "To Mr George Kirby of Bury my base vyoll with the case and all my bookes of vyoll lessons. To Mr George Kirby of Bury my Setts of bookes of ffancies &c. together with all my dutch Roiall ruled paper." RCM 684 must therefore have been copied before 1621, when the will was drafted.[8] The differences in the italic script of RCM 684 and F 1-28 could easily result from the passage of a decade or more.[9] Given the overall impression of order and neatness of the Royal College set (by comparison with Hamond's own collections), it seems very likely that Hamond undertook to copy the partbooks as a gift for this member of his musical circle, and in the process drew upon the manuscripts of their mutual friend, George Kirbye, whose "blacke bookes" he would use again a few years later for his own collection.

Pl. 13a.   Bodleian MS Mus. F 20, fol. 25. The hand of Thomas
Hamond.
(By kind permission of the Bodleian Library)

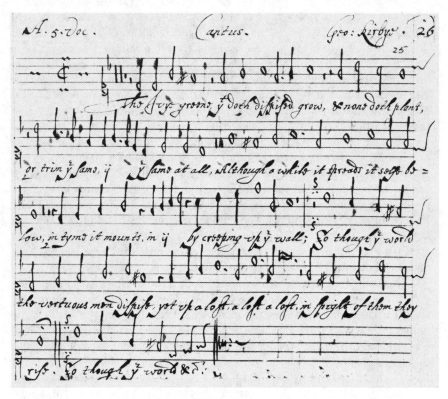

Thus, in addition to the musical connections pointed out by Margaret
Crum, Hamond must have been an important member of the musical circle of
this other avid musical amateur from Suffolk, whose manuscript collection, to
judge by his will, may have been as ample as Hamond's own. A few additional
clues may help us to add a few more names to their group. On folio 2 of F 4,
Hamond goes on to say that Kirbye's black books "weare sould after the
decease of the said Geo: To the right worshipful S^r Jo: Holland: in the yeare
1634 ... And he pai'd/Kirbies Maid/as 'twas said 40^ss." Pamela Willetts has
pointed out that among the manuscripts consulted in connection with the large
collection of viol music belonging to Sir Nicholas Le Strange of Norfolk was
one belonging to "Holland," whom she identifies with the Sir John Holland
mentioned in story 465 of Harleian MS 6395, Le Strange's collection of "Merry
passages and Jeasts."[10] This must be the same Holland whom Hamond
mentions; Holland's manuscript which Le Strange consulted may ultimately

Pl. 13b.   Bodleian MS Mus. F 20, fol. 63. The hand of Thomas
Hamond.
(By kind permission of the Bodleian Library)

derive from Kirbye's collection. In addition, Firmage bequeathed his English
and Italian set to "Mr Robert Drury of Roucham" and "To Mr John Drury of
Rougham my Sett of Latin Mottetts to 4. 5 and 6 voices, and all other my Setts
of Singing bookes unbequeathed." "Drury" is another of the names mentioned
in Le Strange's manuscripts, and it is equally possible that one of these two
could be the Drury in question, though Pamela Willetts puts forward other
possibilities from among the many Norfolk and Suffolk Drurys.[11] Thus, even
though never mentioned by name, both Firmage and Hamond might be
connected, rather tenuously perhaps, with Le Strange's wide circle of musical
contacts. It is an interesting coincidence that among the last pieces which
Hamond entered in F 16-19 we find an unpublished *Mercy dear Lord* by John
Jenkins and *Gloria tribulater* by Thomas Brewer (from Hilton's *Catch that
Catch Can,* 1652), both of whom were in the service of Le Strange.

One can therefore establish with some certainty when and where Thomas
Hamond was active, the nature of the musical sources available to him, and the

Pl. 14a.   Royal College of Music MS 684, Cantus, fol. 49v. The
hand of Thomas Hamond?
(By permission of the Director, Royal College of
Music, London)

sorts of musicians, whether professional or amateur, whom he probably knew.
He represents the eastern counties equivalent of the Londoner, Thomas
Myriell, on the one hand, and the west country lay clerk, John Merro, on the
other. But most of Hamond's activity dates from a few years later than Merro's
and as much as several decades later than Myriell's. Hamond is our prime
identifiable representative of the English musical amateur interested in voices
and viols during the period of Charles I and the Commonwealth.

Hamond's frequent scribblings on flyleaves of his partbooks provide a
much clearer view of his personality than we can piece together about Myriell.
The notes and scraps of doggerel which he jotted down betray a penchant for
sober moralizing and a tendency to comment upon the evils of the times:

> Wise men labour, Good men grieve,
> Knaves invent, & fooles believe,
> Then help us Lord, & stand unto us,
> Or knaves & fooles will quite undoe us.
>   A° 1642, 1643, 1644, 1645, 1646, &c
>   (F 2, fol. 2)

Pl. 14b.   Royal College of Music MS 684, Cantus, fol. 46ᵛ. The
            hand of Thomas Hamond?
            (By permission of the Director, Royal College of
            Music, London)

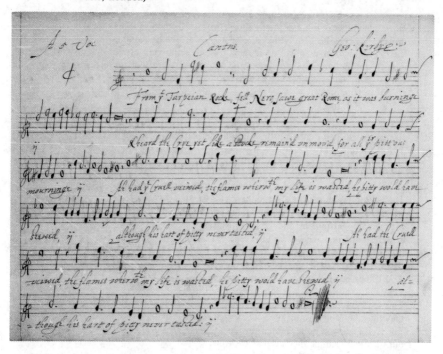

The rise of Cromwell and the Roundheads obviously met with little sympathy
from Hamond the Royalist:

Epitaph

Here lyes Jacke Presbyter, void of all pitty,
who ruin'd the Country, & fooled ye City:
He turned preaching to prating, & telling of lyes,
Caus'd jarrs & dissenssions in all ffamilies.
He invented new oaths, Rebellion to raise,
Deceiving the Commons, whilst on them he prayes.
He made a new Creed, dispised the old
King, State, & Religion by him bought & sold,
He four years consulted, & yet could not tell
the Parliament yᵉ way, Christ went into hell.
Resolved therein, he never could bee,
therefore in great haste, he's gone thither to see.
        They went in July. 1647. & are not yet return'd.
            (F 23, fol. 108ᵛ)

During those hard times Hamond occupied himself with music. Unlike Myriell, who may have been motivated by the prospect of profit or advancement, Hamond copied music strictly for his own amusement:

> He y^t buy paper & write & pricke songs, & value them at so low a rate as I have set them downe, will begg his bread if he have no othere meanes to maintaine him selfe withall. But these & all my othere bookes w^t songs & lessons for instruments or voyces, wch I w^t much cost, trouble & labour have collected and written out, ware done for recreation & to prevent Idlenesse. In witnesse whereof, I heere unto set my hand. December. A°. 1661, per me
> Tho: Hamond
> (F 3, fol. 2)

It is also possible, of course, that he was seeking distraction from the pestering of a nagging wife. He includes numerous misogynous verses, some of which seem to indicate that it was not Thomas Hamond who ruled Cressners:

> The world growes mad in these unhappy dayes;
> when Goodwife rules, & goodman foole obeys;
> for men are fearfull least they should displease;
> & wives imperious, give them little ease.
> ffor 'tis most frequent, both in high & lowe;
> that Men must cackle, & the women crowe;
> And if they bee but troubled wth the twitches
> They must forbeare, & give their wives the Britches.
> This is ye case of men that are uxorious
> they must be fooles, to make ye women glorious.
> For God at first appointed Men to rule
> but they more simple then an oxe, or Mule:
> deprived themselves of pow'r, & dominion
> & now are subject to their wives opynion.
> Thus may you see how Men for lacke of Grace,
> have brought themselves into a slavish case,
> God make them wise in tyme, that they may gaine
> their Glory lost, & once more rule againe.
> If otherwise, it shall be my conclusion
> that they are borne to worke their owne confusion.
> (F 16, fol. ii)

Whatever his motives, Hamond was less concerned than Myriell with musical quality. The Suffolk landowner gives precisely the impression of having dabbled in music, any music, to pass cold winter evenings. He was quite ready to copy whatever came to hand, whether an Italian madrigal, a catch from Hilton's 1652 *Catch that Catch Can,* a motet from *Cantiones Sacrae* of 1575, or a musical example from Morley's *Plain and Easy Introduction.* Clearly, however, Hamond valued music and his music collection highly. His brief will, dated 16 February 1661, otherwise given over entirely to bequests of land or money, concludes with a final reference to his manuscript collection:

"My bookes of songes of four, five or six voices &c &c to John Hammond my sonne, whome I appointe sole executor."[12]

One of the most striking features about Hamond's collection, even given his relative lack of discrimination, is the manner in which it carries on the musical traditions of Myriell and Merro. Hamond's musical taste proves to be notably Elizabethan and Jacobean, with very few concessions to the musical generation from the death of James I to the Restoration. The two little pieces from *Catch that Catch Can* represent practically the only samplings of roughly contemporary rather than retrospective music.

The composers present in Hamond's books, as Margaret Crum points out, include many associated with the eastern counties, and with Cambridge in particular.[13] One might expect this since more than two dozen Norfolk and Suffolk Hamonds appear in the records of the university, including John Hamond, son of Thomas, of Cressners-in-Hawkedon, who matriculated in 1648.[14] Furthermore, the William Firmage of RCM 684 matriculated in Easter term 1602, as mentioned above. So Hamond must have had access to music from Cambridge, as becomes obvious from the appearance in F 25-28 of the commencement exercises of both John Tomkins, organist of King's College from 1606 to 1619, and Robert Ramsey (Mus. B, 1616), organist of Trinity College from 1628 until 1644. In addition, Hamond's books are the only other source for two anthems in the Peterhouse Caroline partbooks, which were compiled during roughly the same period: Osbert Parsley's *This is the day* (F 16-19) occurs anonymously at Peterhouse,[15] while the anonymous *Arise O Lord* in F 20-24, actually a contrafactum of Byrd's *Exsurge Domine* (1591), otherwise appears only at Peterhouse, though misattributed there to Tallis.[16]

Aside from such special Cambridge connections, the list of musicians represented confirms some of the trends apparent in Myriell. Among the most prominent individuals are those who published the later, more contrapuntal, "instrumental," and "serious" sets of partbooks, having less to do with the Elizabethan madrigal of the Morleian variety: Michael East, John Amner, John Ward. As in the majority of the Jacobean manuscript collections, Morley himself puts in the most fleeting of appearances. But in some ways Hamond contrasts with other manuscript compilers. Neither Weelkes nor Wilbye appears very prominently, while William Byrd, who had suffered considerable neglect in earlier secular manuscript collections after 1610, here crops up on several occasions. Orlando Gibbons, so inexplicably absent from Myriell and Merro—and, indeed, from most other manuscript collections—provides no less than sixteen works from his 1612 *First Set of Madrigals and Motets.*

Among those composers providing unpublished music, the four most prominent are Ramsey, Kirbye, Peerson, and Ravenscroft. Ramsey was obviously one of Hamond's Cambridge connections, while Kirbye lived very close at hand at Bury-St.-Edmunds. But the best represented of the four are

Peerson and Ravenscroft, who in Hamond's books seem almost to work in harness: both turn up in two sections of F 16-19, one devoted to five-part Latin motets and the other to English anthems, and in both instances they follow one another. Ravenscroft and Peerson probably had frequent dealings with one another in connection with their London dramatic activities. Ravenscroft had been a chorister under Edward Pearce at St. Paul's (where Peerson later served as master of the choristers), and included several songs from plays performed by the St. Paul's boys in his *Pammelia* (1609), *Deuteromelia* (1609), *Melismata* (1611), and *A Brief Discourse* (1614). The last of these publications also contains a laudatory poem by Peerson "In Approbation of this ensuing *Discourse,* and the *Author* therof my deare friend, Maister THOMAS RAVENSCROFT."[17] A Thomas Rangcroft from Pembroke Hall, Cambridge, received his B. Mus. in 1605.[18] Peerson, on the other hand, was a native of Cambridgeshire, but had already set up house in London by 1604, and in 1606 held a share in the company of the Children of the Queen's Revels at the Blackfriars.[19] It seems, therefore, that Hamond must also have maintained some close links with musical goings-on in the British capital, where these two were active.

When one turns to the madrigals in Hamond's manuscripts now in the Bodleian, one receives an interesting and somewhat unusual view, especially by comparison with those in RCM 684. The Firmage set seems to have been prepared as a presentation copy devoted to the English madrigal in its heyday (though even this set notably neglects Thomas Morley). Hence, among the most prominent sources we find *Musica Transalpina* (1588), and *Italian Madrigals Englished* (1590), two of the most popular and influential prints of the time; also Wilbye's 1609 set and Kirbye's of 1597, plus a smattering of Morley, Weelkes, Lichfield, and minor figures. There is virtually no overlap with Hamond's choices for his own sets, where the most prominent figures are Byrd, Bateson, Gibbons, Ward, and Amner, none of whom finds a place in RCM 684. Of these, only Bateson represents the Italianate Elizabethan madrigal in a lighter mood. Furthermore, the Bodleian manuscripts contain few samplings of Italian pieces in English: only five from *Musica Transalpina* and none from *Italian Madrigals Englished.* While Hamond transmits two unpublished works by Wilbye (*Homo natus est* in F 1-6 and *Oh, who shall ease me* in F 20-24), he includes few of Wilbye's published madrigals. Thus, though Hamond must have had access to examples of the Elizabethan madrigal *par excellence* when he compiled the partbooks for Firmage, for his own sets he turned to the later prints and to the less madrigalian composers.

The one madrigalist shared by both the Bodleian and Royal College sets is the local figure, George Kirbye. Between them, these sources add some eighteen new pieces to the canon of Kirbye madrigals. Unfortunately, only the solitary example for four voices in RCM 684, *Farewell false love,* survives complete, while the other seventeen lack one or two parts. They nevertheless expand significantly our view of Kirbye as a madrigalist beyond that apparent from his 1597 publication, which provided the sole basis for previous assessments of his work. While in many respects they confirm the standard conception, several of these pieces provide new insights into Kirbye's musical development.[20]

In the matter of Kirbye's choice of texts, the unpublished madrigals throw significantly different light upon the composer, and, interestingly enough, once again show Hamond making distinctions between the sort of madrigals appropriate to his own partbooks as opposed to Firmage's. Kerman has described the verse of Kirbye's 1597 set as "entirely Italianate, with the exception of the lament from *The Shepherd's Calendar.*"[21] The madrigals in Firmage's set confirm this view, offering all the expected Petrarchan devices. Indeed, one of them may surpass any from the published set in bringing together so many of the favorite phrases:

I.

My Lady wept, & from her crystal fountains,
Not tears but liquid pearls I saw proceeding,
Wat'ring a plain, between two stately Mountains,
Where Love lay fast asleep, no danger dreading.
And keeping on their delightful swelling,
Like Thames' swift streams or tides of angry Humber,
For liberty against their banks rebelling,
Awak't the lovely God from his sweet slumber.

II.

But when himself bebathed he espied,
Nor wist from whence such floods should have their springing,
He lept & wept, & wept & lept, & cried,
His tender hands most pitifully wringing.
And but his wings a present counsel gave him,
No doubt he had been drowned, & none to save him.

The references to the Thames and Humber may provide a British context, but the hints at Ferrabosco's *I saw my lady weeping*[22] belie the local references, which one might almost suppose to have been substituted for the Arno and Tiber.

The content of this poem may be predictable enough, but the sonnet form which it also shares with the unpublished *Mourn now, my Muse* is much more unusual. Joseph Kerman has pointed out that "all the real madrigalists together attempt only...five sonnets: none by Morley, Weelkes, Farnaby, Bennet, Farmer, Kirbye, or East, and a single one each by Wilbye, Ward, Vautor, Pilkington and Bateson."[23] Kirbye's unpublished sonnet settings therefore seem to betray a certain musical ambition that rarely appears among the genuine madrigalists. For English sonnet settings we must look to composers in the native song tradition: Byrd, who set eight, and Richard Carlton, who set two. Kirbye's flirtation with the sonnet perhaps represents a link with that older aesthetic.[24]

A look at the Kirbye works which Hamond chose for his own manuscripts betrays still stronger links with that native poetic style favored particularly by Byrd, Gibbons, and Carlton. Hamond chose only one or two pieces whose texts fall into line with the accepted view of Kirbye. One offers up the familiar conceits, garnished with one classical reference:

> My mistress is a paragon, the fairest fair alive,
> Alcydes and Aeacydes for fair (less fair) did strive.
> Her colour fresh as damask rose, her breath as violet,
> Her body white as ivory, as smooth as polished jet,
> As soft as down, and were she down Jove might come down and kiss
> A love so fresh, so sweet, so white, so smooth, so soft as this.

The other rejects the whole tradition more strongly than the isolated satirical, anti-Petrarchan pieces of Wilbye, Weelkes, Pilkington, and Bateson, and without any of their subtlety:

> The tyrant love shall never wound my breast.
> I will not love, nor yet beloved be.
> The lover's life I do in heart detest,
> Which now in mirth are straight in misery.
> I being free, do Cupid's custom scorn,
> Reject his laws, disdain his wounding dart.
> And let who will be with his passions torn,
> He neither can nor shall possess my heart.

Having thus denied the Petrarchan tradition, Kirbye's other madrigals turn to an older style, in which elaborate Petrarchan conceits give way to much plainer language, amatory intrigues to proverbial or sententious themes, and highly personal expression frequently to an impersonal mood. One or two expound the familiar old Elizabethan themes of the simple life and quiet mind, but with bitter barbs at the taste of the time:

> A wise man poor is like a sacred book that's never read.
> To himself he lives and to all else seems dead.
> This age thinks better of a gilded fool
> Than of a threadbare saint in wisdom's school.

The final couplet brings to mind the conclusion to Gibbons's *The Silver Swan,* which Hamond also includes in his collection. A similar string of moralizing similes occurs in *See what is life:*

See what is life if life do lack content,
A weedy garden, lacking pleasant flowers,
A tree all sere where juice & sap is spent,
A withered grass that lacks the dropping showers,
A house that stands by props, foundation gone—
Such is my life & such may be my moan.

But in this instance the final line suddenly transforms the impersonal mood (which the piece shares with the previous example) into a more personal utterance. As in the previous example, the lines are characteristically iambic, and in this case the rhyme scheme, *ababcc,* corresponds to that usually present in the older Elizabethan style, and especially in the songs of William Byrd.[25] It is quite possible that both texts originally included additional stanzas, to be sung strophically to the music of verse 1. Hamond may simply have neglected to copy them.[26] *Sleep aye fond hope,* which reflects the same *ababcc* rhyme scheme, might have involved additional stanzas as well. It reveals the same trend toward melancholy and despair observed in *See what is life:*

Sleep aye fond hope, the stumbling block is laid,
At which thou needs must fall through proud disdain.
And sad despair his pageants he have played,
To wreak thy woe and make me much complain.
Sleep aye fond hope, the uttermost is wrought,
And thou forlorn art made but spite's disport.

This is certainly not the Kirbye of *The First Set of English Madrigals.* Admittedly, one or two examples there, such as no. 6, *Sleep now, my Muse,* or nos. 12-13, *Sorrow consumes me/O heavens, what shall I do,* dwell upon a similar discontent, but never with the sober similes of earlier "plain style" verse. These three unpublished madrigals not only seem to portray Kirbye harkening back to older poetic conceits, but also infected prematurely by the somber, melancholy sentiments observed in Gibbons and the Jacobean "madrigalists," as described by Jacquot and Mellers.[27]

Hamond also chooses three other "madrigals" by Kirbye which, while wanting the tone of melancholy and despair, still indulge in the old, traditional, sententious poetic style, which would have appealed so strongly to Hamond, judging by his own poetic efforts. They form a little trilogy in the manuscripts, held together by their iambic meter, their *ababcc* rhyme scheme (in two cases), and by their various references to plantlife. The first makes use of a straightforward simile like *A wise man poor:*

The ivy green that doth dispised grow,
And none doth plant or trim the same at all,
Although awhile it spreads itself below,

> It mounts in time by creeping up the wall.
> So though the world the virtuous men dispise.
> Yet up aloft, in spite of them they rise.

The work which follows *The ivy green* in Hamond's books might be a response to it, with its warning against too rapid success:

> That man that climbeth up too fast to top of Cedar tall,
> Had need take heed that in his haste he catcheth not a fall.
> For being fall'n, it's ten to one his bruise will be so great,
> That all his days, by all assays on foot he ne'er shall get.
> Wherefore climb not by my consent,
> Keep mean estate, seek sweet content.

This exaltation of the simple life, reminiscent of the poem from *The Arbor of Amorous Devices* (1597) set by Nathaniel Patrick in B.L. Add. MSS 17786-91: "Climb not too high for fear thou catch a fall," and Richard Carlton's "Content thyself with thy estate/Seek not to climb above the skies," published in 1601,[28] employs the solid old "fourteeners" of the Elizabethans, which were completely absent from Kirbye's published set. The final poem of this little trilogy offers further plays on words of the sort found in *My mistress is a paragon*. But in this case the confusion of "thyme" and "time" and two possible meanings of "rue" leads to an "excess of art," for by the time one has arrived at its final couplet the point of the poem is severely clouded by the general confusion (enhanced by the uniformity of the spelling of "time" throughout the original text):

> Use thyme whose tender plant untimely cropped
> Doth take revenge on spoilers' foul abuse.
> When other herbs do thrive tho' often lopped,
> Thyme will not bear such common overplus.
> If thyme you plant, of springtime make thy choice,
> For spring once past, thyme uttereth not her voice.
> But rue for thyme will speak, whose kind is but to rot.
> Thus rue's reward for thyme's neglect do fall to fools by lot.

From the external evidence we cannot date these unpublished works any more precisely than "before 1621" for those in RCM 684 and "before 1634" for those in the Bodleian Library. Arkwright, who first called attention to the unpublished madrigals, suggested that they might have been intended for a second publication, which could be implied by the dedication to the *First Set*.[29] As we shall see, however, the pieces preserved in Hamond's manuscripts were almost certainly early, "student works," which Kirbye chose not to publish. The stylistic contrasts between the Firmage madrigals and the published collection are hardly as marked as the differences between the Hamond pieces and later works. Indeed, the gap separating the Firmage madrigals from those in the 1597 set virtually closes at several points. But the overall stylistic picture they present, and especially their links with the Hamond pieces, suggest that the unpublished works in RCM 684 represent Kirbye's first experiments in the Italian vein. It seems unlikely that they date from after 1597 and were intended for a later publication, as Arkwright suggested.[30]

Although our musical appreciation of these unpublished pieces is hampered by their fragmentary state of preservation, we can still glean a great deal from their remains. Several features confirm the generally accepted view of Kirbye's style. The basically gloomy sentiments of the texts of the madrigals matches well the extraordinary, old-fashioned neglect in their musical settings of the major mode, which, as Kerman observed,[31] was also entirely missing from the published collection. The continued absence of happy sentiments could also explain the lack of contrasting sections in triple time, which are practically nonexistent in the *First Set* as well. These pieces also offer little to contradict Kerman's view of Kirbye as the most harmonically conservative of the English madrigalists,[32] with nothing more startling than the juxtaposition of G major and E major chords in *From the Tarpeian Rock* ("Ah, had the cruel viewed"), likewise the boldest gesture in the 1597 set.

The musical style of the pieces in Hamond's manuscripts suggests, however, that Kirbye's first madrigalian attempts favored a less Italianate approach to secular song than we find in his *First Set*, where, as Kerman writes, "there are no pieces reminiscent of the old-fashioned native style."[33] The Bodleian examples, on the other hand, have more in common with those of another easterner, Richard Carlton of Norwich, which share both their traditional style and rather deficient technique. The settings of the more sententious, "plain" style verses, *A wise man poor, See what is life, The ivy green, That man that climbeth up too fast,* and *Sleep aye fond hope,* all employ the traditional ABB form, in which the musical repetition emphasizes the slightly contrasting, or more pointed, final couplet for all but *See what is life.* In that work the repetition involves only the last line which bears the main point of the stanza.

These works are largely given over to regular sets of imitative entries, often based upon points of a markedly "learned" character, as the opening of *A wise man poor* shows (see ex. 1). Indeed, *A wise man poor* could easily be a consort song disguised as a "madrigal" by the addition of words to its lower parts. In typical consort song fashion, the top part enters last, after an extended introduction in the lower parts, and presents only a single statement of each textual phrase. During the rests which separate the phrases of the "first singing part," the lower parts introduce new points in imitation. The text underlay of these lower parts, in contrast to that of the top line, involves considerable textual repetition, and a certain amount of inelegant word-setting, which strengthens the impression that the lower parts were originally conceived

Ex. 1.   *A wise man poor*

without words. The awkwardness of the opening point in this instance seems to confirm the possibility that Kirbye was still struggling to master the niceties of contrapuntal technique. Movement in whole-notes and half-notes predominates, with very few passages in quarter-notes and eighth-notes, far fewer than occur, by contrast, in the Royal College examples. In addition, these pieces show less tendency to fall into familiar style, maintaining the linear independence of the parts more consistently than those in Firmage's manuscripts. Indeed, on some occasions Kirbye seems to be working especially hard to achieve unusual dissonance through the collision of individual lines (see "than of a threadbare saint" from ex. 1).[34] Furthermore, a number of the cadences in the Hamond pieces avoid the stereotyped V-I with raised leading tone, or resolve in an unconventional manner, so that they retain a stronger modal flavor (see ex. 2). Many of the successions of harmonies appear archaic or irregular by comparison with the more Italianate works (see ex. 3).

Ex. 2.   *That man that climbeth up too fast* (sop. 2 reconstructed) and
         My mistress is a paragon (sop. 2 reconstructed)

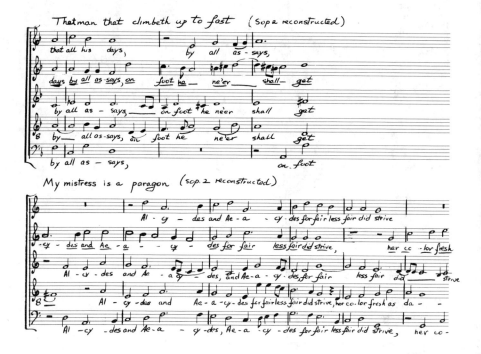

Kerman points out that in the published collection "Kirbye illustrates his text at every point, though always cautiously."[35] But these works, like the majority of the works in the older consort song tradition, offer relatively few opportunities for word-painting. There is nothing in the text of *A wise man poor,* for instance, that calls to mind a suitable musical image. As Philip Brett has suggested in discussing the songs of William Byrd,[36] the generalized nature of such verses, with their numerous moral comments, do not lend themselves to

Ex. 3. *The tyrant love*

a detailed depiction of every image. Kirbye therefore indulges in madrigalian commentary on their texts only rarely. But should an obvious opportunity present itself (e.g., *That man that climbeth up too fast* or "yet up aloft" in *The ivy green),* he does not allow it to pass unnoticed, even in these pieces. Thus, just as Kirbye first drew upon the older native style of poetry in several of the works from F 20-24, he also began with the older native musical style of Byrd. This witness to Kirbye's earlier musical development which Hamond preserves may explain why his 1597 collection, which Kerman has characterized as "completely Italianate," could still reveal elements that Kerman deems "serious," "conservative," "restrained," and "basically regular."[37]

In addition to shedding new light upon Kirbye's initial approach to the madrigal, the large corpus of unpublished pieces in the Bodleian and Royal College manuscripts also reveals extensive experiments with a technique usually regarded as somewhat "forward-looking": the use of structural repetition. But, on the basis of what we have seen in his "student works," Kirbye's use of the device may best be understood as another witness to his indebtedness to the native tradition. The reappearance of earlier musical sections or ideas within the course of a composition, except as required by strophic, ballet, carol, or canzonet forms, was a rarity in English music during the reigns of Elizabeth and James I. Up to now its importance has been emphasized largely in connection with Thomas Weelkes, whose use of the device David Brown regards as relatively novel.[38] It is interesting, therefore, to encounter something similar in the work of an older composer overlooked by Brown. We find some hints of structural repetition in Kirbye's *First Set,* which appeared, interestingly enough, in the same year as Weelkes's earliest collection. Kerman has pointed out the presence of varied repetitions of the opening sections in no. 3, *What can I do, my dearest,* and no. 18, *If pity reign with beauty.*[39] But, in addition to these canzonet-like repetitions, the same set offers one instance of long-range repetition in no. 6, *Sleep now my Muse.* In this case, the textual similarity between the opening of the last couplet and the madrigal's first line induced Kirbye to introduce a musical variation upon the opening of the piece (see ex. 4). It is this latter form of structural repetition which receives attention in the unpublished madrigals.

Ex. 4.   *Sleep now my Muse*

To judge by *Sleep aye fond hope,* preserved in Hamond's manuscripts, Kirbye had already begun to experiment with this device long before the publication of his 1597 collection. Again, the opening textual phrase of the final couplet matches the first line, so Kirbye chose to return to the music of the opening. But in this instance, the reminiscence is much more exact; Kirbye simply reintroduces the opening four bars quite literally (see ex. 5).

In the madrigals from the Royal College manuscripts the technique appears more prominently than it did in either the Hamond madrigals or the printed collection. The only four-voice piece, *Farewell false love,* concludes with this same textual phrase in its final line, which again suggests a musical repetition to Kirbye. But in this case the correspondence is greatly obscured: the solo treatment of "Love" is retained, but for the final line the essential fall of a fourth from A to E is not only divested of the intervening passing notes, but also presented in an entirely different rhythmic configuration (see ex. 6).

Ex. 5. *Sleep aye fond hope*

Two more examples occur among the six-part madrigals from RCM 684, in which Kirbye slightly varies the procedure outlined above. In *O help alas,* Kirbye does not simply repeat the opening musical material when the initial textual phrase reappears. Instead, for the musical reminiscence he omits the one-and-a-half-bar "introduction" to the piece and then redistributes the lines among the different voices (see ex. 7). For "with one smile" he also employs a variation of the point which had appeared for "let pity move thee," and does not fail to stress the madrigalian possibilities of the new text.

The last example, *Mourn now my Muse,* a madrigal in two parts, uses the technique over a longer time scale. At the end of part 2, the phrase "Then mourn my Muse" introduces the final couplet, and Kirbye takes its similarity to the first line of part 1 as an incentive to return to the music of the opening. But in this instance what we find is not a transitory reminiscence of the opening, but a quotation of more than a dozen bars, substituting the words of the final couplet and incorporating a few musical variations.

Ex. 6.   *Farewell false love*

Kirbye's use of structural repetition may become slightly more sophisticated during the course of these madrigalian experiments, but in every instance the musical relationship is plain and invariably derives from the text. The composer takes the textual rhyme as an excuse to employ the time-honored device of musical rhyme. The source of Kirbye's inspiration in adopting the technique remains unclear. Musical restatements sparked by textual repetitions do occur in the Italian madrigal, and precisely the same principle is at work in Marenzio's *I will go die for pure love* from *Musica Transalpina*. But in the light of what we have seen of Kirbye's early development as reflected in the Hamond pieces, it is equally plausible to suggest thet his concern with poetic form and the tendency to seek out verses lending themselves to such a musical treatment (or perhaps to write them himself), may represent a last link with the older, Elizabethan aesthetic in which the shape of the verse remained as important a concern as its content.

Kirbye was not alone in his use of structural repetition, of course, which turns up in works by several of the later English madrigalists, most notably Thomas Weelkes.[40] Although even that most madrigalian of English madrigalists seems to have used the technique primarily to order and unify the wealth of contrasting musical images that abound in his works, the younger Weelkes

Ex. 7. *O help alas*

may have followed a path not unlike Kirbye's, to judge by the kind of poetry he set and the manner in which he treats it. Indeed, in some instances (e.g., *Come clap thy hands, What, have the gods their comfort sent?, Thule, the period of cosmography*) Weelkes employs verbal and musical refrains which have much in common with Kirbye's practice, though the older composer tends toward an

"ABA" rather than Weelkes's "ABCB" form. Both composers, then, may share what Brett, in a recent reassessment of Weelkes, has called "a conscious awareness of that formal approach to poetry observed by Byrd and others in the native tradition, and...a determination not to lose its advantages in writing madrigals."[41]

Aside from George Kirbye, Thomas Ravenscroft is among the more prominent purveyors of unprinted madrigalian pieces in Hamond's manuscripts. Five such works appear in the final sections of F 11-15, forming the largest corpus of unpublished madrigals by this composer:

no. 39	*To Sestos young Leander*
no. 40	*Nymphs and fairies sweetly sing*
no. 41	*Fair shepherds' queen*
no. 42	*Lure, faulkners, lure*
no. 53	*Such was old Orpheus' cunning*

Margaret Crum suggests that perhaps they were intended as illustrations to some sort of essay on modes, since they bear the annotations "Hipolidion cum Hipo-phrygian," "Comedians modulation," etc.[42] In character they are hardly sober or academic, however, for they are all either ballets or the lighter sort of madrigal, such as Ravenscroft had included in his treatise, *A Brief Discourse*, mentioned above.

Lure, faulkners, lure actually appears in that publication, in a four-part version attributed to John Bennet.[43] It seems that Ravenscroft took a fancy to Bennet's contribution to *A Brief Discourse* and rewrote it himself after the fashion of a sixteenth-century parody. Ravenscroft transposes the original down a fourth from C to G (a key for which he seems to have had a special preference), and expands it to five voices, which he combines in a much more imitative setting than Bennet's. The resulting work is twice as long as the printed version, the added length resulting from the extensive imitation. As a rule, Ravenscroft adopts the pre-existent imitative points from Bennet's original where possible, but is much more lavish in their repetition. Sections of text which Bennet passed over after a single homophonic statement receive a more expansive treatment here. For some sections, such as "and stiff winds blow," or "then long too late we faulkners cry," Ravenscroft adopts Bennet's soprano line for use as an imitative point, while in others, such as "the Nyase hawk will kiss the azure sky" he creates a new point of his own (see ex. 8). Ravenscroft also could not pass by the possibilities of "Die fearful ducks" in a mere three bars. He expands Bennet's brief gesture into a seven bar *alla breve* section, indulging cautiously in suspensions and chromatic alterations (see ex. 9). The emotional inflation makes the passage faintly ridiculous, an effect which, one wonders uncomfortably, Ravenscroft may not have intended.

Ex. 8.   *Lure, faulkners, lure*

Such was old Orpheus' cunning, which is separated from Ravenscroft's other madrigalian works by an intervening group of anthems, is in fact a setting of Michael Drayton's dedicatory poem to Thomas Morley's *First Book of Ballets to Five Voices* (1595):

Mᵣ M.D. TO THE AVTHOR

Such was old Orpheus' cunning,
That sencelesse things drew neere him,
And heards of beastes to heare him,
The stock, the stone, the Oxe, the Asse came running.

Morley! but this enchaunting
To thee, to be the Musick-God is wanting.
And yet thou needst not feare him;
Draw thou the Shepherds still and Bonny-lasses,
And envie him not stocks, stones, Oxen, Asses.

Ex. 9.   *Lure, faulkners, lure*

Bennet

Ravenscroft

Ravenscroft sets it in amusing and light-hearted fashion, taking full advantage of the opportunity to illustrate "came running" in extended passages of eighth- and sixteenth-notes. Interestingly enough, he lightly underscores the textual similarities of lines four and nine, before tacking on his whimsical conclusion (see ex. 10).

When we turn from the secular to the sacred, we find that Hamond's choices of purely vocal sacred music are in many ways highly idiosyncratic. It seems somewhat bizarre, for example, to find Byrd's Masses *a 3* and *a 4* in the midst of the "English and Latin Songs" of F 16-19, though, interestingly enough, they do occur as neighbors to selections from *Gradualia,* which are not often found in manuscript. Another notable feature about Hamond's taste in Latin music by Englishmen is the dearth of early Elizabethan motets, which appear quite frequently in some seventeenth-century manuscripts (e.g., Drexel 4180-5, Add. 37402-6, Tenbury 807-11). Perhaps by the 1630s and later they were finally just too archaic to be of interest (though someone like the historically minded John Merro was still transmitting them in relatively large numbers as late as the 1620s). Aside from the pieces from Byrd's *Gradualia,* and one or two motets by Morley, Hamond confines himself to the "moderns." These include the odd example by Kirbye, Wilbye, Dering, and John Tomkins, but primarily pieces by Ravenscroft and Peerson. These eighteen five-voice motets, three by Ravenscroft and fifteen by Peerson, provide another indication that Hamond may have been closely linked with this pair.[44]

Ex. 10. *Such was old Orpheus' cunning* (tenor part missing)

There are, of course, also a large number of Latin motets by foreigners in F
1-6, copied from Kirbye's black books, but these probably tell us more about
George Kirbye's taste than Hamond's. Kirbye must have had a wide exposure
to foreign composers, not just to Philips and Ferrabosco, whose music was
common enough, but also to singularly obscure individuals such as Albino
Fabritio, whose single publication, *Cantiones sacrae sex vocum... Authore
Albino Fabritio. Graecii, quae est metropolis Styriae, excudebat Georgius
Widmanstadius* (1595),[45] provided at least thirteen motets for Kirbye and
hence for Hamond.

Hamond's selection of full anthems is divided between a number of the
almost inevitable old war-horses (Hooper's *Behold, it is Christ,* Tallis's *I call
and cry,* Mundy's *O Lord I bow the knees of my heart,* etc.) and others by the
more modern composers. Apart from a few full anthems from Amner's *Sacred
Hymns,* his choices were unpublished. Ramsey and Ravenscroft offer several,
again attesting to Hamond's close links with them. More unusual, perhaps, are
the isolated piece by one "Mr Taylor" a singing man at Westminster Abbey in
1625, and the *When David heard,* anonymous here, but ascribed elsewhere
(Add. 29427, Add. 29366-8) to the mysterious William Bearsley.

Among the scattered full anthems appears a four-voice setting of *O Lord
turn not away thy face* from the 1561 psalter, ascribed in two partbooks to
"W:B:."[46] Such an ascription is, of course, immediately suggestive of Byrd, but
there is at least one other "W.B." represented in Hamond, though anonymously: William Bearsley, so obscure that he can offer little to aid any attempt to

ascribe that work on the basis of musical style. To make matters worse, such an attempt is hampered by the disappearance of one voice part, the cantus. Even without the top part, the harmony is unusually full, with some effective moments. The composer shows a concern with balancing the imitative outer sections around a brief turn to homophony at the opening of the second section, and the overall result is quite attractive and unpretentious (see ex. 11). One would hesitate to assign it to Byrd on such slim evidence, however.

Ex. 11.   *O Lord turn not away thy face* (cantus part reconstructed)

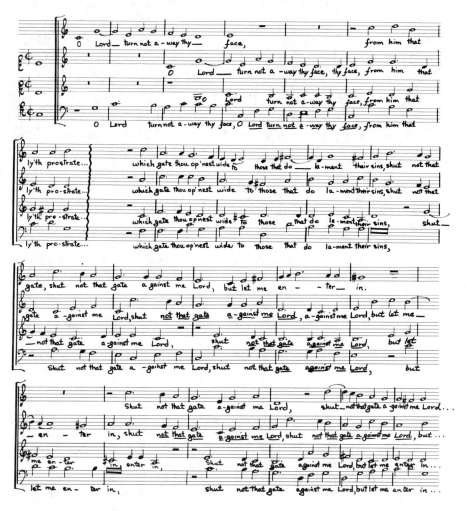

Although we know that Hamond took some interest in viol music, as mentioned at the outset of this chapter, music for voices and viols does not appear with unusual prominence in the extant Hamond partbooks. But nevertheless what there is makes an interesting comparison with that in secular sources of a decade or two earlier. On the whole, Hamond's collection shows the same trend which became increasingly pronounced after 1610 away from the solo consort song. He totally ignores the old Elizabethan playsong repertory. In fact, he shows virtually no evidence at all of an interest in the playsongs of any period, beyond his inclusion of works in other styles by the sometime theatrical composers, Peerson and Ravenscroft. But as we shall see later, these playsongs for voices and viols may have been largely a special London-Oxford phenomenon during the Stuart era. Also notably absent are the various "Cries." Hamond must have known them, for they appear in the set compiled for Firmage, where, given the rest of the repertory, they seem singularly out of place. Their absence from Hamond's own collection remains inexplicable.[47]

Also a relative anomaly is Hamond's interest in Byrd's 1611 *Psalms, Songs and Sonnets,* a real rarity in most manuscript sources. Indeed, as mentioned earlier, Hamond's abiding interest in Byrd so late in the century is quite unusual, matched only in Merro's manuscripts. It could, of course, be purely coincidental that the set came into his hands, but his choice of pieces from the print shows too much discrimination to be purely accidental. Three of his five choices are for voices and viols. Thus, he copies all of the available verse music from the set except the carol for New Years, *O God that guides,*[48] while almost totally ignoring the music for voices alone. It would seem, therefore, that Hamond may have had a special interest in Byrd's music for voices and viols. Yet, if that were so, one would be hard pressed to explain why he ignores *From Virgin's Womb, An earthly tree,* and the extremely popular *Christ rising* from the 1589 *Songs of Sundrie Natures,* which provided twenty-nine pieces for F 11-15, including the choruses for the first two of these verse anthems.[49]

Hamond falls right into line with other musical amateurs in his interest in the verse music of Michael East. His concern is overwhelmingly with East as a composer of music in the verse idiom rather than as a composer of strictly choral pieces. Hamond may include two pieces from East's 1606 collection (East's last to ignore the verse idiom) and one "Neopolitan" from the *Third Set* of 1610, but such full pieces are far outnumberd by the many verse anthems from the 1610 and 1624 publications. The version of *Haste thee O God/But let all those* in F 20-24, unlike East's other anthems in the same manuscript, is not based upon a print, but upon an earlier, prepublication version which also survives in Add. MSS 29366-8. Hamond thus acts as a further witness to the wide circulation of East's verse anthems in manuscript, even long after later versions had appeared in print.[50] He also attests to East's popularity in manuscript sources as a composer of verse rather than full music. Indeed, practically all East's anthems to survive in manuscript sources are verse anthems.

John Amner's *Sacred Hymns* is the other printed source which provided verse music for Hamond's collection. Except for no. 25, *My Lord is hence removed*, Hamond copied all the available verse anthems from the set, plus another eight full anthems. Aside from John Merro, Hamond was the only other music collector to take the trouble to copy Amner's works, which in Hamond's case may be explained by Amner's musical activity at Ely, within the boundaries of Hamond's musical sphere.

Hamond's unpublished verse music features only three composers, Ramsey, Peerson, and Ravenscroft. Ramsey is represented by a three-part work in memory of Prince Henry, *O tell me, wretched shape,* "Dialogues of Sorrow, upon the death of the late Prince Henry. 1615." This is the last of a group of pieces dated 1615 which Margaret Crum suggests may have been prepared for publication, but apparently did not appear.[51] The other texts are set for full choir in the madrigalian style, but for the more solemn lament, Ramsey followed the model of William Byrd in choosing voice and viols as the suitable medium.

The prominence of Ravenscroft, again as a neighbor to Peerson, once again attests to Hamond's apparent connection with this pair. Hamond's collection in fact preserves more verse music by Ravenscroft than any other source, though Christ Church MSS 56-60 and Add. 29372-7 follow as close seconds. One of these anthems, *O woeful ruins,* here consists of three sections, the first full and the others verse. The other source for the work, Christ Church MSS 56-60, transmits only the first section as an independent full anthem. In addition, Ravenscroft provides a setting of *Ah helpless wretch,* Hunnis's text originally set by William Mundy. Though Ravenscroft's setting bears no relationship to the tune given in Hunnis's *A Handful of Honisuckles,* where the text appears, the style of the piece captures most of the sobriety and relative restraint of Mundy's earlier setting. The use of a single soloist, the conservative treatment of his melodic lines, and the extremely brief chorus concluding the stanzas, which simply treats the final melodic phrase in imitation for four bars, contrasts with the more exuberant style of some of Ravenscroft's other verse compositions, and perhaps was meant as a conscious attempt to conform to the decorum appropriate to this old Elizabethan text (see ex. 12).

Hamond likewise proves one of the major sources for Martin Peerson, Ravenscroft's constant companion. Only Myriell and Tenbury 1162-7 contain more examples of Peerson's work, and it is perhaps suggestive that all of the verse anthems by Peerson in Hamond also occur in Tenbury 1162-7.[52] Hamond once again falls in line with other secular scribes in his tendency to include Peerson's verse compositions rather than his works for full chorus. As all the other scribes, he totally ignores the works of Peerson's *Mottects or Graue Chamber Musique* (1630).

Ex. 12.   *Ah helpless wretch.* (The top alto viol part is missing from
Hamond, and has been taken from Add. MSS 29372-7)

Hamond, therefore, seems to have been one of England's most avid, if less discriminating, music collectors before the Restoration, working in an unusually wide circle of musical contacts. Although in finer details his musical taste may appear somewhat less refined in its preferences than some earlier copyists', he does nevertheless represent the continuation of several broader trends from earlier in the century: a single-minded adherence to Elizabethan and Jacobean music, even as late as 1650; an apparent preference for the more serious, less madrigalian style of the later printed collections of Ward, Amner, and Michael East, and even the less common Gibbons; and an interest in the verse idiom—an interest that, though less pronounced than in other sources, reflects the same decline in emphasis upon the solo consort song and the continued preference for the "moderns," East, Peerson, and Ravenscroft. Of his own individual *penchants,* the relatively late interest in Byrd, and the 1611 *Psalms* in particular, seems noteworthy, while his preference for the earlier, more sober works of George Kirbye reveals a new and important side to this distinguished minor figure of the Elizabethan madrigal, which, but for Hamond, would have been lost altogether.

folio[1]	no.	Title	idiom	Composer	Prints
5	1	Dolci sdegni dolci ire[2]		S. Felis	
5ᵛ	2	Dice la mia bellissima licori[3]	f	H. Vecchi	1589[4]:9
6		[Untitled]		S. Molyne	
6ᵛ	3	Cara mia Dafne	f	H. Vecchi	1589[4]:10
7	4	O saette d'amor[2]		Violanti	
7ᵛ	5	Clorinda hai vinto		H. Vecchi	1589[4]:8
8ᵛ	6	Nifa io per te vivo [moro?][3]	f	" "	" :17
9	7	D'amor le riche gemme[2]		A. Stabile	1583[5]
9		Felice[2]			
9ᵛ	8	Mirava alla mia Ninfa[3]	f	V. Bona	1601[6]:6
10ᵛ	9	Son puntentir mordieci	f	" "	" :8
11ᵛ	10	Dimmi ti prego Amori	f	" "	" :10
12ᵛ	11	Riposta: Non sai Damon	f	" "	" :11
13ᵛ	12	Mirabile misterium	f	A. Ferrabosco	
14ᵛ	13	Deus qui beatam Mariam	f	P. Philips	
15ᵛ	14	Nuntium vobis fero de supernis	f	A. Ferrabosco	
16ᵛ	15	Al bel de tuoi capelli[3]	f	H. Vecchi	
17ᵛ	16	Se desio di fuggir[3]	f	" "	
18ᵛ	17	Se tra verdi ar buscelli[3]	f	" "	
19ᵛ	18	Miracol' in natura[3]	f	G. Gastoldi	1583[5]
20ᵛ	19	Sancta Nicola e Christi (i)	f	S. Felis	
21	20	Adesto nostris precibus (ii)	f	" "	
21ᵛ	21	Gaudeamus omnes in Domino	f	P. Philips	
22ᵛ	22	Cum iucunditate nativitatem	f	" "	
23ᵛ	23	Respice in me (i)	f	S. Felis	
24	24	Tribulationes cordis mei (ii)	f	" "	
24ᵛ	25	Vide Domine afflictionem meam	f	" "	
25	26	Miserere mei fili David	f	" "	
25ᵛ	27	Au pres de vous[2]		A. Ferrabosco	
26	28	In qual parte del ciel[2]		R. Paradiso	
26ᵛ	29	O seigneur Dieu[3]	f	A. Pevernage	
27	29	Seigneur, j'ay mis entente	f	" "	
27ᵛ	30	Je vieux mon dieu	f	" "	
28ᵛ	31	Trois fois heureux	f	" "	
29ᵛ	32	Fay que je vive	f	" "	
30ᵛ	33	Recherche qui voudra[3]	f	" "	
31ᵛ	34	In diebus illis	f	S. Felis	
32ᵛ	35	Et stans retro secus pedes	f	" "	
33ᵛ	36	Ad Dominum cum tribularer	f	A. Ferrabosco	
34ᵛ	37	Chacun corps est mortel[3]	f	A. Pevernage	
35	38	Ad Dominum cum tribularer (i)	f	S. Felis	
35ᵛ	39	Fei mihi quia incolatus (ii)	f	" "	
36	40	Di vale filia[2]			
36ᵛ	41	Tanto tempore vobiscum	f	" "	
37	42	[Untitled]		T. Lupo	
37ᵛ	43	Sancti mei qui in carne	f	P. Philips	
38ᵛ	44	O Maria mater, et Joannes	f	" "	
39ᵛ	45	Judica me, Domine (i)	f	A. Ferrabosco	
40	46	Vide humilitatem (ii)	f	" "	
40ᵛ	47	Domine ne in furore (i)	f	S. Felis	
41	48	Miserere mei Domine (ii)	f	" "	
41ᵛ	49	De la mia ruda sorte (i)[3]	f	H. Vecchi	
42	50	Ahi sorte priva (ii)[3]		[" "]	
42ᵛ	51	Ave verum corpus	f	P. Philips	
43	52	Confirma hoc deus	f	W. Byrd	Gr1607:34
43ᵛ	53	Factus est repente	f	" "	" :35
44	54	Veni sancte spiritus, reple	f	" "	" :33
44ᵛ	55	Veni sancte spiritus (i)	f	" "	" :36
45	56	O lux beatissima (ii)	f	" "	" :36
45ᵛ	57	Da tuis fidelibus (iii)	f	" "	" :36

---

1 Modern foliation (from F 1)

2 These pieces are textless in the source.

3 These pieces likewise occur in RCM MS 684.

4 *Madrigali a Cinque Voci...Libro Primo*, 1589.

5 *Harmonia Celeste...Nvovamente Raccolta per Andrea Pevernage...Anversa*, 1583.

6 *Madrigali et Canzoni a Cinque Voci...Libro Primo*, 1601.

folio	no.	Title	idiom	Composer	Prints
46	58	Alleluia. Emitte spiritum tuum	f	W. Byrd	Gr1607:32
46ᵛ	59	Haec dies quam fecit Dominus	f	" "	" :21
47	60	Dominus in Sina	f	" "	" :27
47ᵛ	61	Pascha nostrum immolatus est	f	" "	" :24
48	62	Non vos relinquam orphanos	f	" "	" :37
48ᵛ	63	Spiritus Domini replevit	f	" "	" :31
49	64	Exurgat Deus	f	" "	" :31
49ᵛ	65	Viri Galilei, quid admiramini	f	" "	" :25
50	66	Omnes gentes plaudite	f	" "	" :25
50ᵛ	67	O Rose [Rex] gloria	f	" "	" :30
51	68	Alleluia, ascendit Deus	f	" "	" :26
51ᵛ	69	Ascendit Deus in iubilatione	f	" "	" :28
52		(blank scrap)			
52ᵛ		Ascendit Deus (another copy)			
53	70	Psallite Domine	f	" "	" :29
53ᵛ	71	Gloria Patri et Filio[1]	f	" "	" :20

(fols. 54-54ᵛ blank, unruled)

(Table to songs for six voices)

(six-part pieces)

folio	no.	Title	idiom	Composer	Prints
56	1	Madonna bella sette[2]		S. Felis	
56ᵛ	2	Il dolce marmorio	f	P. Philips	
57ᵛ	3	O Crux benedicta	f	S. Felis	
58	4	Da pacem Domine	f	" "	
58ᵛ	5	Cantate Domino	f	A. Fabritio	1595[3]:12
59ᵛ	6	Dilectus meus mihi	f	T. Victoria	
60ᵛ	7	Exaudiat [te] Domine	f	A. Fabritio	" :25
61ᵛ	8	Diligete iustitiam	f	Massaini	
62ᵛ	9	Anima mea liquifacta est	f	"	
63ᵛ	10	Gaudent in caelis	f	A. Fabritio	" :1
64ᵛ	11	Si mi dicesti ed io	f	P. Philips	
65	12	Ardi ed gela a tua voglia	f	H. Vecchi	
65ᵛ	13	Poi che voi non volete[4]	f	P. Philips	
66		Et exultavit spiritus meus	f	G. Croce	
66ᵛ	14	Bocca mia che midai si dolci	f	G. Gastoldi	
67	15	Si cari e dolci	f	" "	
67ᵛ	16	Exultavit omnium turba	f	A. Fabritio	1595[3]
68ᵛ	17	Alma redemptoris mater	f	" "	" :20
69ᵛ	18	Com' al primo apparir (i)	f	G. Ferretti	1575:1
70ᵛ	19	Cosi al vostro tornar (ii)	f	" "	" :2
71ᵛ	20	Ho in te so dir al molti	f	" "	" :8
72	21	Bon cacciator gia mai	f	" "	" :22
72ᵛ	22	Su su su, non piu dormir	f	" "	" :9
73	23	O che vezzosa Aurora[2]		H. Vecchi	
73ᵛ	24	Beati omnes qui timent Dominum	f	R. del Mell	
74ᵛ	25	Hodie rex caelorum	f	A. Fabritio	1595[3]:5
75ᵛ	26	Deus canticum novum cantabati	f	" "	" :24
76ᵛ	27	O bone Jesu (i)	f	P. da Monte	
77ᵛ	28	Ergo Jesu propter nomen (ii)	f	" "	
78ᵛ	29	O amantissime Jesu (iii)	f	" "	
79ᵛ	30	Credo, quod redemptor	f	A. Ferrabosco	
80	31	Homo natus de muliere	f	J. Wilbye	
80ᵛ	32	Nunc scio vere (i)	f	W. Byrd	Gr1607:38
81	33	Domine probasti me (ii)	f	" "	" :38
81ᵛ	33	Venite exultemus Domino	f	" "	" :46
82ᵛ	34	Levavi oculos meos	f	A. Fabritio	1595[3]:22
83ᵛ	35	O sacrum convivium	f	" "	" :2
84		Quia fecit mihi magna	f	G. Croce	
84ᵛ	36	Tu solus creator	f	A. Fabritio	" :10
85ᵛ	37	Scio quod redemptor meus vivit	f	" "	" :11
86ᵛ	38	Tu es Petrus	f	W. Byrd	Gr1607:41
87ᵛ	39	Quodcunque ligaveris	f	" "	" :44
88ᵛ	40	Laudate Dominum omnes gentes	f	" "	" :45

---

1 Part 3 of *Resurrexi, et adhuc tecum*.

2 These pieces textless in the source.

3 *Cantiones sacrae sex vocum*, 1595.

4 These pieces also occur in RCM MS 684.

folio	no.	Title	idiom	Composer	Prints
89^v	41	Laboravi in gemitu	f	T. Morley	
90^v	42	Ad te, levavi oculos meos	f	A. Fabritio	1595[1]:15
91^v	43	Ascendit Deus in iubilatione	f	" "	" :19
92^v	44	Benedictus deus	f	" "	" :23
93	45	Non porta ghiaccio aprile	f	L. Marenzio	
93^v	46	Constitues eos Principes (i)	f	W. Byrd	Gr1607:39
94	47	Pro patribus tuis (ii)	f	" "	" :39
94^v	48	Et exultavit spiritus meus	f	G. Croce	
95		Sicut erat in principio	f	" "	

(fol. 95^v blank, ruled)

(fols. 96-96^v: various scribblings)

(fol. 97 blank, unruled)

1 *Cantiones sacrae sex vocum,* 1595.

folio[1]	no.	Title	idiom	Composer	Prints
2		Mine eye, why didst thou light	f	T. Hamond	
2ᵛ	i	Whoever thinks or hopes of love	f	[J. Dowland]	1597:2
3ᵛ	ii	Unquiet thoughts	f	" "	" :1
5ᵛ	iii	Now, oh now, I needs must part	f	" "	" :6
6ᵥ	iiii	Think'st thou then	f	[" "]	" :10
6	v	Come away, sweet love	f	" "	" :11
7	vi	If my complaints	f	[" "]	" :4
7ᵛ	vii	Sleep wayward thoughts	f	[" "]	" :13
8	viii	Can she excuse my wrongs	f	[" "]	" :5
8ᵛ	ix	Rest awhile	f	" "	" :12
9	x	My thoughts are winged	f	" "	" :3
9ᵛ	xi	Dear, if you change	f	[" "]	" :7
10	xii	Go, **crystal** tears	f	" "	" :9
10ᵛ	xiii	Come again, sweet love	f	" "	" :17
11	xiv	His golden locks	f	" "	" :18
11ᵛ	15	Burst forth my tears	f	" "	" :8
12ᵛ		Away with these self-loving lads	f	" "	" :21
13		Jockie, thine horn pipes dull	f	T. Weelkes	1608:2
13ᵛ		Some men desire spouses	f	" "	" :3
14		Come sirrah Jack, ho	f	" "	" :6
14ᵛ		The nightingale	f	" "	" :25
15		The ape, the monkey	f	" "	" :10
15ᵛ	1	My choice is made	f[2]	F. Pilkington	1605:2
16	2	Beauty sat bathing	f	" "	" :18
16ᵛ	3	Can she disdain	f	" "	" :3
17	4	Alas, fair face	f	" "	" :4
17ᵛ	5	Rest, sweet nymphs	f	" "	" :6
18	6	Now let her change	f	" "	" :8
18ᵛ	7	Underneath a cypress shade	f	" "	" :9
19	8	Sound woeful plaint	f	" "	" :10
19ᵛ	9	You that pine	f	" "	" :11
20	10	**Look, mistress mine**	f	" "	" :12
20ᵛ	11	Climb, oh heart	f	" "	" :13
21	12	Thanks, gentle moon	f	" "	" :14
21ᵛ	13	I sigh as sure	f	" "	" :15
22	14	*Down a down:thus Phillis sung*	v	" "	" :16
22ᵛ	15	Diaphenia like the daf down dillie	f	" "	" :17
23	16	Music, dear solace	f	" "	" :19
23ᵛ	17	With fragrant flowers	f	" "	" :20
24	18	Now peep bo peep	f	" "	" :1
24ᵛ	19	Whither so fast	f	" "	" :5
25	20	Aye me, she frowns	f	" "	" :7
25ᵛ	21	Sweet was the song	f	T. Hamond[3]	

1 Modern foliation (from F 7).

2 One part untexted.

3 Hamond composed the two inner parts for this piece.

no.	Title	idiom	Composer	Prints

(three-part pieces)

no.	Title	idiom	Composer	Prints
0	See, mine own sweet jewel	f	T. Morley	1593:1
1	Lord in thy rage rebuke me not	f	W. Byrd	1589:1
2	Right blest are they whose wicked sins	f	" "	" :2
3	Lord in thy wrath	f	" "	" :3
4	O God which art most merciful	f	" "	" :4
5	Lord hear my prayer instantly	f	" "	" :5
6	From depth of sin, O Lord	f	" "	" :6
7	Attend mine humble prayer	f	" "	" :7
8	Susanna fair	f	" "	" :8
9	The nightingale so pleasant[3]	f	" "	" :9
10	When younglings first on Cupid (i)	f	" "	" :10
11	But when by proof they find (ii)	f	" "	" :11
12	Upon a summers day (1)	f	" "	" :12
13	Then for a boat (ii)	f	" "	" :13
14	The greedy hawk	f	" "	" :14

(four-part pieces)

no.	Title	idiom	Composer	Prints
15	Is love a boy (i)	f	W. Byrd	" :15
16	Boy pity me (ii)[2]	f	" "	" :16
17	Wounded I am (i)	f	" "	" :17
18	Yet of us twain (ii)	f	" "	" :18
19	From Citheron the warlike boy (i)	f	" "	" :19
20	There careless thoughts (ii)	f	" "	" :20
21	If love be just (iii)	f	" "	" :21
22	O Lord my God, let flesh and blood	f	" "	" :22
23	While that the sun	f	" "	" :23
24	Rejoice with heart and voice	f	" "	" :24
25	Cast off all doubt	f	" "	" :25

(five-part pieces)

no.	Title	idiom	Composer	Prints
26	Weeping full sore	f	W. Byrd	" :26
27	Penelope that longed	f	" "	" :27
28	Compel the hawk	f	" "	" :28
29	See those sweet eyes	f	" "	" :29
30	Fair Ladies that to love (i)	f	O. Gibbons	1612:10
31	'Mongst thousands good (ii)	f	" "	" :11
32	Fair is the rose	f	" "	" :16
33	What is our life	f	" "	" :14
34	Now each flowery bank	f	" "	" :12
35	O that the learned poets	f	" "	" :2
36	O how glorious art thou O God	f	R. White	
37	O Lord I bow the knees of my heart	f	W. Mundy	
38	O give thanks unto the Lord	f	N. Giles	
39	To Sestos young Leander	f	T. Ravenscroft	
40	Nymphs and fairies sweetly sing	f	" "	
41	Fair shepherds' queen	f	" "	
42	Lure, faulkners, lure	f	" "	
43	O woeful ruins of Jerusalem (i)	f	" "	
44	*Those sacred walls (ii)*	v	" "	
45	*O how these graceful piles (iii)*	v	" "	
46	*Wrapt up, O Lord (i)*	v	" "	
47	*Thy power and mercy (ii)*	v	" "	
48	*Yet from this depth of sin (iii)*	v	" "	
49	Behold, now praise the Lord	f	" "	
50	Best is the man	f	" "	
51	Such was old Orpheus' cunning	f	" "	
52	*Ah helpless wretch*	v	" "	
53	*I called upon the Lord (i)*	v	M. Peerson	
	All nations (ii)	v	" "	
	They kept me in (iii)	v	" "	
54	*They came about me (iv)*	v	" "	
55	*O God when thou wentest forth*	v	" "	
56	*Fly, ravished soul (i)*	v	" "	
57	*Rest but awhile (ii)*	v	" "	
	Muse still thereon (iii)	v	" "	
58	*Rain eyes (iv)*	v	" "	

---

1 Catalogue based upon F 11, the most complete of the partbooks.

2 In place of *Boy, pity me*, F 11 includes a second copy of *Yet of us twain*.

3 This piece also occurs in RCM 684

BODLEIAN MSS MUS. F 16 - 19[1]

folio[2]	no.	Title	idiom	Composer	Prints
		(three-part pieces)			
4	1	Sure there is no God of love	f	T. Tomkins	1622:3
4^v	2	Our hasty life	f	" "	" :1
5^v	3	No more I will thy love	f	" "	" :2
$5a^v$	4	Fond men that do so highly prize	f	" "	" :4
6^v	5	Love, cease tormenting	f	" "	" :6
7^v	6	O stay dear life	f	J. Ward	1613:3
8^v	7	How great delight	f	T. Tomkins	1622:5
9^v	8	Sweet, those trammels	f	T. Bateson	1618:6
10^v	9	Love is the fire	f	" "	" :1
11	10	My mistress after service due	f	" "	" :2
11^v	11	One woman scarce of twenty	f	" "	" :3
12^v	12	Flourish, ye hillocks	f	J. Wilbye	1609:2
13^v	13	If I seek to enjoy	f	T. Bateson	1618:4
14^v	14	I have been young	f	W. Byrd	1611:7
15	15	Ave Maria	f	" "	Gr1607:9
15		Cantate Domino	f	" "	" :1
15^v	16	Kyrie Eleison	f	" "	Mass *a 3*
15^v		Et in terra pax	f	" "	" " "
16^v	18	Patrem omnipotentem	f	" "	" " "
18^v	22	Sanctus	f	" "	" " "
19	23	Benedictus	f	" "	" " "
19^v	24	Agnus Dei	f	" "	" " "
20	25	Notum fecit Dominus	f	" "	Gr1607:2
20^v	26	Domine probasti me	f	" "	" :20
21	27	Deus iuditium tuum	f	" "	" :10
21^v	28	Beauty is a lovely sweet	f	T. Bateson	1604:1
22	29	Your shining eyes and golden hair	f	" "	" :6
22^v	30	Aye me, my mistress scorns	f	" "	" :4
23^v	31	Come follow me	f	" "	" :5
24^v	32	Love would discharge	f	" "	" :2
25		Gloria tribulatur	f	T. Brewer	1652[3]:116
25^v		Mercy, dear Lord (i)	f	J. Jenkins	
26	34	Mercy, dear Lord (ii)	f	" "	
26^v	35	O Domine Jesu Christe	f	R. Dering	
27	36	**Gloria Patri**	f	Barnwell	1652[3]:118
27		Gloria Patri	f	T. Heardson	" :120
27^v	37	Come follow me	f		
28^v	38	Great and marvelous are thy works	f		
		(four-part pieces)			
33	1	Kyrie Eleison	f	W. Byrd	Mass *a 4*
33		Et in terra pax	f	" "	" " "
34^v	4	Patrem omnipotentem	f	" "	" " "
36^v	8	Sanctus	f	" "	" " "
37	9	Benedictus	f	" "	" " "
37^v	10	Agnus Dei	f	" "	" " "
38	11	Quare tristis es anima (i)	f	G. Kirbye	
38^v	12	Convertere anima mea (ii)	f	" "	
39^v	13	Ave verum corpus	f	W. Byrd	Gr1607:5
40		This is the day which the Lord hath made	f	O. Parsley	
40^v	14	Ecce quam bonum (i)	f	W. Byrd	" :9
41^v	15	Quod descendit (ii)	f	" "	" :9
42	16	Agnus Dei	f	T. Morley	
42^v	17	Domine fac mecum	f	" "	
43	18	Viderunt omnes	f	W. Byrd	" :2
43^v	19	Dies sanctificatus	f	" "	" :3
44	20	Tui sunt coeli	f	" "	" :4
44^v	21	Hodie Christus natus est	f	" "	" :6
45^v	22	O magnum mysterium	f	" "	" :8
46	23	Beata virgo	f	" "	" :9
46^v	24	Surge, illuminare	f	" "	" :15
47	25	Viderunt omnes	f	" "	" :5
47^v	26	Jesu nostra redemptio	f	" "	" :19
48^v	27	Tu esto nostrum gaudium	f	" "	" :19
49	28	Eheu sustulerunt Dominum	f	T. Morley	P&E1608[4]

1 Catalogue based upon F 19, the most complete of the partbooks.

2 Modern foliation.

3 John Hilton, *Catch that Catch Can*, 1652.

4 *Plain and Easy Introduction to Practial Music*, (1608 edition)

folio	no.	Title	idiom	Composer	Prints
49^V	29	Perche	f	T. Morley	P&E1608[1]
50	30	Ard'egn hora	f	" "	"
50^V	31	Monsieur Mingo	f	O. Lassus	
51^V	32	O my son Absalom	f		
52	33	O Lord turn not away thy face	f	"W:B:"	

(five-part pieces)

folio	no.	Title	idiom	Composer	Prints
55	1[2]	Laboravi in gemitu	f	T. Ravenscroft	
55^V	2	O Domine Jesu Christe	f	" "	
56^V	3	Ne laeteris	f	" "	
57^V	4	Deus omnipotens	f	M. Peerson	
58^V	5	Redemptor	f	" "	
59^V	6	Pater fili	f	" "	
60^V	7	Levavi occulos (i)	f	" "	
61^V	8	Ecce non dormitabit (ii)	f	" "	
62^V	9	Mulieres sedentes (i)	f	" "	
63^V	10	Christus factus est (ii)	f	" "	
64^V	11	Hora nona Dominus Jesus (i)	f	" "	
65^V	12	Latus eius (ii)	f	" "	
66^V	13	O rex gloriae	f	" "	
68	14	Quid vobis videtur	f	" "	
69^V	15	O Domine Jesu Christe	f	" "	
71	16	Laboravi in gemitu	f	" "	
72^V	17	Nolite fieri (i)	f	" "	
73^V	18	Multa flagella (ii)	f	" "	
74^V	19	*Praise the Lord (i)*	v	" "	
74^V		*O put not your trust (ii)*	v	" "	
75^V	20	*I am small*	v	" "	
77	21	O Metaphysical tobacco	f	M. East	1606:22
77^V	22	*When Israel came out (i)*	v	" "	1610:4
78^V	23	*What aileth thee (ii)*	v	" "	" :5
79^V	24	Hence stars	f	" "	1606:21
80^V	25	The nymphs and shepherds	f	Marson	1601:6
81^V	26	Come Lovers forth	f	G. Ferretti	Mo1598:4
82^V	27	Retire my troubled soul	f		

1 *Plain and Easy Introduction to Practical Music* (1608 edition).

2 Numbers 1-19 bound in after 20-27 in F 17.

folio[1]	no.	Title	idiom	Composer	Prints
		(five-part pieces)			
4	1	A wise man poor	f	G. Kirbye	
4ᵛ	2	Remember not, Lord our offences	f	J. Amner	1615:13
5ᵛ	3	Now doth the city	f	" "	" :16
6ᵛ	4	He that descended man to be	f	" "	" :17
7ᵛ	5	Arise, O Lord[2]	f	[W. Byrd]	
8ᵛ	6	Sweet Philomel cease thy songs	f	J. Ward	1613:13
9ᵛ	7	See sylvan nymphs (ii)	f	" "	" :14
10ᵛ	8	Flora, fair nymph	f	" "	" :15
11ᵛ	9	Upon a bank with roses	f	" "	" :18
12ᵛ	10	Hope of my heart	f	" "	" :17
13ᵛ	11	Almighty God, the fountain	f	T. Tomkins	
14ᵛ	12	Behold it is Christ	f	E. Hooper	
15ᵛ	13	I will sing unto the Lord	f	Taylor	
16	14	*I have roared (i)*	v	M. East	1624:4
16ᵛ	15	*I am brought (ii)*	v	" "	" :5
17	16	*My loins are filled (iii)*	v	" "	" :6
17ᵛ	17	*As they departed (i)*	v	" "	" :1
18ᵛ	18	*But what went you out to see (ii)*	v	" "	" :2
19ᵛ	19	*For this is he (iii)*	v	" "	" :3
20ᵛ	20	Thus sings that heavenly choir	f	J. Amner	1615:14
21ᵛ	21	The heavens stood amazed (ii)	f	" "	" :15
22ᵛ	22	I will sing unto the Lord	f	" "	" :18
23ᵛ	23	My mistress is a paragon	f	G. Kirbye	
24	24	Blessed be thy name[3]	f	T. Tallis	
24ᵛ	25	See, what is life	f	G. Kirbye	
25	26	The ivy green	f	" "	
25ᵛ	27	That man that climbeth up too fast	f	" "	
26ᵛ	28	Use time whose tender plant	f	" "	
27ᵛ	29	Sleep, aye, fond hope	f	" "	
28	30	When David heard	f	[W. Bearsley]	
28ᵛ	31	The tyrant love	f	G. Kirbye	
29	32	Come life, come death	f	M. East	1610:6
29ᵛ	33	Liquid and watery pearls [5]	f	L. Marenzio	MT1588:31
30	34	With bitter sighs	f	T. Bateson	1618:19
30ᵛ	35	Have I found her	f	" "	" :13
31ᵛ	36	Sleep, mine only jewel (i)	f	S. Felis	MT1588:28
32ᵛ	37	Thou bring'st her home (ii)	f	" "	" :29
33ᵛ	38	Lady, that hand of plenty [5]	f	Bertani	" :38
34ᵛ	39	My heart, alas [5]	f	Conversi	" :39
35ᵛ	40	Camilla fair tripped	f	T. Bateson	1618:15
36ᵛ	41	Why do I dying live	f	" "	" :20
37ᵛ	42	Up [down!] the hills Corinna	f	" "	" :14
39ᵛ	43	Come, sorrow, help me	f	" "	" :24
40	44	All the day I waste (i)	f	" "	" :22
40ᵛ	45	Why dost thou fly me (ii)	f	" "	:23
41	46	Those sweet delightful lilies	f	" "	1604:13
41ᵛ	47	*Triumph with pleasant melody*	cs	W. Byrd	
43	48	Who prostrate lies	f	T. Bateson	" :20
43ᵛ	49	Sweet Gemma, when I first (i)	f	" "	" :15
44ᵛ	50	Yet stay alway (ii)	f	" "	" :16
45		The silver swan	f	O. Gibbons	1612:1
45ᵛ	51	Heark, hear you not	f	T. Bateson	1604:22
46ᵛ	52	Alas, where is my love	f	" "	" :18
47ᵛ	53	And must I needs depart	f	" "	" :14
48	54	Crowned with flowers	f	W. Byrd	1611:22
48ᵛ	55	I call and cry[4]	f	T. Tallis	
49ᵛ	56	Trust not too much	f	O. Gibbons	1612:20

---

1 Modern folation from F 20.

2 Adaptation of the motet, *Exsurge Domine,* from CS1591.

3 Adaptation of the motet, *Mihi autem nimis,* from CS1575.

4 Adaptation of the motet, *O sacrum convivium,* from CS1575.

5 These pieces also occur in RCM MS 684

folio	no.	Title	idiom	Composer	Prints
50ᵛ	57	Nay, let me weep (i)	f	O. Gibbons	1612:17
51ᵛ	58	Ne'er let the sun (ii)	f	" "	" :18
52ᵛ	59	Yet if that age (iii)	f	" "	" :19
53ᵛ	60	Lais now old that erst	f	" "	" :13
54ᵛ	61	Dainty fine birds	f	" "	" :9
55	62	How art thou thrall'd (i)	f	" "	" :7
55ᵛ	63	Farewell all joys (ii)	f	" "	" :8
56ᵛ	64	Ah, dear heart	f	" "	" :15

(six-part pieces)

folio	no.	Title	idiom	Composer	Prints
61	1	*In vain [How vain] the toils*	cs	W. Byrd	1611:32
61ᵛ	2	*Have mercy upon me, O God*	v	" "	" :25
62ᵛ	3	Oft have I tendered	f	J. Ward	1613:20
63ᵛ	4	Cupid in a bed of roses (i)	f	T. Bateson	1618:25
64		Cithera smiling (ii)	f	" "	" :26
64ᵛ	5	Her hair the net	f	" "	" :27
65ᵛ	6	Fond love is blind (i)	f	" "	" :28
66ᵛ	7	Ah Cupid, grant (ii)	f	" "	" :29
67ᵛ	8	Die not fond man	f	J. Ward	1613:25
68ᵛ	9	Oh, who shall ease me	f	J. Wilbye	
69	10	Retire, my troubled soul	f	J. Ward	" :19
69ᵛ	11	*O ye little flock (i)*	v	J. Amner	1615:19
70ᵛ	12	*Fear not (ii)*	v	" "	" :20
71ᵛ	13	*And they cry (iii)*	v	" "	" :21
72ᵛ	14	*Lo, how from heaven (i)*	v	" "	" :22
73ᵛ	15	*I bring you tidings (ii)*	v	" "	" :23
74ᵛ	16	A stranger here	f	" "	" :24
75ᵛ	17	With mournful music	f	" "	" :26
76ᵛ	18	Weep forth your tears	f	J. Ward	1613:28
77ᵛ	19	Out from the vale	f	" "	" :21
78ᵛ	20	O divine love	f	" "	" :22
79ᵛ	21	If the deep sighs	f	" "	" :23
80ᵛ	22	There's not a grove	f	" "	" :24
82	23	*Ah silly soul*	cs	W. Byrd	1611:31
82ᵛ	24	I have entreated	f	J. Ward	1613:26
83ᵛ	25	Come sable night	f	" "	" :27
84ᵛ	26	She with a cruel frown	f	T. Bateson	1618:30
85ᵛ	27	Dear if you wish	f	" "	1604:23
86ᵛ	28	Merrily my love	f	" "	" :27
87ᵛ	29	Phillis, farewell	f	T. Bateson	" :12
88ᵛ	30	Fair Hebe, when dame Flora	f	" "	" :24
89ᵛ	31	Thirsis on his fair Phillis	f	" "	" :26
90ᵛ	32	Woe I am constrained	f	R. Ramsey	
91ᵛ	33	How doth the city	f	" "	
92ᵛ	34	*O clap your hands (i)*	v	T. Ravenscroft	
93ᵛ	35	*God reigneth (ii)*	v	" "	
94ᵛ	36	Sing joyfully	f	W. Byrd	
95ᵛ	37	*Haste ye, O God (i)*[1]	v	M. East	1618:21
96ᵛ	38	*But let all those (ii)*	v	" "	" :22
97ᵛ	39	When Oriana walked	f	T. Bateson	1604:unnum.
98ᵛ	40	If plaint "-Aᵒ 1615"	f	R. Ramsey	
99ᵛ	41	Since no desert can move thee	f	" "	
100ᵛ	42	Part we must (i)	f	" "	
101ᵛ	43	Yet of us (ii)	f	" "	
102ᵛ	44	Why dost thou say "ay me"	f	" "	
103ᵛ	45	*O tell me wretched shape (i)*[2]	v	" "	
104ᵛ	46	*What dire mishap (ii)*	v	" "	
105ᵛ	47	*Gone is the world's delight (iii)*	v	" "	
106ᵛ		O my son Absalom	f	T. Weelkes	

---

1 This anthem was not copied from the print, but from an earlier, pre-publication version.

2 "-Dialogues of Sorrow, upon the death of the late Prince Henry. 1615."

folio[1]	no.	Title	idiom	Composer	Prints
3^V	2	Call to remembrance	f	J. Hilton	
4^V	3	Phillis, I fain would die	f	T. Morley	1595:21
5^V	4	Cantate Domino	f	J. Tomkins	
6^V	5	Are lovers full of fire	f	R. Jones	1607:25
7^V	6	Inclina Domine	f	R. Ramsey	
9^V	7	You blessed bowers	f	J. Farmer	1599:17
10^V	8	The more I burn	f	R. Jones	1607:26
11	9	Diliges Dominum	f	W. Byrd	CS1575:25
11^V	10	Mio cor, mio bene	f	B. Ratti	

1 Modern foliation, from F 25.

folio[2]	no.	Title	Composer	Prints

(three-part pieces)

folio	no.	Title	Composer	Prints
1	1	Do you not know	T. Morley	1593:16
1[V]	2	Aye me, can every rumor	J. Wilbye	1598:3
2	3	See Amarillis shamed	M. East	1606:2
2[V]	4	Oh, what shall I do (i)	J. Wilbye	1609:6
3	5	At thy feet I fall (ii)	" "	" :6
3[V]	6	O do not run away	M. East	1604:6
4	7	I live and yet methinks	J. Wilbye	1609:7-8
4[V]	8	Ah, cruel Amarillis	" "	" :3
5	9	Come shepherd swains	" "	" :1
5[V]	10	Ah, silly John (i)	E. Johnson	
6	11	That I love her (ii)	" "	

(fols. 6[V]-8[V] blank, unruled)

folio	no.	Title	Composer	Prints
9	19	Ah, Phillis still I love thee [Ahi Filli anima mia]	Scaletta	1590[3]:4
9		Though she ever were cruel [Perche Barbara sia questa]	"	" :6
9		Farewell, though my beloved [Amor tutte le leggi]	"	" :2
9[V]	20	O love with haste relieve me [Amor per qual caggione]	"	" :1
9[V]		Say love, what doth displease thee [Di che ti lagni Amante]	"	" :3
10	21	Sweetheart I know you love me [S'un tempo]	Mortaro	1590[4]:1
10		If I part from my jewel [Era al sol il mio sole]	"	" :2
10[V]	22	All comfortless thus left [Son per morir]	"	" :7
10[V]		With pity now relieve me [Gran cosa a se mi pare]	"	" :9
10[V]		In Cloris [Nel seno di mia Clori]	"	" :6
11	23	Tormented, yet my pain groweth [Io ardo e l'ardor mio]	Scaletta	1590[3]:20
11		Cast down with grief [Profondi laghi e voi]	"	" :21
11[V]	24	Mine own sweet heart [Che ve penseu]	"	" :10
11[V]		Alas when she disdain me [Donna s'io vi non lunge]	"	" :8
11[V]		Where shall I rest my hopes [Quelli occhi ladri]	"	" :9

(fols. 13-13[V]: table of pieces for four voices)

(four-voice pieces)

folio	no.	Title	Composer	Prints
14	1	O grief, if yet my grief	Donato	MT1588:5
14[V]	2	False love, now shoot	Prenestino	" :4
15	3	Farewell false love	G. Kirbye	
15[V]	4	Fair shepherds' queen	L. Marenzio	IM1590:5
16	5	Lady, your look so gentle	Verdonck	MT1588:12
16[V]	6	Lo, here my heart	G. Kirbye	1597:1
17	7	Alas, what hope of speeding	" "	" :2
17[V]	8	Say, gentle nymphs	T. Morley	1594:20
18	9	What meanest love to nest him	Prenestino	MT1588:8
18[V]	10	Clorinda false, adieu	T. Morley	1594:2
19	11	Help, I fall	" "	" :5
19[V]	12	Farewell, my love, I part	G. Kirbye	1597:5
20	13	Sleep now, my Muse	" "	"
20[V]	14	Zephyrus breathing	L. Marenzio	IM1590:4
21	15	Change me, O heavens	J. Wilbye	1609:11
21[V]	16	In vain he seeks for beauty	P. da Monte	MT1588:7
22	17	Farewell, cruel and unkind	L. Marenzio	IM1590:3
22[V]	18	As matchless beauty	J. Wilbye	1609:15
23	19	Happy, oh happy who not affecting	" "	" :16
23[V]	20	I love, alas, yet am not loved	" "	" :14
24	21	When Cloris heard of her Amintas	" "	" :9
24[V]	22	Woe am I, my heart dies	G. Kirbye	1597:4
25	23	Adieu, sweet Amaryllis	J. Wilbye	1598:12
25[V]	24	What can I do my dearest	G. Kirbye	1597:3
26	25	When first my heedless eyes beheld	L. Marenzio	IM1590:1

1 Aside from the "Cries" and *New Fashions* all the pieces in the partbooks are "full".

2 Modern foliation.

3 *Vilanelle alla Romana a tre voci...Libro Primo*, 1590.

4 *Il secondo libro delle fiamelle amorose, a tre voci*, 1590.

folio	no.	Title	Composer	Prints
26[V]	26	The fair Diana	G. de Macque	MT1588:2
27	27	Joy so delights my heart	Prenestino	" :3
27[V]	28	Sweet love when hope was flowering	"	" :9
28	29	O come gran martire	A. Pevernage	1591[1]
28[V]	30	A che piu strali	C. Verdonck	"
29	31	Voi volete ch'io morire	P. Philips	"
29[V]	32	More quasi il mio core	Prenestino	"
30	33	Ma per me lasso	L.Marenzio	1587[2]:23
30[V]	34	Rendi mir il finto	Farina	
31	35	Sei del finto si vago	"	
31[V]	36	Su'l caro del lamente (i)	L. Marenzio	" :24
32	37	Vedi ch'eglia (ii)	" "	" :25
32[V]	38	Donna s'io sono il sole	Farina	
33	39	Tu sei signore il sole	"	
33[V]	40	Moriro cor mio	"	1591[1]
34	41	Hor vedi amor	L. Marenzio	1587[2]:7
34[V]	42	Nova angeletta	" "	" :10
35	43	Dissi a Pamata mia lucida	" "	" :2
35[V]	44	O bella man che mid' istringi (i)	" "	" :4
36	45	Candido leggia (ii)	" "	" :5
36[V]	46	Ecco di fiori e di vermiglie	Farina	
37	47	Amor sei i bei rubin (i)	P. Philips	1591[1]
37[V]	48	Perche non poss (ii)	" "	"

(fol. 38: blank, unruled)

(fols. 38[V]-39[V]: table of songs for five voices)

(five-part pieces)

folio	no.	Title	Composer	Prints
40	1	When shall I cease lamenting	Faignient	MT1588:21
40[V]	2	I must depart all hapless	L. Marenzio	" :22
41	3	When from myself sweet cupid	" "	IM1590:16
41[V]	4	Sweet singing Amarillis	" "	" :17
42	5	All ye that joy in wailing	Nanino	" :20
42[V]	6	Hills and woods, crags and rocks	Quintiani	MT1597:11
43	7	That muse which sang the beauty	G. Kirbye	1597:16
43[V]	8	See what a maze of error	" "	" :17
44	9	If pity reign with beauty	" "	" :18
44[V]	10	Sweet honey-sucking bees (i)	J. Wilbye	1609:17
45	11	Yet, sweet take heed (ii)	" "	" :18
45[V]	12	Come clap thy hands (i)	T. Weelkes	1598:19
46	13	Phillis hath sworn (ii)	" "	" :20
46[V]	14	From the Tarpeian rock	G. Kirbye	
47	15	I saw my lady weeping (i)	A. Ferrabosco	MT1588:23
47[V]	16	Like as from heaven (ii)	" "	" :24
48	17	Thirsis enjoyed the graces	" "	" : 42
48[V]	18	Fancy retire thee	L. Marenzio	IM1590:18
49	19	So far dear life	G. Eremita	MT1597:3
49[V]	20	Sweet love, oh cease thy flying	G. Kirbye	1597:15
50	21	Lady, that hand of plenty	L. Bertani	MT1588:38
50[V]	22	The nightingale so pleasant	A. Ferrabosco	" :43
51	23	The white delightful swan	H. Vecchi	MT1597:1
51[V]	24	Cinthia, thy song	G. Croce	" :4
52	25	Lady, if you so spite me	A. Ferrabosco	MT1588:40
52[V]	26	My heart, alas, why dost thou love	G. Conversi	" :18
53	27	Zephyrus brings the time	A. Ferrabosco	" :52-3
53[V]	28	Fly if thou wilt	G. Eremita	MT1597:5
54	29	Sound out my voice	Palestrina	MT1588:30
54[V]	30	Liquid and watery pearls	L. Marenzio	" :31
55	31	Within a greenwood	Ferretti	" :33
55[V]	32	Sometime when hope relieved me	del Melle	" :34
56	33	What, shall I part	G. Kirbye	1597:11
56[V]	34	Rubies and pearls and treasure	A. Ferrabosco	MT1588:35
57	35	O sweet kiss full of comfort	" "	" :36
57[V]	36	Sometime my hopeful weakly	" "	" :37
58	37	Lo, she flies	T. Morley	1595:18
58[V]	38	Sweetheart, arise	L. Marenzio	IM1590:14- 5
59	39	Sweet eyes admiring you	Venturi	MT1597:16
59[V]	40	The nightingale so pleasant	O. Lassus	MT1588:32
60	41	Alas, where is my love	L. Marenzio	IM1590:13
60[V]	42	Since my heedless eyes	" "	" :10
61	43	A silly sylvan kissing	J. Wilbye	1609:26
61[V]	44	O my grief were it disclosed	H. Lichfield	1613:6

1 *Melodia Olympica...Nvovamente Raccolta da Pietro Philippi Inglese...Anversa, 1591.*

2 *Madrigali a Quatro Voci...Libro Primo...Venetia, 1587.*

folio	no.	Title	Composer	Prints
62	45	In every place I find my grief	[Palestrina]	MT1588:15
62^V	46	Thirsis to die desired (i)	L. Marenzio	" :16
63	47	Thirsis that refrained (ii)	" "	" :17
63^V	48	Though faint	" "	IM1590 :9
64	49	Ah, sweet alas when first I saw	G. Kirbye	1597:7
64^V	50	My lady wept and from her chry-stal fountains (i)	" "	
65	51	But when himself bebathed (ii)	" "	
65^V	52	Weep, mine eyes	J. Wilbye	1609:23
66	53	Why [what] doth my pretty darling	L. Marenzio	MT1588:27
66^V	54	All ye that sleep in pleasure	H. Lichfield	1613:1
67	55	Ah cruel, hateful fortune	F. Dentico	
67^V	56	From what part of heaven (i)	P. da Monte	MT1588:13
68	57	In vain he seeks (ii)	" " "	" :14
68^V	58	Dolorous mournful cares	L. Marenzio	MT1597:9
69	59	Resveillez-vous, chacun fidelle	A. Pevernage	
69^V	60	D'estre si long	" "	
70	61	Chacun corps est mortel^1	" "	
70^V	62	Al bel de tuoi capelli^1	H. Vecchi	
71	63	Dice la mia bellissima^1	" "	1589^2:9
71^V	64	Cara mia Dafne^1	" "	" :10
72	65	Di lauri e mirti il tuo	L. Quintiani	1588^3:1
72^V	66	Recherche qui voudra les apparens^1	A. Pevernage	
73	67	La franc d'ambition (ii)	" "	
73^V	68	Se desio di fuggir^1	H. Vecchi	
74	69	Se tra verdi ar buscel^1	" "	
74^V	70	Miracol' in natura^1	G. Gastoldi	1583^4
75	71	Nifa io per te vivo [moro?]^1	H. Vecchi	1589^2:17
75^V	72	Mirava alla mia ninfa^1	V. Bona	1601^5:6
76	73	O Seigneur Dieu qui vois ma passion^1	A. Pevernage	
76^V	74	Picciol far falla arder	V. Bona	" :20
77	75	Ameni colli vaghi	" "	" :22
77^V	76	Polimira un che t'honora	L. Quintiani	1588^3:14
78	77	Se le virtu che'n voi chi udite	" "	" :5
78^V	78	Sapeti amanti	" "	" :9
79	79	De la mia cruda sorte^1	H. Vecchi	
79		Ahi sorte priva^1		
79^V	80	Vermiglio e vagho fiore	V. Bona	1601^5:13
80	81	Parto O non parto	L. Marenzio	
80^V	82	Credete voi ch'i vina	" "	
81	83	Ardemno insieme	P. Nenna	1609^6:15
81^V	84	Suggeste mi il sangue	" "	" :17
82	85	Fuggite pur fuggite crudel	" "	" :19
82^V	86	La bella man vi stringo	L. Marenzio	
83	87	Lamorego veleno	P. Nenna	" :10
83^V	88	Filli mia s'al mio seno (i)	" "	" :8
84	89	Coridon del tuo petto (ii)	" "	" :9
84^V	90	Non veggio il mio bel sola	" "	" :11
85	91	Godea: La mia ninfa	" "	" :2
85^V	92	In due: Vidd'io purpura rosa	" "	" :3
86	93	Soglie ver ch'io vadore	" "	" :1
86^V	94	Con le labra di rose	" "	" :5
87	95	Cruda Amarilli	C. Monteverdi	
87^V	96	Non si fos col horror	P. Nenna	
88	97	All'amoroso fonte	Bartolini	
88^V	98	Luci, luci serene e chiare	C. Monteverdi	
89	99	Voi pur dami partire anima	" "	
89^V		The Cries of London	O. Gibbons	

(fols. 92-93 : blank)

| 93^V | | The Country Cry | R. Dering | |
| 94^V | | New Fashions | W. Cobbold | |

(fol. 96: blank)

(fols. 96^V-97^V: table of pieces for six voices)

---

1 These works also occur in Bodleian MSS Mus F 1-6.

2 *Madrigali a Cinque Voci...Libro Primo*, 1589.

3 *Il Primo Libro De Madrigali A Cinque Voci...Venetia*, 1588.

4 *Harmonia Celeste...Nvovamente Raccolta per Andrea Pevernage...Anversa*, 1583.

5 *Madrigali et Canzoni a Cinque Voci...Libro Primo...Venetia*, 1601.

6 *Il Settimo Libro de Madrigali a Cinque voci...Venetia*, 1609.

folio	no.	Title	Composer	Prints
		(six-part pieces)		
98	1	O gracious and worthiest of each	G. Croce	MT1597:19
98ᵛ	2	Love, quench this heat consuming	B. Palavicino	" :17
99	3	Cruel, why dost thou fly me	" "	" :18
99ᵛ	4	Long have I made these hills	J. Wilbye	1609:34
100	5	Poor is the life that misses	Ferretti	
100ᵛ	6	O help, alas, let pity move thee	G. Kirbye	
101	7	Oh, shall I die	" "	
101ᵛ	8	I sung sometime (i)	L. Marenzio	MT1588:56
102	9	Because my love (ii)	" "	" :57
102ᵛ	10	Shall I live so far	" "	MT1597 :20
103	11	Up then, Melpomene (i)	G. Kirbye	1597:22
103ᵛ	12	Why wail we thus (ii)	" "	" :23
104	13	Life, tell me	M. East	1610:21
104ᵛ	14	Cruel, behold	J. Wilbye	1598:28
105	15	Lo, here my heart in keeping	"Incerto"	MT1588:50
105ᵛ	16	Zephyrus brings the time (i)	Conversi	" :52
106	17	But with me wretch (ii)	"	" :53
106ᵛ	18	As lives the salamander	L. Marenzio	Mar1594:3
107	19	Lo, where I lie in grief	G. Croce	
107ᵛ	20	Dainty white pearl	L. Marenzio	" :18
108	21	The fates, alas, too cruel	" "	IM1590:27
108ᵛ	22	Love hath proclaimed war	A. Striggio	" :26
109	23	Unkind, alas, why do you grieve me	G. Kirbye	
109ᵛ	24	Oh when my love had me disdained	" "	
110	25	Unkind, oh stay thy flying	L. Marenzio	IM1590:25
110ᵛ	26	Now must I part	" "	MT1588:51
111	27	My heavy heart	S. Felis	
111ᵛ	28	Must I part, O my jewel	G. Kirbye	1597:21
112	29	Ah, cannot: to pity me	J. Wilbye	1609:30
112ᵛ	30	Thirsis to die desired (i)	B. Palavicino	MT1588:16
113	31	Thirsis that heat refrained (ii)	" "	" :17
113ᵛ	32	Thus, these two lovers (iii)	" "	" :18
114	33	In chains of hope and fear	L. Marenzio	IM1590:22
114ᵛ	34	O hear me, heavenly powers	" "	" :21
115	35	So saith my fair and beautiful Licoris	" "	MT1597 :21
115ᵛ	36	With angel's face and brightness	G. Kirbye	1601:29
116	37	Hard by a chrystal fountain	G. Croce	MT1597:24
116ᵛ	38	I will go die for pure love	L. Marenzio	MT1588:46
117	39	O wretched man	**J. Wilbye**	1609:27
117ᵛ	40	Ah, cruel, hateful fortune	G. Kirbye	1597:19
118	41	Draw on, sweet night	J. Wilbye	1609:31
118ᵛ	42	Where most my thoughts (i)	" "	" :28
119	43	Dispiteful (ii)	" "	" :29
119ᵛ	44	Mourn now my Muse (i)	G. Kirbye	
120	45	As sudden death (ii)	" "	
120ᵛ	46	So far from my delight (i)	A. Ferrabosco	MT1588:48
121	47	She only doth (ii)	" "	" :49
121ᵛ	48	Thou art but young	J. Wilbye	1598:29
122	49	Pianger filli	L. Marenzio	
122ᵛ	50	Laura serena (i)	" "	
123	51	Le quale spargea (ii)	" "	
123ᵛ	52	Questa chel cor m'ancide	F. Anerio	1590[1]:4
124	53	Laura dolce	" "	" :3
124ᵛ	54	Deh non misar	G. Croce	
125	55	Bocca soave e care	" "	
125ᵛ	56	Ecco ch'el ciel (i)	L. Marenzio	
126	57	Ecco che mill'augei (ii)	" "	
126ᵛ	58	Almor morar	G. Gastoldi	
127	59	Adio: Caro il mio Tirsia	G. Croce	
127ᵛ	60	Frai vaghie bei crind'o	Feliciani	
128	61	Occhi: sereni e chiari	L. Marenzio	
128ᵛ	62	Come marti de l'aba (i)	" "	
129	63	Cosi questa (ii)	" "	
129ᵛ	64	Dono Cinthia a Damone	" "	
130	65	Per duo coralli	" "	
130ᵛ	66	O che vezzosa[2]	H. Vecchi	
131	67	Felice amante	G. Gastoldi	
131ᵛ	68	Valli profunde (i)	G. Croce	
132	69	Erme cam vag' (ii)	" "	
132ᵛ	70	Poi che voi non volete[2]	P. Philips	
133	71	Creci bel verd'alloro	Meldert	
133ᵛ	72	Laura che noi circonda	F. Anerio	1590[1]:2
134	73	Godi leggiadre filli	" "	" :14
134ᵛ	74	Come ne caldi	" "	" :15

1 *Primo Libro De Madrigale a sei Voci...Venetia*, 1590.

2 These works also occur in Bodleian MSS Mus. F 1-6.

folio	no.	Title	Composer	Prints
135^V	75	Giunta qui dori	Cavaccio	
135^V	76	Baci soavi e care (i)	L. Marenzio	
136	77	Baci mentre (ii)	" "	
136^V	78	Baci affamato (iii)	" "	
137	79	Baci cortesi (iv)	" "	
137^V	80	Baci ohime (v)	" "	

British Library Additional MSS 29366-8

Time has not dealt kindly with this set of manuscripts. Once described as "A perfect set of Anthem & fansie Six par:" on the cover of 29367, today only the cantus, quintus, and bassus books survive. Many of the works contained therein are rendered even more fragmentary by their omission from one or other of the remaining partbooks (e.g., Bearsley's *When David heard* settings and the anonymous *Wounded with sin extremely*). Indeed, in their present state, with some pieces out of sequence or missing altogether from one or more books, the contents are so jumbled that one exasperated antiquarian was prompted to write:

> NB: These books want examination; the severall pieces mention'd being promiscuously written, it requires an index & to Number ye Pages.
>   (29366, fol. 1)

In addition to the designation of the individual voice parts, the cover of each book bears the inscription in ink, "Io: Browne:". Hughes-Hughes suggested that this probably referred to the seventeenth-century music printer of St. Dunstan's, Fleet Street. Because some of the motets from the manuscript bear the monogram "AF," he further suggested that the books were copied by Alfonso Ferrabosco the Elder.[53] Edward Thompson altered the latter suggestion to Alfonso Ferrabosco II,[54] but the possibility of ownership by the St. Dunstan's music printer has passed on unchallenged,[55] for want of any other hypothesis.

Hughes-Hughes's identification of the copyist must be discounted since Ferrabosco Senior was dead before some composers in the partbooks were born. Given the fact that Ferrabosco the Younger was quite generally referred to simply as "AF," a monogram which recurs in many different hands in all manner of sources, Thompson's nomination of Ferrabosco the Younger as the scribe seems hardly more plausible.

What of the possibility that the "Io: Browne:" on the covers refers to the music publisher? Hughes-Hughes's suggestion apparently stemmed from the fact that Browne was the publisher of Alfonso Ferrabosco II, who composed some of the motets at the end of the manuscripts. Motets by the Ferraboscos appear most commonly in sources from the London area (e.g., Tregian's anthologies, Myriell's collection, Madrigal Society MSS G44-47 and 49, Yale University Music Library, Filmer MS 1, etc.). Many of the other works and composers in 29366-8, on the other hand, have much in common with sources from the eastern counties and Cambridge.

The set contains a comparatively large number of works by Robert Ramsey:

O how fortunate they
Cease now thy grief
Hear my prayer, O Lord
Since no desert can move thee

The first of these also occurs in Tenbury 1162-7 (see chap. 7) and the last in Hamond's partbooks, Bodl. MSS Mus F 20-24. The other two works are apparently unique to 29366-8. Ramsey may have enjoyed sufficient prominence locally for his works to find their way into sources from the area, or even into an Oxford source (Add. MSS 17786-91). His works put in only rare appearances in London sources.[56]

The source also contains a significant number of other concordances with manuscripts from the Cambridge area. Like Hamond's, it includes the *When David heard that Absalom was slain* by William Bearsley,[57] in addition to the only surviving part of *When David heard that Jonathan was slain* by that singularly obscure composer. Another link with Hamond appears in Michael East's *Haste Thee, O God/But let all those,* which both Hamond and 29366-8 transmit in an earlier prepublication version. It must have remained in circulation in the eastern counties long after 1618 for Hamond to have copied it sometime after 1630. Like Hamond, 29366-8 also contains *Cantate Domino a 7* by John Tomkins, which also survives, significantly enough, in Add. 18936-9, a manuscript from the Paston orbit, which belonged to Stephen Aldhouse of Norfolk. John Tomkins, who served as organist of King's College from 1606 until 1619, composed this motet as a commencement exercise for his Mus.B. at Cambridge in 1608. Add. 29366-8 is again linked to Stephen Aldhouse's partbooks by its inclusion of John Wilbye's solitary consort song, *Ne reminiscaris.*[58] The anthem *Wounded with sin extremely* reappears in another Cambridge source, Drexel 5469, Henry Loosemore's organ book, which also happens to include Wilkinson's *I am the resurrection,* otherwise known only from 29366-8 and the Peterhouse "Caroline" partbooks.

Thomas Wilkinson represents the most important link to Cambridge. Add. 29366-8 is, in fact, one of the major sources for Wilkinson's works; only the Durham and Peterhouse partbooks contain more. Wilkinson is one of the most obscure Elizabethan or Jacobean figures, whose sacred works appear prominently at Durham. This has given rise to the suggestion that he may have been a singing man at the cathedral there, although no archival record exists at Durham to substantiate such a possibility.[59] On the other hand, Wilkinson's few known secular works appear most frequently in sources from the eastern counties. *Say Galatea* appears in Aldhouse's set, Add. 18936-9. The more popular *A sea nymph sat,* which also appears in Add. 18936-9 and Tenbury 1162-7, is ascribed to Wilkinson in Paris Rés. 1186, which Robert Creighton[60] apparently compiled at Cambridge during the 1630s, to judge by the dates appended to several pieces in that source. Therefore the presence of another of

Wilkinson's madrigals, *O lovely loveless sweet,* plus ten of his fourteen verse anthems in 29366-8 (including one not even found at Durham), seems to indicate a close link with the Cambridge area. John Morehen has documented the extensive interactions between the Cambridge college, Peterhouse, and Durham Cathedral during the 1630s, when their partbooks were compiled.[61] But to judge by 29366-8, Wilkinson's anthems may have been known in Cambridge during the 1620s, *before* the compilation of the Peterhouse and Durham manuscripts. In this light, Peter le Huray's suggested identification of the composer with the Thomas Wilkinson who was listed as a choirman at King's College, Cambridge in 1579-1580 and 1595-1596 seems very plausible.[62] It is quite possible, therefore, that Wilkinson's works found their way from Cambridge to Durham, rather than *vice versa,* in the course of the later interchange between the two important centers of sacred music during the reign of Charles I.

One or two more tenuous links in 29366-8 may also point to the Cambridge area. Byrd's *Sing joyfully,* though anonymous in the surviving partbooks, is ascribed to "Mr Mudd of Peter [borough]" in the later table of contents on folio 1 of 29366, which perhaps took the ascription from one of the partbooks now lost.[63] The Mudds, John and Thomas, whom musical historians cannot entirely separate, were connected with Cambridge, and both served as organists of nearby Peterborough Cathedral. The name also appears in the Peterhouse manuscripts and in Creighton's keyboard source apparently compiled at Cambridge. It is also equally common in the manuscripts of nearby Ely Cathedral. Although the name also occurs occasionally at Durham, it is otherwise relatively rare. The Mudds, then, were largely eastern counties figures, and it seems most probable that the appearance of the name in 29366-8 indicates some connection with that region.

Finally, Add. 29366-8 preserve the only three surviving voices of a five-part full anthem, *I am the resurrection,* attributed to Orlando Gibbons.[64] Not only is this the sole full anthem ascribed to Gibbons to survive incomplete, it is also the only full anthem to appear in a secular source. Why did the work fail to circulate widely like most of Gibbons's other full anthems, and why should it occur in 29366-8? Although it is difficult to gain much of an impression of the finer details of the work from its fragmentary state, it might possibly represent one of Gibbons's earlier efforts, written during his time at King's College,[65] where the "mundum books" record various payments to the youthful composer for special occasions.[66] The nature of the text suggests that *I am the resurrection* may have been composed for a funeral at the college, after which the anthem was largely forgotten, never finding its way into any of the sacred sources of the time. But, as we have seen, John Tomkins's *Cantate Domino,* the concordance with Loosemore's organ book, and perhaps the numerous Wilkinson anthems, testify to a possible connection between 29366-8 and

King's College. Such a link might have led the scribe to this anthem, which otherwise would have survived only as a single anonymous alto part in Add. 29427.

Thus, the evidence to connect Add. 29366-8 with Cambridge is not insubstantial. Furthermore, the physical characteristics of the partbooks suggest that they might have been compiled in such a communal environment. As a rule, the other important secular sources, such as Add. 29372-7, Add. 17786-91, Add. 17792-6, Drexel 4180-5, Bodl. Mus. F 1-28, and Tenbury 1162-7, reveal the work of a single scribe who attempts to organize his materials according to the number of voices, the types of compositions, the composers, etc. But in 29366-8, although there is some attempt to order the works by type, the order frequently breaks down, primarily because several scribes had a hand in the copying. Perhaps 29366-8 was compiled by a group of Cambridge musicians who had access to the works of local figures such as Ramsey, John Tomkins, and Wilkinson. It may be more than mere coincidence, then, that the following notes appear in the records of Peterhouse and Trinity Colleges:

Peterhouse Bursar's Book, 1655-60:

1658:   'To Mr. Browne ye Musitian' (ls. 8d)
1660:   'To Mr. Browne ye Musitian' (ls. 8d)

Trinity College Junior Bursar's Accounts, 1620-1660:

1651:   'Paid Mr. Browne the wages for ye Waits pro A° 1651' (£ 3)
1654:   'Paid to Mr. Brown ye Musitian his wages for this yeare' (£ 3)
1656:   'Mr. Browes [sic] wages ye Musician' (£ 3)
1658:   "Paid to Mr. Brown the waytes their wages (£ 3)
1659:   'Paid to Mr Brown the wages for the waytes' (£ 3)
1660:   'To Mr. Brown ye wages for ye waites' (£ 3)[67]

Thus, we find one of the University Waits, "Mr Browne," appearing repeatedly in the records of Robert Ramsey's old college, where there exist numerous other references to the waits for the periods shortly before and after the Restoration. John Morehen quotes only those which link Browne to both Peterhouse and Trinity. It is tempting, therefore, to connect the John Browne of 29366 with this University Wait. The references are admittedly somewhat late for connection with this source, and "John Browne" was hardly an unusual name in the early seventeenth century. Indeed, a John Brown served as one of the four lay clerks and as a music copyist at Worcester Cathedral shortly after the Restoration.[68] Furthermore, 29366 does not contain the sorts of music which Waits normally played, at least in their official capacity. But Morehen seems to imply that the University Waits may have served the college chapels in some capacity,[69] and such music would not be outside their capabilities, at least if they were comparable to the Norwich Waits of the Elizabethan age, whom Will Kempe described in glowing terms:

Such Waytes fewe Citties in our Realme have the like, none better; who besides their excellency in wind instruments, their rare cunning on the Vyoll and Violin, theyr voices be admirable, everie one of them able to serve in any Cathedrall Church in Christendome for Quiristers. *(Nine Days Wonder)*[70]

A search through the other Cambridge records may reveal references to a "John Browne" among the University Waits of a slightly earlier date, for music was frequently a family profession during the seventeenth century. In any event, given the accumulated evidence, it seems as probable that Add. 29366-8 were compiled for use in Cambridge as that they were owned by the London music printer.

If this account of the provenance of the set seems reasonable, then it provides a few clues to the date of compilation. The several laments for Prince Henry and the description of Martin Peerson as "Bacc: Mu:" indicate that the earliest possible date must be ca. 1613. But these works remained popular long after Henry's death, as we see from their inclusion in Hamond's partbooks. There is no reason, therefore, why the partbooks could not have been compiled somewhat later. Robert Ramsey, the Trinity College organist who appears prominently here, does not turn up in Cambridge records until 1616, when he received his Mus. B. degree, and did not take up his post at Trinity College until 1628. Therefore, a date sometime in the 1620s is perhaps the most reasonable hypothesis.

Add. 29366-8 reflect the same essential patterns of musical taste that have recurred frequently in the other sources associated with voices and viols. The proposed connection with Cambridge and the University Waits may explain the few idiosyncracies of the set. Judging the contents as a whole, among its more notable features is the total neglect of published music. East's *Haste Thee, O god/ But let all those,* the only piece in the collection to appear in print before Barnard's *The First Book of Selected Church Music,* occurs here in a prepublication version, as mentioned above. In this respect 29366-8 reflects the same pattern present in Add. 17786-91 and Christ Church 56-60. Like 56-60, 29366-8 were compiled by several scribes concurrently, presumably for use at their musical gatherings. It is quite possible that the members of the group also brought along to these gatherings whatever musical prints they happened to own individually, to supplement the contents of the manuscripts.[71] Hence, unlike individual copyists such as Myriell, Merro, or Hamond, who may have lacked such a communal library, perhaps the scribes of 29366-8 did not feel compelled to recopy works from prints to enhance the variety at their musical gatherings.

It is interesting to note that, like Add. 29427, Add. 17786-91, Add. 17792-6, and Christ Church 61-66, sources with a strong instrumental emphasis, Add. 29366-8 begin with a group of fantasias. Another section of fantasias appears later in the partbooks, perhaps segregated from the previous group because they are by Italians (or "Italianized" Englishmen). Dering, Ferrabosco II, Coperario, and Lupo all represent the second generation of viol composers. The scribes were not interested in the older works of Byrd, Bull, or Ferrabosco Senior. But, on the other hand, they do not include examples by the next generation of viol composers (e.g., Jenkins, Coleman, Ives). This strengthens the possibility that the set was compiled during the early 1620s, before the members of the youngest generation had achieved much prominence.

The madrigal, on the other hand, occupies a very minor place in 29366-8. Of the half dozen examples, most are by Cambridge figures—Ramsey, who provides three, and Wilkinson, who provides a single example. The source for the translation of Pallavicino's *Donna, se quel Ohime* remains a mystery, though we do know that such translations were popular in the Cambridge area, to judge by RCM 684. Adjacent to the only anonymous madrigal, *Stay Daphne, stay*, a scribe began to enter another example, *In vain, poor eyes*, but he never got beyond copying the opening few lines of text into 29367.

The partbooks reveal the same abiding interest in laments for Prince Henry which so frequently turn up in the manuscript sources. In addition to Weelkes's extremely popular *O my son Absalom* and *O Jonathan*, they include two by the obscure and perhaps local figure, William Bearsley,[72] who provides the only extant English setting of II Samuel 1:25, *When David heard that Jonathan was slain*.

The few full anthems in the source are notable for their pronounced secular orientation. Only two of them appear in sacred sources. Byrd's immensely popular and rather madrigalian *Sing joyfully* was somehow misattributed to "Mr Mudd of Peter [borough]," as mentioned above. Thomas Tomkins's seven-part *O sing unto the Lord* also reappears in other secular sources, Drexel 4180-5 and the related sources, Add. 17786-91 and Tenbury 1382; John Morehen suggests that the last of these may originally have been intended for secular use.[73] Its appearance next to John Tomkins's Mus. B. exercise, also for seven voices, and its ascription to "Th. Tomkins Bachel: of Mus. orga: Wigorniensis," an honorific otherwise rare in 29366 (though applicable to at least eight of the composers in the source), suggests that perhaps it was originally composed as the Worcester organist's B. Mus. exercise for Oxford in 1607.[74] Gibbons's *I am the resurrection* might have been an early occasional piece for a funeral, as suggested above. The last two anthems, *Wounded with sin extremely* and *Bow down thine ear*, which appear as neighbors in the partbooks, are perhaps the most unusual, for they represent English adaptations of Italian madrigals. The former is based upon Palestrina's popular *Io son ferito*, while the latter is a retexting of Peter Philips's *Cantai mentre*.[75] They may provide an additional indication of the enthusiasm for the Italian style in Cambridge, as mentioned by both Peacham and Mace.[76]

The scribes show no interest in the Elizabethan motet, which continued to crop up in retrospective collections such as Add. 37402-6, Drexel 4180-5, and Add. 17792-6. Instead, they concern themselves primarily with the more modern examples of Alfonso Ferrabasco II that also appear in *Tristitiae Remedium* and, significantly, in Creighton's keyboard manuscript from Cambridge, Paris, Rés. 1186.

A look at the works for voices and viols reveals, predictably enough, a total lack of interest in the solo consort song, which is represented by an isolated piece, John Wilbye's *Ne reminiscaris.* Of the nineteen examples that include a chorus, surprisingly few are by the more prominent members of the younger generation:

> *Haste Thee, O God* (i), M. East
> *But let all those* (ii), M. East
> *I will magnify Thee,* M. Peerson

Both younger men have tenuous Cambridge connections, of course.[77] The rest of the verse anthems show a strong local bias, and, by contrast with the full anthems, a marked ecclesiastical orientation. By far the most prominent figure is Thomas Wilkinson, who provides ten verse anthems. While a few of his most popular works appear as isolated examples in *Tristitiae Remedium, Christ Church 56-60,* and Add. 37402-6, the vast majority are limited to sacred sources, primarily at Durham.

The next most important composer, William Simms, provides three verse anthems, his entire corpus of extant sacred music. In addition to the tremendously popular *Rise O my soul,* we find *Away fond thoughts,* otherwise known from Tenbury 1162-7 and Christ Church 56-60. But 29366-8 is the only set to preserve the incomplete *Haste Thee, O God.* Could the prominence of Simms in the source perhaps indicate that he was in some way connected with Cambridge? Simms is another of those very obscure composers about whom next to nothing is known, aside from the fact that he was for a time in the service of Thomas Sackville, first Earl of Dorset (1536-1608). An entry in the Sackville papers records:

> 17 Mar. 1608: Paid to William Symmes late one of your Lordship's musicians for his wages due to him for 4 months ended this last January 1607/8 the sum of twenty nobles by warrent of your Lordship 6 li. 13s. 4d.[78]

By 1608 Simms was no longer in Sackville's service, and perhaps moved subsequently to the Cambridge area.[79] It is impossible to confirm this hypothesis at present, however.

Robert Ramsey, Thomas Tomkins, and Thomas Warwick each provide a single verse anthem for the partbooks. Apart from Add. 29427, Add. 29366-8 is the only secular source to preserve the Tomkins piece, while the Ramsey work is unique to this set, and his only verse anthem surviving outside the sacred sources. Warwick's extant sacred works consist of a single full anthem and the verse anthem in 29366-8. While the texts are both to be found in Harl. MS 6346 and Bodl., Rawl. Poet. MS 23, the music for the verse anthem survives only in this source and in Christ Church 56-60. Warwick, the son of Bull's successor at Hereford, was primarily a London figure, who by 1611 had achieved sufficient renown to be described in Davies's *Scourge of Folly* as an "expert Master in the liberall science of Musicke."[80] He replaced Orlando Gibbons as organist of the Chapel Royal, and was also listed as one of the London Waits and as a member of the "Royal Band" in 1641.

A Cambridge bias may in part account for the absence of so many prominent composers of the time. The omission of works by Morley, Weelkes, and Wilbye might be explained either by a basic lack of interest in the madrigal on the part of the scribes or by their neglect of printed sources. As other sources have shown, the madrigals of Morley were, in any case, a rarity by this time. Although the same explanation might account for the almost total neglect of William Byrd, whose single contribution appears under the undistinguished name of Mudd, it may simply be another confirmation of the trend so often found in other sources, which seemed to judge Byrd's music, and especially the works in the verse idiom, too old-fashioned for late Jacobean and Caroline ears.

folio[1]			no.	Title	idiom	Composer	Prints
-66	-67	-68					
3	1	1		[Fantasia]		R. Dering	
3ᵛ	1ᵛ	1ᵛ	2	["]		"	
4ᵛ	2ᵛ	2ᵛ	3	["]		" "	
5	3	3		*Ne reminiscaris Domine*	cs	J. Wilbye	
5ᵛ	3ᵛ	4	4	[Fantasia]		R. Dering	
6	4	4ᵛ	5	["]		" "	
6ᵛ	4ᵛ	5ᵛ	6	*Put me not to rebuke*	v	T. Wilkinson	
7ᵛ	5ᵛ	6ᵛ	7	*Help, Lord*	v	" "	
8ᵛ	6ᵛ	7ᵛ	8	*O Lord, my God, in thee*	v	" "	
9ᵛ	7ᵛ	8ᵛ	9	*O Lord consider my distress*	v	" "	
10ᵛ	8ᵛ/ 9ᵛ[2]	9ᵛ		*Preserve me, O Lord, from those*	v	" "	
11ᵛ	10ᵛ	10ᵛ		*O Lord, let me know mine end*	v	T. Tomkins	
12ᵛ	12ᵛ	12ᵛ		Cruel, unkind, adieu[3]	f	B. Palavicino[4]	
13ᵛ	13ᵛ	13ᵛ		*Rise, O my soul (i)*	v	W. Simms	
				And thou, my soul (ii)	v	" "	
				To thee, O Jesu (iii)	v	" "	
15	13	13		*Haste thee, O God*	v	" "	
15ᵛ	14ᵛ	14ᵛ		Sing joyfully	f	[W. Byrd][5]	
16	15	15		*Awake [away] fond thoughts*	v	W. Simms	
18	17	18		O how fortunate they	f	R. Ramsey	
18ᵛ	17ᵛ	18ᵛ		Cease now thy grief	f	" "	
19ᵛ	18ᵛ	19ᵛ		*Haste thee, O God (i)*[6]	v	M. East	1618:21
20	19 19ᵛ	20		*But let all those (ii)* *In vain, poor eyes*[7]	v	" "	" :22
20ᵛ	20ᵛ	20ᵛ		Stay, Daphne, stay	f		
21	21	21		O lovely, loveless sweet	f	T. Wilkinson	
21ᵛ	21ᵛ	21ᵛ		I am the resurrection	f	O. Gibbons	
22	22	22		*I lift my heart up to the hills*	v	T. **Warwick**	
22ᵛ	22ᵛ	16ᵛ		*Hear my prayer, O Lord*	v	R. Ramsey	
24ᵛ	24ᵛ	22ᵛ		Since no desert can move thee	f	[" "]	
25ᵛ	25ᵛ	23ᵛ		*I will magnify thee*	v	M. Peerson	
26ᵛ	26ᵛ	29		*Lord, how are they increased*	v	T. Wilkinson	
27	27ᵛ	29ᵛ		*Deliver me, O Lord from lying lips*	v	" "	
28ᵛ	11ᵛ	11ᵛ		O my son Absalom	f	T. Weelkes	
29	12	12		O Jonathan	f	" "	
29ᵛ				When David heard that Absalom	f	W. Bearsley	
30				When David heard that Jonathan	f	" "	
30ᵛ				Wounded with sin extremely[8]	f	[Palestrina]	
31ᵛ	29ᵛ	31ᵛ		Bow down thine ear[9]	f	P. Philips	
32	31ᵛ	32		*I am the resurrection (i)*	v	T. Wilkinson	
32	31ᵛ	32ᵛ		*I know that my redeemer (ii)*	v	" "	
	32ᵛ	33ᵛ		Cantate Domino	f	J. Tomkins	
		34ᵛ		O sing unto the Lord	f	T. Tomkins	
33ᵛ	33ᵛ	35ᵛ		[Fuga dunque] (i)		G. Coperario	
33ᵛ	33	35ᵛ		[Fantasia] (ii)		" "	
34ᵛ	34ᵛ	36ᵛ	3	[Fantasia]		A. Ferrabosco [II]	
34ᵛ	34ᵛ	37	4	["]		" " [II]	
35	35	37ᵛ	5	["]		" " [II]	
35	35	37ᵛ	6	["] (ii)		" " [II]	
35ᵛ	35ᵛ	38	7	["]			
36	35ᵛ	38ᵛ	8	[Alte parole]		T. Lupo	
37ᵛ	36ᵛ	24ᵛ	1	Ego sum resurrectio	f	A. Ferrabosco [II]	
	37	25	2	Quare derelinquerunt	f	" " ["]	
38	37ᵛ	26ᵛ	3	O nomen Jesu	f	" " ["]	
38ᵛ	38	26ᵛ	4	Ego dixi Domine (i)	f	" " ["]	
39ᵛ	38ᵛ	27	5	Convertere Domine (ii)	f	" " ["]	
39ᵛ	39		6	Domine Deus meus (i)	f	" " ["]	
40ᵛ	39ᵛ	26ᵛ	7	Noli me projecere (ii)	f	" " [■]	
40ᵛ	40	28	8	Ubi duo vel tres (i)	f	" " [■]	
41ᵛ	40ᵛ	28ᵛ	9	Libera me, Domine (ii)	f	" " ["]	
41ᵛ	28ᵛ	30		*Praise the Lord, O ye servants*	v	T. Wilkinson	

1 Modern foliation

2 First copy incomplete

3 Adaptation of the madrigal, *Donna, se quel ohime.*

4 Attribution from later index (late 17th or early 18th century?)

5 Attributed to "Mr Mudd of Peter" in later index.

6 An earlier, pre-publication version

7 Incomplete (words only)

8 Adaptation of the madrigal, *Io son ferrito.*

9 Adaptation of the madrigal, *Cantai mentre.*

4

The West Country

John Merro's Manuscripts

Several years ago Pamela Willetts first called attention to the musical scribe, John Merro, whose name occurs in Bodl. MSS Mus. Sch. D 245-7, and whom Willetts identified as the copyist of British Library Add. MSS 17792-6.[1] In addition to suggesting that Merro was connected with the West of England, Miss Willetts also established that 17792-6 later passed into the hands of the Oxford musical enthusiast, Dr. Matthew Hutton (1638-1711). But John Merro's full musical significance only became clear when Philip Brett indicated the presence of his hand in a larger and more important source, New York Public Library, Drexel MSS 4180-5:

> A large collection of motets, anthems, madrigals and instrumental music compiled between about 1600 and 1620. Most of it is in the hand of John Merro. Like Me2 [Add. 17792-6], it may subsequently have belonged to Matthew Hutton, since it contains annotations which appear to be in his hand.[2]

Finally, in 1967, Andrew Ashbee showed that John Merro had served as a lay-clerk at Gloucester Cathedral from as early as 1609, and lived on well into the 1630s.[3] Merro seems to have been a music compiler on a par with Thomas Myriell and Thomas Hamond. Indeed, his largest collection, Drexel 4180-5, is even more extensive than the monumental *Tristitiae Remedium*. Furthermore, when viewed as a whole, Merro's musical activity contrasts significantly with that of Myriell, the London clergyman, and provides some insight into the state of English musical life in the western provinces, less closely in touch with London and the court circles.

Drexel MSS 4180-5

This, the largest and oldest of Merro's sets of partbooks, is also the most varied in its contents and the most ambiguous in terms of its paleography. While some details remain constant (e.g., the formation of treble, bass, and c-clefs), some

Pl. 15a.   New York Public Library, Drexel MS 4184 quintus,
fol. 1. John Merro's more formal, square hand.
(By kind permission of the Drexel Collection, Music
Division, The New York Public Library, Astor, Lenox
& Tilden Foundations)

aspects of the paleography reveal considerable variation in both the music, which ranges from a relatively formal square notation to a more flowing, round notation (see pls. 15a and 15b), and in text, which varies from a stiff secretary to a very florid italic. But the manuscripts are entirely the work of one man and the notational variety results from changes in Merro's hand during the dozen or more years when the copying took place.

The more archaic of these notational extremes appears primarily in the sections of four- and five-part sacred pieces by Tallis and his generation at the beginning of the partbooks. The combination of square notation and secretary hand, with the opening words set off in bolder lettering, seems very appropriate to the older generation of Elizabethan composers represented here, of whom

William Byrd is the most junior member, and shows a marked similarity to the
layout of older Elizabethan sources, such as Christ Church MSS 984-8 (the
Dow partbooks) and Add. MS 22597. This may indeed have been a conscious
affectation on Merro's part, a gesture towards decorum in penmanship and
towards a historical sense which he seems to possess.

This combination of features, which is limited to folios 1-16^V, 18^V-38^V, 40-
43, 54^V-57, and 64^V-68,[4] must represent the oldest layer of the partbooks. It
seems most likely that the four-part and five-part sacred sections were begun
simultaneously on folios 0^V and 23^V, respectively. The section in this "original
hand" beginning on folio 54^V proves more difficult to interpret. Like *O God
give ear,* which opens the five-part section, the four consort songs on folios 54-
55^V were probably copied directly from William Byrd's 1588 *Psalms.* Merro
may have conceived folios 54-55^V as the start of a section of consort songs,

Pl. 16.   British Library Additional MS 17792, fol. 111ᵛ. A
              typical example of Merro's later hand, which
              predominates in this source.
              (Reproduced by permission of the British Library)

which he began simultaneously with the five-part full pieces on folio 23ᵛ. It
makes sense that he should begin with Byrd's *Lullaby,* one of the most famous
of all consort songs.[5] He began the last of the original groups, four full anthems
for five to eight voices, on folios 64ᵛ-68.

Some of the blank leaves were soon filled with other repertories, still in the
oldest hand. The blank folios which preceded the Amner four-part pieces
indicate that these works were intended as a separate section, probably copied
at the same time as the addition of the five-part Amner anthems to the five-part
section. It is possible, on the other hand, that Amner's six-part verse anthems
were entered on some of the blank leaves *before* the last group of full anthems
on folios 64ᵛ-68. In addition, Merro apparently planned a section of five-part
madrigals as a group, to judge by the blank sides before folio 40. This, the only
other layer in the "original hand," contains the seven sections of Palestrina's
Vergine cycle.

The other paleographic extreme appears in the last hundred folios where we find a much greater preponderance of round notation and a less frequent use of secretary script. Perhaps the most obvious difference is the formation of the annotations "5 voc" and "6 voc," which in this section correspond to their equivalents in Merro's later source, 17792-6 (cf pls. 15b and 16). These folios represent the latest layer in 4180, and may have been completed concurrently with 17792, at least to judge by the last few vocal entries.

Beginning on folio 158ᵛ of 4180 we find a final group of full anthems, a haphazard mixture in five to twelve parts. These are also among the last entries in 17792. But in the latter source Merro made a more consistent attempt to maintain his groups *a 5, a 6* and *a 7*. Thus, he took John Mundy's *O give thanks unto the Lord* from folio 163 of 4180 and entered it as the first piece of his six-part group on folio 115 of 17792. The next piece in the Drexel source, Hugh Davies's *Awake up my glory,* was likewise used to open a section *a 7* on folio 160ᵛ of 17792. But the next work in 4180 was *a 5* (Tomkins's *Lord enter not into judgment*), so Merro appended it to the five-part section of 17792, on folio 149ᵛ. Tomkins's anthem was followed in 4180 by another seven-part piece, Weelkes's *O Lord arise,* which Merro methodically entered as the second work of his seven-part section on folio 161 of 17792. By this time Merro had exhausted the available space in 4180, so when he happened upon William Randall's six-part *Give sentence with me,* he was forced to enter it on one of the earlier blank folios between the blocks of Weelkes and Tomkins madrigals (folio 122aᵛ). But in 17792 he could simply add the anthem to the blank folios of his six-part section. The same is true of Thomas Ford's five-part *Let God arise:* while Merro could enter it quite simply enough after *Lord enter not into judgment* in his five-part section of 17792, for 4180 he again had to backtrack to the nearest vacant folios, between the Weelkes and Tomkins madrigals. The distinctive and consistent calligraphy of *Awake up my glory, Lord enter not into judgment, O Lord arise, Give sentence with me,* and *Let God arise* in 4180 confirms this interpretation, and makes clear the fact that Merro had arrived at these two points simultaneously in his two sources. He went on to fill up the remainder of his five-part and six-part sections in 17792 by searching further back into 4180.

What, then, was the date of these latest insertions in 4180? Several entries in the later calligraphy are datable with some certainty in the early 1620s. The large block of Tomkins madrigals on folios 124ᵛ-138 obviously comes directly from the *Songs* of 1622. It has been suggested that Bateson's only extant sacred work, *Holy Lord God almighty a 7* (fol. 160), was composed as the exercise for his M.A. degree, which he received from Trinity College, Dublin in 1622.[6] Byrd's popular anthem for the sovereign, on the other hand, occurs on folio 89ᵛ as *O Lord make thy servant James,* which indicates that it was entered before

1625. Thus, the evidence of 4180 itself points to a date of 1622-25 for these sections. As Pamela Willetts has pointed out,[7] however, Bodl. MS Mus. Sch. D 245, which, like this section of 4180 is in Merro's later hand, contains Merro's comments upon Samuel Hoard's *God's love to Mankind*, published in 1633. The scribe must therefore have been at work during the 1630s, and it is not impossible that the very latest entries in 4180 and 17792 were made after 1630.

The date at which the copying was begun is more difficult to establish with certainty. The opening four- and five-part sections are retrospective in character, and therefore provide no clues toward the dating. As mentioned above, however, the entries from John Amner's *Sacred Hymns* (1615) exhibit all the scribal characteristics of the oldest layer. It seems reasonable to assume, therefore, that Merro began his collection, not ca. 1600 as Philip Brett suggests, but approximately fifteen years later.

Given Merro's affiliation with Gloucester Cathedral, it is not surprising that his manuscripts should be rich in works by west countrymen. The only composers associated with specific locations in the manuscripts are from the West: "Mr Hugh Davies of Hereford," "Mr Tomkins of Woster," "Smith of Salop" (i.e., Shropshire), "Smith of Gloucester." Aside from the Oxfordian Richard Nicolson, all of the most obscure composers are west countrymen and tend to appear primarily in sources from that part of the country.[8] Merro's manuscripts also contain several concordances with the pre-Restoration Gloucester bassus book, which John Morehen believes may be in the hand of John Okeover.[9] Of the twelve full anthems in that source, eight also occur in 4180, including the relatively rare *Awake up my Glory* by Davies and *O sing unto the Lord* by Amner. Merro must have borrowed frequently from the cathedral music library, for over thirty of the anthems which he entered in his partbooks appear in no other secular source.

The subsequent ownership of 4180 remains unclear. I have been unable to discover the annotations in the hand of Matthew Hutton mentioned by Philip Brett (see above), who seems to have been mistaken in this instance, and I should therefore tend to doubt that these partbooks had been in Hutton's possession.[10] The set, like the other Drexel manuscripts, were formerly in the collection of the musical antiquarian, Edward Rimbault, whose methods of acquisition were not always entirely reputable. Christ Church Library, for one, seems to have suffered at his hands.[11] In this case it seems unlikely that Christ Church was his source, for none of the Library's early lists contains an entry which might correspond to 4180-5. Rimbault, in publishing several anthems from the manuscripts, described them as:

> formerly in the possession of the celebrated John Evelyn, and now forming one of the many musical rarities in the library of the Editor.

This valuable set of ancient Part-books consists of six small oblong volumes in the original binding, and with the Arms and Badge of Edward the Sixth stamped on the sides... The writing commences in the reign of Edward the Sixth, and ends in that of Charles the First; the last composition entered being an Ode composed by Orlando Gibbons for the marriage of that king with the Princess Henrietta Maria.[12]

Evelyn's own catalogue of his library, *Catalogus Evelynianus 1687,* MS 20a does not mention such a set of partbooks specifically amongst the musical items on page 190.[13] Had the manuscripts belonged to Evelyn they should bear the press mark, Cove E ☿ on the covers or flyleaves. These do not appear there today, though it is not impossible that they disappeared when the manuscripts were rebound in New York.[14] It is interesting to note that the auction catalogue for Rimbault's library makes no mention of Evelyn in its description of the partbooks.[15]

Work on 4180-5 seems to have begun around 1615 and was probably completed around 1630. It is, then, roughly contemporary with Thomas Myriell's *Tristitiae Remedium.* A comparison of the two sources provides a picture of the state of secular music in the provinces at roughly the time when Myriell was compiling his up-to-date collection in London.

Merro must have intended 4180 initially as a vocal collection of a highly serious nature. His initial entries were large retrospective groups of full anthems in four and five parts, perhaps drawn from the Gloucester Cathedral library. Throughout the compilation the copyist continually returned to the full anthem, which accounts for more than seventy works in the collection. Significantly, the most modern entries, aside from those by local luminaries, are by Amner and Tomkins, whose musical styles related more closely to earlier generations than do the styles of the "moderns" such as East and Peerson. Indeed, those more extrovert members of the younger generation, frequently encountered in Myriell's source, are notably absent.[16] Instead, the majority of the full anthems in Merro's source still look back to the generation of Tallis and William Mundy. Perhaps it is not fanciful to suggest that Merro, like Edward Paston, who was concerned with another and even older repertory, sought to preserve a tradition which was fast vanishing as one set of choirbooks, worn out by frequent use, was replaced by another.

The English madrigal represents the next most prominent genre. Unlike Myriell, Merro makes all his entries from a particular madrigal print in large blocks, rather than entering them a few here and a few there after Myriell's fashion. But in his choice of madrigals Merro confirms the pattern found in Myriell: a preference for the best, the most popular, or the more serious. All but a handful come from only four prints:

Songs (1622), Tomkins, 16
Ballets (1598), Weelkes, 14
First Set (1598), Wilbye, 13
The Triumphs of Oriana (1601), Morley, ed., 7

The prominence of Tomkins's publication may be due in part to the proximity of Gloucester to Worcester, where Tomkins was organist; Tomkins and Merro must have known one another.[17] Weelkes (another cathedral organist), whose *Ballets* enjoyed sufficient popularity to warrant a second edition in 1608, is usually regarded, in terms of madrigal composition, as second only to Wilbye, whom he barely manages to surpass, at least in terms of numbers, in this source. The *Triumphs*, like the Weelkes set, had also enjoyed sufficient popularity to necessitate a second edition; but its representation here does not extend to the music of the mind behind it. As in Myriell's collection, the figure most notably absent is Thomas Morley, who increasingly leaves the impression of a career brilliant but soon forgotten, in the seventeenth century at least, if not the twentieth. One might note again in passing the total neglect of Orlando Gibbons's *First Set* of 1612, which Myriell and virtually all scribes but Hamond likewise ignored.

Merro, like Myriell, shows an interest in the English translations of Italian madrigals, copying eleven pieces from *Musica Transalpina* (1588), six from *Italian Madrigals Englished* (1590), and two from *Musica Transalpina II* (1597). Luca Marenzio is again the most popular of the Italians, with ten pieces, followed, predictably enough, by Ferrabosco. But significantly, the composer from the Italian anthologies to be given pride of place was William Byrd, whose four-part setting of *This sweet and merry month of May* for *Italian Madrigals Englished* was the first madrigal to be entered in the manuscripts. It is followed by Marenzio's *Every singing byrd* (Merro's witty tribute to England's leading composer?), which like the former madrigal is texted throughout. All the other "Englished" Italian pieces are textless but for their titles. This remarkable treatment seems an extreme example of the common English reaction to Italian madrigals (and indeed, French chansons), which were very frequently left textless in English manuscripts, owing to the Englishman's inability to cope with the foreign tongues.

This attitude toward the Italian madrigal is carried even further in the case of those madrigals for which no English translations were available. In some cases Merro does not even bother to provide their titles, but simply describes them as "Italian 1," "Italian 2," etc. (see fols. 62^v-64^v); presumably he intended them to serve simply as viol pieces. Such a treatment hardly simplifies the task of identifying these works. It has nevertheless proved possible to uncover the source for a few of them: Hans Leo Hassler's *Madrigali a 5. 6. 7. & 8. voci,* 1596. Merro's use of the Hassler print confirms the impression that his interest in the Italian madrigal ranged further afield and toward more unusual examples than that of his contemporaries, even if he was hardly concerned with preserving their integrity as madrigals. Among the other Italian works (for which Merro at least provides titles, if not attributions), we find Palestrina's *Vèrgine* cycle (published in 1581), the only Italian works which form a part of the original layer of the manuscripts. Relatively late in the course of the compilation Merro added another block of Italian pieces for more massive forces, employing eight to twelve voices (see fols. 139ᵛ-149). It is quite probable that in this instance we had as his source a three-volume publication from Nurnberg, *Gemmae Musicalis: Selectissimae Varii Stili Cantiones, Quae Madrigali et Napolitane Italis dicunter, Quatuor, Quinque, Sex & plurium vocum, continens,* which had appeared in three installments in 1588, 1589, and 1590.[18] This seems to be the only publication from which Merro might have obtained all these works as a group. It also happens to contain the two other isolated Italian madrigals, Marenzio's popular *Dolorosi martir* (fol. 65) and the less common *Tutt'eri foco* (fol. 156) by Pallavicino, both of which were apparently entered as afterthoughts on blank folios, perhaps concurrently with the other madrigals from the print on folios 139ᵛ-149.

Merro's interest in the Latin motet likewise contrasts with that of Myriell, who, aside from three of Byrd's most popular motets, devotes himself almost entirely to the more modern motets of Ferrabosco, Morley, and Thomas Lupo. With the exception of a single motet by Morley inserted as an afterthought, the motets of these later composers do not receive the slightest attention from Merro, who turns instead to native Englishmen from the generation of Tallis, Shepherd, and Mundy. Merro thus recalls older sources such as Christ Church 979-83, 984-88, Bodl. Mus. Sch. E 423, or the more modern sources such as Add. 37402-6 or Tenbury 807-11. But by the time Merro came to copy these works, their composers had been dead for as much as sixty years, which helps to explain why so many of the motets occur anonymously or are ascribed in error.

In addition, relatively late in the compilation Merro added several continental motets by the ever-popular Lassus and the rarer Clemens non Papa. The well-known Lassus pieces, *Veni in hortum* and *Angelus ad pastores,* which had been finding a place in English sources for at least forty years, are treated in the same fashion as motets by Lassus's English contemporaries. But the motets by Clemens, which were probably relatively late additions inserted as filler (see the four-part *Circumdederunt/Quoniam tribulatio* in particular), received the same treatment as the continental madrigals: they appear with no text beyond their titles, further evidence of Merro's strangely insular attitude toward foreign composers in whatever language their works may appear.

Music for voices and viols plays a relatively small role in 4180, especially by comparison with Myriell's collection. This again could be a sign of the difference between the musical life of London and that in the provinces. The *solo* consort song, on the other hand, retains greater prominence than in the London sources, perhaps another sign of Merro's "historical" sense, seen at its most extreme in the archaic *In paradise* and *Abradad,* or of his comparative insularity. The most important contributor to the solo song in 4180 is William Byrd, who, in addition to four works from the 1588 print, provides two unpublished pieces. As mentioned above, Merro may have entered the four songs from 1588 concurrently with the layers at the beginning of the partbooks, intending them as the start of a larger section of consort songs. The four are obviously taken from the 1588 *Psalms,* but Merro has converted them back into consort songs by omitting the words from all but the "first singing part."[19] As one might safely predict, the first to be entered was that recurrent favorite, the *Lullaby.* The two unpublished Byrd songs form a group with the anonymous *In paradise a 7.* Only *Come pretty babe* actually bears an attribution to Byrd,[20] but *Delight is dead* may be added to the Byrd canon on the basis of the attribution in *Tristitiae Remedium.*

Between the published and unpublished Byrd pieces appear another three consort songs, which also form a group. *Abradad,* which opens the group, sets the tone for all three, which all must date from well before the turn of the century and which would have appeared decidedly archaic to a London audience around 1620, when Merro must have copied them. It will be remembered that in 1616 Myriell had apparently deemed *Abradad* too old-fashioned for inclusion in *Tristitiae Remedium.* But outside of London it would still do for a few more years. Indeed, when viewed as a whole, Merro's solo consort song repertory appears very ancient, with nothing that need have been written after Byrd's 1588 collection. We find none of the newer approaches to the consort song showing the influence of the lute ayre, such as occur in profusion in Add. 17786-91 and 17797, which both probably antedate Merro's collection.

But in his choice of pieces for viols plus solo and chorus Merro begins to make concessions to current taste. Of course, almost half of his verse anthems were copied from Amner's *Sacred Hymns* (1615), upon which he had also drawn for a number of full pieces. The others include works which reappear repeatedly. In addition to the inescapable *Rise O my soul,* perhaps the most popular Jacobean verse anthem to appear in secular sources, Merro includes East's *When Israel came out of Egypt,* not in the printed version of 1610, but in the earlier manuscript version which likewise appears in the secular sources Add. 37402-6 and Tenbury 1162-7. Merro's other verse anthem, *Sing we merrily,* also by Michael East, is again based upon a prepublication source which probably dates from 1618 to 1624. These three works are the only verse anthems from manuscript sources to appear in Merro's partbooks.

Merro falls right into line with current taste by including the two most popular "Cries": Gibbons's *London Cry* and Dering's *Country Cry.* His third choice, the anonymous *Cry of London,* appears to have been less well-known. Merro's version of Gibbons's *Cry of London* differs from Myriell's in several details. However, 4180, like Myriell's earlier source, Add. 29427, reverses the order of the two sections of the piece. Interestingly enough, both compilers' later collections, Add. 29372-7 and 17792-6, rectify this mix-up.[21]

In his verbal text, Merro differs from all the other sources for Gibbons's popular piece. The various "Cries" were, of course, all subject to a great deal of variation in text underlay. But Merro's textual additions or alterations are especially extensive, and uniformly rude. Thus, "Buy a new cover for a close-stool" crops up in the first tenor part early on in the piece, and somewhat later the description of the lost mare presents the variant, "she hath but one eye, and that is almost out, and a hole in her arse and there your snout." This particular passage presents a great deal of variation among the sources,[22] but Merro's stands out as especially hearty. Such variants and several others in Merro's text present the serious, somewhat old-fashioned John Merro in a rather different light than the rest of his collection.

The last of Merro's secular verse pieces, which has some of the characteristics of a later insertion, is unique to this manuscript: Orlando Gibbons's *Do not repine fair sun,* written for the visit of James I to Scotland in 1617.[23] How this work, so intimately connected with life at court, should find its way into Merro's provincial collection, which otherwise seems isolated from both London and courtly circles, is puzzling. One possible connection suggests itself, however. The text for the piece was the work of one Joseph Hall (1574-1656), the active and well-traveled cleric who had served as chaplain to Henry, Prince of Wales, and who accompanied James I to Scotland in 1617, when *Do not repine* was performed. Shortly before the Scottish progress, the King nominated Hall dean of Worcester (1616), a post which he occupied until 1627. In 1624 he was offered the see of Gloucester which he refused, but became bishop of Exeter in 1627. Hall was a noted pluralist and obviously would not have been a frequent visitor to Worcester. But nevertheless, he seems the most obvious link between this courtly composition and Merro in the western counties.[24]

British Library Additional MSS 17792-6

In Drexel 4180 Merro had already expressed considerable interest in consort music by his inclusion in the main body of the manuscript of some fantasias and In Nomines by Lupo, Dering, Byrd, Ferrabosco, and Parsons, as well as numerous textless and even titleless Italian madrigals presumably intended for instrumental performance. At the end of the partbooks the more modern fantasias of Gibbons, Ives, and Jenkins, presumably added later, attest to a growing interest in music for viols. This enthusiasm for viol playing must have inspired Merro to undertake the compilation of another set of manuscripts, intended primarily as a repository for instrumental compositions, Add. 17792-6. These partbooks provide evidence of somewhat greater forethought in their planning than the scribe's earlier set: where 4180 looks like an *ad hoc* collection, 17792 was definitely a planned one. Merro maintains the organization into sections *a 3, a 4, a 5, a 6,* and *a 7* more rigidly, and benefits from his previous miscalculations by leaving more blank folios between sections than he had done in the Drexel source, where the space for four-part works was too quickly exhausted.

The scribe apparently began by providing separate sections for In Nomines, fantasias, and pavans of three to six parts. These reveal a much more modern orientation than Merro's older source, and include works by all the most up-to-date Jacobean instrumentalists who had just begun to appear in the final section of 4180: Thomas Tomkins, Ferrabosco II, John Jenkins, Simon Ives, Richard Mico, William White, Thomas Ford, Richard Dering, and Thomas Lupo. Notably absent, however, are the more archaic In Nomines and Parsons's *De la courte* from 4180.

For present purposes the primary interest rests in the vocal pieces which Merro includes, frequently by recopying them from 4180. On folios 22-25[V] the scribe simply lifts as a group the four-part Amner anthems and a subsequent madrigal from the older set, using them to fill up some of the blank folios between the three- and four-part fantasias. The other block of four-part vocal music, "Mr Luges short service" (fols. 54[V]-58), was obviously a later addition, for the ink contrasts markedly with that of the surrounding instrumental pieces. On the basis of Merro's interest in west countrymen, it seems probable that the Lugge in question is the John Lugge of Exeter. Anglican service music is a rarity in secular partbooks and its presence here provides further evidence of Merro's close connection with cathedral music.

Also in a contrasting ink, and therefore probably somewhat later, is the section of solo consort songs on folios 68[V]-71[V], between the five-part pavans and the five-part fantasias. Again Merro reaffirms his interest in William Byrd already apparent from 4180. But, whereas in 4180 Merro had as his source Byrd's 1588 print, in this case the scribe had access to original, prepublication consort song versions of pieces which Byrd had published with words in all parts in 1588 and 1589.[25] In addition, Merro includes three unpublished consort songs, one of which, *Methought of late,* bears an ascription to Byrd, which Philip Brett has called into question on the basis of musical style.[26] An examination of the song readily confirms Brett's suggestion. The opening presents one of the most common imitative figures in Elizabethan and Jacobean music, based upon a filled-in triad, a figure which Byrd seems to avoid quite consciously in his manuscript songs. In the rare instances where a similar figure occurs,[27] the shape of the point and its treatment are worlds removed from that of *Methought of late,* inevitably involving less regular entries, a more varied harmonic matrix, and a broader sense of the phrase as a whole. In this case, however, the point is merely three half-notes long, and its brevity is only emphasized by the regularity of the successive entries. The second point, which enters squarely on the cadence in the middle of bar 5, is simply an ornamented version of the preceding one, and again is treated very squarely.

The composer's short-sightedness in musical phrasing, on the other hand, seems especially prominent at bars 12-13 and 15-18. In the former case the phrygian cadence of bar 12 gives way two beats later to a cadence on D, followed in turn by a move toward C, all within the space of a bar-and-a-half. In addition, the suspension in the middle of bar 13 seems too inelegant for Byrd, just as the passage as a whole lacks his superior sense of long-range tonal direction. Bars 15-18, on the other hand, get bogged down in a totally regular series of suspensions, onto which the composer tacks a gratuitous simultaneous false relation in bar 17, a device which Byrd would have reserved to emphasize expressive moments in the text.

These more obvious moments in the piece, plus several other more fleeting ones, are quite incongruous with Byrd's style. Given Merro's tendency toward misattributions, so frequently revealed in 4180, this could easily be a scribal oversight, especially since *Methought of late* has been sandwiched between two authentic works published in the 1588 collection.

In any event, the four authentic Byrd songs in this section, probably one of the latest additions to 17792, show that Merro did not flag in his interest in the solo song style, especially as practiced by William Byrd—a marked contrast with the more fashionable circles, where by 1620 both the solo consort song and Byrd, its chief exponent, suffered neglect.

The consort songs are followed by two madrigals with Italian titles from Morley's *Ballets* of 1595. These are the only new Italian pieces to find their way into the later collection, where they appear, predictably enough, without texts. This large block of later additions concludes with William Byrd's *Browning,* also absent from 4180. Merro's version contrasts with that in all other sources for the piece by texting the popular tune at each of its appearances.

Folios 114v-131 are devoted to verse anthems, primarily drawn from 4180. Merro ignores the verse pieces from Amner's 1615 *Sacred Hymns* which had appeared in his previous set, but recopies all the other verse anthems from 4180 with the exception of Gibbons's *Do not repine fair sun.* The three "Cries" again form a block, followed by another section consisting of the three anthems attributed to Michael East in the older partbooks, here systematically joined into a single group. Merro fills out the section with two verse anthems absent from 4180. Tomkins's *Rejoice, sing and rejoice* (with eight-part chorus, *Blessed Virgin Mary*) survives only in 17792-6 and the Gloucester bassus book. The last verse anthem, *O go not from me* by Martin Peerson, may attest to new contacts with the younger generation which had been rising to the fore in London circles for some fifteen years. But the connection could hardly have been intimate, for Merro misattributes the work to a "Mr Palmer."

The slightly paler ink of the section of five-part full anthems beginning on folio 131^V contrasts quite strongly with that of surrounding sections, and it appears that this section was not begun concurrently with the instrumental pieces, but slightly later.[28] With the exception of only four works, the entire corpus is drawn from 4180. But Merro's choices reveal a slight change in focus: only three of the works which he transfers from 4180 come from Tallis's generation, which was so prominent in the earlier source. Instead we find a greater preponderance of Jacobeans, another hint that Merro was perhaps beginning to change with the times.

As mentioned previously, it seems quite likely that the six-part and seven-part full sections were begun concurrently with the entry of the same pieces in 4180. But after Merro had entered the pieces from folios 163-168 and 122a^V-124 of 4180 into 17792 he had to backtrack in order to fill out the five-, six-, and seven-part sections in the later source. During this process some six-part pieces crept into the seven-part section, including an arrangement of the *Te Deum* from William Byrd's *Great Service*, which appears in the pale ink of the latest additions. This version of the *Te Deum* provides yet another link with Worcester, for it is the only extant version which agrees with the major variants of the Worcester pre-Restoration tenor book, MS A 3.3. Like the Lugge *Short Service* (acquired and entered concurrently?), it also testifies to Merro's ready access to cathedral music rarely found in secular manuscripts.

The concluding folios are given over to groups of motets in four and five parts. Of these, the following are in the paler ink of the very latest additions:

> *In resurrectione,* W. Byrd
> *Incipit Lamentatio,* T. Tallis
> *Heth,* etc., R. White
> *O quam gloriosum,* W. Byrd
> *Tristitia et anxietas,* W. Byrd

Only the first two appear in 4180. Like the full anthems, the motets of 17792, when compared with the entire source, may reveal a turning away from the earlier Elizabethans. Of the more modern English motets available from 4180, Merro takes the two by Byrd and Nicolson's example, rejecting only Morley's *O amica mea,* and also adds two new ones by Byrd. Of the fourteen motets from Tallis's generation, he rejects eight, though he does add White's *Lamentations.* Of the foreign motets, he recopies the two by Lassus, but ignores the five by Clemens.

Thus, when viewed as a whole, and in comparison with 4180, 17792 not only confirms some of Merro's preferences, but also hints at a slightly different focus. The later set ignores the English madrigal almost totally. Merro only allows the two most anthem-like examples from Tomkins's *Songs*: no. 26, *Woe is me that I am contrained to dwell* and no. 28, *Turn unto the Lord*. Merro had already revealed a certain disregard for the Italian madrigal, as evidenced by its treatment in 4180. It comes as no surprise, therefore, that the Italian madrigal is hardly in evidence at all in 17792. The only concordance with the earlier set, *O grief, if yet my grief* (fol. 25ᵛ) probably slipped in on the coat tails of the four-part Amner anthems which it follows in the older source. Perhaps Merro even mistook it for another anthem of penitential character, an understandable mistake, given the title alone. This same lack of interest in things foreign reappears in Merro's attitude toward the motet, for aside from the long-familiar examples by Lassus, he omits all the foreign importations, which he had already left textless in 4180.

But Merro's interest in the English anthem abides, though with a hint of a more modern outlook. He rejects all the four-part Elizabethan anthems, transfering only the more modern four-part pieces from Amner's 1615 collection. While the older generation continues to appear in the five-part section, it has relinquished some of its prominence to the Jacobeans.

Any hints of modernity in Merro's attitude toward the verse idiom are barely perceptible, however. His primary concern remains the solo consort song, which by the 1620s was hardly cultivated in more up-to-date circles. Furthermore, his choice of solo consort songs is entirely retrospective, admitting nothing which need be more modern than Byrd's 1588 *Psalms, Sonnets and Songs*. Indeed, William Byrd remains the predominant figure in Merro's list of solo songs, providing eight published and two unpublished (plus another of questionable attribution discussed above) of the total of seventeen in 4180 or 17792. Merro's serious interest in Byrd is further emphasized by his having preserved these works as consort songs, not part songs, and having procured prepublication versions of some of them for his later manuscript collection.

But perhaps the greatest evidence of Merro's relative isolation is his neglect of pieces combining chorus with solo voices, a genre which had achieved increasing prominence during the reign of James I. Merro does reflect the general fascination with the "Cries," which enjoyed great popularity. He also falls prey to the dubious charms of the inevitable *Rise O my soul,* whose attractiveness to Jacobean ears remains a mystery. But otherwise Merro includes only a very meager handful of examples, and does not bother to recopy either Amner's six-part verse pieces or Gibbons's *Do not repine.*[29]

John Merro, then, leaves the impression of a musician with strong enthusiasm, if rather provincial outlook. His strictly instrumental choices for the later 17792 may reveal a certain modernity, but his taste in choral music or works for voices and viols clearly lags behind the times. While Jacobean composers may make some inroads in the realm of the full anthem, their works in the verse idiom receive scanty consideration. In contrast to what we have seen in London and the eastern counties, John Merro seems relatively hidden away in Gloucester. He either disliked, or lacked access to, the verse anthems of the younger, more fashionable composers such as Peerson and Ravenscroft, whose rise to prominence in London is reflected so clearly in Myriell's *Tristitiae Remedium,* and who still remained popular in the eastern counties some twenty years later, to judge by Hamond's manuscripts. By contrast with all the other late Jacobean and Caroline manuscript compilers, Merro retains an interest in the older, more traditional solo consort song. It is William Byrd whom Merro still seems to admire above all other composers, not only for his consort songs, but for his anthems and motets as well. Despite the recently deceased composer's apparent decline in popularity in other, less isolated musical circles, where the more fashionable Jacobeans are cultivated, Merro clings to his memory and in the process provides us with at least one small gem, the lullaby *Come pretty babe,* that would otherwise have been lost to posterity.

Merro and Gloucester offer a vivid portrait of provincial music making at its most conservative, one which accords well with the presence at nearby Worcester of that sturdy conservative, Thomas Tomkins. It is indeed a different view of musical life from that encountered in the London sources, especially, and in the Cambridge and Suffolk collections. As we move from the far west country back toward London once more, we shall have good reason to pause at England's other major university town. In Oxford, the home of the manuscripts that occupy the next chapter, we find yet another profile of Jacobean musical life, one as sharply etched and as fully detailed as we have yet encountered, and one that creates a new balance between old and new.

-80[7]	-81[7]	folio -82[7]	-83[7]	-84[7]	-85[7]	Title	idiom	Composer	Prints
						(four-part pieces)			
0[v]	0[v]	1[v]	1			O Lord the maker	f	[W. Mundy]	
1	1	2	1[v]			O Lord give thy holy spirit	f	[T. Tallis]	
1[v]	1[v]	2[v]	2			Give alms	f		
2[v]	2[v]	3[v]	2[v]			My God look upon me	f	Mr Smith of Salop	
3[v]	3	4	3[v]			If ye love me	f	[T. Tallis]	CN1560
3[v]	3[v]	4[v]	3[v]			I give you a new commandment	f	[J. Shepherd]	"
4[v]	4[v]	5[v]	4[v]			Hear the voice	f	[T. Tallis]	"
5	5	6	5			Let us now laud	f	Mundy	
6	6	7	5[v]			A new commandment	f	"	
6[v]	6[v]	7[v]	6			This is my commandment	f	[Mundy/Tallis/Johnson]	
6[v]	7	8	6[v]			If ye be risen	f	[C. Tye]	
7[v]	7[v]	8[v]	7[v]			Rejoice in the Lord	f	N. Strogers	
8[v]	8[v]	9[v]	8			A new commandment	f	T. Tallis	
9	9	10	8[v]			Submit yourselves	f	[J. Shepherd[	CN1560
9[v]	9[v]	10[v]	9			He that hath my commandment	f	[Mundy]	
10	10	11[v]	9[v]			He that hath my commandment	f	[T. Coste]	
10[v]	10[v]	12	10			Behold it is Christ	f	[W. Mundy]	
11	11[v]	12[v]	10[v]			Praise the Lord	f	[Mundy]	
11[v]	12	13[v]	11			O Lord from us	f		
12[v]	12[v]	14	12			I will always give thanks	f		
13	13	14[v]	12[v]			This sweet and merry	f	W. Byrd	LM1590:8
14	14	15[v]	13			Every singing byrd	f	L. Marenzio	" :6
15	15	16[v]	14			When first my heedless	f	" "	" :1
15[v]	15[v]	17	14[v]			O merry world	f	" "	" :2
16	16	17[v]	15			Zephyrus [breathing]	f	[" "]	" :4
16[v]	16[v]	18	15[v]			Fair shepherd's queen	f	" "	" :5
17	17	18[v]	16			Circumdederunt me	f	[Clemens non Papa]	
17[v]	17[v]	19	16[v]			Quoniam tribulatio (ii)	f	[" " "]	
18[v]	19	20	18			Saint Marie now (i)	f	J. Amner	1615:9
18[v]	19	20	18			At length (ii)	f	" "	" :10
19	19[v]	20[v]	18[v]			But he the God of love (iii)	f	" "	" :11
19[v]	20	21	19			Sweet are the thoughts	f	" "	" :7
	21	22	20			Woe is me that I am	f	[" "]	" :12
21	21[v]	22[v]	20[v]			Come let's rejoice	f	" "	" :8
21[v]	22	23	21			O grief, if yet	f	[Donato]	MT1588:5
22[v]	23	24	21[v]			My heart, why hast	f	T. Morley	1597:8
23	23[v]	24[v]	22			Still it frieth	f	" "	" :9
						(five-part pieces)			
23[v]	24	25	22[v]	1		O God, give ear	f	W. Byrd	1588:1
24	24[v]	25[v]	23	1[v]		O mortal man	f	"W. Byrd"[1]	
25	25[v]	26[v]	23[v]	2[v]		O Lord I bow the knees	f	W. Mundy[2]	
26	26[v]	27[v]	24[v]	3a[v]		Grant unto us	f	N. Strogers	
26[v]	27	28	25[v]	3b		Wipe away my sins[3]	f	T. Tallis	
27[v]	28	29	26[v]	4		Deliver me from mine enemies	f	[R. Parsons][4]	
28	29	29[v]	27	4[v]		Lord, who shall dwell	f	R. White	
29[v]	30	31	28[v]	6		Prevent us O Lord	f	W. Byrd	
30	30[v]	31[v]	29	6[v]		Blessed by thy name[5]	f	T. Tallis[6]	
30[v]	31	31[v]	29[v]	7		Set up thyself	f	Mr Smith of Gloucester	
31	32	33[v]	30	7[v]		Almighty God, the fountain	f	Mr Tomkins of Woster	
32	33	32[v]	31	8[v]		I will sing unto the Lord	f	J. Amner	1615:18
32[v]	33[v]	33	31[v]	9		The heavens stood	f	" "	" :15
33	34[v]	34[v]	32	9[v]		He that descended	f	" "	" :17
33[v]	35	35	32[v]	10		Now doth the city	f	" "	" :16

---

1 Anonymous in the only other source, Christ Church MS 439.

2 In 4180: "Mr Tallis"; corrected in other partbooks.

3 Adaptation of the motet, *Absterge Domine,* from CS1575.

4 Attributed to "Mr White" in the source.

5 Adaptation of the motet, *Mihi autem nimis,* from CS1575.

6 In 4180 "Mr Byrd"; corrected in other partbooks.

7 4180: cantus, -81: altus, -82: tenor, -83: bassus, -84: quintus, -85: sextus.

| --- | --- | --- | --- | --- | --- | --- | --- | --- | --- |
34	35^V	35^V	33	10^V		*When Israel (i)*	v	M. East	1610:4
						What aileth thee (ii)	v	" "	" :5
35^V	36^V	36^V	34	11^V		*Rise O my soul (i)*	v	[W. Simms][1]	
						And thou, my soul (ii)	V	["]	
						To thee. O Jesu (iii)	V	["]	
37	38	38^V	35^V	13^V		*Do not repine fair sun*	v	O. Gibbons	
40	41	43	39	17		Vergine bella[2]		[Palestrina]	1581:1
40^V	41^V	43^V	39^V	17^V		Vergine saggia		["]	" :2
41	42	44	40	18		Vergine pura		["]	" :3
41^V	42^V	44^V	40^V	18^V		Vergine santa		["]	" :5
42	43	45	41	19		Vergine sol'al [mondo]		["]	" :6
42^V	43^V	45^V	41^V	19^V		Vergine chiara		["]	" :8
43	44	46	42	20		Vergine quante [lagrime]		["]	" :9
43^V	44^V	46^V	42^V	20^V		[Fantasia] the first		T. Lupo	
44	45	47	43	21		["] the second		" "	
44^V	45^V	47^V	43^V	21^V		["] the third		R. Dering	
45	46	48	44	22		["] the fourth		" "	
45^V	46^V	48^V	44^V	22^V		The white delightful swan[2]		[H. Vecchi]	MT1597:1
46	47	49	45	23		Cinthia [thy song]		[G. Croce]	" :4
46^V	47^V	49^V	45^V	23^V		"Larissinall" [i.e., Le Rossignol]		[A. Ferrabosco]	MT1588:43
47	48	50	46	24		When I would thee embrace		[G.B. Pinello][3]	" :41
47^V	48^V	50^V	46^V	24^V		When shall I cease		[Faignient]	" :21
48	49	51	47^V	25^V		I must depart		[L. Marenzio]	" :22
48^V	49^V	51^V	47^V	25^V		Susanna fair		[O. Lassus]	" :19
49	50	52	48	26		So gratious		[Ferretti]	" :25
49^V	50^V	52^V	48^V	26^V	1^V	*In paradise*	cs		
50	51	53	49	27		*Delight is dead*	cs	[W. Byrd]	
50^V	51^V	53^V	49^V	27^V		*Come pretty babe*	cs	" "	
51	52	53^V	50	28		*Abradad*	cs		
52	52^V	54^V	50^V	28^V		*Farewell the bliss*	cs		
53	53	55	51	29		*Come Charon*	cd		
54^V	53^V	55^V	51^V	29^V		*Lullaby (i)*	cs	W. Byrd	1588:32
						Be still (ii)	cs	" "	" :32
55^V	54^V	56	52	30^V		*Prostrate O Lord*	cs	" "	" :27
54	55	56^V	52^V	31		*In fields abroad*	cs	" "	" :22
55^V	55^V	57	53	31^V		*Constant Penelope*	cs	" "	" :23

(section for mixed number of parts)

-80	-81	-82	-83	-84	-85	Title	idiom	Composer	Prints
56^V	56	57^V	53^V	32	2^V/ 10^V	O sing unto the Lord	f	T. Tomkins	
57^V	57	58^V	54^V	33	3^V	*Sing we merrily (i)*	v	M. East	1624:14
57^V	57	58^V	54^V	33		*Take the psalm (ii)*	v	" "	" :15
58	57^V	59	55	33^V	4	*Blow up the trumpet (iii)*	v	" "	" :16
59	58^V	61	56	34^V	4^V	Why dost thou shoot	f	J. Wilbye	1598:30
59^V	59	61^V	56^V	35	5^V	Of joys and pleasing pains	f	" "	" :26
60	59^V	62	57	35^V	6	My throat is sore	f	" "	" :27
60^V	60^V	62^V	57^V	36^V	7	*O ye little flocks (i)*	v	J. Amner	1615:19
61^V	61	63^V	58	37	7^V	*Fear not (ii)*	v	" "	" :20
62	61^V	64	58^V	37^V	8	*And they cry (iii)*	v	" "	" :21
62^V	62^V	64^V	59	38	8^V	*Lo how from heaven (i)*	v	" "	" :22
63	62	65	59^V	38^V	9	*I bring you tidings (ii)*	v	" "	" :23
63^V	63	65^V	60	39^V	9^V	A stranger here	f	" "	" :24
64	63^V	66	60^V	40	10	*My Lord is hence removed*	v	" "	" :25
64^V	64	66^V	61	40^V	12^V	Sing joyfully	f	W. Byrd	
65^V	65	67^V	61^V	41^V	13^V	O God the proud	f	T. Tomkins	
66	65^V	68^V	62^V	43^V		Christ rising (i)	f	[T. Tallis]	
						Christ is risen (ii)	f	["]	
67^V	67	69^V	63^V	44^V		O Lord how long wilt thou	f		
68^V	68	70^V	64^V	45^V		Salvator Mundi	f	T. Tallis	CS1575:1
69	68^V	71	65	46		Absterge Domine	f	" "	" :2
70	69^V	72	66	47		Lamentations	f	" "	
71^V	71	73^V	67^V	48^V		In resurrectione	f	W. Byrd	CS1589:17
72	71^V	74	67^V	49	15^V	Adolescentulus sum	f	[Mundy]	
73	72^V	75	68^V	50	16^V	Jerusalem plantabis	f		
73^V	73^V	75^V	69	50^V	17^V	Credo quod redemptor	f	R. Parsons	
74			69^V	51		O sacrum convivium	f	T. Tallis	CS1575:9
74^V	74	76	70	51^V	18	[Homo] quidam fecit	f	["]	

1 Attributed to Michael East in the source.

2 All the madrigals in this group are textless in the source.

3 Attributed to Ferrabosco in the source.

-80	-81	-82	-83	-84	-85	Title	idiom	Composer	Prints
75	75^V	77^V	70^V	52		In Nomine		W. Byrd	
75^V	76	78	71^V	52^V		" "		R. Parsons	
58	76^V	78^V	71^V	53		" "		A. Ferrabosco	
58^V	77	79	72	53^V		" "		"Brewster"	
59	78^V	79^V	72^V	54		De la courte (i)		[R. Parsons]	
59^V	77^V	80^V	73	54^V		De la courte (ii)		[" "]	
62^V	79	81^V	73^V	55^V		Italian 1[1]			
63	79^V	82	74	56		[Ma la fiamma]		[H.L. Hassler]	1596[2]
61^V	80	82^V	74^V	56^V	18^V	[Musica e lo mio core]		[" "]	"
63^V	80^V	83^V	75	57	19^V	Italian 4			
64	81	84	75^V	57^V		Italian 5			
64^V	81^V	84^V	76	58		[Care lagrime mie]		[" " "]	"
65	82	85	76^V	58^V		Dolorosi [martir][3]		L. Marenzio	
65^V	82^V	85^V	77	59	20	Now must I part		" "	MT1588:51
66	83	86	77^V	59^V	20^V	So far from my delight		A. Ferrabosco	" :48
66^V	83^V	86^V	78	60	21	[She only doth not feel]		" "	" :49
67	84	87	78^V	60^V	21^V	I sung sometime		L. Marenzio	" :56
67^V	84^V	87^V	79	61	22	[Because my Love]		" "	" :57
68	85	88	79^V	61^V	22^V	Laudate pueri	f	[W. Byrd]	Cs1575:17
69^V	86	91		62^V	23^V	Deus misereatur	f	[J. Shepherd]	
71	88	89	80^V	64	25	Deus misereatur	f	[R. White][4]	
72^V	89^V	92^V	81^V	65^V	26^V	Domine non exaltatum	f	W. Mundy	
73^V	90^V	93^V	82^V	66^V	27^V	[Libera nos] salva	f	[J. Shepherd]	
74	91	94	83^V.	67	28	[Libera nos] salva	f	[" "]	
74^V	91^V	94	82^V	67		Essurientes[5]		[" "]	
74^V	92	94^V	84	69		Jerusalem surge		Clemens non Papa	
75	92^V	95	84^V	69^V		(part 2)		" " "	
75^V	93	95^V	85	70		Veni electa mea (i)		" " "	
76	93^V	96	85^V	70^V		Audi filia (ii)		" " "	
76^V	94	96^V	86	68		Dum transisset	f	"Mr Tallis"	
77^V	94^V	97^V	86^V	71		Cantate Domino	f	R. Nicolson	
78	95^V	98^V	87	71^V		Blessed art thou that fearest	f		
79	96^V	98	88	72^V		Veni in hortum	f	[O. Lassus]	
79^V	97	100	88^V	73		Angelus ad pastores	f	[" "]	
80	97^V	100^V	89	73^V		Sermone blando[6]		[W. Mundy]	
80^V	98	101	89^V	73^V	28^V	Cante, cantate		[R. Parsons]	
81	98^V	101^V	90	74		Johnson's knell		[R. Johnson]	
8	99a	102	91	75		Alas, alack			
82^V	$99a^V$	102^V	91^V	75^V		Holy, holy, holy	f	[R. Parsons]	
83^V	$99b^V$	103^V	92^V	76^V		All ye people, clap[7]	f	W. Byrd	
84	100	104	93	77		O lord turn thy wrath (i)[8]	f	" "	
84^V	100^V	104^V	93^V	77^V		Bow thine ear (ii)	f	" "	
85^V	101^V	105^V	94^V	78^V		Out of the deep	f	" "	
86^V	102^V	106^V	95 v	79^V		Behold, how good and joyful	f	" "	
87^V	103^V	107^V	96^V	80^V		How long shall mine enemies	f	" "	
89^V	104^V	108^V	97^V	81^V		O Lord, make thy servant, James	f	" "	
90^V	106^V	109^V	98			O fools can you not	f	[J. Wilbye]	1598:8
91^V	107	110	98^V			Alas, what hope	f	[" "]	" :9
92^V	107^V	110^V	99			Lady, when I behold	f	[" "]	" :10
93^V	108^V	111^V	99^V			Thus saith my Cloris	f	[" "]	" :11
94	109	112	100			Adieu, sweet Amarillis	f	[" "]	" :12
94^V	109^V	112^V	100^V	82		Die, hapless man	f	[" "]	" :13
95	110	113	101	82^V		I fall	f	[" "]	" :14
95^V	110^V	113^V	101^V	83		Unkind O stay	f	[" "]	" :20
96	111	114	102	83^V		Flora gave me	f	[" "]	" :22
96^V	111^V	114^V	102^V	84^V		I sung sometimes	f	[" "]	" :21
97^V	112^V	115^V	103^V	85^V		When David heard	f	Mr Smith	
98	113	116	104	86		O give thanks	f	N. Giles	
99	114	117	105	87		Behold it is Christ	f	E. Hooper	
100	115	118	106	88		Rejoice in the Lord	f	Mr.Hugh Davies of Hereford	

---

1 The next six madrigals lack both title and text in the source.

2 *Madrigali a 5. 6. 7. & 8. voci*, 1596.

3 The next six madrigals lack their texts in the source.

4 Attributed to "Mr Mundy" in the source.

5 The next five Latin works are textless in the source.

6 The next four pieces are textless in the source.

7 Adaptation of the motet, *Alleluia, Ascendit Deus*, from Gr1607.

8 Adaptation of the motet, *Ne irascaris/Civitas sancti tui*, from CS1589.

-80	-81	-82	-83	-84	-85	Title	idiom	Composer	Prints
101^V	116^V	119^V	106^V	89^V		O God, whom our offences	f	W. Byrd	
102^V	117^V	120^V	107^V	90^V		Hear my crying	f		
104	119	122	108^V	92		All people clap	f	T. Weelkes	
105	119^V	123	109^V	92^V		O Lord rebuke me not	f		
106	121	124	110^V	94		Christ rising (i)	f	[E. Tucker]	
						Christ is risen (ii)	f	[" "]	
107a^V	122^V	125^V	112	95^V		*The Country Cry*	v	[R. Dering]	
109^V	125^V	128	114^V	98^V		*The London Cry (i)*	v	[O. Gibbons]	
						A good sausage (ii)	v	[" "]	
112^V	127^V	130^V	116^V	101^V		*The Cry of London*	v		
114	129	132	118	103		O amica mea^1			
114^V	129^V	132^V	118^V	103^V		All at once well met	f	T. Weelkes	1598:1
115	130	133	119	104		To shorten winter's	f	" "	" :2
115^V	130^V	133^V	119^V	104^V		Whilst youthful	f	" "	" :4
116	131	134	120	105		On the plains	f	" "	" :5
116^V	131^V	134^V	120^V	105^V		Hark all ye lovely	f	" "	" :8
117	132	135	121^V	106		Say, dainty dames	f	" "	" :9
117^V	132^V	135^V	121	106^V		In pride of May	f	" "	" :11
118	133	136	122	107		We shepherds sing	f	" "	" :17
118^V	133^V	136^V	122^V	107^V		I love and have my love	f	" "	" :18
119^V	134^V	137	123	108		Give me my heart	f	" "	" :7
120	136a	137^V	123^V	108^V		Now is my Cloris	f	" "	" :22
120^V	136a^V	138	123^V	109	29^V	Cease now delight	f	" "	" :24
121^V	135^V	139	124^V	111		Come clap thy hands	f	" "	" :19
122a	136a	139^V	125	111^V		Phillis hath sworn	f	" "	" :20
122a^V	136b^V	140	125^V	112	30^V	Give sentence with me	f	W. Randall	
123^V	138^V	142	127^V	114		Let God arise	f	T. Ford	
124^V	139^V	143^V	128^V		32	To the shady woods	f	T. Tomkins	1622:13
125	140	144	128^V		32^V	Too much I once lamented	f	" "	" :14
126^V	140^V	144^V	129^V		33 ^{V}	Come shepherds	f	" "	" :15
127^V	141^V	145	130		34^V	Cloris, why still	f	" "	" :16
128^V	142	145^V	130^V		35^V	See the shepherd's queen	f	" "	" :17
129^V	142^V	146	131^V		36^V	Phillis now cease	f	" "	" :18
130^V	143	146^V	132^V		37^V	When David heard	f	" "	" :19
131^V	143^V	147^V	133^V		38^V	Phillis, yet see him	f	" "	" :20
132^V	144^V	148^V	134		39^V	Fusca, in thy starry eyes	f	" "	" :21
133^V	145^V	149	134^V		40^V	Adieu ye city prisoning towers	f	" "	" :22
134^V	146^V	149^V	135	115^V	41^V	When I observe	f	" "	" :23
135^V	147^V	150^V	135^V	116^V	42^V	Music divine	f	" "	" :24
136^V	148^V	151^V	136^V	117^V	43^V	Oft did I marle	f	" "	" :25
137^V	149^V	152^V	137^V	118^V	44^V	Woe is me	f	" "	" :26
138^V	150^V	153^V	138^V	119^V	45^V	It is my well-beloved's voice	f	" "	" :27
138	151^V	154^V	138	120^V	46^V	Turn unto the Lord	f	" "	" :28
139^V	152	155	139^V	121	47	A le quancie de rose^2		[A. Gabrieli]	GM1588^3
140^V	152^V	155^V	140^V	121^V	47^V	Ecco vinegio		["]	"
141^V	153^V	156^V	141^V	122^V	48^V	Sacri [di Giove]		[G. Gabrieli]	GM1589
142^V	154^V	157^V	142^V	123^V	49^V	O passi sparsi		[A. Gabrieli]	"
143^V	155^V	158^V	143^V	124^V	50^V	A dio [dolce mia vita]		[G. Gabrieli]	GM1588
144^V	156	159^V	144	125^V	51^V	D'un si bel foco		[A. Striggio]	"
145^V	156^V	160^V	144^V	126^V	52^V	Quei vinto dal furor		[A. Gabrieli]	GM1589
146^V	157^V	161^V	145	127	53^V	Ecco l'alma beata		[G. Croce]	"
147^V	158^V	162^V	145^V	127^V	54^V	Basti [fin qui]		[L. Marenzio]	"
148^V	159^V	163^V	146^V	128^V	55^V	Lieto godea [sedendo]		[G. Gabrieli]	GM1588
149	160	164	147	129^V	56^V	O misero mio core		[G. Eremita]	GM1590
149^V	160^V	164^V	147^V	130^V		Hence stars	f	[M. East]	1601:unnum.
150^V	161^V	165^V	148^V	131^V		With angel's face	f	[D. Norcomb]	" :1
151^V	162^V	166^V	149^V	132^V		Lightly she whipped	f	[J. Mundy]	" :2
152^V	163^V	167^V	150^V	133 ^{V}		Long live fair Oriana	f	[Ellis Gibbons]	" :3
153^V	164^V	168^V	151^V	134^V		All creatures now	f	[J. Bennet]	" :4
154^V	165^V	169^V	153^V	135^V		Fair Oriana	f	[J. Hilton]	" :5
155	166^V	170	152^V	136		Sing shepherds all	f	[R. Nicolson]	" :9
156^V	167^V	171^V	154^V	137^V		Tutteri foco^4		[B. Palavicino]	
157^V	168^V	172^V	155	138^V		[untitled]			
158^V	169^V	173^V	155^V	139^V	57^V	O sing unto the Lord	f	J. Amner	
160	170	175	156^V	140^V	60^V	Holy Lord God almighty	f	J. Bateson	
160^V	171^V	175^V	157^V	141^V	62	Out of the deep	f	W. Byrd	
162	172^V	176^V	158^V	142^V	63^V	Rejoice in the Lord	f	M. Jeffreys	
163	173^V	177^V	159^V	144	64^V	O give thanks	f	[J. Mundy]^5	

1 This piece is textless in the source.

2 The next eleven madrigals are textless in the source.

3 These eleven works may ultimately derive from *Gemma Musicalis...Noribergae*, 1588, 1589, 1590.

4 The next two pieces are textless in the source.

5 Attributed to "Mr Byrd" in the source.

-80	-81	-82	-83	-84	-85	Title	idiom	Composer	Prints
164^V	175	179^V	160^V	145^V	65^V	Awake up my glory	f	Mr Hugh Davies of Hereford	
166	176	180^V	161^V	147		Lord enter not into judgment	f	T. Tomkins	
167^V	176^V	181	162^V	147^V	68^V	O Lord arise	f	T. Weelkes[1]	
166^V	177^V	181^V	163^V	148^V	69^V	O praise the Lord, all ye heathen	f	T. Tomkins	
168^V	179^V	183^V	165^V	150^V	71^V	Fantasia		W. Byrd	
169^V	180^V	184^V	166^V	151^V		"		" "	
	181	185	167	152		Dorick		J. Bull	
	184^V	185^V	167^V		72^V	Fantasia		[S. Ives]	
	181^V	186^V	168^V		73^V	"		[" "]	
	182^V	187^V	169^V		74^V	"		[J. Jenkins]	
	183^V	188^V	170^V		75^V	"		[" "]	
	185^V	189^V	171^V		76^V	"		[S. Ives]	
	186^V	190	172^V		77^V	"		[" "]	
	187^V	191^V	173^V		78^V	"		[A. Ferrabosco]	
169^V	188^V		174	152^V	79^V	"			
			174^V	153^V	80^V	"	1	[O. Gibbons]	
			175^V	154	81^V	"	2	[" "]	
			176^V	154^V	82^V	"	3	[" "]	
			177^V	155	83^V	"	4	[" "]	
			178^V	155^V	84^V	"	5	[" "]	
			179	156	85	"	6	[" "]	
			179^V	156^V	85^V	"	7	[" "]	
			180^V	157	86^V	"	8	[" "]	
			181	157^V	87^V	"	9	[" "]	
					88^V	"	9	" "	

---

1 Attributed to Thomas Tomkins in 4180; corrected in the other partbooks.

	f o l i o								
-92	-93	-94	-95	-96	4180	Title	idiom	Composer	Prints
	1^V	1^V	1^V		174^{V1}	Fantasia 1		O. Gibbons	
	2v	2^V	2^V		175^V	" 2		" "	
	3^V	3^V	3^V		176^V	" 3		" "	
	4^V	4^V	4^V		177^V	" 4		" "	
	5^V	5^V	5^V		178^V	" 5		" "	
	6^V	6^V	6^V		179	" 6		" "	
	7^V	7^V	7^V		179^V	" 7		" "	
	8^V	8^V	8^V		180^V	" 8		" "	
	9^V	9^V	9^V		181	" 9		" "	
	10^V	10^V	10^V			" 10		G. Coperario	
	11v	11^V	11^V			" 11		T. Tomkins	
	12^V	12^V	12^V			" 12		[T. Lupo]	
	13	12^V	12^V			" 13		[" "]	
	13^V	13^V	13^V			" 14		[" "]	
	14^V	14^V	14^V			" 15		[" "]	
	15^V	15^V	15^V			Almaine 1		J. Jenkins	
	15^V	15^V	15^V			" 2			
	16	16	16			" 3		" "	
	16^V	16^V	16^V			" 4		S. Ives	
	17	17	16^V			" 5			
	17	17	17			" 6			
	17^V	17^V	17			" 7			
	18	18	17^V			" 8			
1^V			1			In Nomine		T. Tomkins	
2^V			1^V			" " 2		" "	
3^V			2^V			Fantasia 3		" "	
4^V			3^V			" 4		" "	
5^V			4^V			" 5		" "	
6^V			5^V			" 6		" "	
7^V			6^V			" 7		" "	
8^V			7^V			" 8		" "	
9^V			8^V			" 9		" "	
10^V			9^V			" 10		" "	
11^V			10^V			" 11		" "	
12^V			11^V			" 12		" "	
13^V			12^V			" 13		" "	
14^V			13^V			" 14		" "	
15^V			14^V			" 15		" "	
						(four-part pieces)			
22	21	21	22	18^V		Saint Marie now (i)	f	J. Amner	1615:9
22^V	21^V	21^V	22^V	18^V		At length to Christ (ii)	f	" "	" :10
23	22	22	23	19		But the God of love (iii)	f	" "	" :11
23^V	22^V	22^V	23^V	19^V		Sweet are the thoughts	f	" "	" :7
24^V	24^V	24^V	24^V	21		Come let's rejoice	f		" :8
25^V	23^V	23^V	25^V	21^V		O grief, if yet	f	[B. Donato]	MT1588:5
30	29^V	29^V	30			Fantasia 1		A. Ferrabosco	
30^V	30^V	30^V	30^V			" 2		" "	
31^V	31^V	31^V	31^V			" 3		" "	
32^V	32^V	32^V	32^V			" 4		" "	
33^V	33^V	33^V	33^V			" 5		" "	
34^V	34^V	34^V	34^V			" 6		" "	
35^V	35^V	35^V	35^V			" 7		" "	
36^V	36^V	36^V	36^V			" 8		" "	
37^V	37^V	37^V	37^V			" 9		" "	
38^V	38^V	38^V	38^V			" 10		" "	
39^V	39^V	39^V	39^V			" 11		" "	
40^V	40^V	40^V	40^V			" 12		[" "]	
41^V	41^V	41^V	41^V			" 13		" "	
42^V	42^V	42^V	42^V			" 14		" "	
43^V	43^V	43^V	43^V			" 15		" "	
44^V	44^V	44^V	44^V			" 16		" "	
45^V	45^V	45^V	45^V			" 17		" "	
46^V	46^V	46^V	46^V			" 18		" "	
47^V	47^V	47^V	47^V	167^{V1}		" 19		S. Ives[2]	
48^V	48^V	48^V	48^V	168^V		" 20		" "	
49^V	49^V	49v	49^V	169^V		" 21		J. Jenkins	
50^V	50^V	50^V	50^V	170^V		" 22		" "	
51^V	51^V	51^V	51^V	171^V		" 23		S. Ives	
52^V	52^V	52^V	52^V	172^V		" 24		" "	
53^V	53^V	53^V	53^V	173^V		" 25		A. Ferrabosco	

1 The foliation in these groups is taken from Drexel 4183.

2 The attributions for fantasias 19-24 are in the hand of Matthew Hutton.

-92	-93	-94	-95	-96	4180	Title	idiom	Composer	Prints
54^V	54^V	54^V		54^V		Come let us sing	f	J. Lugge	
55^V	55^V	55^V		55^V		We knowledge thee	f	" "	
57	57	57		57		My soul doth magnify the Lord	f	" "	
58	58	58		58		Lord, now lettest thou thy servant	f	" "	

(five-part pieces)

-92	-93	-94	-95	-96	4180	Title	idiom	Composer	Prints
58^V	58^V	58^V	28	$58^V/72^V$		Preludium		[W. Byrd]	
74	59^V	59^V	29^V	59^V	80	Sermone blando		[W. Mundy]	
60	60	60	30	60		Pavin 1		T. Tomkins	
60^V	60^V	60^V	30^V	60^V		" 2		" "	
61	61	61	31	61		" 3		" "	
61^V	61^V	61^V	31^V	61^V		" 4		A. Ferrabosco	
62	62	62	32	62		" 5		" "	
62^V	62^V	62^V	32^V	62^V		" 6		" "	
63	63	63	33	63		" 7		" "	
63^V	63^V	63^V	33^V	63^V		" 8		T. Weelkes	
64	64	64	34	64		" 9		R. Mico	
64^V	64^V	64^V	34^V	64^V		" 10		" " 1	
65	65	65	35	65		" 11		" "	
65^V	65^V	65^V	35^V	65^V		" 12			
66	66	66	36	66		" 13			
66^V	66^V	66^V	36^V	66^V		" 14			
67	67	67	37	67		" 15			
67^V	67^V	67^V	37^V	67^V		" 16		R. Carlton	
68	68	68	38	68		" 17		T. Tomkins	
68^V	68^V	68^V	38^V	68^V		The funerals		[A. Holborne]	
68^V	**69**	69	39	68^V		*My heart doth pant*	cs		
69	69	69^V	39^V	69		*Why do I use*	cs	W. Byrd	1588:33
69^V	69^V	70	40	69		*Methought of late*	cs	"W. Byrd"2	
69^V	70	70^V	40	69^V		*Thou Amaryllis*	cs	" "	" :12
70	70^V	71	40^V	69^V		*When I was otherwise*	cs	" "	1589:30
71	71	71^V	41	70		*Susanna fair*	cs	" "	1588:29
71^V	71^V	71^V	41^V	70		*My mind to me*	cs		
71^V	72	72	42	70^V		Vezzosette3		[T. Morley]	1595:1
72	72^V	72^V	42^V	70^V		Pia cher		[" "]	" :9
72^V	73	72^V	43	71		Browning4		[W. Byrd]	

(different section in 17795; see separate page)

-92	-93	-94	-95	-96	4180	Title	idiom	Composer	Prints
74^V	74^V	74^V	74^V	74^V		Fantasia		W. White	
75^V	75^V	75^V	75^V	75^V		" 2		[T. Ford]	
76^V	76^V	76^V	76^V	76^V		" 3		[" "]	
77^V	77^V	77^V	77^V	77^V		" 4		[" "]	
78^V	78^V	78^V	78^V	78^V		" 5		[" "]	
79^V	79^V	79^V	79^V	79^V		" 6		[" "]	
81	80^V	80^V	80^V	80^V		" 7			
82^V	81^V	81	81^V	81		" 8			
83	82	81^V	82	81^V		" 9		[G. Coperario]	
83^V	82^V	82^V	82^V	82^V		" 10		[" "]	
84^V	83^V	83^V	83^V	83^V		" 1		R. Dering	
85^V	84^V	84^V	84^V	84^V		" 2		" "	
86^V	85^V	85^V	85^V	85^V		" 3		" "	
87^V	86^V	86^V	86^V	86^V		" 4		" "	
88^V	87^V	87^V	87^V	87^V		" 5		" "	
89	88^V	88^V	88^V	88^V		" 6		" "	
89^V	89^V	89^V	89^V	89^V		" 1		T. Lupo	
89^V	89^V	89	89	89		" 2		" "	
90^V	90^V	90^V	90^V	90^V		" 3		" "	
91^V	91^V	91^V	91^V	91^V		" 4		" "	
92^V	92^V	92^V	92^V	92^V		" 5		" "	
93^V	93^V	26^{V5}	93^V	93^V		" 6		" "	
94^V	94^V	93^V	94^V	94^V		" 7		R. Dering	
95^V	95^V	94^V	95^V	95^V		" 1		J. Ward	
96^V	96^V	95^V	96^V	96^V		In Nomine 1		S. Ives	
97^V	97^V	96^V	97^V	97^V		" " 2		A. Ferrabosco	
98^V	98	97^V	98^V	98^V		" " 3		" "	
99^V	98^V	98^V	99^V	99^V		Fantasia 1		W. White	
100^V	99^V	99^V	100^V	100^V		" 2		J. Oker	

1 17792: "Mr Wilks"

2 Attribution queried by Dr Philip Brett.

3 These two madrigals are textless in the source.

4 Merro adds words to the tune, *The leaves be green,* whenever it occurs in the piece.

5 In the hand of Matthew Hutton.

(six-part pieces)

-92	-93	-94	-95	-96	4180	Title	idiom	Composer	Prints
101ᵛ	100ᵛ	100ᵛ	101ᵛ	101ᵛ		Fantasia 1		W. White	
102ᵛ	101ᵛ	101ᵛ	102ᵛ	102ᵛ		" 2		" "	
103ᵛ	102ᵛ	102ᵛ	103ᵛ	103ᵛ		" 3		[" "]	
104ᵛ	103ᵛ	103ᵛ	104ᵛ	104ᵛ		" 4		" "	
105ᵛ	104ᵛ	104ᵛ	105ᵛ	105ᵛ		" 5		" "	
106ᵛ	105ᵛ	105ᵛ	106ᵛ	106ᵛ		" 6		" "	
107ᵛ	106ᵛ	106ᵛ	107ᵛ	107ᵛ		" 1		J. Ward	
108ᵛ	107ᵛ	107ᵛ	108ᵛ	107ᵛ		" 2		" "	
109ᵛ	108ᵛ	108ᵛ	109ᵛ	108ᵛ		" 3		" "	
110ᵛ	109ᵛ	109ᵛ	110ᵛ	109ᵛ		" 4		" "	
111ᵛ	110ᵛ	110ᵛ	111ᵛ	110ᵛ		" 5		" "	
112ᵛ	111ᵛ	111ᵛ	112ᵛ	111ᵛ		" 6		" "	
113ᵛ	112ᵛ	112ᵛ	113ᵛ	112		" 7		[W. Cranford][1]	
114ᵛ	113ᵛ	113ᵛ	114ᵛ	112ᵛ	107aᵛ	*The Country Cry*	v	[R. Dering]	
117ᵛ	116ᵛ	116	117ᵛ	114ᵛ	109ᵛ	*The First London Cry*	v	[O. Gibbons]	
119ᵛ	119ᵛ	118	120ᵛ	117	112ᵛ	*The Second London Cry*	v		
120ᵛ	121	121	121ᵛ	118	34	*When Israel came out of Egypt (i)*	v	M. East	1610:4
						What aileth thee (ii)	v	" "	" :5
122ᵛ	122ᵛ	122ᵛ	123	119ᵛ	35ᵛ	*Rise, O my soul (i)*	v	[W. Simms][2]	
						And thou, my soul (ii)	v	[" "]	
						To thee, O Jesu (iii)	v	[" "]	
124ᵛ	124ᵛ	124	125	121	57ᵛ	*Sing we merrily (i)*	v	M. East	1624:14
						Take the psalm (ii)	v	" "	" :15
						Blow up the trumpet (iii)	v	" "	" :16
126	126ᵛ	125ᵛ	126ᵛ	122ᵛ		*Rejoice, sing, and rejoice*	v	T. Tomkins	
128	128ᵛ	127ᵛ	128ᵛ	124	84	*O Lord turn thy wrath*	f	W. Byrd	
129ᵛ	130	129	130	125ᵛ		*O go not from me*	v	[M. Peerson][3]	

(five-part full anthems)

-92	-93	-94	-95	-96	4180	Title	idiom	Composer	Prints
131ᵛ	132ᵛ	130ᵛ	131ᵛ	126ᵛ		Deliver us O Lord	f		
132ᵛ	131ᵛ	131ᵛ	132ᵛ	127ᵛ	31	Almighty God the fountain	f	T. Tomkins	
133ᵛ	133ᵛ	132ᵛ	133ᵛ	128ᵛ	99	Behold, it is Christ	f	E. Hooper	
134ᵛ	134ᵛ	133ᵛ	134ᵛ	129ᵛ		Stir up we beseech thee	f		
135	133aᵛ134ᵛ	133ᵛ	130ᵛ	67ᵛ		How long shall mine enemies	f	[W. Byrd]	
136ᵛ	134aᵛ135ᵛ	136ᵛ	131ᵛ	26ᵛ		Wipe away my sins[4]	f	[T. Tallis]	
138	136	155	138	133	30	Blessed be thy name[5]	f	[" "]	
138ᵛ	136ᵛ	155ᵛ	138ᵛ	133ᵛ	98	O give thanks	f	[N. Giles]	
139ᵛ	137ᵛ	156ᵛ	139ᵛ	134ᵛ	100	Rejoice in the Lord	f	[H. Davies]	
140ᵛ	138ᵛ	157ᵛ	140ᵛ	135ᵛ	82ᵛ	Holy Lord God	f	[R. Parsons]	
141ᵛ	139ᵛ	158ᵛ	141ᵛ	136ᵛ		Remember not, Lord	f	[J. Amner]	1615:13
142	140ᵛ	159	142ᵛ	137ᵛ	25	O Lord I bow the knees	f	[W. Mundy]	
143ᵛ	141ᵛ	160	143ᵛ	139		With all our hearts[6]	f	[T. Tallis]	
144ᵛ	142ᵛ	160ᵛ	144ᵛ	139ᵛ	32	I will sing unto the Lord	f	[J. Amner]	1615:18
145	143	161	145	140	33	He that descended	f	[" "]	" :17
145ᵛ	143ᵛ	161ᵛ	145ᵛ	140ᵛ	101ᵛ	O God whom our offences	f	W. Byrd	
146	144ᵛ	137	146ᵛ	141ᵛ	104	All people clap	f	[T. Weelkes]	
147	145ᵛ	137ᵛ	147ᵛ	142ᵛ	105	O Lord rebuke me not	f		
148ᵛ	146ᵛ	138ᵛ	155	143ᵛ	106	Christ rising (i)	f	[E. Tucker]	
						Christ is risen (ii)	f	[" "]	
149ᵛ	147ᵛ	139ᵛ	149ᵛ	145ᵛ	166	Lord, enter not into judgment	f	[T. Tomkins]	
150ᵛ	148ᵛ	140ᵛ	150ᵛ	146ᵛ	123ᵛ	Let God arise	f	[T. Ford]	
151ᵛ	149ᵛ	141ᵛ	151ᵛ	147ᵛ	85ᵛ	Out of the deep	f	[W. Byrd?]	
152ᵛ	150ᵛ	142ᵛ	152ᵛ	148ᵛ	78	Blessed art thou that fearest	f		
153ᵛ	151ᵛ	143ᵛ	153ᵛ	149ᵛ	102ᵛ	Hear my crying	f		

(six-part full anthems)

-92	-93	-94	-95	-96	4180	Title	idiom	Composer	Prints
155	153	145	156ᵛ	151ᵛ	163	O give thanks unto the Lord	f	[J. Mundy]	
156ᵛ	154ᵛ	146ᵛ	157ᵛ	152ᵛ	122aᵛ	Give sentence with me	f	[W. Randall]	
158	155ᵛ	147ᵛ	158ᵛ	153ᵛ	64ᵛ	Sing joyfully	f	[W. Byrd]	
158ᵛ	158ᵛ	148ᵛ	159ᵛ	154ᵛ		With angels and archangels (a 5)	f		

---

1 Attributed to John Ward in the MSS.

2 Attributed to Michael East in the MSS.

3 Attributed to Mr Palmer in the source.

4 Adaptation of the motet, *Absterge Domine*, from CS1575.

5 Adaptation of the motet, *Mihi autme nimis*, from CS1575.

6 Adaptation of the motet, *Salvator mundi*, from CS1575.

-92	-93	-94	-95	-96	4180	Title	idiom	Composer	Prints
159^V	156^V	149^V	160^V	155^V	137^V	Woe is me that I am constrained to dwell	f	T. Tomkins	1622:26
160	157	150	161	156	138	Turn unto the Lord	f	" "	" :28

(section primarily for seven parts)

160^V	157^V	150^V	161^V	156^V	164^V	Awake up my glory	f	[Hugh Davies]	
161^V	159^V	151^V	162^V	157^V	167^V	O Lord arise	f	T. Weelkes	
162^V	160^V	152^V	163	158^V	158^V	O sing unto the Lord...let	f	[A. Amner]	
163^V	161^V	153^V	164^V	159^V	162	Rejoice in the Lord, O ye righteous	f	M. Jeffreys	
164^V	162^V	154^V	165^V	160^V	160	Holy Lord God almighty	f	T. Bateson	
165	163^V	162^V	166^V	162		Te Deum [Great Service]	f	W. Byrd	

(five-part motets)

173	172	171	173	164/ 169	71^V	In resurrectione	f	W. Byrd	CS1589:17
173^V	172^V	171^V	173^V	169^V	76^V	Dum transisset	f	["Tallis"]	
174	173^V	172^V	174^V	170^V	77^V	Cantate Domino	f	[R. Nicolson]	
175	174^V	173^V	175	171	79	Veni in hortum	f	[O. Lassus]	
175^V	175	174^V	175^V	171^V	79^V	Angelus ad pastores	f	[" "]	
175a	176^V	175	176	172	69^V	Deus misereatur	f	[J. Shepherd]	

(five- and six-part motets)

164^{V1}	178	176^V	177^V	173^V	71	Deus misereatur		[R. White]	
166	179^V	178^V	180	174^V	72	Adolescentulus sum ego		[W. Mundy]	
167	180^V	179^V	181	163^{V1}	68	Laudate pueri		W. Byrd	CS1575:17
168	181^V	180^V	182	164^V	72^V	Domine non exultatum		[W. Mundy]	
168^V	182^V	181^V	183	165^V	73	Jerusalem plantabis			
169	183	182	183^V	166	70	Lamentations		T. Tallis	
170^V	184^V	183^V	184^V	167^V		Heth, etc.[2]		R. White	
173^V	187	186	187^V	170^V		O quam gloriosum (i)		W. Byrd	CS1589:22
						Benedictio et claritas(ii)		" "	" :23
174^V	188^V	187	188^V	171		Tristitia [et anxietas]		" "	" :6
176^V	190^V	164^V	190^V			Fantasia[3]		R. Dering	

---

1 Original foliation ends: the following numbers are taken from the modern foliation.

2 The White *Lamentations* and the following Byrd motets are textless in the source.

3 Copied by Matthew Hutton.

fol.	Title	Composer
44^V	[Fantasia]	
47^V	[untitled]	
54^V	["]	
55^V	Ne irascaris	[W. Byrd]
56^V	Mall Simms for 2 bass viols	
57^V	Galliard 2 viols	
58^V	[untitled]	

(fol. 59 cut; stub remains)

60^V	[untitled]	
61^V	["] 1 for 3 bass viols	
62	["] 2 for 3 bass viols	
62^V	["] 3 for 3 bass viols leero sett	
63$_V$	["] 4 for 3 bass viols leero sett	
63$_V$	["] 5 for 3 bass viols leero	
64	["] 6 for 3 bass viols leero sett	

"Almains and Ayers for Base and Treble violls"

64^V	Almain 1	
64^V	" 2	
65^V	" 3	
65^V	" 4	
66^V	" 5	
66^V	" 6	
67^V	" 7	
67^V	" 8	
68^V	" 9	
68^V	" 10	
69^V	" 11	
70^V	" 12	
70^V	" 13	
71^V	" 14	
71^V	" 15	
72^V	" 15 [sic]	

(folios 44^V - 64 are in tablature)

5

The Oxford Sources

British Library Additional MSS 17786-91

British Library Additional MSS 17786-91, the largest, and probably the earliest, of the Oxford sources, have frequently drawn the attention of musical scholars during the last decades. Peter Warlock employed them for both his *Elizabethan Songs...for One Voice and...Four Stringed Instruments,* (Oxford, 1926), and his *Six English Tunes from the XVI and early XVII Centuries,* (Oxford, ca. 1926). More recently the partbooks proved an important source for *Consort Songs (MB* XXII). But although several scholars, most notably John Ward[1] and Gordon Spearritt,[2] have considered Add. MSS 17786-91 in connection with special topics, the set has never been the subject of an extensive study in its own right.

The six volumes, contained in vellum bindings devoid of any ornamentation beyond the designation of each part on the cover,[3] seem to have been the work of a single scribe with considerable copying skill. Certain inconsistencies in both text and musical notation require explanation, however. The opening fifteen folios of 17786-89 and 17791 give the impression of a careful, precise, slowly working hand. For the fantasias of John Okeover, John Ward, and Martin Peerson, on the other hand, the notation becomes more sprawling and "flamboyant," as illustrated, for example, by the differences in the formation of the g-clefs in the superius partbook. The contrast between the two writing styles appears most clearly at the end of no. 3, the six-part fantasia by William Byrd. As first copied, this piece concluded some nine breves early, without a return to duple time, as is quite clearly shown by the original fermata and the annotation, "ffinis Mr Byrd," which has been erased and covered by the additional music. At some later date the scribe added the concluding duple section. This was accomplished with some difficulty, however, for it was necessary to paste additional staves into some of the partbooks to accommodate the extra music. We thus find the austere and more flamboyant styles of writing juxtaposed on a single page (see pl. 17). The differences in the hand are perhaps best explained if we suppose that the more sprawling notation dates from a later period.

Pl. 17.   British Library Additional MS 17789, fol. 4ᵛ. The
scribe's "austere" and "flamboyant" hands, juxtaposed
on a single page.
(Reproduced by permission of the British Library)

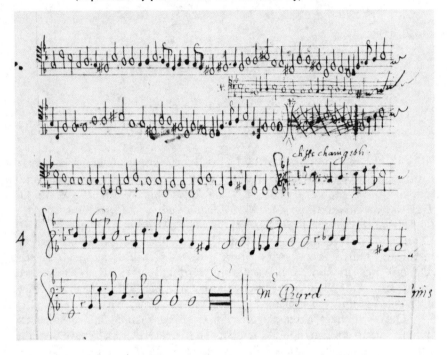

Although we cannot say precisely how much later the conclusion to the Byrd
six-part fantasia was inserted, it was probably added after some years.[4]
Because the Okeover, Peerson, and Ward fantasias appear in the less austere
hand, they must have been copied at a later date as well.

Despite the relative neatness and legibility of the text, the pieces are not
without numerous inaccuracies, whether missing or incorrect rests, incorrect
note values, or occasional incorrect pitches. This unreliability also extends to
the attributions of individual pieces. Number 7, *Abradad,* here ascribed to
Robert Parsons, is attributed to Richard Farrant in Christ Church MSS 984-8
(the Dow MSS). The most recent scholarly writing on the subject gives greater
credence to the Christ Church source, which is "earlier and generally more
reliable."[5] The eighth composition, *My little sweet darling,* here attributed to
William Byrd, appears anonymously in all other sources, including Christ
Church 984-8. Although the ascription has long been accepted,[6] considerable
doubt has been thrown on the matter, largely because of the nonimitative
character of the instrumental parts, which disagree with Byrd's usual practice

in consort song accompaniments.[7] Though he may be considered a proficient scribe, the compiler of Add. 17786-91 therefore cannot always be trusted, either in matters of notation or attribution.

The absence of the words from many of the consort songs points to the necessity of a seventh partbook, now lost, similar in character to 17790, which provides words and duplicates the principal melodic line for a number of songs, whose musical texts are complete in the remaining five books.[8] On the basis of Add. 17786-91, only those songs can be completely reconstructed for which verbal texts are found in 17790. It is useful to attempt a reconstruction of the contents of the missing volume, however tentative it may be:

7. *Abradad*, R. Parsons
9. *Climb not too high*, N. Patrick
11. *Daphne**, anon.
13. *Joan quoth John*, R. Nicolson
14. *This merry pleasant spring*, anon.
18. *Sweet youth**, anon
20. *There is a garden*, [R. Jones]
21. *Come hither*, W. Wigthorpe
22. *Orlatto*, anon.
23. *Smiths are good fellows*, W. Wigthorpe
27. *Sweet was the song*, anon.
28. *What meat eats the Spaniard*, anon
29. *I am not I of such belief*, W. Wigthorpe
35. *Of all jolly pastimes*, anon.
37. *Lift up your eyes**, J. Holmes
38. *Prepare to die*, N. Patrick

1. *Fantasia 1*, J. Coperario
2. *Fantasia 2*, J. Coperario

O Lord Arise, T. Weelkes
O sing unto the Lord, T. Tomkins

Three of these pieces take the form of a dialogue: *Joan quoth John, Come hither*, and *I am not I of such belief*. The additional partbook must have contained missing stanzas of their texts, which are incomplete as they stand.[9] Those songs with asterisks in the catalogue of the missing partbook could simply have been instrumental pieces. No. 11, *Daphne*, exists in several other sources as a purely instrumental work,[10] but because it is grouped with a number of vocal pieces in 17786-91 it seems quite probable that this was a vocal version with words and melody contained in the missing partbook.[11] No. 37, *Lift up your eyes* by "Mr Holmes Winton" is more problematic. Another version entitled *Lift up your eyes to the skies* occurs as a virginal piece by R. Creighton in Paris, Rés. 1186, folio 21. On the other hand, the obvious madrigalism at the opening of the piece seems to cry out for texting, and indeed, the initial phrase treats an ascending point in imitation (see ex. 1). The title has an obvious Biblical ring about it, though there is no verse which begins precisely in this fashion.[12] Neither Simpson[13] nor Sternfeld and Greer[14] reveals a parallel among secular texts. It is therefore impossible to state definitely that the Holmes piece was intended for vocal performance by the compiler of 17786-91.

Ex. 1. *Lift up your eyes*

The two viol pieces by Coperario included in the conjectural catalogue are needed to complement the parts which are extant in 17790. It is impossible to say if and where the organ part was included. There are no pieces by Coperario in 17786-89 or 17791.

One of the most interesting questions raised by the "sextus" and missing seventh partbooks is the possibility of an alternative method of performance to that normally assumed for the consort song. Arkwright has suggested that the textless versions of the songs in 17786-91 were meant for use in a purely instrumental performance, when there was no singer available.[15] It would have been an exorbitant waste of time, however, to copy the principal melodic parts twice, once with text and once without, simply to make the collection "apt for voices and viols." The duplication must have been made to provide a separate part for both a viol player and a singer, to be used concurrently. *Smiths are good fellows* offers further confirmation for this hypothesis. In this instance, the "singing part" (17790) does not simply double the part in 17786 throughout, but introduces rests for the instrumental interlude of bars 24-27.[16] The scribe must have wanted the voice and viol to perform together for the rest of the song. By extension, the same would apply to the rest of the collection, when 17786 and 17790 duplicate one another. It is probable, therefore, that the singer would be doubled by an instrumental part: the ensemble would consist of a singer and *five* viols, rather than a singer and four viols.[17]

One may reasonably surmise that the performance practice implied by 17786-91 could also extend to the other sources discussed above where verse anthems occur. In partbooks such as Myriell's *Tristitiae Remedium* or Merro's Drexel 4180-5, where some portions of a musical part are texted, it seems unlikely that viols would have stopped playing when words appeared in their parts. The singers must simply have joined them at that point, while the viols continued to play.[18]

The manuscripts are subdivided into groups of pieces for five, six, and seven parts, an arrangement which is followed very consistently, the only exception being the Byrd six-part fantasia and the two two-part fantasias by Coperario in 17790. Within these sections we find groups of pieces of similar character, and on the basis of the variations in the hand described above, it may be possible to establish the order in which the groups were entered in the manuscripts.

The partbooks open with a set of six instrumental pieces by Robert Parsons, William Byrd, and anonymous. The Parsons and Byrd pieces must have been composed long before the compilation of the manuscripts. The piece which follows the Byrd fantasias, here simply entitled *A Toy*, is in fact a five-part setting of the popular tune, "Wilson's Wild" (unrelated to the "Wolseys Wild" attributed to Byrd in the *Fitzwilliam Virginal Book*, however). The last two, *Hollis berrie* and *The Wyche*, are similar in character to *A Toy*.[19] *The Wyche* apparently served for Jonson's *The Masque of Queens* (1609).[20] After this initial group of instrumental pieces, a large number of consort songs and dialogues appears (nos. 7-29). The first six, like the opening instrumental works, are quite early. Thus, the works on the first six folios of the manuscripts largely comprise the "old-fashioned" section of the five-part pieces, copied first.

With no. 13, *Joan quoth John*, the scribe turned his attention to the more modern generation, for as a rule, songs 13-29 date from around 1610. Nicolson, who had become master of the choristers at Magdalen College, Oxford ca. 1594-5, was active at the university at this time. Wigthorpe was organist of New College, Oxford, from 1598-1610. Robert Jones's *Ultimum Vale*, containing no. 20, *There is a garden*, appeared in 1605. By far the most common composer in this section is William Wigthorpe, whose name appears with no less than six of the seventeen pieces in the group. Two of these, *Sorrow come* and *To plead my faith*, are consort versions of lute ayres by Dowland and Bachelor, respectively. It has been suggested that *There is a garden, Daphne*, and *Sweet was the song* are also Wigthorpe arrangements,[21] and it is quite likely that others are his work as well.

No. 22, which goes under the title *Orlatto*, remains one of the more puzzling pieces in the source. As the example shows (ex. 2) one part is especially prominent, entering after a three-bar introduction in the lower parts. No ready explanation comes to mind to make sense of this strange line, which presents countless repeated eighth-notes, or jumps about on the notes of the underlying triads. Perhaps *Orlatto* was intended as a piece for some solo instrument with

Ex. 2.   *Orlatto*

four-part accompaniment, or it might even have been a prototype for Charles Butler's music for bees, where the parts contain similar repeated patterns.[22] The real solution to the mysteries of this odd work may have vanished with the missing partbook. The four-part introduction has much in common with those found in consort songs, while the monotone solo part is very reminiscent of the vocal lines in the popular "Cries." In addition, the short middle section in triple time recalls similar passages in the "Cries," or the lighter, more modern play songs. It is possible, therefore, that *Orlatto* was originally intended as a "Cry"-like consort song, but has escaped notice since its text did not survive.

Two playsongs in the collection, nos. 7 and 10, are headed with titles, *Abradad* and *Pandolpho*, rather than with their opening lines. Perhaps *Orlatto*, too, was a song from a play in which "Orlatto" was either a character or a part of the title. A search through early seventeenth-century play titles has failed to yield a character or title corresponding exactly to "Orlatto." But the name is remarkably like "Orlando," which, before one or two scribal errors, could have been the original form. At this period "Orlando" usually refers to Ariosto's *Orlando Furioso*. An English play by Robert Greene, *The History of Orlando Furioso*, had been performed in 1591 and printed in 1594.[23] One other piece of music at least, entitled *Orlando* or *Orlando sleepeth*, may have been intended for this play, as John Ward has conjectured.[24] Perhaps the present work might also have found a place in some production of this popular story. It seems quite likely that *Orlatto* is another of Wigthorpe's arrangements, occurring as it does between two pieces bearing his name in the manuscripts. Indeed, the rather unskillfull part-writing, not without some parallel fifths or octaves, is characteristic of the New College organist.

No. 28, *What meat eats the Spaniard*, might also be a Wigthorpe arrangement, and it comes from a play, *Blurt, Master Constable*, produced in London. Like *Come hither, Smiths are good fellows*, and *I am not I of such belief*, all ascribed to Wigthorpe by name in the manuscripts, its text involves more than one protagonist. Such songs seem to have been a favorite with Wigthorpe. Furthermore, as pointed out in *Consort Songs*,[25] the version of *What meat eats the Spaniard* in 17786-91 appears to be an elaboration of an original five-part composition. We have seen that Wigthorpe was very fond of making such arrangements, and it seems reasonable to suppose that he was responsible for this work as well. It is possible, therefore, that eleven of the seventeen more "modern" songs (nos. 15 and 20-29) were Wigthorpe's work, making him by far the best-represented composer in the collection.

After this large group of consort songs the scribe turned to purely instrumental music for nos. 30-34. The first two of these form an interesting pavan-galliard pair: *Mr Dowland's Lachrimae* and *James his Galliard*. The version of the pavan in 17786-91 virtually duplicates the treble and bass of Dowland's *Flow my tears* as it appears in his *Second Book* of 1600, while differing slightly from Dowland's *Lachrimae or Seaven Teares* of 1605. The British Library arrangement is not in a-minor like Dowland's, however, but in d-minor, like the version in Morley's *First Book of Consort Lessons* (1599), which, however, it closely duplicates only in its bassline.

The original source therefore must have been Dowland's *Second Book,* which the five-part consort arrangement most closely follows. This possibility is strengthened by the fact that the only other Dowland arrangement in the manuscripts, *Dowland's Sorrow* (i.e., *Sorrow stay*), follows *Lachrimae* in the 1600 collection. It is also quite likely that Wigthorpe was responsible for the *Lachrimae* arrangement as well as for *Dowland's Sorrow,* for his inexpert contrapuntal technique could be revealed in the many parallel fifths or octaves.[26] In making the arrangement, Wigthorpe probably transposed the piece to d-minor to make it fit with the galliard.

James his galliard was clearly a popular dance, judging by the number of sources in which it appears. A version ascribed to Byrd occurs in the *Fitzwilliam Virginal Book,* again paired with the *Lachrimae Pavan,* transposed to d-minor. *Lachrimae* and *James his galliard* are also associated in a bass viol book in the Cambridge University Library (Dd 5.20).[27] Other copies turn up in British Library Add. 30826-8, Cambridge, Fitzwilliam Museum, Lord Herbert of Chirbury's lute book, and Yale University Music Library Filmer MS 2. The galliard was published on the continent as a five-part instrumental piece in 1607 as part of Füllsack's *Auserlesene Paduanen.* Keyboard versions are known from Berlin, Preussische Staatsbibliothek Mus. MS 40316, fol. 12 ("Mr James his Galliard"), and Paris, Rés. 1185, p. 112. Finally, another arrangement entitled "Galliarda Ferrabosco" (!) appeared in the seventeenth-century Dutch publication *'t Uitnemend kabinet.*[28] The nature of the consort arrangement in 17786-91 is similar to that of *Lachrimae,* and very probably by the same composer. The less than expert control of the contrapuntal lines, with occasional parallel fifths and octaves, once again suggests Wigthorpe.

The group of pieces from no. 35 through no. 40, mixing instrumental pieces, consort songs, and a madrigal, contradicts the systematic groupings encountered in the previous portions of the manuscript. Numerous scribal details suggest that the compiler was trying to fill out the gathering as best he could.[29] The various pieces at his disposal were insufficient to use up the remaining folios, so he was forced to spread them out as much as possible, adorning the unused staves with circular scribbles. The result was a musical miscellany gathering up various loose ends, quite inconsistent with the relatively systematic structure of the earlier sections of the partbooks.

Grace my lovely one, fair beauties, the only canzonet piece in madrigalian style in nos. 1-40, was entered after a few folios left blank, probably to receive more consort songs. The madrigal must have been entered separately and perhaps slightly later than the earlier layers, since the ink is much lighter than that on the surrounding folios. *Grace my lovely one* is known from one other source which is believed to be in Weelkes's own hand,[30] and which has twice passed through Sotheby's in recent years. On this holograph, the madrigal is described "Sir: Frances Steward, his Canzonett." According to Foster,[31] Frances Steward matriculated at Oxford on 15 March 1603/04 at the age of 15, and received his B.A. degree on 26 February 1605/06. On 15 March 1616 the M.A. degree was conferred upon him. Anthony Wood provides the following description of Steward:

> 1616: July 9. *Francis Stewart* of *Ch. Ch.* (Knight of the *Bath*) one of the Sons of Earl *Murrey,* was actually created Master of Arts. -He was a learned Gentleman, was one of Sir *Walt. Raleigh's* Club at the *Meremaid* Tavern in *Fryday-Street* in *London,* and much venerated by *Ben Johnson,* who dedicated to him his Comedy called *The Silent Woman.* He was a Person also well seen in marine Affairs, was a Captain of a Ship, and, as I have been informed by those who remember him, did bear the Office for sometime of a Vice, or Reer, Admiral.[32]

According to Foster, Steward must have been in Oxford between 1603/04 and 1605/06. Thomas Weelkes received his B. Mus. from New College in 1602. Wigthorpe took his B. Mus. in 1605. Weelkes might have become acquainted with this artistic relation of the king during Steward's sojourn in Oxford. More probably, however, they met at the Mermaid Tavern circle, of which Weelkes must have been a member, to judge by the text of *The ape, the monkey and baboon* from his 1608 *Ayres.*[33] Indeed, *Grace my lovely one* is perhaps closest in style to this, Weelkes's latest collection, and the apparent occasional nature of its text also reflects a trend from that set. The character of the text strongly suggests a wedding:

> Grace my lovely one, fair beauties,
> Every Nymph show me your duties,
> fa la la...
> Attend with mirth and fa la laes,
> Whilst this my love so kindly stays,
> and then ile Joy that Joyes of mine,
> shall thus be graced by graces nine,
> fa la la...

As yet, no information about Steward's marital history has come to light. The so-called Weelkes holograph is headed "Sir Frances Steward," which seems to indicate that it was not copied until after June 1610, the date when Sir Frances became a Knight of the Bath. Most probably this corresponds roughly to the date of composition. The scribe of 17786-91 might have acquired it either through his connection with Thomas Weelkes or through his connections with dramatic circles, an interest which Steward apparently shared, to judge by Jonson's dedication of *The Silent Woman.*

Beginning with folio 18 we encounter a change, both in the character of the hand and in the nature of the pieces, for nos. 41-55 are all purely instrumental. As mentioned above, the hand becomes much more sprawling, by comparison with the precise, closely spaced notation at the beginning of the manuscript, and persists until folio 30. As the catalogue of the partbooks reveals, the scribe was very meticulous in providing attributions for the instrumental compositions. Among this group only nos. 50 and 51 are recorded without the names of their composers, but number 50 appears in a number of other sources with an attribution to Richard Dering.

The difficulties in dating this section are largely caused by one "John Okeover Wellensis," who dominates folios 18-30. According to Wyn K. Ford,[34] it is reasonable to assume that he was born about 1600 and died sometime after 1662. Anthony Wood writes of him:

1633 Batch of Music. *July 5. John Okeover* of *New* Coll. Organist and Vicar choral of the Church of *Wells.* -He hath composed several Ayres of 2 and three Parts for the violin and Viol, which, I think, are extant. He succeeded in the said Organist's place one *Rich. Browne,* an eminent Musician, 16 *Feb.* 1619.[35]

Okeover was a practicing musician at least as early as 1616[36] and must have been actively composing in the 1620s, when he held the organist's post at Wells. Perhaps before Okeover took his degree from New College in 1633 his instrumental fantasias came to the attention of the scribe of 17786-91. Sometime around 1620 the scribe must have renewed his interest in the viol fantasia. When copying the Okeover, Ward, and Dering pieces into the partbooks, he may have discovered a longer version of the six-part Byrd fantasia entered years before at the beginning of the partbooks. Considerable alteration of the partbooks proved necessary in order to update the Byrd piece, and extra staves had to be added in some cases. This would explain the juxtaposition of the "old" and "new" hands on folio 4^V of the partbooks (see pl. 17).

After an entire gathering of blank folios (ignored in the modern foliation), the section of six-part compositions begins on folio 32^V. The numbering of the pieces only begins with the second, Byrd's *Laudate pueri,* however. This work, which opens the sixth gathering, is quite definitely in the "old" hand and must have been copied around the same time as the earliest section of the five-part works. The hand of nos. 2-5 and no. 7 is ambiguous. The Dering pieces (nos. 3 and 4) were presumably not composed until around 1610.[37] The Ramsey piece must be of similar date. The composer did not receive his B. Mus. from Cambridge until 1616, and was still active in 1644 at Trinity College. His earliest datable composition to my knowledge is *What tears, dear Prince,* inspired by the death of Prince Henry in 1612. No. 6, "for 6 voc: Tho: Weelkes," is very problematic. The script is much less elegant than that of the rest of the manuscript. The musical notation, too, is quite different, and finds its nearest parallel in that of the two Patrick pieces, nos. 38-39. It seems that the Weelkes piece was crammed into two blank staves at some later date.

The unnumbered Weelkes *Gloria in excelsis Deo* of folio 32ᵛ is quite definitely in the "later" hand. It is the only one of the six-part vocal pieces not for the combination with two basses. The scribe must have discovered it too late to include it with the other six-part vocal works. He had no alternative but to insert it on some of the blank pages at the end of the fifth gathering, presumably intended for five-part compositions. This explains why the numbering of the six-part works only begins with the Byrd piece.

It is interesting to note the "instrumental" character of the six-part vocal works. The six-part combination with two basses was one normally associated with instrumental consort music, where the usual six-part viol consort consisted of two trebles, two tenors, and two basses. Byrd's *Laudate Pueri* probably expresses this instrumental bias. As Joseph Kerman has pointed out,[38] the motet is an adaptation of an earlier instrumental piece, appearing in Christ Church MSS 979-83:

> There exists a contemporary adaptation to English words, *Behold now praise the Lord*, deviating musically from the motet only in rhythmic detail...The entire "anthem" left textless for instrumental performance, occurs in Add. 17786-91 under the title "Laudate pueri .6 voc. 2 basses."

The rest of the six-part section is devoted to fantasias and almains by Martin Peerson, systematically arranged into fantasia-almain pairs. Once again the hand appears in its later version. Presumably they were added at the same time when the scribe's renewed interest in viol fantasias led him to copy the five-part pieces, nos. 41-55.

At the conclusion of the partbooks, after seventeen blank folios (ignored in the modern foliation), the scribe has included a pair of unnumbered seven-part pieces: Weelkes's *O Lord arise* and Tomkins's *O sing unto the Lord a new song*. A proper section of seven-part pieces must not originally have been conceived as part of the manuscripts. Whilst the scribe was careful to begin the six-part section after several blank folios but at the beginning of a gathering, the seven-part pieces are simply inserted at the very end of the partbooks, apparently an after-thought. Evidently David Brown was not the first to realize that these two works were tangibly related.[39] Perhaps the compiler of 17786-91 reached the same conclusion and decided to add this later seven-part section at the very end of his partbooks.

This extended discussion of the overall character of 17786-91 helps to clarify the central questions about its date and provenance. Although most of the evidence has already been put forward in previous pages, it might be well to summarize it here.

First, the majority of the composers represented in 17786-91 have some connection with Oxford. The following matriculated or received degrees at Oxford between 1590 and 1635:

1595:	Richard Nicolson	(Magdalen)
1597:	Robert Jones	(St. Edmund Hall)
1602:	Thomas Weelkes	(New College)
1605:	William Wigthorpe	(New College)
1607:	Thomas Tomkins	(Magdalen)
1610:	Richard Dering	(Christ Church)
1613:	Martin Peerson	(Lincoln)
1633:	John Okeover	(New College)

In addition, Sir Frances Steward, whose canzonet appears on folio 17^v, was at Christ Church from 1603/04 to 1605/06.

The connections with New College are particularly strong, and those with Magdalen are likewise noteworthy. The two composers of vocal music in 17786-91 whose compositions are most numerous, Thomas Weelkes and William Wigthorpe, were both connected with New College. John Okeover, represented by no less than nine instrumental works, received his B. Mus. through New College in 1633. Furthermore, the fact that the partbooks contain a work by the comparatively obscure composer, John Holmes, organist of Winchester, seems more than coincidental, for Winchester is the site of the other Wykhamist foundation, Winchester College, where Thomas Weelkes had been organist in the years before he took his B. Mus. from New College in 1602.

The Oxford provenance is confirmed by the previously unrecognized connection of 17786-91 with Tenbury MS 1382. This single tenor partbook has been extensively described by John Morehen,[40] who suggested that it may have been compiled at the behest of Jarves Jones in Oxford between 1612 and 1617, possibly by a professional scribe. Morehen further suggests that Jones may have consulted Thomas Fido (B.A. Magdalen, 1606) about the choice of music, which would explain the large number of works in Tenbury 1382 by John Fido, assistant organist to Thomas Tomkins at Worcester, and also the large number of pieces by Tomkins himself.

The Tenbury source has four concordances with 17786-91:

	17786	1382
Gloria in excelsis	32^v	62
Laudate pueri	33^v	63
O Lord arise	45^v	64^v
O sing unto the Lord	46^v	65^v

The discussion of 17786 has shown that *Laudate pueri* was the first work to be copied in the six-part section of the MS. The text duplicates that in 1382 exactly, except for two half-notes, which in 1382 are divided to accommodate separate syllables of text. The text of Weelkes's *Gloria in excelsis deo,* on the other hand, which had been added later on blank folios before *Laudate pueri* in 17786, shows several differences in the two sources, the most significant being the translation of the opening Latin phrase of text in 1382 and the omission of the repetition of the entire "Gloria in excelsis" section before the "Amen" in that source. For the two seven-part works not only are the readings virtually identical (in *O Lord arise* 17786 breaks up one ligature and combines shorter notes in two repetitions of the concluding word, "alleluia"; in *O sing unto the Lord* 17786 adds a redundant sharp to the second of two repeated notes; there are also a few discrepancies in spelling—"New" versus "newe," etc.), but the layout on the page, with the same amount of music per stave, is the same. Clearly both manuscripts must derive from a common source, or perhaps one might even have been copied from the other.

Morehen points out that 1382 shows strong connections with Magdalen College. Add. 17786-91, on the other hand, shows equally strong connections with New College. The strongest candidate as scribe would be William Wigthorpe, or at least a close associate.[41] Wigthorpe could scarcely be called a first class composer; his works never achieved national renown, and he was not among the contributors to *The Triumphs of Oriana,* by contrast with several other relatively obscure composers. Add. 17786-91 is the largest known collection of his works. Indeed, he is represented in only three other sets of manuscripts: Bodl. MS Mus. D 162, Bodl. MSS Mus. E 23-25 (both sets originating from New College), and Tenbury MS 791. As has been shown, several of the compositions or arrangements which are not attributed to him in the partbooks may be his own. The following is a tentative list (compositions bearing Wigthorpe's name in the partbooks have an asterisk):

11. *Daphne*
15. *Dowland's Sorrow**
20. *There is a garden*
21. *Come hither**
22. *Orlatto*
23. *Smiths are good fellows**
24. *Were I made juror**
25. *Venus birds*
26. *To plead my faith**
27. *Sweet was the song*
28. *What meat eats the Spaniard*
29. *I am not I of such belief**
30. *Mr. Dowland's Lachrimae*
31. *James his galliard*

This makes a total of fourteen compositions, of which almost half bear attributions. The total is greatly out of proportion to the composer's skill or renown. Surely no one but the composer himself or a close associate would have had access to, or an interest in, so many of Wigthorpe's works.

Unfortunately, very little is known of Wigthorpe's life. He was apparently a chorister at Winchester Cathedral, since his name was carved on Bishop Gardiner's chantry in 1592, and appears in the cathedral records of 1597 in this capacity.[42] In the following year he moved to New College, where he matriculated on 19 May 1598. He is described as "of Hampshire" and "plebeus," the lowest grade on the social scale at matriculation, in the Matriculations Register. Wigthorpe supplicated for the degree of B. Mus. on 2 July and was admitted on 4 July 1605. With the last reference is a note that he was of New College and had been a student of music for ten years.[43] He remained at New College as organist until 1610, after which he disappears from sight. It has proved impossible to find an authentic signature of Wigthorpe to compare with the hand in 17786-91. There is no record of a signature at New College, and the entry in the Oxford Subscription Register appears to have been made by someone who copied several names in a row into the Register.

These records show that Wigthorpe was in Oxford at the same time as Nicolson, Weelkes, Tomkins, and Frances Steward, who all bear some relation to the present partbooks, and also at the same time as Thomas Fido of Magdalen, who John Morehen suggests may have been important to the compilation of Tenbury 1382. Interestingly enough, Wigthorpe and those composers of his own generation or younger (John Bennet, Thomas Weelkes, John Okeover, John Ward, Richard Dering, Robert Ramsey, Martin Peerson—like John Fido in 1382) are not referred to as "Mr.," a title reserved for composers presumably older and more venerable than the copyist (Mr Byrd, Mr Parson, Mr Richard Farrant, Mr Nicolson, Mr Dowland, Mr Holmes). The exceptions to this rule are few. Patrick is treated ambivalently; Weelkes rates a "Mr" only at the very end of the partbooks. It seems likely that Wigthorpe or some close associate first copied the "oldest layer" of the manuscripts, the older instrumental pieces and the consort songs represented by nos. 1-12 (fols. 1-7), and the Byrd *Laudate pueri* (fol. 33^V). These were followed immediately or shortly thereafter (ca. 1610-15) by the more up-to-date songs (nos. 13-29, fols. 8-13^V, and no. 35, fol. 15^V), more modern instrumental pieces (nos. 30-34, fols. 14-15), and a madrigal or two (no. 40, fol. 17^V and no. 2, fol. 34^V).

A considerable time may have passed before the manuscripts were taken up again in earnest. Perhaps because of some new stimulus in the direction of the instrumental fantasia, nos. 41-55 (fols. 18-30^V) and nos. 8-20 (fols. 38^V-44^V) were added, probably in the early 1620s, and the correction was made in the Byrd six-part fantasia (fol. 4^V). The passage of time may explain the change in the scribe's hand. Nos. 36-39 (fols. 15^V-17^V), the Weelkes *Gloria in excelsis* (fol. 32^V), nos. 3-7 (fols. 35^V-38), and the two seven-part compositions (fols. 45^V-46^V) remain ambiguous. Possibly they were added intermittently in the period between the "early" and "late" layers.

Add. 17786-91 offers a revealing view of one side of musical life during the first half of the reign of James I, providing a link between the few older sources of the late Elizabethan period and the proliferation of manuscripts from the latter half of James's reign. The earlier period is poorly represented by manuscripts for voices and viols, and therefore the Oxford set becomes more important for a comprehensive view of the verse idiom during the Jacobean period.

The scribe was guided primarily by two central interests: music for viol consort and music for the theater. These basic interests may in part explain his concentration upon secular music, by contrast with several of his contemporaries (e.g., Myriell, Merro, James Pearson, and somewhat later, Thomas Hamond), who all admit many works of a sacred character, either in English or Latin. Indeed, it is significant that two of the four "anthems" which the scribe includes, Weelkes's *Gloria in excelsis deo* and *Hosannah to the Son of David,* were probably intended for secular rather than liturgical occasions, and hold their places in the modern cathedral repertory primarily because of the taste of twentieth-century musicians, whose ideas of musical decorum differ from those of the Jacobean era, when these pieces probably bore much more tenuous links to church and chapel.[44] The omission of Latin motets is also notably at odds with many of the other secular sources which express an interest in the verse idiom. As mentioned above, Byrd's *Laudate Pueri,* the only recognizable "motet," is in fact a wordless version of an English adaptation, here intended for performance as a fantasia. A look beyond the incipit of the other ecclesiastical sounding title, *Resurrexit a mortuus,* reveals a macaronic text of decidedly secular bent.

The compiler placed little reliance upon printed collections, considerably less than most of the other important manuscript sources.[45] Indeed, the influence of the prints is still less direct, since the few works taken from them are as a rule subjected to some sort of rearrangement.[46] It is also interesting to note that the few printed sources form part of the lute ayre repertory, to the total exclusion of madrigalian publications. Indeed, the scribe is notably rigorous in his exclusion of the madrigal, represented by only two isolated (and relatively undistinguished) examples which never appeared in print. This may, however, be attributed as much to the scribe's neglect of purely vocal music as a whole as to some dissatisfaction with the madrigalian aesthetic. One can also not rule out the possibility that the scribe had ready access to madrigal prints and felt no need to duplicate them.

The interest in strictly instrumental music may have provided the original impetus for the compilation. That is what is suggested by the fact that both the five- and six-part sections originally began with instrumental groups, including some works dating back at least twenty-five years. By comparison with these older, relatively large-scale works by Byrd and Parsons, the rather slight little pieces such as *The Witch* seem very insubstantial. Such arrangements of popular tunes for viols are less common as a rule than those for lute or keyboard, and again might be another reflection of Wigthorpe's penchant for arranging pre-existent materials, in this instance for viols alone. Since they occur in the midst of so many play songs, it seems quite probable that they served as incidental music for such dramatic entertainments. *The Witch* seems especially suitable for some sort of stylized stage business, for it contains several bars of sustained chords interspersed throughout the piece and emphasized by fermatas in this source. Indeed, as mentioned earlier, David Fuller has identified it as "the first Witches' Dance" from Jonson's *The Masque of Queens* of 1609.[47] Perhaps other of these brief pieces once fulfilled a similar function.

The continuing interest in instrumental music is likewise reflected by the later additions to the manuscripts: the fantasias (and almains) by Okeover, Peerson, Ward, and Dering. These in fact represent the scribe's only real concession to the "modern" trends of ca. 1610-20. Much like Merro in Add. 17792-6, the scribe of this Oxford source draws his most up-to-date materials from the strictly instrumental repertory, ignoring the contemporary works for voices and viols or for voices alone by Peerson, East, Ward, Simms, or Ravenscroft.

But 17786-91 is of greatest interest as a purveyor of works in the verse idiom during the earlier part of the Jacobean era, apparently a period during which this older genre was in a state of flux, adapting and absorbing elements from newer musical developments such as the madrigal and lute ayre. One encounters an unusually strong emphasis upon the solo consort song, which here provides some seventeen examples, more than in any other important source with the exception of Paston's books. The scribe's inclusion of so many consort songs is primarily an expression of his interest in the theater, an interest not confined to contemporary theatrical pieces, but also affording special prominence to play songs from Elizabeth's reign. These include, in addition to such relatively popular pieces as *Abradad* and *Pandolpho,* a number of others, *O Jove from stately throne, Send forth thy sighs, Prepare to die,* all by N. Patrick, unique to this source. The Patrick pieces probably reaffirm the connection with Worcester, via the Fido family prominent in Tenbury 1382 (John Fido succeeded Patrick as organist in 1595).[48] The only other source with a comparable number of Elizabethan play songs is Robert Dow's much earlier collection, more nearly contemporary with this musico-dramatic phenomenon. Perhaps the scribe of 17786-91 found these old songs too good to ignore (the most popular of them would, after all, continue to be recopied until about 1615). Or perhaps, having found their way to Oxford in Dow's collection, they were adopted for use in modest dramatic productions in New College choir school or for choir training, to which the more modern dramatic songs and dialogues would be equally suited.[49]

The remaining body of the consort songs, on the other hand, reflects later musical developments, whether in the realm of the lute ayre or of music for the Jacobean stage. Wigthorpe was especially drawn to the lute ayre, then enjoying its heyday. It seems reasonable for him to turn to this genre rather than to the madrigal because of the greater similarity between the musical aesthetic of consort song and lute ayre, not only with regard to the basic idea of combining solo voice and instruments, but also with regard to the choices of poetry and the similar manner of projecting the texts. Wigthorpe's method in *Sorrow stay* from Dowland's *Second Book* and *There is a garden* from Jones's *Ultimum Vale* consists of preserving tune and bass line quite literally, while adding new inner parts. The musical results are usually not much more contrapuntal or imitative than their lute originals, and stay closer to their models than, for example, the other consort arrangement of the Dowland song in Add. MSS 37402-6.[50]

Aside from these lute ayre arrangements, the remainder of the consort songs can be connected with Jacobean drama, either through external evidence or on the basis of textual or musical similarities to identified play songs. The text of the narrative comic interlude, *What meat eats the Spaniard*, for example, appears at the end of Act I of *Blurt, Master Constable*, published in 1602.[51] No. 25, *Venus Birds*, on the other hand, may also have originated in a play, as Mary Chan suggests on the basis of the textual variants in other sources.[52] Another half dozen pieces might also fall into this category, though no concrete references to them in plays have yet come to light:

13.   *Joan quoth John**, R. Nicolson
21.   *Come hither**, W. Wigthorpe
22.   *Orlatto*, anon.
23.   *Smiths are good fellows**, W. Wigthorpe
29.   *I am not I of such belief**, W. Wigthorpe
35.   *Of all jolly pastimes*, anon.

Of these, four are dialogues (marked with asterisks), either for different voices singing different verses or for a duet over three accompanying viols. In addition, *Of all jolly pastimes* may originally have involved two soloists as well.[53] Their similarity to the known playsong, *What meat eats the Spaniard*, suggests that they, too, might have fulfilled a similar dramatic role. While there are no extant examples of such dialogues from the older play song repertory,[54] they became popular after the turn of the century, chiefly through the lute ayre.[55]

In addition to the duos, there are also a few pieces incorporating a chorus at their conclusions: no. 17, *Born is the babe* and no. 23, *Smiths are good fellows*. In both instances the choral sections are utterly simply, merely involving a varied repetition of the final solo phrase. Here again, there was some precedent for such "verse anthem-like" conclusions, chiefly in the works of William Byrd.[56] The trend in evidence here also appears in the roughly contemporary Add. MSS 37402-6, and also finds its way into print concurrently in collections such as Michael East's *Third Set* (1610), Ravenscroft's *Deuteromelia* (1609), and *Melismata* (1611), all of which include brief, uncomplicated pieces for solo voices and viols, concluding with choruses, and attest to the increased popularity of this simple manifestation of the verse idiom, for which 17786-91 provides some of the earlier examples.

More than anything else 17786-91 seems to represent the musical character of one man, or at least, one circle of instrumentalists. It may have been the prominence which consort songs allow to viol players that originally prompted the inclusion of so many songs here, for otherwise the scribe shows relatively little interest in vocal music. But in any event, he provides one of the clearest witnesses to the development of the dramatic song for voices and viols during the reigns of Elizabeth I and James I. While the source continues to transmit the contrapuntal songs of the Elizabethan stage tradition in unusual numbers, it also reveals new elements, largely derived from the lute ayre, which simplify the consort song, infusing it with a lighter tone and less complex texture. These later works, probably also intended for the stage, present a simpler manifestation of the verse idiom, one which contrasts with the other Jacobean form—the longer, elaborate, more contrapuntal verse anthems of Peerson, East, and Ravenscroft, which became popular in other sources during the second decade of the century.

While Add. 17786-91 may be connected closely with the taste of one Oxford musician, this taste was not peculiarly his own. It may, in fact, have been a special Oxford phenomenon, as the next source will show.

folio[1]	no.	Title	idiom	Composer	Prints

(five-part pieces)

folio[1]	no.	Title	idiom	Composer	Prints
1	1	De la courte		R. Parsons	
2ᵛ	2	Fantasia		W. Byrd	
3ᵛ	3	" (a 6)		" "	
4ᵛ	4	A toy			
5	5	Hollis berrie			
5	6	The wyche			
5ᵛ	7	*Abradad*	cs	R. Parsons	
6	8	*My little sweet darling*	cs	"Mr Byrd"[2]	
6ᵛ	9	*Climb not too high*	cs	N. Patrick	
6ᵛ	10	*Pandolpho*	cs	R. Parsons	
7	11	*Daphne*	cs		
7ᵛ	12	*O Jove from stately throne*	cs	R. Farrant	
8	13	*Joan quoth John. A Dialogue*	cd[3]	R. Nicolson	
8ᵛ	14	*This merry pleasant Spring*	cs		
9	15	*Dowland's Sorrow*[4]	cs	W Wigthorpe	
9ᵛ	16	*Eliza, her name gives honour*	cs	J. Bennet	
9ᵛ	17	*Born is the babe*	v		
10	18	Sweet youth			
10ᵛ	19	Resurrexit a mortuus	f		
11	20	*There is a garden*	cs	[R. Jones]	1605:10
11	21	*Come hither. A Dialogue*	cd	W. Wigthorpe	
11ᵛ	22	*Orlatto*	cs?		
11ᵛ	23	*Smiths are good fellows*	v	W. Wigthorpe	
12	24	*Were I made juror*	cs		
12ᵛ	25	*Venus birds*	cs	J. Bennet	
12ᵛ	26	*To plead my faith*[5]	cs	W. Wigthorpe	1610:6
13	27	*Sweet was the song*	cs		
13ᵛ	28	*What meat eats the Spaniard*	cd		
13ᵛ	29	*I am not I of such belief*	cd[6]	W. Wigthorpe	
14	30	Mr Dowland's Lacrimae			
14ᵛ	31	James his galliard			
14ᵛ	32	Tickle my toe			
15	33	Strawberry leaves			
15	34	My Robin is to the [greenwood gone]			
15ᵛ	35	*Of all jolly pastimes*	cd		
15ᵛ	36	Pavan		T. Weelkes	
16	37	Lift up your eyes		"Mr Holmes Winton"	
16ᵛ		*Prepare to die*	cs	N. Patrick	
16ᵛ		*Send forth thy sighs*	cs	" "	
17ᵛ	40	Grace my lovely one	f	T. Weelkes	
18	41	Pavan		J. Okeover	
18ᵛ	42	"		" "	
18ᵛ	43	Fantasia		" "	
19ᵛ	44	"		" "	
20ᵛ	45	"		" "	
21ᵛ	46	"		" "	
22ᵛ	47	"		" "	
23ᵛ	48	"		" "	
24ᵛ	49	"		J. Oker	
25ᵛ	50	"		[R. Dering]	
26ᵛ	51	"			
27ᵛ	52	"		J. Ward	
28ᵛ	53	"		" "	
29ᵛ	54	"		" "	
30ᵛ	55	"		" "	

(fols. 31ᵛ - 32 are blank)

(six-part pieces)

folio[1]	no.	Title	idiom	Composer	Prints
32ᵛ		Gloria in excelsis deo	f	T. Weelkes	
33ᵛ		Laudate pueri[7]		W. Byrd	
34ᵛ	2	Wilt thou unkind now leave me	f	R. Ramsey	
35ᵛ	3	Fantasia		R. Dering	
36ᵛ		"		" "	

---

1 Modern foliation

2 Questionable attribution.

3 Only the man's verses are extant.

4 Adaptation of Dowland's *Sorrow stay*.

5 Adaptation of Bachelor's *To plead my faith*.

6 The woman's reply is missing from the dialogue.

7 Words omitted from all parts.

folio	no.	Title	idiom	Composer	Prints
37^V	5	Pavan		T. Leetherland	
37^V	6	[untitled]		T. Weelkes	
38	7	Hosannah to the Son of David	f	" "	
38^V	8	Fantasia		M. Peerson	
39	9	Almain 1		" "	
39	10	Fantasia 2		" "	
40	11	Almain 2		" "	
40^V	12	Fantasia 3		" "	
41	13	Almain 3		" "	
41^V	14	Fantasia 4		" "	
42	15	Almain 4		" "	
42^V	16	Fantasia 5		" "	
43	17	Almain 5		" "	
43^V	18	Fantasia 6		" "	
44	19	Almain 6		" "	
44^V	20	Almain 7		" "	

(seven-part pieces)

folio	no.	Title	idiom	Composer	Prints
45^V		O Lord arise	f	T. Weelkes	
46^V		O sing unto the Lord...let	f	T. Tomkins	

fol.	no.	Title	idiom	Composer
1	3	Fantasia		W. Byrd
2	8	*My little sweet darling*	cs	
2^V	10	*Pandolpho*	cs	R. Parsons
3^V	12	*O Jove, from stately throne*	cs	R. Farrant
4	13	*John Quoth Joan. A Dialogue.*	cd	R. Nicolson
4^V	15	*Sorrow come*	cs	W. Wigthorpe
5^V	16	*Eliza, her name gives honour*	cs	J. Bennet
6^V	17	*Born is the babe*	v	
7^V	21	*Sir, what do you desire* [*Come hither*]	cd	W. Wigthorpe
8	23	*Smiths are good fellows*	v	" "
8^V	24	*Were i made juror*	cs	" "
9	26	*To plead my faith*	cs	" "
9^V	28	*What meat eats the Spaniard*	cd	
10	29	*I am not I of such belief*	cd	" "
10^V	35	*Of all jolly pastimes*	cd	
11	39	*Send forth thy sighs*	cs	N. Patrick

(fol. 12 blank)

| 12^V | 1 | Fantasia for two [bass] viols | | J. Coperario |
| 13^V | 2 | "   "   "   "   " | | "   " |

(fol. 14^V-15 blank)

15^V		Gloria in excelsis Deo	f	T. Weelkes
16^V		Laudate Pueri		W. Byrd
17^V	2	Wilt thou unkind now leave me	f	R. Ramsey
18^V	3	Fantasia		R. Dering
19^V	4	"		" "
20^V	5	Pavan		T. Leetherland
20^V	6	[untitled] for two basses		T. Weelkes
21	7	Hosannah to the son of David	f	" "
21^V	8	Fantasia 1		M. Peerson
22	9	Almain 1		" "
22^V	10	Fantasia 2		" "
23	11	Almain 2		" "
23^V	12	Fantasia 3		" "
24	13	Almain 3		" "
24^V	14	Fantasia 4		" "
25	15	Almain 4		" "
25^V	16	Fantasia 5		" "
26	17	Almain 5		" "
26^V	18	Fantasia 6		" "
27	19	Almain 6		" "
27^V	20	Almain 7		" "
28^V		O Lord arise	f	T. Weelkes
29^V		O sing unto the Lord	f	T. Tomkins

British Library Additional MS 17797

This little set of partbooks, all bound together in a single volume, is in many ways a companion to its nearby neighbor on the British Library shelves, Add. 17786-91. For 17797, all the external evidence points even more strongly toward Oxford as its point of origin. The most prominent composer, definitely responsible for seven compositions, and very likely the composer of several of the anonymous ones, is Richard Nicolson, master of the choristers at Magdalen College, Oxford, and the first Heather Professor of Music at the university. In addition, two verse anthems appended to the end of the collection bear the name of William Stonnard, organist of Christ Church, Oxford, from 1608 until 1630. Furthermore, the three anonymous consort songs based on church tunes, *Come Holy Ghost, O Lord of whom I do depend,* and *O Lord turn not away thy face,* survive in only one other source, Christ Church MSS 984-88, where they appear in the same sequence. The Christ Church partbooks originally belonged to Robert Dow, a fellow of All Souls' College, Oxford, from 1577 until his death in 1588, who may have copied these three works from the same source used by the scribe of 17797, as Philip Brett suggests.[57] Thus, 17797 is given over almost entirely to Oxford music and Oxford musicians.

The time of compilation, on the other hand is much less certain. The final verse anthems could not have been entered before 1608, since their composer is described as "Mr Will Stonnard Bach Musick," a distinction not attained by the Christ Church organist until that year. The three psalms, on the other hand, are decidedly archaic; they must date from before 1588, the year the other copyist, Robert Dow, died, and they may well be earlier still. The Nicolson pieces might have been composed any time after ca. 1595, when he became master of the choristers at Magdalen. Thus, one has very little to go on in pinning down the time when the set was compiled. Sometime between 1610 and 1620 might be most reasonable.

The identity of the copyist remains a puzzle. The prominence of Richard Nicolson, who provides the majority of the works in the set, immediately suggests that the hand might be his own or that of an intimate of his musical circle. Such a possibility is strengthened by the fact that while both Byrd and Stonnard are called "Mr," Nicolson's attributions range from "Mr Nicolson" to "R. Nic" to the simple. "RN." A problem arises, however, from the fact that another Oxford set, Bodl. MSS Mus. Sch. D 212-216 (discussed below), which also contains pieces by Nicolson and abbreviated attributions, including "RN," and which John Bergsagel suggests may have been copied by the Magdalen organist,[58] does not match the hand in 17797. There is no conclusive evidence to reveal which, if either, could be Nicolson's own handwriting, since he has left no sample of his hand in the archives of either Oxford University or Magdalen College. But when all the evidence has been considered, D 212-216 seems the more probable choice, as will be shown later. The abbreviations in 17797 could simply attest to Nicolson's prominence in Jacobean musical circles in Oxford. As organist of Magdalen and later as the first Heather Professor of Music, he must have been one of the leading lights of academic musical life, where his initials alone would leave no question as to the name implied.[59] Therefore, until further evidence comes to light, one can say nothing more than that this manuscript was probably the work of some member of Nicolson's musical circle in Oxford.

A glance at the layout of the partbooks suggests that two sections may originally have been intended, one devoted to consort songs and the other to "full" pieces of madrigalian character. With the exception of *What sudden change* all the works from *Cuckow* to *O Lord turn not away thy face* were intended for voice and viols. All those from *Thou marvailst much* to *Come infirmity/Come then sweet pity* are purely vocal, save *Sweet they say such virtue lies*, which despite its madrigalian character and texture lacks words in the three lower parts.[60] The opening madrigal and motet in the manuscript may have been added after this scheme had been conceived.

The character of Nicolson's consort songs in 17797 has much in common with the more modern examples in the Wigthorpe manuscripts, Add. 17786-91, which also happen to contain a song by Nicolson, as well as Wigthorpe's own setting of a text also set by the Magdalen organist. As we have seen, much of Wigthorpe's original inspiration derived from the lute ayre, some examples of which he actually arranged as consort songs. While there is no evidence to suggest that Nicolson (whose compositional skills quite definitely surpassed those of the New College organist) approached the consort song as an "arranger" of other composers' works, the style of his consort songs neverthe-less corresponds essentially to Wigthorpe's. Again, the works are often largely homophonic, with little or no imitation. The sole exception to this rule is *Cuckow,* the only consort song not actually ascribed to Nicolson in the source. The solo line clearly predominates over the accompaniment, which rarely even provides an introduction. Thus, the voice and viols are not on a relatively equal footing as they had been in Elizabethan consort songs, particularly those of William Byrd.

The presence of Nicolson's alternative setting of *I am not I of such belief,* also set by Wigthorpe in 17786-91, offers a rare opportunity to observe two different settings of the same text, a kind of comparison more frequently possible for the English madrigal but quite uncommon for the consort song.[61] It very likely testifies to the interchange between New College and Magdalen, and perhaps grew out of a spirit of friendly rivalry between the two choral foundations, still perceptible today. The rather cryptic text runs to two stanzas in Wigthorpe's version, where we find the heading, "A dialogue. man. woman." Only the man's verses survive:

1.
I am not, I, of such belief
That tears are always signs of grief;
That ev'ry face and varnish'd hue
Is nature's grace and beauty true;
That things which seem are so in deed;
That Pater noster is the Creed:
For women, for women,
I way no more you know my meaning.

2.
I cannot be induc'd to think
That all do sleep when as they wink.
That to dislike is to say "Fie!"
That to say no is to deny;
That heart affects when tongue doth gloze;
That each red flower is a rose:
for women...

The version in 17797, on the other hand, includes only the first stanza and lacks any suggestion that it might have been a dialogue. It is quite possible, of course, that the scribe simply neglected to add the extra stanzas.

Certain similarities between the two settings suggest that they were not composed in isolation, though one would be hard pressed to ascertain which came first. Both Wigthorpe and Nicolson obviously desired to stress the final couplet, (which for Wigthorpe's setting also serves as a refrain), and both chose the popular ABB form, so common in the consort song, allowing a total repetition of the final section. In addition, both include several reiterations of "for woman," the only fragment of text emphasized in this way in either version. Furthermore, as the following summaries of the cadences at the end of each line show, both Nicolson and Wigthorpe wished to make a major articulation in the middle of the stanza, where we find a return to the tonic, complete with a strong cadence, in both settings:

Nicolson   V   V   V   I   VII   V   ‖: I :‖

Wigthorpe   V   V   V   I   II   I   ‖: I :‖

Interestingly enough, both composers begin the fifth line with the melodic fragment that opened their song.

But, aside from these largely formal considerations, the approaches of the two composers differ significantly. While in Nicolson's setting (as in his consort songs in general), the primary attention is focused upon the voice, in Wigthorpe's version imitative counterpoint of a simple sort retains greater importance. This is also generally true of the other consort songs by the New College organist, whose contrapuntal orientation might derive from the many older, Elizabethan consort songs which appear in 17786-91. Thus, Wigthorpe begins with a very brief introduction in which tenor viol II anticipates the voice, while Nicolson simply opens with a tonic chord, with the singer's first note in the top viol part. The Magdalen version is interrupted repeatedly by rests in all parts, between vocal phrases. In the New College setting, on the other hand, simple imitations bridge these gaps. In his B-section, Wigthorpe again animates his setting through imitative interchange on the point, "for women," while Nicolson simply draws out the vocal line through sequential repetition of the same fragment in the voice. Further evidence of Nicolson's concentration upon the vocal line appears in his tendency to repeat melodic fragments: each of the first three couplets opens with the initial melody of the piece, either transposed or slightly modified. This is another feature which reappears in many other of Nicolson's works, both consort songs and madrigals, and may, again, reflect further influence of the lutenist song writers.

The three songs, *Come Holy Ghost, O Lord of whom I do depend,* and *O Lord turn not away thy face,* which reveal a more serious character and a more archaic style, show special ingenuity in their combination of the In Nomine tune in an inner part with Church Tunes from the "Old Version" psalters. The fact that in the source all three occur under the number "6" may indicate that the scribe conceived them as forming a whole because of these common features. Peter le Huray, perhaps following the lead of *The Catalogue of Manuscript Music in the British Museum,*[62] adds these works to the Nicolson canon on the basis of an attribution to "RN."[63] In neither 17797 nor the alternate source, Christ Church MSS 984-8, however, do we find such an attribution. More recently David Wulstan has written that "though anonymous, these songs are almost certainly by Nicolson ... The artistry which he brings to bear upon this three-fold *tour de force* again shows Nicolson to have been no mean contrapuntist."[64] The other source for these songs was compiled between 1581 and 1588, however, as Philip Brett has shown.[65] Simply on external evidence, therefore, it seems highly unlikely that Nicolson was their composer.

More interesting, perhaps, is the fact that they were still considered worth recopying more than twenty years after their entry in the Dow manuscripts. It would be very difficult to imagine Thomas Myriell for example, entering them in *Tristitiae Remedium.* But a comparison of Nicolson's own consort songs (or several of the more modern ones from the "companion set," 17786-91, for that matter) with *Come Holy Ghost, O Lord of whom I do depend,* and *O Lord turn not away thy face* shows that Nicolson probably would not have felt such a great discrepancy. Although his word-setting, use of shorter note values, and repetition of shorter vocal phrases might contrast with the practice in these three sacred songs, his harmonic style reveals little to set it apart from that in these Elizabethan examples. He avoids all the more modern gestures, which younger composers such as Michael East and Martin Peerson seemed consciously to emulate from 1610 onward. It is interesting that the sole example of the more up-to-date Italianate cadence with the stereotyped series of suspensions, $\begin{smallmatrix}7\,6\,5\\5\text{-}4\text{-}4\text{-}3\\3\end{smallmatrix}$, appears in *Sweet they say such virtue lies* (bars 46-47), which, as mentioned above, was probably a madrigal.[66]

A look at Nicolson's madrigals also makes it clear that he was hardly among the more *avant-garde* composers of his day in this genre. In his approach to the madrigal he seems to have been of two minds: on the one hand, attempting to follow the example set by Morley, Weelkes, and Wilbye, but on the other, continuing to think in terms of what Joseph Kerman has called "The Native Tradition of Secular Song."[67] With the exception of *Sing shepherds all,* Nicolson's contribution to *The Triumphs of Oriana,* all of his extant madrigals, appear in 17797, where three bear his name. As with the anonymous consort songs (except the psalms), it seems highly probable that the anonymous madrigals may also be his.[68] In *Sing shepherds all,* Nicolson's only work published during his lifetime, the composer seems consciously to emulate the lighter madrigalian style of the 1590s as best he can. We find considerable variety in texture, scoring, and range of note-values, with a preponderance of quarter-notes and eighth-notes.[69] Considerable imitation based on quick canzonet figures abounds. As in his consort songs, Nicolson offers little variety in his choice of imitative materials. The harmonic style is predominantly chordal, with frequent pedals, combined with the stereotyped cadential patterns so common in Morley's madrigals.

Some of the works from 17797 conform to this general pattern, as one can frequently predict from their texts alone. *What sudden change* and *Thou marvail'st much* both involve the common "burning" and "cold" of the afflicted lover, while *Sweet needle spare my Flora's hands* (anon.) draws upon the analogy between the wounds of the needle and the ones that Cupid inflicts. Of the madrigals in 17797, these three follow most closely the model of *Sing shepherds all* in their shorter note-values, frequent sprightly figures, contrasts in scoring and texture, and madrigalian harmonic idiom.

But a look at the other madrigals finds Nicolson's style set on a different tack. Many of their texts, while not given over to the sober moralizing often found in those set by Byrd, Mundy, Carlton, and Alison, betray traditional traits which at times seem more reminiscent of the Elizabethan play song than the madrigal. The text of *Farewell the joys* is obviously a lament on the death of a lover:

(i)
Farewell the joyes that erst I have conceived
To hear the birds and Philomellae's notes
Sith cruel fate hath me of him bereaved
On whom though dead my fancy always dotes.
Such were the tunes and lais he daily had
As would have made poor Titius to be glad.

(ii)
Come therefore, sorrow, sit and sigh awhile
And sighing weep and weeping wring they hands.
Speak out my grief, though in no lofty style,
That he who loss of dear things understands
May know I purpose while I draw my breath
By this to show my sorrow for his death.

With its classical names and its alliterative "sorrow sit and sigh" and "weep and weeping wring," it could have served as the text of an earlier play song like the ones which appear in profusion in 17786-91.

Of the anonymous madrigals, two have texts of a somewhat similar character. The text of *And so an end,* though relatively short, receives a rather extended musical setting:

And so an end; but yet before I end,
Remember well the pains that I do prove.
The sighs, the tears, the passions of a friend,
And not to be expressed pangs of love.
When this is done and thou hast made reply,
I and my hope will be content to die.

In isolation, the opening line and especially its musical setting seems a bizarre *nonsequitur,* which would make more sense if part of some dramatic context.[70] The text recalls the rhetorical set speech of the older playsongs, and the musical setting, with the endless repetition of "be content to die," seems especially reminiscent of the Elizabethan tradition.

The rhetorical posture of *Come infirmity* is equally pronounced:

(i)
Come, come infirmity this thy triumph day,
Perfection yielded hath and conquer'd here doth lay,
Conquer'd by blindness, sight by no eyes, eyes,
As mischief's instruments to whom affection flies.
What Homer blind or else Tyresias wounded,
No, but Argus was and Argus ever turned.

(ii)
Come then sweet pity, come and extinguish
These candles two which nature light, or else I languish.
Love's oratrix hath sent forth streams of treason.
The basilisk hath wounded me, and die I must by reason.

Again we find the classical references (the basilisk, for example was a mythical lizardlike monster whose breath and glance proved fatal), the appeal to an abstract principle (infirmity, pity), and possibly some implied dramatic setting. With its convoluted, obscure expressions, it is far removed from the conventional lovers' laments of madrigalian literature.

The musical settings of these texts also have less in common with the madrigal than with the older consort song style. They are by and large sober in character, moving consistently in half-notes, and often with carefully maintained series of imitative points of a "learned" character rather than the lively figures of the works discussed above. Nicolson proves surprisingly reticent to indulge in word-painting in his settings of these texts. There are occasional blatant examples, such as the extended cadence which opens *And so an end*. But quite often the rather "abstract" points are not especially descriptive of their particular textual ideas, and, in fact, may do service for several in the course of the same piece.

These characteristics are perhaps clearest in *Farewell the joys*. One might even think the first three lines a disguised consort song in the style of Orlando Gibbons. In this section, which opens with a five-bar "introduction" for the lower parts in consort song fashion, there is little textual repetition.[71] The top part, always the last to enter, simply presents the first two lines of text once, largely in long note-values, though it repeats the third line, to emphasize the major articulation at that point in the piece. Although the second half of part 1 involves slightly greater textual repetition, the first three lines of part 2 of the piece introduce only single statements of each line in the top part, as in part 1.

The piece is higly imitative, with each point finding its way into every part. All the parts are kept busy most of the time, and the five-part texture is relatively unrelieved. The individual direction of the lines has not succumbed to harmonic considerations to the extent that we often find in the madrigal, and a remarkable number of cadences in the work involve a descent by a step in the bass, with a 7-6 suspension above (a type of cadence for which Nicolson shows a special fondness). Only a single example of the Morleian cadence with the stereotyped series of suspensions, $\begin{smallmatrix} 7 & 6 & 5 \\ 5\text{-}4\text{-}4\text{-}3 \\ 3 \end{smallmatrix}$, appears in part 2, perhaps a conscious attempt to paint the text, "Speak out my grief *though in no lofty style*" (bars 51-55).

The text of the anonymous *Muse not fair love* reflects the spirit of the lighter poems mentioned above:

> Muse not, fair love, if after love's offence
> Love, bettered and content best pleased we find.
> Music, next love, chief ravisher of sense,
> Falls best when discords harsh sweet concords bind.
> All our life is for love's preeminence,
> And our dissension, who should most be kind.
> O sweet uniting strife, O dear dissension,
> When love grows sweeter by sweet love's contention.

But its musical setting has as much in common with the sober style of *Farewell the joys* as it does with the lighter madrigalian style one might expect for such a text.[72] Again the imitation is consistently maintained and the texture unvaried. The lines move primarily in long note-values, with only a few shorter notes in passing. As one might anticipate, the most extensive experiments with word-painting involve the two lines dealing with "Music, next love," the only passage in which the composer departs from the otherwise restrained harmonic idiom of the remainder of the piece. For "chief ravisher of sense" he introduces the traditional phrygian cadence, one of Nicolson's favorite cadential patterns, here used for expressive purposes. "When discords harsh sweet concords bind," on the other hand, deserved a more extreme treatment, and therefore the composer resorted to both the old-fashioned simultaneous false relation (bars 17 and 19), and to a series of the more expressive Morleian suspensions, which makes its only appearance in the piece at this point. In one instance, no third is present (bar 17), which often happens when Nicolson attempts this device.

The anonymous *And so an end* reveals some of the same stylistic ambivalence apparent in *Muse not, fair love.* Once again we find the sober, highly imitative style of the previous examples, with movement in long notes. Indeed, shorter values are virtually nonexistent in this work. But, while the harmonic style of the opening section conforms to the practice of the previous two examples, beginning at "the pains that I do prove" the composer plunges into more expressive harmonic waters in which he had only dabbled for *Muse not fair love.*[73] More than a quarter of the entire piece is given over to the expressive setting of this phrase, which together with the remainder of the piece is chiefly a study in suspensions, and may reveal Nicolson somewhat out of his depth. Examples of the newer, more expressive suspensions abound, but often lack the third above the bass or introduce especially uncouth dissonances.

But, on the other hand, there are also madrigals in which Nicolson shows the relative security apparent from his contribution to *The Triumphs of Oriana.* In the more madrigalian *Thou marvail'st much,* for example, one line of text, "But cruel love that I may prove," demands an expressive treatment of the sort just discussed above. In this instance the musical setting is simpler, less prolix, and generally more assured.[74] Could this work possibly represent a later, more mature conception, written after Nicolson had more or less come to terms with the madrigalian aesthetic as we see it in *Sing shepherds all, What sudden change,* and *Sweet needle, spare my Flora's hands?* It is possible that *Farwell the joys, And so an end,* etc., are earlier works. *Farwell the joys* does contain some awkward moments, including a few blatant parallel fifths. In the closing section, the transition from "while I draw my breath" to "by this to show my sorrow" seems rather inelegant, largely because of the awkward motion in the tenor and soprano II.[75] In addition, the final cadence seems particularly cursory and anticlimatic. In *And so an end,* the composer seems somewhat at a loss as to how he could best cope with the more modern idiom. It is possible, therefore, that Nicolson, like George Kirbye, approached the madrigal first from the school of Byrd, Mundy, and Carlton, and only later came to attempt the lighter, more Italianate variety (perhaps when invited to contribute to *The Triumphs of Oriana?*). But, unlike Kirbye, Nicolson never seems quite at home (or adept) in the lighter madrigal style, and, ironically enough, appears happiest in its successor, the decontrapuntalized consort song, as we have seen in *I am not I of such belief.*

The view of Richard Nicolson provided by 17797, though admittedly a rather limited one, suggests that he must have been an active member of that Oxford musical circle which, as we surmised from the contents of 17786-91, was more involved in consort song than madrigal. As in the other Oxford source, it seems likely that some of the pieces might possibly have been intended to fulfill some sort of dramatic function. Frederick Boas has written that "at Oxford there appear to have been only three chief theatrical centres— Christ Church, Magdalen, and St. Johns."[76] Indeed, the earliest recorded performance at Oxford University, *Quem quaeritis,* took place at Magdalen in 1487.[77] Despite the lack of extant plays to confirm the fact, dramatic productions must have been an important aspect of the artistic life of the college. Again, to quote Boas:

> These [lists of plays whose names are known] form, of course, only a fraction of the tragedies, comedies, and miscellaneous "shows" produced on College stages during the Tudor period. This is most strikingly illustrated in the case of Magdalen College, Oxford. Though it was one of the greatest centres of academic acting, there is no extant play which can be said without doubt to have been performed there before the death of Elizabeth.[78]

In addition, several more plays took place at Magdalen during the reign of James I,[79] and, to judge by Boas's statement, there must have been numerous others as well. Perhaps several of Nicolson's works in 17797 were first heard in the course of these dramatic presentations.

Aside from madrigals and consort songs, 17797 contains a motet, a full anthem, and two verse anthems. The motet is anonymous here, but attributed to Nicolson in Drexel 4180-5, which preserves a reading close enough to that in 17797 to suggest that both originated from a common source. The motet thus serves as further evidence of the links between John Merro and Oxford.

The full anthem, *O praise our Lord, ye Saints,*[80] here ascribed to "Mr Byrd," is especially puzzling, and has provoked comment because of its unusual style and conflicting attributions. The entire anthem appears again in the highly reliable Paston source, British Library Add. MS 31992 with an ascription to Byrd, while sections 3 and 4 survive in the less reliable Add. 18936-9 with an ascription to "Alfonso."[81] The piece is most akin, perhaps, to Byrd's vernacular motets published in the 1611 *Psalms, Songs and Sonnets,* which share numerous features with it. The anthem might best be understood as a less successful attempt at the style of the 1611 print, one Byrd himself ultimately chose to suppress.

The two verse anthems, *Hearken all ye people* and *Behold how good and joyful,* are unique to Add. 17797, and have been inserted at the very end of the partbooks, perhaps as an afterthought. Aside from 17797, William Stonnard's few extant sacred works occur only in the sacred sources from Peterhouse, Cambridge and Durham, with isolated examples in Tenbury MS 791 and the related source, Royal College of Music MSS 1045-51. To judge by *Behold how good and joyful,* Stonnard was neither very adept in his art nor among its more adventurous practitioners.[82] While some details of the word-setting, such as the attempts at lively declamation (e.g., "in unity," "It is like a precious ointment"), sequential repetition of brief phrases (e.g., "Brethren to dwell," "down to his skirts," which reveal a musical correspondence), and enthusiastic word-painting (e.g., "That ran down unto the beard"—almost surely bound to raise unseemly titters from the singers), clearly mark it as Jacobean, the other stylistic features are more retrospective. The harmonic idiom, for example, shows none of the more up-to-date features which begin to creep into the verse anthems of East and Peerson during the first and second decades of the century. Most of the unusual harmonic moments result simply from the composer's awkward part writing, which is also rather liberally sprinkled with parallel fifths and octaves. Therefore, Stonnard's contributions to 17797 reinforce the basic musical aesthetic of the collection, though they may lag behind the works of Nicolson in their level of musical competence.

Taken as a whole, then, 17797 largely confirms the view of Oxford musical life evident from 17786-91. To judge by these two sources, the secular circles around two of Oxford's choral foundations, Magdalen and New College, may have been more at home with the consort song for voices and viol, well suited to viol teaching and choir training, than with the madrigal. The Nicolson source concentrates upon a modern kind of consort song which also appeared in the

Wigthorpe manuscripts in company with numerous older, Elizabethan examples. This modernity involves a simplification of the texture and a more lively declamation of the text, perhaps reflecting the influence of the lute ayre rather than that of the madrigal, which, on the other hand, seems to have appealed more strongly to the younger verse anthem composers on the Ely-Cambridge-London circuit, led by Michael East and Martin Peerson.

As mentioned above, many works in both sources might have been intended for some sort of dramatic presentation by the New College or Magdalen choir schools. But we have seen that 17786-91 also involved a great deal of music for viols alone. It is equally plausible, therefore, that an especially strong interest in viol playing may have prompted the inclusion of so many consort songs in these two sets of manuscripts. Consort songs, after all, could provide occupation for both those who wished to sing and those who wished to play.

In the light of these two sources, the original stipulations of William Heather's endowment of the Oxford music professorship are of special interest. Among them we read:

> Thirdly, I do appoint that the said Master bring with him two boys weekly, at the day and time aforesaid [Thursday afternoons], and there to receive such company as will practice Musick, and to play Lessons of three Parts, if none other come.[83]

Richard Nicolson, it will be remembered, became the first Heather Professor of Music under William Heather's endowment. It is not unlikely that he may have advised Oxford's musical benefactor as to the most suitable working arrangement for the Music School's activities. Perhaps Heather's Thursday meetings, then, were modeled on an older, unofficial practice, largely supported by Oxford's more musically minded colleges. Both 17786-91 and 17797, with their very similar repertories, may originally have met the needs of such older meetings. In fact, the numerous dialogues in the Wigthorpe manuscripts and the version of *Sweet they say such virtue lies* for two sopranos and viols in 17797 might even reflect the original precedent for Heather's stipulation that two boys should attend the official weekly meetings established in 1627.

As yet, no concrete evidence has come to light to prove the existence of regular, informal musical afternoons in Jacobean Oxford, which could have served as Heather's models. But the last of the Oxford pre-Restoration sources, Bodl. MSS Mus. Sch. D 212-216, probably represents one attempt to meet the needs of the official musical Thursday afternoons established by Heather, as the following discussion will show.

C	A	T	B	Q	no.	Title	idiom	Composer
1ᵛ	19ᵛ	37ᵛ	55ᵛ	73ᵛ	1	And so an end	f	
2ᵛ	20ᵛ	38ᵛ	56ᵛ	74ᵛ	2	Cantate Domino	f	[R. Nicolson]
3ᵛ	21ᵛ	39ᵛ	57ᵛ	75ᵛ	3	*Cuckow*	cs	
4	22	40	58	76		*In the merry month of May [i.e., In a merry May morn]*	cs	R. Nicolson
4ᵛ	22ᵛ	40ᵛ	58ᵛ	76ᵛ	4	*No more good herdsman*	cs	" "
5	23	41	59	77		*I am not I of such belief*	cs	" "
5ᵛ	23ᵛ	41ᵛ	59ᵛ	77ᵛ	5	What sudden change	f	" "
6ᵛ	24ᵛ	42ᵛ	60ᵛ	78ᵛ	6	*Come Holy ghost²*		
6ᵛ	24ᵛ	42ᵛ	60ᵛ	78ᵛ		*O Lord of whom I do depend*		
7	25	43	61	79		*O Lord turn not away thy face*		
7ᵛ	25ᵛ	43ᵛ	61ᵛ	79ᵛ	7	Thou marvail'st much	f	R. Nicolson
8ᵛ	26ᵛ	44ᵛ	62ᵛ	80ᵛ	8	Sweet needle spare my Flora's hands	f	
9ᵛ	27ᵛ	45ᵛ	63ᵛ	81ᵛ	9	Muse not, fair love	f	
10ᵛ	28ᵛ	46ᵛ	64ᵛ	82ᵛ	10	*Sweet, they say such virtue lies³ (i)*	cd	
11	29	47	65	82ᵛ		*Since the virtue, then, is such (ii)*	cd	
11ᵛ	29ᵛ	47ᵛ	65ᵛ	83ᵛ	11	O praise our Lord (i)	f	
11ᵛ	29ᵛ	47ᵛ	65ᵛ	83ᵛ		Extoll the greatness (ii)	f	
12	30	48	66	84		Praise him on tube (iii)	f	
12	30ᵛ	48ᵛ	66ᵛ	84ᵛ	12	The gladsome sound (iv)	f	
13	31	49	67	84ᵛ		Let all the creatures (v)	f	"Mr Byrd."
13ᵛ	31ᵛ	49ᵛ	67ᵛ	85ᵛ	13	Farewell the joys (i)	f	R. Nicolson
14	32	49ᵛ	68	86		Come therefore sorrow (ii)	f	" "
14ᵛ	32ᵛ	50ᵛ	68ᵛ	86ᵛ	14	Come infirmity (i)	f	
15	33	51	68ᵛ	87		Come then sweet pity (ii)	f	
				87ᵛ	15	And hath good grace		" "
16ᵛ	34ᵛ	52ᵛ	70ᵛ	88ᵛ	16	*Hearken all ye people*	v	W. Stonnard
18	36	54	71ᵛ	90		*Behold how good and joyful*	v	" "

1 Modern foliation.

2 These three consort songs are textless in the source.

3 This piece was probably conceived as a madrigal; in the present version the lower three parts have been left textless for instrumental performance.

Bodleian MSS Mus. Sch. D 212-216

Bodl. MSS Mus. Sch. D 212-216 form another set of pre-Restoration partbooks in which music for voices and viols rubs shoulders with strictly instrumental pieces. In this instance the greater part of the manuscripts consists of a collection of instrumental In Nomines, to which ten anthems have been appended, presumably because the verse anthems among them also require viols for their performance. The ten anthems quite definitely form a separate layer in the manuscripts, however, one which reveals features more common in strictly sacred sources of the time.

Unfortunately, there is scanty information to help establish when the books became part of the Music School collection; the first mention of them does not occur until 1682, in the list made at the death of Edward Lowe (MS Mus. Sch. C 204* [R]):

Folio Books in Vellam with green strings   5[84]

But they apparently found their way into the Music School before the Restoration since in this list the manuscripts occur among the volumes kept in "ye Long Cupboard," reserved for pre-Restoration acquisitions.

Clearly the opening group of In Nomines at one time formed a collection of separate sheets, for some of them are now very badly aligned in the partbooks, while others have lost parts of their titles or attributions. The collection of anthems, on the other hand, is copied on different paper stitched in gatherings at the end of the partbooks, and has suffered no losses from the binder's knife. Perhaps it was the Music School authorities who determined to bind this gift of loose pages into a more practical form, and at the same time decided to insert extra gatherings of a different paper at the end of each volume.

It was probably after the books had returned from the binder that the small group of anthems was copied on the new gatherings which formed an appendix to the In Nomine collection. Since there were not enough partbooks to allow for the three anthems in six parts, the scribe undertook to enter the sixth voice of *Sing Joyfully, Almighty God who by the leading of a star,* and *O Lord consider my distress* on blank folios in the oldest set of manuscript books in the Music School, MSS Mus. Sch. E 376-81, the only manuscript partbooks among the forty-three sets originally presented by William Heather in 1627. In MS Mus. Sch. E 381 these three anthems are headed "Sixt part in the ~~wait~~[sic] white books" (fol. 55v), our clue that D 212-216 had already received their white vellum bindings before the anthems were entered.

John Bergsagel has suggested that either Richard Nicolson or William Heather might have been responsible for the copying.[85] But on the basis of Heather's sample signatures preserved in the University Archives, and also given the fact that Richard Hinde's anthem is dated "1632" in Peterhouse MS 45 (p. 41),[86] five years after Heather's death, one may rule him out as a possible scribe. Nicolson, on the other hand, seems a very plausible candidate. As the first Heather Professor of Music at Oxford, he was responsible for both the music books and the musical instruments, which were not to "be lent abroad upon any pretence whatsoever, nor removed out of the Schoole and place appointed."[87] Of the ten anthems in this collection, three are ascribed to Nicolson, the only composer who provides more than a solitary example. One of them, *When Jesus sat at meat,* was obviously composed for Magdalen College, where Nicolson was organist, and is unique to this source.

Furthermore, as pointed out in the earlier discussion of Add. 17797, the Heather Professor was required to bring two boys along to the Thursday afternoon meetings at the Music School, and there to make music with whatever musicians should appear, or else simply to play instrumental pieces in three parts. It is interesting, therefore, that of the verse anthems in D 212-216, Bull's *Almighty God,* Nicolson's *When Jesus sat at meat,* Hinde's *O sing unto the Lord,* and Hilton's *Teach me, O Lord* all require two boy's voices. In addition, the version of Tomkins's *Above the stars,* unique to this source, "has a verse part for soprano as well as alto and could be sung either as a duet with string accompaniment or as a solo for either voice with strings,"[88] and requires two boys for the final chorus. The version of *O Lord consider my distress,* on the other hand, includes another mean part in E 381, which duplicates the one in D 212 for all but the verse "for thee have I offended," when the former is silent. The last of the verse anthems, Martin Peerson's *Blow out the trumpet,* also requires two boy's voices. Finally, of the three full anthems, all but *O pray for the peace of Jerusalem* require two cantus parts. Thus, nine of the ten anthems seem to have been entered with two boys in mind, as if the copyist were trying his best to provide enough music to keep both occupied during the musical Thursday afternoons at the Music School—just the sort of "practical musicianship" one might expect of the Heather Professor himself, especially if he had previous experience with unruly choristers as *Informator Choristarum* at Magdalen.

Finally, of the attributed pieces in D 212-216 all but Nicolson's include the honorific "Mr" or "Dr." It is true, as we have see, that Nicolson was the only composer in Add. 17797 whose works sometimes lacked the title "Mr." But in the Music School set he is *never* "Mr Nicolson," but "Rich: Nicolson," "Richard Nicolson," or simply "RN." Thus, when all the evidence is considered, it seems much more probable that D 212-216 are in the hand of the first Heather Professor, while Add. 17797 was the work of a member of his musical circle.

If Nicolson were in fact the copyist, it becomes possible to pinpoint quite closely the date of compilation. As mentioned earlier, Hinde's *O sing unto the*

Lord was probably composed in 1632. Nicolson died around 1639. Therefore, the anthems were probably entered sometime during this seven-year period. A final scrap of evidence may substantiate this hypothesis. Crammed into an empty space on the title page of the bassus book appears the name "Jo: Evelyn" in a browner ink. The only John Evelyn listed in Foster for this period is the well-known diarist, who matriculated at Balliol in 1637,[89] and by 1640 was at the Middle Temple. Evelyn was an enthusiastic musician, who has left some personal reactions to his musical experiences in Oxford.[90] Perhaps he observed or took part in the musical Thursday afternoons at the Music School during his sojourn in Oxford between 1637 and 1640, and furtively left his mark in the bassus book from this set of In Nomines and anthems.

But although these manuscripts were compiled for use in the Music School, in many respects they have much in common with sacred sources of the time. The term "mean," the common designation for a boy's voice in sacred sources, occurs at one verse of *O Lord consider my distress* in D 212, while the Latin form, "medius," recurs repeatedly in both D 212 and D 216. Furthermore, instructions for the use of decani or cantoris sides of the choir, totally inappropriate to a secular source, appear at least half-a-dozen times in these anthems.[91] This probably indicates that they were copied directly, and quite literally, from sacred partbooks, perhaps those in use at Magdalen College.

The repertory as a whole shows a marked ecclesiastical orientation. When one has discounted Mundy's *O give thanks unto the Lord,* Bull's *Almighty God who by the leading of a star,* and Byrd's *Sing joyfully,* all among the most popular pieces of the age in both sacred and secular manuscripts, and the two works unique to this source, Nicolson's *When Jesus sat at meat* and Hilton's *Teach me O Lord,* practically all the others occur only in sacred manuscripts before the Restoration. Nicolson's *O pray for the peace of Jerusalem* is a borderline case, since, in addition to strictly sacred sources, it occurs in the Oxford source mentioned in connection with 17786-91, Tenbury MS 1382, which may possibly have been created in a secular context, as John Morehen suggests.[92] Peerson's most popular anthem, *Blow out the trumpet,* on the other hand, is one of only three out of more than twenty by this composer considered appropriate for liturgical use by pre-Restoration scribes.[93]

The choice of anthems may also have been governed at least in part by personal connections with their composers. The link with Nicolson is, of course, obvious; D 212-216 contain all three of his surviving sacred works in English. It is likewise the unique source of Hilton's *Teach me, O lord.* Hilton, though a native of Oxford (and perhaps a chorister there?), took his Mus.B. from Cambridge in 1626. In 1627 he dedicated his *Ayres or Fa La's* to William Heather, who endowed the music professorship at Oxford that same year. Margaret Crum has suggested that Hilton may have presented a copy of his *Ayres* to his patron's new foundation,[94] at which time he might also have transmitted his verse anthem to the first Heather Professor. Finally, the presence of Richard Hinde's *O sing unto the Lord* may attest to a connection with Lichfield Cathedral, where Hinde served as organist. Not only do we find the Hinde anthem at Oxford, but Nicolson's *O Pray for the peace of Jerusalem* also survives in manuscripts at Lichfield, the only non-Oxford sources for the piece, and perhaps for any of Nicolson's anthems.[95]

O Lord consider my distress, attributed to "RN" in E 381, is especially puzzling, for another anthem with this title appears in the pre-Restoration partbooks from Durham, attributed to Edward Smith (d. 1611). Although the Durham sources contain numerous differences, there can be little doubt that these are two versions of the same piece.[96] The Smiths were prominent musical figures at Durham, where the cathedral manuscripts include works by William Smith, Edward Smith, and the somewhat later Elias Smith. Both Edward Smith and his father, William Smith Senior, before him served as organists of Durham, while William Smith Junior, probably a chorister at the cathedral from 1609 until 1613, served as minor canon, sacrist, and precentor from 1627 until 1645, during which time he copied literally hundreds of pages of music into the Durham pre-Restoration manuscripts.[97] Although William Smith did not copy this anthem of his ancestor, the actual scribes, Henry Palmer, a minor Durham musician and composer who entered the piece in the organ book MS A5, and Toby Brooking, who probably copied some of the vocal parts,[98] should be equally trustworthy in their attributions.[99]

D 212-216, on the other hand, represent our most reliable source for the works of Nicolson. It seems that somehow Edward Smith's verse anthem fell into the hands of the Magdalen organist. Perhaps Nicolson acquired only an organ part and the vocal parts, which he then determined to rewrite in a version for viols. It is obvious that the scribe of D 212-216 was working from a score and not simply copying from other partbooks, for after completing a line near the end of the verse "For thee alone have I offended" in one of the contratenor books, his eye absent-mindedly wandered onto the wrong contratenor part, at a point where both parts were quite similar. Very probably this was Nicolson's own score of his revised version of the anthem.

The changes which Nicolson introduced into *O Lord consider my distress* are certainly extensive enough to warrant the addition of his initials to the part in Mus. Sch. E 381. Not only has he composed new viol parts, including extensive revisions of the outer voices from Smith's version, but he has also significantly enlarged the role of the chorus.

In Smith's version, the text by Sternhold and Hopkins was divided into four sections, punctuated by choruses, which repeat the final pair of lines for each section (choruses in italics):

O Lord consider my distress
  and now with speed some pity take.
My sins remit, my faults redress,
  Good Lord for thy great mercy sake.
Wash me O Lord, and make me clean
  from this unjust and sinful act.
And purify yet once again
  my heinous crime and bloody fact.

Remorse and sorrow do constrain
  me to acknowledge mine excess.
My sins, alas, do still remain
  before thy face without redress.
For thee alone I have offended,
  committing evil in thy sight.
And if I were therefore condemned
  yet were thy judgement just and right.

Turn back thy face and frowning ire,
  for I have felt enough thy hand.
And purge my sins I thee desire,
  which do in number pass the sand.
Make new my heart within my breast
  and frame it to thy holy will.
Thy constant spirit in me let rest,
  which may these raging enemies kill.

Lord unto Sion turn thy face.
  Pour out thy mercies on thy hill.
And on Jerusalem, thy grace,
  build up the walls and love it still.

Interestingly enough, Smith employs the same music for the first two choruses, which differ only in their texts, while the third chorus is also related to them through its headmotif and homophonic texture. Even Smith's final chorus employs a somewhat similar opening melodic figure, though it later becomes more contrapuntal, treating points from the previous section in imitation (see ex. 3).

Nicolson, on the other hand, while preserving these four choruses more or less intact as the major sectional articulations of his reworking, introduces additional shorter choruses in the first two sections, intended to set off the natural break after the fourth line in each of them. The four-bar chorus in the midst of section 1 repeats the fourth line of text and employs a variation of the melodic line from the previous contratenor solo (see ex. 4). The more extended chorus in the middle of the second large section repeats the last two lines (and some of the musical ideas) of the previous solo.

Aside from these changes which were largely intended to articulate the form of the text and to enrich the contrasts of solo and chorus in typically Jacobean fashion, Nicolson was apparently concerned primarily with updating

Ex. 3.   The openings of the choruses from Smith's *O Lord consider my
distress* (contratenor 1 missing throughout)

the scoring of the solo sections. Although the fragmentary state of Smith's
anthem obscures somewhat the composer's original intention,[100] it seems that
the first two sections of his anthem involved only single soloists. Nicolson's
mean solo, which joins the contratenor soloist at "Wash me, O Lord," does not
fit the extant organ part at Durham, and at one point the Oxford version
contains an extra semibreve, necessary to make room for the mean entry, "and
purify yet once again." The same sort of discrepancies are apparent in the
second long section ("Remorse and sorrow"), in one instance involving an
additional breve and in another, three semibreves.[101] Thus, it seems likely that
the additional solos are the work of Nicolson.

The third section of Smith's anthem involved a mean and a bass soloist.
Interestingly enough, in this case Nicolson ignores the older bass solo part,
which lay consistently above the organ bass-line, and simply adds the text to his
own revised bass-line. It seems likely that Smith employed two means in the
final section, the climax of the piece, where the organ part contains fragments
of both. He may have allotted the second mean part to the first contratenor, a
practice which Nicolson also follows.

Nicolson's enrichment of the scoring of *O Lord consider* may represent an
attempt to make Smith's anthem conform more closely to the Jacobean taste
for increasingly elaborate textures. But otherwise the Magdalen organist shows

Ex. 4.   Nicolson's *O Lord consider my distress* (the first two sections only)

Ex. 4—*continued*

Ex. 4—*continued*

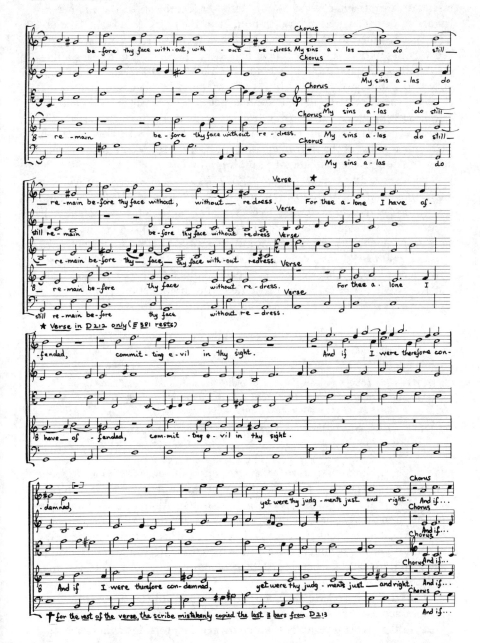

★ Verse in D212 only (E 381 rests)

† for the rest of the verse, the scribe mistakenly copied the last 3 bars from D213

remarkable restraint. Indeed, he introduces nothing to jar with Smith's essentially Elizabethan conception. With the exception of the momentary change to quarter-notes and eighth-notes near the opening to paint "and now with speed some pity take" (which occurs in the earlier version as well), the declamation in both settings is sober and carefully controlled, moving almost entirely in whole-notes and half-notes. Each textual phrase still appears only once in the solo parts until the final verse section, where, in order to affect the climax at the close of the anthem, the final petition, "build up the walls and love it still," appears three times.[102] But this, too, was also present in Smith's earlier version. Though there can be no doubt that Nicolson greatly enhances the harmonic interest of the instrumental parts, he introduces nothing that would upset the underlying aesthetic of Smith's original.

Nicolson's other verse anthem, *When Jesus sat at meat,*[103] provides an interesting contrast with his revision of the anthem by Edward Smith. Everything points to its being a later work, presumably written for the celebration on St. Mary Magdalen's Day (July 23) at Nicolson's college. As we have seen, Nicolson's most significant alterations of the original *O Lord, consider my distress* involved the insertion of additional solos in the verses. This interest in enriching the scoring is carried much further in the later work. Nicolson divides the extended prose text into three sections, employing as many as five soloists in the verses, and inevitably two sopranos:

SS   When Jesus sat at meat in the Pharisee's house, *behold, a woman in the city, which was a sinner:*
Mary, called Magdalen.

SSATB She bought an alabaster box of ointment, and stood behind him, weeping. *And began to wash his feet with tears, and wiped them with the hairs of her head. And kissed his feet, and anointed them with ointment.*

SSAT   *Jesus turned to the woman, and said: Thy sins are forgiven; thy faith hath saved thee. Go thy way in peace.*

In addition, the composer affords ever-greater prominence to the chorus as the piece progresses (choral repetitions of the text appear in italics above), until in the final section the chorus repeats the text in its entirety. Furthermore, the vocal declamation has become much more lively than that of the previous work (see ex. 5). Short melodic fragments pass from part to part in imitation, and frequently appear a second or third time in the same part. In addition, Nicolson quite commonly allots separate syllables to quarter-notes, a practice rare in *O Lord consider my distress.*

The harmonic style of the later anthem is also somewhat more in touch with the Jacobean era. A few concessions to the madrigalian harmonic idiom appear in the occasional use of the stereotyped cadential formula including a suspended seventh over a pedal, a feature entirely absent from the other

Ex. 5.   *When Jesus sat at meat*

Ex. 6.   *When Jesus sat at meat*

anthem, Nicolson's consort songs, and, indeed, from several of his madrigals. In addition, the transposed repetition of "a woman in the city" also has a more modern ring (see ex. 6).

Interestingly enough, Nicolson uses a closely related passage at the words of Jesus in the third section, as illustrated in example 7. The earlier discussion of Nicolson's works in Add. 17797 indicated that the Magdalen organist frequently uses very similar points in the course of a piece. But in this case he seems consciously to have planned the first and third sections symmetrically.

Ex. 7.   *When Jesus sat at meat*

Ex. 8.   *When Jesus sat at meat*

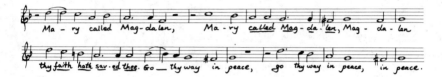

Not only do they both share this striking repetition, in their melodic contours and pitch sets, but they also close with roughly the same bass-line, and the same sort of falling point in the upper parts (see ex. 8). Thus, Nicolson joins the steadily growing number of composers who experimented with "structural repetition," previously emphasized by David Brown only in connection with Thomas Weelkes.[104]

All things considered, Nicolson's *When Jesus sat at meat* proves a rather fine and effective work, with numerous expressive moments. While it may reveal a decidedly different, more Jacobean conception than the older *O Lord, consider my distress,* it still belongs to a different realm than the verse anthems of the more fashionable young Jacobeans such as Peerson, East, Ravenscroft, or Simms, who appear especially prominently in the London sources. Instead, Nicolson seems to cling to an older tradition best represented in Jacobean times by Orlando Gibbons. In Gibbons's work we find the same richness of scoring, with a wider range of forces in the verses, and a livelier declamation than appears in the works of the Elizabethans, but without quite the exuberance of Peerson and his school. Gibbons also shows the same interest in the repetition of short phrases, often organized sequentially. Occasionally we may even come upon passages involving modulations similar to those which Nicolson employed in sections 1 and 3 of his later verse anthem (see ex. 9). Furthermore, Gibbons very often treats the chorus after the same fashion as Nicolson in *When Jesus sat at meat.* Both composers tend to make the choruses rely heavily upon the preceding verse sections. Frequently this involves quite literal restatement, simply repeating the solo lines and adding words to the remaining instrumental parts from the verses in order to transform them into choral parts.[105]

Ex. 9. *See, see the Word is incarnate*

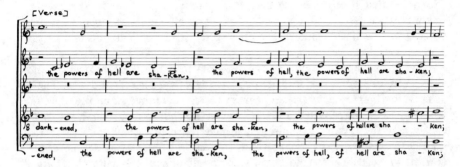

Thus, Nicolson's contributions to D 212-216 testify to the same unmadrigalian, relatively traditional orientation of the other verse anthems in the source. Indeed, this appendix of ten anthems at the back of the partbooks largely confirms the patterns evident in the earlier Oxford sources, Add. 17786-91 and Add. 17797, discussed above. As we have seen, those sources, judged on their own, seemed either largely oblivious or unsympathetic to the madrigalian aesthetic, and derived their more up-to-date features from the lute ayre. Similarly, many anthems in D 212-216, and Nicolson's in particular, are in marked contrast with those in the other major secular sources, whether from London (e.g., Myriell) or from the Cambridge area (e.g., Hamond, or Add. 29366-8). In those manuscript collections, Peerson, East, and other more exuberant, madrigalian verse anthem composers predominate. This seems all the more remarkable since the anthems were probably copied into D 212-216 after 1632, at the same time Hamond was at work in Suffolk, and at least two years after Martin Peerson had published his adventurous collection in the verse idiom, *Mottects or Grave Chamber Music* (1630). D 212-216 reflect instead the more sober school of the Jacobean verse anthem, a contingent led by Orlando Gibbons, and represented in this source especially by Bull, Tomkins, and Nicolson himself.

As mentioned above, the choice of anthems in D 212-216 reveals a marked ecclesiastical orientation. Perhaps this could be the clue, not only to the aesthetic of D 212-216, but also to that of the earlier Oxford sources of a similar outlook. The arbiters of Oxford musical taste, whether Nicolson at Magdalen, Wigthorpe at New College, or Stonnard at Christ Church, were basically church organists whose concerns must have revolved around daily sung services and the activities of the choir schools. It is logical, therefore, that their musical tastes should have been colored by these preoccupations. The remarkably extensive collections of playsongs in Add. 17786-91 and perhaps also in Add. 17797, whether the Elizabethan or more "modern" Jacobean examples, would be suitable for use by the choristers of the Oxford choral foundations, either informally, for choir training, or in connection with the many recorded dramatic performances at the university. Or, on the other hand, they might have served for musical afternoons of singing and playing which could have been the models for those prescribed by William Heather, as suggested earlier.

It is reasonable that the Oxford organists' taste in anthems for voices and viols, even for secular use, should be governed by their ecclesiastical bias. Then, as now, inertia may have been a primary factor governing the choice of music from day to day or month to month. With at least half-a-dozen services to plan each week, the Oxford organists must have relied primarily upon what was readily to hand—the basic staples of their choral libraries, which no doubt consisted primarily of the old, familiar Elizabethan works. Furthermore, when it came to choosing more modern music, whether through the exercise of their own compositional skills or by recopying works by their contemporaries, they were probably drawn, once again, to the style most familiar and comfortable to them and to their choirs. Thus, the anthems of Nicolson in D 212-216 and the less expert attempts by Stonnard in Add. 17797 cling largely to the underlying tenets of an earlier age, introducing little to jar with either its basic musical style or older sense of decorum, in much the same way that most twentieth-century Anglican church music carries on the traditions of Stanford and Parry.

And while Nicolson, Wigthorpe, and Stonnard might be among the leading musical lights of Oxford, they were hardly stellar figures beyond the boundaries of the university. Morley, in beating the bush around the provinces for additional contributors to *The Triumphs of Oriana,* may have flushed out Nicolson, thereby inspiring the Magdalen organist to the highest pitch of madrigalian fervor he would ever achieve. But otherwise these Jacobean Oxford musicians seem to have been content with their own relatively narrow horizons. Unlike Cambridge musicians such as Orlando Gibbons and John Tomkins, who went down from their university to the musical centers of London, Nicolson and Stonnard lived out their lives in Oxford.[106] The university might confer academic distinctions upon some of the more prominent musicians of the day, such as Peerson and Gibbons. But these men only stayed long enough to collect their degrees before returning to the more vital life of London, around the Court, the Chapel Royal, or St. Paul's. Musical life in Oxford continued to follow its own special course, as these sources indicate, either relatively oblivious to many of the newer developments in London circles, or else choosing to ignore them.

BODLEIAN MSS MUS. SCH. D 212 - 216
(and MUS. SCH. E 381)

| f o l i o[1] | | | | | | Title | idiom | Composer |
-12	-13	-14	-15	-16	-81			
71ᵛ	77ᵛ	77ᵛ	76ᵛ	51ᵛ	56ᵛ	*Almighty God, who by the leading of a star*	v	J. Bull
72ᵛ	78ᵛ	78ᵛ	77ᵛ	52ᵛ		O pray for the peace of Jerusalem	f	R. Nicolson
73	79	79	78	53		*When Jesus sat at meat*	v	" "
74	80	80	79	54		*Teach me, O Lord*	v	J. Hilton
75	81	81	80	55		O give thanks unto the Lord	f	[J. Mundy]
76	83ᵛ	82	80ᵛ	56		*Above the stars*	v	T. Tomkins
76ᵛ	84ᵛ	82ᵛ	81ᵛ	57ᵛ	57ᵛ	*O Lord consider my distress*	v	"R N"
78	85ᵛ	83ᵛ	82ᵛ	58ᵛ	55ᵛ	Sing joyfully	f	W. Byrd
78ᵛ	86	84ᵛ	83	59ᵛ		*Blow out the trumpet*	v	M. Peerson
79ᵛ	87	85	83ᵛ² 85ᵛ	60		*O sing unto the Lord*	v	[R. Hinde]

1 Modern foliation.

2 The original *O sing unto the Lord* was canceled because a chorus section had been omitted. In order to recopy it, a new sheet (with 6-line staves) was glued into the partbook.

6

British Library Additional MSS 37402-6

Unfortunately, not all manuscripts preserve the sorts of clues to their origins that we find in the Oxford sources. While the Oxford sets may lack the names of their original owners or the dates of compilation on their flyleaves, the repertories establish their provenance with some certainty. B.L. Add. MSS 37402-6, on the other hand, at first appear promising, for the set includes three different names, "James Pearson," "Elizabeth Babington" (or "Babtoon"), and "Robert Babington," on various leaves. But after a search through the various indices of British wills, the lists of alumni of Oxford and Cambridge, etc., they still remain only tantalizing clues. Add. 37402-6 obstinately refuse to divulge anything concrete about their early history, even after long perusal and a careful study of their repertory.

Indeed, the longer one studies 37402-6 the less there is about this source that appears straightforward. A list of its diverse contents runs the entire gamut of musical forms prevalent in the earliest years of the Jacobean age: Italian madrigals, motets both English and continental, instrumental pieces from previous generations as well as fantasias of the most up-to-date variety, Elizabethen madrigals, consort songs, verse anthems, a lute song, a quodlibet, and, perhaps most surprising of all, even some examples of Anglican service music. But what adds to the interest of the set, and increases its relevance to the present study is the frequency with which things are not what they seem: the apparent fantasias are not fantasias at all, lute songs are in fact consort songs, and even madrigals are transformed. Indeed, the categories that preserve most clearly their original form are the examples of the verse idiom. It is in this connection that Add. 37402-6 become important to our discussion.

The primary layer in the partbooks, undoubtedly copied first, consists of more than seventy Italian madrigals, which form a distinct section having little to do with what follows. They were probably entered as late as 1596, the date of the most recent published source for some of them.[1] The manner of presentation, omitting the words for instrumental performance, illustrates one possible solution to the Elizabethans' problem with pieces in the Italian language, aptly summed up by Nicholas Yonge:

Italian Songs, are for sweetness of Aire, verie well liked of all, but most in account with them that understand the language. As for the rest, they do either not sing them at all, or at the least with little delight.[2]

The possibility raised by Mr. Warwick Edwards that such textless copies were meant to be sol-faed or sung "to the bare note"[3] is overruled in this instance by an annotation to number 66 in Add. 37406: "the last lyne ys to be *played* afore this" [italics added]. Hence, 37402-6 is definitely an anthology for viol players, not madrigal singers.

Sometime around 1600 Add. 37402-6 must have passed from the hands of this viol-playing devotée of the Italian madrigal to a new owner of similar interests, who attests to his purchase in a note on folio 98ᵛ of 37402: "Bought By James Pearson [his] booke [?]." The monogram "IP" appended to a few folios subsequent to the block of Italian madrigals very probably indicates that Pearson was responsible for the coying of these later works. Virtually nothing is known of James Pearson except that 37402-6 were not his only music books. His signature reappears on the cover of a copy of Weelkes's *Ayeres or Phantasticke Spirites* (1608), now in the British Library (K.3.k.13). While Pearson was apparently interested enough in the Italian madrigals to make a few corrections in them and to blacken some especially faint passages, he made no further additions in this genre. For Pearson's primary interest lay closer to home in the works of native Englishmen, and especially in those musical genres which would provide interesting material for viol players.

Pearson's must have been a retrospective mind, for the first large section to follow the Italian madrigals includes a number of works by both English and continental composers dating back to the beginning of Elizabeth's reign. Some of these, without words or even titles in the partbooks, are in fact motets masquerading as instrumental works. The piece on folio 48ᵛ of 37402, for example, simply headed "of sexe parts," is in fact the second part of Lassus's *In te Domine speravi,* entitled *Quoniam fortitudo.* The complete motet, first published in 1564, recurs in another retrospective English source, Add. MS 32377. The succeeding work in 37402-6, simply headed *Timor et tremor,* also proves to be by Lassus, and was first published in the same collection of 1564.[4]

In addition to these continental works, the compiler includes a number of English pieces from the earlier period. On folio 51ᵛ of 37402 there occurs a five-part cantus firmus setting headed simply "Libera." The British Library catalogue incorrectly identified the chant as "Libera me Domine";[5] it is in fact an antiphon for the Trinity, "Libera nos, salva nos, justifica nos, O beata Trinitas." The piece bears the ascription "Talles" but, while it may produce some of the right sorts of stylistic thumbprints, various infelicities, especially the consecutives of bars 14 and 18, make the attribution questionable[6] (see ex. 1). The reliability of the scribe's attributions has also been called into question by Joseph Kerman[7] in the case of the motet, *Decantabat populus,* here ascribed

Ex. 1.   *Libera nos, salva nos*

to "Mr Birde," but occurring anonymously in the Dow MSS (Christ Church MSS 984-8). In this instance the error can probably be explained as a slip on the part of the scribe, who may have intended the attribution for the previous piece, Byrd's *O Lord who in thy sacred tent*, which remains anonymous in the source. The quodlibet, *Peace, I heard a voice*, confirms that such errors were not unknown. It at one time bore an ascription to Gibbons (whose *The Cries of London* follows in the partbooks) which has subsequently been canceled. In addition, each of the six-part "Orianas" after Weelkes's *As Vesta was from Latmos hill* bears the title appropriate to the madrigal which follows it in 37402—further proof of the compiler's lack of interest in these works as madrigals rather than as viol music. It is an interesting conicidence that the last of the old-style motets in 37402-6, a setting of *Dum transisset sabbatum,* happens to be the only other anonymous motet in the Dow manuscripts. The piece must have been a reasonably popular one, however, since it occurs in at least five other Elizabethan and Jacobean sources.[8]

Besides these motets, an additional group of pieces confirms the copyist's continuing interest in Elizabethan music. Of these, only Parsons's ever-popular *De la courte* bears a distinctive title. The work on folio 52ᵛ of 37402 ascribed to "D. Tye" is in fact the composer's *Lawdes deo,* which also appears in Add. 31390 (fol. 52).[9] The three works which follow *Lawdes deo* are the last of the group, and in many ways the most puzzling. The first, bearing the title *la fantisia* is remarkably like the second, headed "Tow [*sic*] Trebles" in 37406 and ascribed to Morley in 37405; indeed, one must be a variation upon the other (see ex. 2). Neither of these works seems especially like a fantasia. Warwick

Ex. 2.

Edwards has, in fact, suggested that they could be studies in the canzonet style which Morley rejected from publication.[10] The strictly homophonic openings of both, quoted above, do seem reminiscent of Morley's ballet style. Indeed, *la fantisia,* which divides into four sections, set off by fermatas, could be in a freely varied ballet form. The opening of the second section seems to be a diminution of the beginning of the work (see ex. 3a). Both sections also employ the same closing progression, with a brief cadence on A before the final cadences on G (see ex. 3b). Sections 3 and 4 on the other hand, both open with the same favorite madrigalian progression emphasizing the triad on the flattened seventh degree of the scale (see ex. 3c). Finally, all four sections are linked by short passages that repeat the same short-winded phrase, rescored

Ex. 3.   *La Fantisia*

a. Opening of section 2

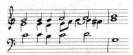

b. End of sections 1 and 2

c. Opening of sections 3 and 4

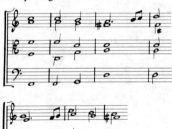

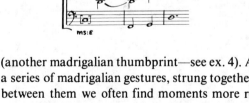

(another madrigalian thumbprint—see ex. 4). All these amount to, however, is a series of madrigalian gestures, strung together rather unsuccessfully. Indeed, between them we often find moments more reminiscent of Anglican church music. The final phrase of *la fantisia,* for instance, could conclude any number of Anglican services (see ex. 5). Despite such ecclesiastical echoes, Warwick Edwards's suggestion seems quite plausible, and, recalling the copyist's tendency to omit titles, as in the case of *Quoniam fortitudo* and *Lawdes deo,* one is left with the uneasy feeling that these could be the madrigalian experiments of some church composer (perhaps Morley, from his days at Norwich?), here in the guise of instrumental fantasias.

Ex. 4.   *La Fantisia*

Ex. 5.   *La Fantisia* (conclusion)

The remaining piece, without any title apart from "v pts", is ascribed to "munday" in all the partbooks. This large bisectional work, twice as long as either of the previous examples, also constrasts with them by being rigidly contrapuntal, excessively so in fact, with predictable entries and extensive passages of literal repetition (see ex. 6). It is, in other words, what one might expect of a motet by William Mundy. It is not unlikely that such it may have been before Pearson deprived it of its text; but an original texted version has yet to come to light.

Ex. 6.   Untitled piece ascribed to "munday"

Sprinkled amongst these archaic motets and "instrumental" pieces we find several other works, dating from shortly before *The Triumphs of Oriana*, which testify once again to James Pearson's concern with music for viols. The first work to follow the block of Italian madrigals is a madrigal by Richard Carlton, *If women could* [i.e., *"can"*] *be courteous,* the thirteenth "madrigal" in the 1601 collection of this master of the choristers and minor canon of Norwich Cathedral and vicar of St. Stephen's in the same city. If our copyist were to turn to a madrigalian publication, there could be few better suited to his needs than Carlton's, which Joseph Kerman aptly describes as "indeed the most solemn of all the English secular publications ... in an abstract contrapuntal style only occasionally touched by madrigalisms."[11] The scribe transforms Carlton's madrigal into an instrumental piece by omitting the text and combining repeated notes into longer values. The fact that he does not transmit the apparent misprints in bars 6 and 16[12] of the print suggests that he was not working from the print, or was quick enough to catch these printer's errors.

Two works that follow shortly after, *Prostrate O Lord* and *O Lord* [*who in thy sacred tent*], are recognizable as components of another highly serious and unmadrigalian set, but one of much greater musical caliber than Carlton's, William Byrd's *Psalms, Sonnets and Songs* of 1588. But despite the fact that the copyist must have entered these songs more than a decade after their publication, he used, not the printed versions, for which the lines had been altered slightly to accommodate the addition of words, but what can clearly be identified as the original consort song versions.[13] The "first singing part" is more or less identical to the printed text of 1588, but the other parts remain more instrumental in character, introducing numerous passing notes and long note values which need not be broken up to accommodate different syllables of the text, as they were in the 1588 collection. It is interesting to note as well that *Prostrate O Lord* provides a repetition of the final section, beginning at "breathed from an inward soul," which fails to appear in either the 1588 print or the other manuscript copy of the consort song version, Harvard MS 30. The Harvard manuscript is a Paston source, and therefore probably bears a close connection with the composer.[14] We have no such concrete evidence for 37402-6. But this sort of repetition is certainly a common enough feature of the consort song in general, and it is quite possible that the compiler of these partbooks felt it was a necessity. As we shall see below, there is evidence that he may have had a penchant for "improving" other musicians' works, and in this instance perhaps it was he who added the first ending, which does not meet Byrd's musical standards.[15]

Aside from these songs which reappear in published sources, this section of the partbooks contains a few other consort songs:

> *The Cry of London,* Orlando Gibbons
> *Like as the day,* Patrick Mando
> *Death the dissolver,* anon.
> *Fye, fye my fate,* "mundye"

The Gibbons work poses one problem in the form of an extra musical section inserted after bar 130[16] which does not appear in any of the numerous other sources for the piece. It seems highly unlikely that these sixteen bars could be from Gibbons's pen. The alto viol part of the Gibbons "Cry" incorporates the In Nomine tune, which, except for ornamentation or digressions of not more than three bars, is always clearly evident until the last few bars of each section, where Gibbons adds short "codas." However the In Nomine tune is entirely absent from this insertion, but resumes immediately afterward. The seams joining the passage to the main body of the work are especially noticeable: the first incorporates some particularly ugly dissonances, while the second marks time for two bars in an uninteresting fashion. The passage as a whole, with its thin textures, dull spacings, and simple-minded harmonic matrix moving squarely from one half-note pulse to the next, bears little resemblance to Gibbons. It is noteworthy that, in contrast to the rest of the piece, the parts never cross in this passage. What it resembles most is a rather amateurish harmonic progression, first worked out at the keyboard (it does lie better under the hands than surrounding passages) and then divided up among the five voices in a straightforward fashion.

With the exception of the Gibbons *Cry,* none of the other pieces in this group is of particular merit. The anonymous *Death the dissolver* is textless in the source, but to judge by the musical style, falls into the category of the Elizabethan consort song (see ex. 7). *Fye, fye my fate,* which seems to be a dramatic rendering of the parable of the Prodigal Son, as Philip Brett points out,[17] achieves special significance because of the attribution in 37406 to "mundye." Two extant verse anthems attest to William Mundy's pioneering interest in the verse anthem, but aside from *Fye, fye my fate* we possess no manifestations of his interest in the secular side of the verse idiom.

Ex. 7.   *Death the dissolver*

The final work in this section of the partbooks, *Sorrow stay* from Dowland's 1600 collection, serves as one of the most revealing witnesses to the scribe's steadfast, one might say obstinate, devotion to the consort song. What we find is someone's (perhaps the scribe's) rather awkward attempt to turn Dowland's lute song into a consort song. A useful comparison presents itself in William Wigthorpe's consort setting of the same work in Add. 17786-91.[18] But whereas Wigthorpe preserves the outer voices and the integrity of Dowland's original, the composer of the version in 37402-6 tries to rewrite the piece in a contrapuntal style reminiscent of the previous generation, and before long finds himself quite out of his depth.

Of all the pieces in Dowland's *Second Book*, none could offer greater appeal to the arranger's specific taste except perhaps no. 2, *Flow my tears*, or no. 14 *Come ye heavy states*. But they do not come so close to capturing the particular flavor of the play songs of the 1570s and 1580s as this lament of "a woeful, wretched wight," a phrase which might come directly from the *Paradise of Dainty Devices* (1576).

The arranger's goal was apparently to create as contrapuntal a setting as possible (see ex. 8, where the song is printed in full). Thus, where Dowland opened his piece with no introduction beyond a single g-minor chord, our arranger tacks on an introductory bar for the viols which is really nothing more that Dowland's bar 1, with the original voice part now allotted to the treble viol. This method of producing additional imitations simply by expanding the original to allow literal repetitions of the vocal phrases by the treble viol is the arranger's standard technique, as for example at bar 42, where he stretches Dowland's piece by three half-notes in order to introduce a literal anticipation of the phrase "I am condemned ever" in the treble viol part before reverting to the plan of Dowland's outer voices at the entry of the voice itself. A few bars later (52-56) he adds an extra breve in order to introduce another literal entry of the voice's "down, down, down, down, I fall" in viol I.

There are passages, however, in which the arranger preserves Dowland's outer parts and still manages to insert imitative entries. Thus, in bars 10-18, by preserving Dowland's outer parts but shifting the bass up an octave, the newer version can produce an additional entry in the tenor (bars. 14-17). But these searches for additional entries can land the arranger in musical situations which prove much less effective than the original. His setting of "Pity, pity, pity," for example, by weaving the declamatory pattern of the voice into all the inner parts, sacrifices Dowland's much more dramatic contrast between simple C-major and A-major chords.

When it comes to striking harmonic gestures, the arranger of 37402-6 is content, quite predictably, to indulge in that favorite Jacobean archaism—the false relation. Thus, in bar 34 the alto viol leaps to an f-natural against the voice's f-sharp in the same octave. The arranger makes the repetition of the

Ex. 8.   *Sorrow stay*

Ex. 8—*continued*

Ex. 8—*continued*

phrase literal enough to retain the clash. As if that were not enough, he alters the cadence of the following bar from Dowland's VII^6-I to a V^{4-3}-I in order to produce a C-sharp in the alto to clash with the voice's entry on C-natural at the same moment. Still not content, he begins another repetition of the point "alas I am condemned" in the treble viol on the C-natural above the tenor's C-sharp in bar 39.

This sort of excess extends to the contrapuntal character as well. In an effort to produce an imitative setting in which all parts are equally busy the arranger gets bogged down in a fussiness which clogs the texture and introduces technical demands beyond his musical skill, as the numerous consecutives show. Indeed, the arranger seems to have become so entangled in his own contrapuntal web that he finally lost heart and gave up with a rather cursory conclusion which avoids the challenge of the varied repetition of the final section by the abrupt note, "pity ://:," tacked on at the end of the vocal part.

The following section in the partbooks further attests to the scribe's apparent preference for voices and viols. The next twenty-five folios contain the complete first edition[19] of *The Triumphs of Oriana*. The compiler has not simply copied the madrigals as he found them in print, but has omitted the words from the lower three parts of the five-part works. In other words, he has tried to transform these pieces taken from one of England's most madrigalian publications into consort songs for vocal duet and three viols.[20] For the six-part pieces he simply omitted the words from all the parts, and, as mentioned earlier, even failed to match the pieces with the proper titles in 37402. He later realized his error, but only bothered to correct the titles of the first few six-part "Orianas." Such a treatment of these works is perhaps the strongest witness in the set to the compiler's basic lack of interest in the madrigal proper and his concern instead with music for viols, or for viols and voices.

The final section of the partbooks consists primarily of verse anthems,[21] or "antoms," as they are called in the source, and represents the sacred side of the scribe's interest in music for voices and viols. Before entering them the scribe added Weelkes's *Cry of London* and two instrumental pieces. The second of these instrumental works, a five-part piece headed "fantasia—attendite," can be identified from a concordance in Christ Church MSS 716-20 as Martin Peerson's fantasia of that title. It offers much to tax the virtuoso viol player, not simply rapid passages in eighth-notes, but also extreme chromaticism, striking as far afield as D-flat, and employing both the augmented second and even enharmonic changes.

Of the small group of verse anthems, all but Wilkinson's *Put me not to rebuke* appear anonymously, but can be identified from concordances. The version of Peerson's *O God when thou wentest forth* is somewhat closer to the one in Tenbury 1162 than to Hamond's text in Bodl. MSS Mus. F 11-15. The Wilkinson piece is closer to Add. 29366-8 than to the version in *Tristitiae Remedium* and Christ Church 56-60. The version of Peerson's *I am brought into so great trouble* appears to be somewhat simpler and therefore probably earlier than that of the only other source, *Tristitiae Remedium.* The text of the ubiquitous *Rise O my soul* by William Simms shows no special affinity with any of the eight other sources for the work.

Michael East's *When Israel came out of Egypt* is of special interest. Like Tenbury 1162-7 and John Merro's sources, 37402-6 present a simpler version than that which East published in 1610. But the version from 37402-6 is unique in several respects. The instrumental portions of the lines consistently bear the designation "orgaine," which perhaps indicates that the voices were accompanied by both viols and organ. This explanation is not entirely satisfactory, however, for in the second half of the work the scribe changes to the method of copying commonly employed in liturgical sources, whereby only the vocal portions are entered and the intervening portions are represented by rests. Significantly, the only part copied in its entirety, including both the instrumental and vocal portions, is the bassus, which bears the annotation, "organ pt" at the outset. The four-breve introduction to part 2 for the treble viol, on the other hand, has been squeezed into 37405, apparently as a later addition. But after this introduction, 37405 provides only the vocal portions like the inner parts. It is possible, therefore, that for part 2 the scribe was attempting to transcribe from an organ score. Or, alternately, he may have intended an accompaniment consisting of a viol on the bass-line, plus an organ filling out the harmony, either from an organ score no longer extant or perhaps even by improvising on the bass-line.[22]

After *When Israel came out of Egypt* the scribe enters one last vocal work, *What first did break thee,* "A love song" in strophic form.[23] Although it is a secular work, the scribe probably chose to enter it here, in the section devoted primarily to "antoms," since it shares with them the alternation of soloists and chorus. It represents an early example of the sort of secular piece for voices and viols that Michael East labeled "verse pastorals" in his *Third Set* of 1610, where such works first began to appear in print.

The partbooks conclude with an instrumental work, simply headed "A Pavinge," and bearing no attribution beyond James Pearson's monogram. But as Warwick Edwards first realized, the piece is in fact a consort version of William Byrd's first pavan for keyboard. It could not have been copied here until more than a decade after John Baldwin had copied the keyboard version into *My Ladye Nevell's Book*. James Pearson could very likely have acquired this original version of Byrd's *First Pavan* from the same source that provided him with the original versions for Byrd's *Prostrate O Lord* and *O Lord who in thy sacred tent*.

This last section has disappeared entirely from 37404. But in its stead we find something equally intriguing: examples of Anglican service music, consisting of the treble part for an entire service (minus the Kyrie) and the opening section (through "he hath put down") of an additional Magnificat. Both services have apparently eluded scholars of Anglican church music, and fail to appear in Daniel and le Huray's *The Sources of English Church Music*. The former can be identified as Thomas Morley's *Verse Service,* while the fragmentary Magnificat occurs in Morley's *Evening Service.* The manner of presentation is similar to that for liturgical sources, in which only the vocal passages are notated. But it seems unlikely that the part could have been used in anything but secular circles, for the small oblong octavo format is hardly common or practical for liturgical surroundings.[24] In addition, the incomplete text, consisting only of incipits for the important phrases[25] is also uncharacteristic for cathedral partbooks. Thus, 37404 apparently belongs to a very small handful of manuscripts which attest to the performance of Anglican service music in secular surroundings.

As mentioned above, the copying of the original layer of Italian madrigals was completed shortly after 1596. Soon afterward James Pearson must have proceeded to enter a large number of works dating from the turn of the century:

> *Sorrow stay,* Dowland (1600)
> *If women could be courteous,* Carlton (1601)
> *The Triumphs of Oriana,* 1st ed., Morley (1601)

The date of his final entry proves more difficult to establish. Of the two other works that also appear in printed sources, William Byrd's six-part fantasia (published in 1611) and Michael East's *When Israel came out of Egypt* (published in *The Third Set of Books,* 1610), both occur in simpler, earlier versions in 37402-6. Given Michael East's apparent eagerness to get all his works into print as soon as possible, it seems probable that the simpler version of *When Israel came out of Egypt* which appears here was composed soon after

1606, the year of East's *Second Set,*[26] and sometime slightly after 1606, perhaps early in the second decade of the century, seems the most reasonable hypothesis for the completion of the manuscripts.

Despite the diversity of its contents, 37402-6 is unified by the compiler's special concern with music for viols. Not only does he include fantasias by Lupo and Byrd (as well as the original consort version of Byrd's "First Pavan"), but he also "transforms" numerous vocal works into instrumental pieces by omitting their texts. Many of these are in fact sixteenth century motets, as we have seen, largely by composers of Tye's generation. Pearson, therefore, was another of those Jacobean copyists, like John Merro, not quite ready to give up the old Tudor motet repertory, even if he no longer treated the works as vocal pieces. Pearson's attitude toward the madrigal, on the other hand, was little different than his attitude toward the motet. He quite happily divested the six-part "Orianas" of their words, and even mixed up some of their titles, revealing in the process how unconcerned he was with their true identity as madrigals. His treatment of the five-part "Orianas" and of Dowland's *Sorrow stay,* on the other hand, was apparently intended to render them more appropriate to voices and viols. Thus, his version of *Sorrow stay* incorporates a viol accompaniment more contrapuntal (and less expert) than Dowland's original, and more akin perhaps to the Elizabethan dramatic lament than to the lute ayre. In the "Orianas" Pearson omits the texts from all but the top two parts— perhaps an oversight, but possibly an attempt to transform them into consort duets.

The only vocal forms which in fact retain their integrity to any great degree at this compiler's hands are the consort songs and verse anthems, which already make provision for his primary interest in viol playing. In this context the copyist reveals a continuing respect for William Byrd, who provides not only consort songs, but also consort music and an anthem. But surprisingly enough, neither of those continuing favorites, *Lullaby* or *Christ rising,* puts in an appearance. Thus, to judge by Pearson's manuscripts, during the first decade of the seventeenth century Byrd still retained some appeal. In the following decade his popularity would wane (as shown by the Myriell sources, for example), in the face of the more "modern" and fashionable output of East, Peerson, and Simms, who already begin to find a place for themselves among the last entries in Add. 37402-6.

(The opening section of the MSS is devoted to seventy-five Italian madrigals; see *Catalogue of MS Music in the British Museum, III*, pp. 222-224.)

folio[1] -02	-03	-04	-05	-06	no.	Title	idiom	Composer	Prints
45	45^V	65	44	46		If women could [can] be courteous[2]		[R. Carlton]	1601:13
45^V		65^V	44^V	46^V		Peace, I heard a voice	f		
46^V	46	66^V	45^V	47^V		*The Cry of London (i)*	v	O. Gibbons	
						A good sausage (ii)	v	" "	
	48	68^V	47^V	49^V		*Like as the day*	cs	P. Mando	
48^V[3]	48^V	69	48	50		[Quoniam fortitudo][2]		[O. Lassus]	
49^V	49	69^V	48^V	50^V		*Timor et tremor*[2]		[" "]	
50	49^V	70	49	51^V		Fantasia		W. Byrd	
51^V	50^V	72	50	54^V		Arise O Lord[2]		" "	
51^V	50^V	71^V	50	54^V		Libera [nos, salva nos][2]		"Talles"	
52	51	71^V	50^V	55		*Prostrate O Lord*[2]		W. Byrd	1588:27
52^V	51^V	71^V	51	55^V		[Lawdes deo][2]		C. Tye	
52^V	51^V	72^V	51^V	56		"la fantasia"			
53^V	52^V	73	52	56^V		[untitled]		"Morley"	
54	53	73^V	52^V	57		["]		Mundy	
54^V	53^V	74^V	53	57^V		*Death the dissolver*[2]			
55	54	74^V	53^V	58		*Dum transisset*[2]			
55^V	54^V	75^V	54	58^V		*O Lord [who in thy sacred tent]*[2]		[W. Byrd]	1588:6
56	55	75^V	54^V	59		*Decantabat [populus]*[2]		"Mr Birde"	
57	55^V	76^V	55^V	60		*Fye, fye my fate*	cs	"mundye"	
57^V	56^V	77	56	60^V		*De la courte*		R. Parsons	
58^V	57	77^V	56^V	61		*Sorrow stay*	cs	[J. Dowland]	
59^V	57^V	78^V	57^V	61^V	i	*Hence, stars*	cd	M. East	1601:unnum.
60^V	58^V	79	58	62	ii	*With angel's face*	cd	D. Norcomb	" :1
61^V	59^V	79^V	58^V	62^V	iii	*Lightly she whipped*	cd	J. Mundy	" :2
62^V	60^V	80^V	59^V	63	iv	*Long live fair Oriana*	cd	E. Gibbons	" :3
63^V	61^V	81	60	63^V	v	*All creatures now*	cd	J. Bennet	" :4
64^V	62^V	81^V	60^V	64	vi	*Fair Oriana*	cd	J. Hilton	" :5
65	63^V	82	61	64^V	vii	*The nymphs and shepherds*	cd	G. Marson	" :6
65^V	64	82^V	61^V	65	viii	*Calm was the air*	cd	R. Carlton	" :7
66^V	65	83	62	65^V	ix	*Thus bonny boots*	cd	J. Holmes	" :8
67^V	66	83^V	62^V	65^V	x	*Sing shepherds all*	cd	R. Nicolson	" :9
68^V	67^V	84^V	63^V	66^V	xi	*The fauns and satyrs*	cd	T. Tomkins	" :10
69^V	68^V	85^V	64^V	67	xii	*Come gentle swains*	cd	M. Cavendish	" :11
70	69	85^V	65	67^V	xiii	*With wreaths of roses*	cd	W. Cobbold	" :12
70^V	70	86^V	65^V	68	xiv	*Arise awake*	cd	T. Morley	" :13
71^V	71^V	87	66	68^V	xv	*Fair nymph*[2,4]		J. Farmer	" :14
72^V	72	87^V	66^V	69	xvi	*The Lady Oriana*[2]		J. Wilbye	" :15
73^V	72^V	88	67	69^V	xvii	*Hark*[2]		T. Hunt	" :16
74^V	73	88^V	68	70	xviii	*As Vesta was*[2]		T. Weelkes	" :17
76^V	73^V	89^V	69	70^V	xix	*Fair Orion*[2]		J. Milton	" :18
77^V	74	90	70^V	71	xx	*Round about*[2]		E. Gibbons	" :19
78^V	74^V	90^V	71	71^V	xxi	*Phoebus*[2] [Bright Phoebus]		G. Kirbye	" :20
79^V	75	91	71^V	72	xxii	*Fair Oriana*[2]		R. Jones	" :21
80^V	75^V	91^V	72	72^V	xxiii	*Fair Cithera*[2]		J. Lisley	" :22
81^V	75^V		72^V	73	xxiv	*Hard by a chrystal*[2]		T. Morley	" :23
83^V	76^V		73	73^V	xxv	*Come blessed*[2]		E. Johnson	" :24
84^V	77		74	74		*The Cry of London*	cs	T. Weelkes	
88	79^V		76^V	76		[untitled]			
89	80^V		77^V	77		Fantasia: attendite		[M. Peerson]	
90	81		78^V	78		*O God [when thou wentest]*	v	[M. Peerson]	
91	82^V		79^V	79		Put me not to rebuke	v	T. Wilkinson	
92	83^V		80^V	80		*Rise O my soul (i)*	v	[W. Simms]	
						And thou my soul (ii)	v	[" "]	
						To thee, O Jesu (iii)	v	[" "]	
93^V	85		82	81^V		*I am brought into to great trouble (i)*	v	[M. Peerson]	
						My heart panteth (ii)	v	[" ."]	
95	87		85	83		Fantasia: the first		T. Lupo	
95^V	87^V		85^V	83^V		["]: the second		" "	
96	88		86	84		["]: the third		" "	
97	89		86^V	84^V		*When Israel came out (i)*	v	[M. East]	1610:4
						What aileth thee (ii)	v	[" "]	" :5
97^V	89		86^V	84^V		*What first did break thee*	v		

1 Modern foliation.

2 These pieces left textless in the source.

3 In the case of compositions in six parts, two parts are entered in 37402, except in the case of the Byrd fantasia, where two parts appear in 37406.

4 In 37402 the scribe failed to provide the correct titles for the six-part "Orianas". He subsequently corrected the first three. In 37403 the last few "Orianas" lack titles.

-02	-03	-04	-05	-06	no.	Title	idiom	Composer	Prints
98^V	91^V		89^V	86^V		Pavinge		[W. Byrd]	
		92				*Te Deum*	v	[T. Morley]	
		93				*Benedictus*	v	[" "]	
		94				*Creed*	v	[" "]	
		94^V				*Magnificat*	v	[" "]	
		95				*Nunc dimittis*	v	[" "]	
		95^V				Magnificat	f	[" "]	

St. Michael's College, Tenbury MSS 1162-7

Tenbury MSS 1162-7, like Add. 29372-7 and Drexel 4180-5, form one of the few major sources of Jacobean and Caroline music for voices and viols to survive complete. Of the ninety-four works contained in the set, almost half employ the verse idiom. By contrast with Myriell and Merro, the scribe of the Tenbury manuscripts carefully segregates the works for voices and viols in the second half of the partbooks.

A considerable degree of organization also extends to small details of the manuscripts. It is quite common for works to be grouped by composer (e.g., five of Michael East's contributions appear together, beginning on p. 59), or by printed source (e.g., all the five-part works from *Musica Transalpina II* occur on pp. 40-42). In addition, the scribe occasionally orders his choices by subject matter; hence, the two "Amyntas" pieces on pages 36-39, the "unkind" pieces, nos. 98-100, and the laments for Prince Henry, nos. 102-4.

But despite this tendency to organize, the scribe never includes composers' names with any of the pieces. Given the neatness of his copying hand, it comes as something of a surprise to find that he can be exasperatingly inaccurate. The entries often reveal omissions in both rests and notes, which make it questionable if the books were ever used in performance.

Judging 1162-7 in isolation, there is little in the way of external evidence to aid in the dating of the source. The set once belonged to James Bartleman (1769-1821), the well-known bass and music collector, and was auctioned off as part of his collection in 1822.[1] The repertory contains nothing printed later than 1618 (East's *Fourth Set of Books),* while all the most modern composers begin to appear in other sources datable from 1613-1616. Thus, in the past the Tenbury source has been dated either "early 17th century,"[2] or more exactly, "*c.* 1615-1625."[3] Indeed, none of the compositions which can be identified by concordances need be any later.

The general style of the music hand, however, resembles none of the sources previously discussed, and has much more in common with manuscripts from a later period. Plate 18b, from Royal College of Music MS 2033, exemplifies this later writing style in a form that reveals numerous similarities to 1162-7 (pl. 18a): the custos, often broadening out at the end of the tail; the

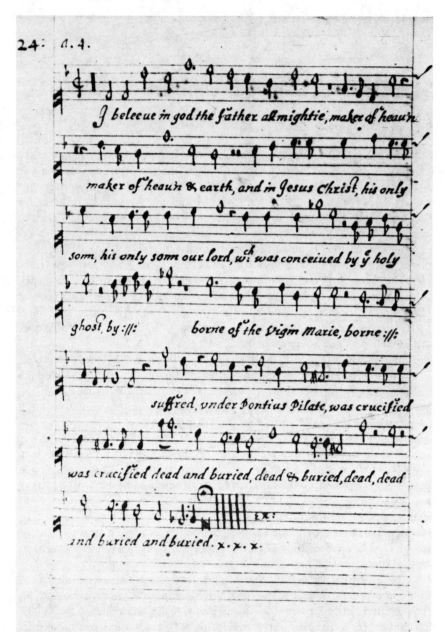

Pl. 18b.   Royal College of Music MS 2033.
(By permission of the Director, Royal College of
Music, London)

time-signature, with a curving blob at the bottom of the stroke through the half
circle (precisely placed on the middle line of the staff); the very stubby flat signs,
often open at the top; the fermata which replaces the central dot with
something like a lop-sided breve; the "x.x.x." ornament at the end of the text.
Indeed, the extent of their similarity has led Robert Ford to suggest that the
scribe of RCM 2033 might actually have been imitating the scribe of 1162.[4] The
Royal College source, however, contains an entirely different repertory from
the Tenbury partbooks: one- and two-voice continuo motets, largely by
Dering, and an English anthem by a considerably later composer, George
Jeffreys (ca. 1610-1685).[5]

Robert Ford has identified the scribe of 1162-7 as the copyist of several
other sources: a set of viol manuscripts belonging to Franklin B. Zimmerman
of the University of Pennsylvania, Philadelphia, Christ Church MS 430,
British Library, Madrigal Society MSS 33-36, and the "Layton Ring
Manuscript."[6] All these sources are devoted primarily or entirely to the work of
William Lawes, a composer who failed to attract the interest of any other scribe
discussed in this volume, and, indeed, a composer who was not active until after
several of the scribes' deaths. The writing style of 1162 and the other sources,

then, goes hand in hand with works of a later era. David Pinto has suggested a date of ca. 1640 for the Zimmerman MSS and for Christ Church 430;[7] it is reasonable to assume that 1162-7 must date from the same period, fifteen to twenty-five years later than previously supposed.

The reappearance of the scribe's hand in these other sources, and in the Zimmerman MSS and Christ Church 430 in particular, suggests London as the point of origin for 1162-7. Both the other sources contain annotations in the hand of John Browne (1608-1691), a seventeenth-century music collector who has been the object of considerable scrutiny in recent years.[8] The son of a prosperous dealer in poultry, Browne read law and was admitted to the Middle Temple in October 1628. He later served as clerk of the Parliaments from March 1636/37 until 1649 and from 1660 until his death.[9] Browne would most probably have acquired the Zimmerman MSS and Christ Church 430 in London around 1640. Although there is no evidence to link 1162-7 with Browne, the reappearance of the same scribal hand in two of Browne's sources raises the possibility that 1162-7 might also have been copied in the capital. The prominence of William Lawes in these concordant sources, and of Richard Dering (who also puts in an appearance in 1162-7), likewise suggests London, because of these composers' strong court connections.

A comparison of the contents of 1162-7 with the sources from previous chapters, however, reveals interesting affinities with the Cambridge area. The Tenbury manuscripts are among the few sources to transmit several compositions by Robert Ramsey, who took his Mus. B. from Cambridge in 1616 and served as organist of Trinity College from 1628 until 1644 and as master of the choristers from 1637 until 1644. Aside from the three works which may be attributed to the Trinity College organist on the basis of concordances, others might also be his work, as will be shown later. Furthermore, apart from 1162-7, the only known source for the anonymous *Wherefore are men so loath to die,* Paris Rés. 1186,[10] is a Cambridge manuscript, apparently compiled during the 1630s by Robert Creighton, educated at Trinity College and professor of Greek at Cambridge from 1625 until 1639.

Thomas Hamond of Hawkedon, Suffolk, maintained ties with Cambridge at roughly the same time as the scribe was at work on Tenbury 1162-7, and it is intriguing to discover a certain overlap in the repertories of Hamond's manuscripts and Tenbury 1162-7. Both are important sources for the anthems of Martin Peerson (a native of Cambridgeshire); Hamond includes five, all of which appear in the Tenbury source. The overlap with Myriell, by contrast, only involves three anthems by Peerson. For the single Peerson anthem shared by all three sources, *Fly ravished soul,* 1162 and Hamond clearly differ from Myriell, not only in adding *Rain Eyes* as a fourth part, but also in transmitting a somewhat different text for their first chorus. The concordances from the works of Thomas Ravenscroft, so frequently a companion of Peerson's in

Hamond, are more unusual. They consist of a ballet, *Nymphs and fairies,* and a madrigal, *Lure, faulkners lure,* attributed to Ravenscroft in Hamond's books. It is interesting that in both sources we find the same version of the latter piece, with the added fifth part, *not* the version *a4* printed in Ravenscroft's *Brief Discourse* (1614) and attributed there to John Bennet. In addition, the last two anthems in Tenbury 1162-7, *Laudate Dominum a8* and *O sing unto the Lord a9,* could quite possibly be Cambridge degree exercises; Hamond had transmitted two such exercises by Ramsey and John Tomkins. All these significant coincidences could indicate that both Hamond and the scribe of Tenbury 1162-7 had access to the same musical repertory.

External evidence thus suggests London as the place of origin for the source, while the contents confirm what we have seen elsewhere: strong musical links between Cambridge and the capital during the period. It is not implausible that Cambridge repertory should find its way to London (or vice versa)—less implausible, perhaps, than that a London scribe might find his way to Cambridge.

The scribe of the Tenbury source set about his task with a clear scheme in mind: a collection devoted specifically and almost exclusively to the madrigal. It is unlikely, however, that the verse pieces were part of this original scheme. They are characterized by a contrasting text hand which had made its first appearance with the last full piece of the five-part section *(To pitch our toils)* and with *Why dost thou shoot* of the six-part section. The copying must already have been at an advanced stage before the first works for voices and viols were entered. The scribe subsequently exhausted all the space available for five-part works before all the verse works were entered, and therefore he had to backtrack to the end of the four-part section to insert *I believe in God* and *He that descended,* which reveal the same text hand as the latter portion of the partbooks.

The fifty or so madrigals that appear in 1162-7 reveal a very specific aesthetic concern, one which contrasts with that of other sources where we find a strong interest in the verse idiom, such as Myriell's or Merro's. The Tenbury scribe was interested above all in the Italian madrigal or in English works which strongly reflect the Italian idiom. The most prominent prints in the partbooks are *Musica Transalpina I* (eight compositions) and *Musica Transalpina II* (six compositions), while *Italian Madrigals Englished* also provides another two pieces. These three collections account for almost half the printed madrigals in the source. Among these Italian works, the madrigals of Marenzio predominate, with seven examples, as compared with the nearest competitor, Ferretti, with three. It is interesting to find Alfonso Ferrabosco totally ignored. Possibly the conservative style of this old Elizabethan and Jacobean favorite seemed simply too old-fashioned to satisfy the taste of this later scribe.

Of the English madrigal sets, both Morley's 1593 *Canzonets* and Wilbye's 1609 *Second Set* follow close on the heels of the second *Musica Transalpina*, with five works apiece. There are also another four from *The Triumphs of Oriana* (including Weelkes's and Wilbye's contributions), and two from Wilbye's *First Set* (1598). Thus, the scribe concerns himself only with the most madrigalian Englishmen. Morley's prominence is especially striking, for he rarely appeared in the other important manuscript sources discussed earlier. His presence here is one of the most striking manifestations of the compiler's primary concern with the madrigal in its first heyday.

The composers whom the scribe ignores are those whose publications tended to be the more prominent in the other major manuscripts which profess an interest in the verse idiom. We find nothing from Byrd's three secular sets of 1588, 1589, and 1611, nothing from Ward's set of 1613, no examples from Tomkins's 1622 publication, and nothing from Gibbons's 1612 *First Set of Madrigals and Motets.*

Of the seventeen unpublished madrigals only a few an be ascribed on the basis of other sources. *O how fortunate those* (p. 32) also occurs in Add. 29366-8 with an ascription to Ramsey, and *Wilt thou unkind now leave me weeping* is ascribed to him in Add. 17786-91. It is not surprising to find him here, given the possible Cambridge connections of the source and Ramsey's particular indebtedness to the Italian style, as outlined by Edward Thompson.[11]

Because of the scribe's tendency to group compositions either by print or by composer, it is possible that the group on pages 32-38, beginning with Ramsey's *O how fortunate those*, might contain other of his works. Edward Thompson has pointed out that Ramsey's texts are "invariably moralistic or pathetic."[12] Not only Ramsey's *O how fortunate those*, but also the works on pages 33-35, conform to this pattern. Furthermore, when the poems are read as a group, their common features seem too numerous to be purely coincidental:

32   O how fortunate those are born untimely,
            Folding the light in everlasting slumber.
            Since alonely to griefe our days we number.

33 (i)   Cease now thy wailing.
            How can a shade endure the substance failing?
            Here ends thy mourning,
            Time with a cypress wreath thy brows adorning.
            False love which beauty staineth,
            Freedom betraying, no pleasure gaineth,
            But breathless sighs, thy life with grief decaying.
            When crooked age assails thee,
            Silver hair strowed,
            What then avails thee?

34 (ii)   Stay then, and first behold the end,
           What may befall it.
           Time lost, thou mayest repent too late,
           Never recall it.
           Then do not waste this treasure,
           To follow vain delights and pleasure.

35   So vain is all their pleasure
           That delight in this worldly treasure,
           That when they joy most
           Pale grief, pleasure adorning
           With mourning, mars all their mirth.
           And life, which youth here borrows,
           Yields for one flying joy a thousand sorrows.
           But death, vain life expired,
           Conveys our souls to rest,
           Sweet quiet slumber,
           Whose end no time can number.

The opening of 35 seems a response to the conclusion of 34, and both employ the "pleasure/treasure" rhyme. The poet's stock of rhymes is in fact very limited, for "slumber/number" crops up in both 32 and 35, while "mourning/ adorning" from 33 also appears in 35. In addition to these recurrent rhymes, the poems also share patterns of syntax, such as gerund constructions (e.g., "the substance failing," "thy brows adorning," "freedom betraying," "with grief decaying" from 33, and "pleasure adorning" from 35), or contracted phrases which seem incomplete (e.g., "How fortunate those *are born untimely"* from 32; "How can a shade endure *the substance failing,"* "False love which beauty staineth, *freedom betraying,* no pleasure gaineth," "When crooked age assails thee, *silver hair strowed,* what then avails thee" from 33; "But death, *vain life expired,* conveys our souls to rest" from 35). It is possible, therefore, that all are the products of a single versifier's limited talents. It is also possible that they were conceived as some sort of cycle, for they make slightly more sense if read in sequence than when considered in isolation.

A look at their musical settings reveals a talent reasonably matched to the poet's. At the highest level the works favor some sort of large-scale repetition. In 32 the final section is repeated, with the top two parts interchanged. In 33 and 34 we find an AA'BB' formal scheme, like a canzonet without the middle section; in the latter the top two parts again interchange for the repetitions. Only 35 avoids such structural restatements. But, like all the others, it makes incessant use of repeated phrases, often stated first in one group of voices and then in another. All four works follow this structural pattern, based upon varied repetition of smaller phrase units.

Viewed on the most general level, the works show the same basically homophonic texture, where the imitative counterpoint remains clearly within the confines of the successions of relatively stereotyped harmonies and moves in half-notes and quarter-notes with dogged insistence. The composer occasionally attempts to break the rhythmic straight-jacket of four-in-a-bar, but inevitably in the same way, either within the bar, "♩ ♩. ♪ ♩," or across the bar, " ♩ ♩♩♩♩ ♩ " (see exx. 1 and 2).

Harmonically all the pieces make use of similar devices intended to vary the otherwise regular succession of chords. Thompson has characterized Ramsey's work as offering "expressive harmonies abounding in 'false relations'"[13]—a fine example appears at the opening of *O how fortunate those,* the one piece definitely attributable to Ramsey (see ex. 1). Less striking examples recur in the other works (see ex. 2). A preoccupation with false relations was, of course, typical of Jacobean composers. But these works are linked by other harmonic features. The pieces show an interest in the juxtaposition of triads a third apart, when the latter has as its root the third of the former (see ex. 2).

Ex. 1.

32.   *O how fortunate they*

35.   *So vain is all their pleasure*

Furthermore, *O how fortunate* and *Cease now thy wailing* have in common the same means of varying their second endings, a method which shows no great imagination: the first ending is simply repeated with the time values doubled, a device which also reappears in Ramsey's *If plaints, laments or sorrow* in Hamond's manuscripts, F20-24.

Ex. 2.

In addition, so far as the movement of their voice parts is concerned, all the works betray the same lack of real contrapuntal activity. Those sections which are not blatantly homophonic simply ring the changes on a rudimentary idea, usually based on a triad, tossing it from voice to voice in very regular fashion. The idea is rarely more than a bar long, and its repetition usually does not introduce any harmonic variety. In some cases, as at "folding the light" of 32 (bar 11ff) and "one flying joy" of 35 (bar 39ff), the points and their treatments are virtually identical (see ex. 3).

Thus, the group of pieces on pages 32-35 share a great deal in common, both in terms of their texts and musical settings. Because of their many similarities, it seems that not only 32, but the entire group, could well be the work of Robert Ramsey.

Ex. 3.

This group is followed in the source by two more anonymous pieces, having in common a concern with the tribulations of one "Amyntas." These two works reflect the same approach to the madrigal style apparent in the previous group. The first, again seems quite Ramseian, presenting the familiar cross rhythm, "♩ ♩ ♩. ♪ ♩," the succession of chords a third apart, the usual brief, very square figures tossed from part to part with complete regularity, including figures that appeared in both *O how fortunate those* and *So vain is all their pleasure.*

The other work, *O wretched Amyntas,* must represent an Englishman's attempts to cope with the Monteverdian madrigal style. By contrast with all the preceding works of the group except number 35, this work is through-composed, and attempts to capture all the images of its madrigalian verse. It shows less tendency to lapse into totally predictable repetitions of short phrase groups, and indeed, differs from the other works in its more varied and contrasting sections, whose range of note values is wider than that of the pieces discussed above. The opening, with its striking chordal declamation of the text, seems consciously to imitate the later Italian madrigal (see ex. 4).

In addition to this declamatory passage, the madrigal is especially notable for its affective dissonance and harmony, obviously in imitation, again, of

Ex. 4.   *O wretched Amyntas*

some later Italian madrigalists. Several passages prove far more adventurous than anything in the previous pieces. The results are indeed striking, if at times somewhat awkward, especially by comparison with the works of the more skillful Italians, which must have provided the models for the present composer (see ex. 5). *O wretched Amyntas* seems to carry still further the enthusiasm for the Italian style also apparent in Ramsey's work. It may attest once again to the common interest in Italian music at Cambridge, to which both Peacham and Mace bear witness.

After another group of some seven madrigals from Thomas East's and Thomas Watson's collections there occur three unpublished ballets and a madrigal. The latter, *Lure, faulkners, lure,* had been ascribed to Weelkes in the table of contents, and the attribution was subsequently altered to Bennet by someone familiar with the *Lure, faulkners, lure* in Thomas Ravenscroft's *A Brief Discourse* (1614). But a closer look at the *Lure, faulkners, lure* in 1162-7 reveals that this is not Bennet's piece, but another version in five parts, the same version that turns up in Thomas Hamond's Bodl. MSS Mus. F 11-15, where we also find its neighbor in 1162, *Nymphs and fairies,* as mentioned above.

The anonymous pieces that preceded *Nymphs and fairies* are also ballets (the only others in the source), and have much in common with Ravenscroft's in terms of their approach to the light madrigalian idiom. A liking for

Ex. 5.   *O wretched Amyntas*

sequential passages, as revealed by the first "fa-la" of *Nymphs and fairies*
reappears for the corresponding section of *O help me soon*. Several shorter
sequences also occur in Ravenscroft's *Such was old Orpheus' cunning* from
Hamond's manuscripts. Both *O help me soon* and *Out alas, what should I say*
are less homophonic than Ravenscroft's *To Sestos young Leander* or *Nymphs
and fairies*, which become extensively contrapuntal only during their "fae-
laes." The character of the two anonymous ballets is therefore closer to that of
Such was old Orpheus' cunning, Fair shepherds' Queen, or *Lure, faulkners,
lure*. They all share a fascination with ostinato-like repetitions of short, lively
figures, often in eighth-notes, and occasionally even in sixteenths, which skip
from part to part, much of the time in parallel thirds and sixths. Like the
attributed pieces, *O help me soon* and *Out alas, what should I say* pay more
attention to irregular entries and harmonic variety than the anonymous works
in the Ramsey group above, for example. Often the anonymous *O help me
soon* and *Out alas, what should I say* introduce figures which reappear in the
pieces bearing Ravenscroft's name. For example, not only does the point from
bar 7 of *O help me soon* occur again, beginning at bar 28 of *Out alas,* it also
reappears at bar 46 of *Fair shepherds' Queen* and at bar 73 of *Such was old
Orpheus' cunning*, where the treatments have a certain amount in common (see
ex. 6). Whether or not these two anonymous ballets are actually by

Ravenscroft, the scribe was quite justified in grouping them with the attributable works on the basis of the stylistic uniformity which pervades the group as a whole.

Ex. 6.

Having begun with the Elizabethan madrigal in its heyday, the works of Morley, Wilbye, and the "Englished" Italians, the scribe turned to a later generation of Englishmen, of whom Ramsey and Ravenscroft are identifiable, who indulge in the modernisms of the Italians, but with somewhat less expertise than their predecessors. The scribe's next step takes him decidedly further afield, for, after a hodge-podge of Oriana madrigals, a full anthem, and a hunting piece, *To pitch our toils,* he turns to the native idiom of voices and viols. There follow some forty works for voices and viols, an unusually large number for a source previously devoted to a still greater number of examples of the Elizabethan madrigal *par excellence.* But while the scribe obviously intended a clear separation of the two genres, these verse pieces are hardly divorced from what has preceded them, for they show in many respects the infiltration of the native style by the Italian, madrigalian idiom, whether in some external manner, such as the use of an Italian text for a consort song, or in the enthusiastic adaptation of various madrigalian features to the consort idiom as inherited from the Elizabethans. This source presents in a nutshell the historical outcome of the interaction between these two genres. During the later years of the reign of James I a few madrigals continued to be written, frequently less expert and successful than their Italian or late Elizabethan models: here, the pieces by Ramsey, Ravenscroft, or anonymous. But in general the trend was directed away from the madrigal toward a greater diversification of styles, sometimes based upon the time-honored combination of voices and viols, now infused with more modern elements, either Italian in origin, or adapted from the lute ayre. The results, as we shall see, are not necessarily so successful as either the old consort song or the madrigal in their own right.

The person who best represents this musical interaction historically, Michael East, also occupies the pivotal position in this source. After having published two collections devoted entirely to madrigals in 1604 and 1606, East broadened the scope of his *Third Set* of 1610 to include "Pastorals, Anthemes, Neopolitanes, Fancies, and Madrigals." The composer's later publications continue to reveal the same diversification. East's block of contributions to Tenbury 1162-7 all appeared in either the crucial *Third Set* or in his *Fourth Set* of eight years later:

59   *Cantate nimphe e pastori* (i), (1610)
      Ahi me, purche sospirar (ii), (1610)
      Ma pace (iii), (1610)
60   *When Israel came out of Egypt* (i), (1610)
61   *What aileth thee* (ii), (1610)
62   *O clap your hands* (i), (1618)
63   *God is gone up* (ii), (1618)

Not only do these works provide a sampling of English music in transition, the versions in Tenbury 1162-7 also happen to represent East's first thoughts, for all the works were later revised before being sent to the printer. A comparison of East's first and second thoughts throws new light upon his musical development. We first see the young composer, shortly before 1610, still not quite in control of the basic techniques of composition, experimenting with the characteristic devices of the madrigal and the verse idiom. Then, *O clap your hands,* composed a few years later, shows East as a more mature composer, ready to shift his attention to large-scale musical problems governing the shape of a piece of music as a whole. It therefore seems worthwhile to consider these works in some detail for what they can tell us, on the one hand, about the changes in English musical style in the middle years of James's reign, and, on the other, about East's own musical growth.

The works on page 59 through folio 61[V], when printed, served as the opening five pieces of *The Third Set* (1610). It is interesting to note that four of the five "Neopolitanes" which conclude the same collection employ Italian models for both music and text.[14] This makes it all the more intriguing to find in 1162-7 versions of the opening three "verse pastorals" from the same print, (i) *Sweet Muses,* (ii) *Aye me, wherefore sighs,* (iii) *My peace and my pleasure,* provided with an *Italian* text: (i) *Cantate nimphe e pastori,* (ii) *Ahi me, purche sospirar,* and (iii) *Ma pace.* The variations in text do not represent the only differences between the two versions of the work, however, for the 1610 print proves to be quite an extensive reworking of the original.

A comparison of the English and Italian texts shows that this may be another instance in which East has borrowed an original Italian text (somewhat obscured by the Jacobean spellings). Both texts are set out side-by-side for comparison in table 1. Perhaps the music, too, is based upon some Italian original, for certain details of the musical setting correspond more closely to the Italian than to the English. The opening roulade, for instance, was undoubtedly conceived for "Cantate" rather than for the nondescript "Sweet Muses."[15] When the same figure reappears for bars 19-24 of the print it falls to the insignificant "after," while in the Tenbury version it is again associated with "cantate." The second and third parts follow the Italian closely, but the opening section betrays a greater freedom. Interestingly enough, the "shrillest notes" of the translation of the second line match more the high g's of the solo line than do the "accenti dolci" of the Italian. The English version, after translating the Italian for part 1, adds an entirely new section, beginning "Now join we altogether." These added lines were probably intended to form a clearer transition to part 2 by introducing one of the protagonists from the second section. As we shall see, the music for the added lines also bears little relation to the manuscript version.

Table 1.   Italian-English Comparison of Three Texts

1162-7	1610 print
Cantate Nimphe e Pastori	Sweet Muses, Nymphs and shepherds sporting,
Con accenti dolci e sonori.	Sound your shrillest notes of joy consorting.
Fauni, Satyri, e tu Eccho,	Fauns and Satyrs, and thou, Echo,
Cantate, Ta na na na no.	Sing after me, Ta na na na no.
	Now join we all together,
	To welcome Sylvia hither.
	And sweetly sing,
	Ta na na na no.
Ahi me, Purche sospirar Sylvia	Aye me, wherefore sighs the fair Sylvia
Pur suouen Syrenio?	(Alas) for her Syrenio?
Purche Rhodanthe bella	But why Rodan the fairest
Pur suo savi Silvio?	For her sweet Sylvio dearest?
Ahi me, Eccho risoni,	Aye me, Echo sweetly sing,
Nimphe e Pastori.	Nymphs and shepherds reporting.
Ma pace, amore,	My peace and my pleasure,
Pace et amore,	Love and chiefest treasure,
Dona ta diva Pallas,	Lady, thou goddess, Pallas,
Et suo satyro.	And all thy satyrs.

The differences in the musical settings of this little poem provide a rare example of a Jacobean composer's second thoughts about an earlier work. The changes which East introduces seem designed to make the piece, on the one hand, better suited to voices and viols, and, on the other, more up-to-date and Italianate. Part 1 in the 1610 print begins with what appears to be an extensive rewriting of the first eight bars of the manuscript version (see ex. 7). In place of the original four bars of strict homophony, East employs a six-bar introduction in which each viol enters with the opening figure from the vocal parts. It seems that he intended something more akin to the imitative opening of the traditional consort song, but the result, which runs about in a basically static series of thirds and sixths, bears only a superficial resemblance to the time-honored form. It is also telling that he reorganizes the cadence over the pedal-D to create a $\begin{smallmatrix}7\ 6\ 5\\5\text{-}4\text{-}4\text{-}3\\3\end{smallmatrix}$ series of suspensions, an obvious earmark of the Italian style, which had been a rarity in the older consort song. Thus, from the introduction alone, we see native style and Italian influence jostling one another.

Once the voice has entered, the correspondence to the manuscript version is more exact, but still shows small alterations, usually intended either to increase the contrapuntal activity or to enrich the cadences. Thus, at bar 9 of

Ex. 7. *Sweet Muses*

(printed version)

(manuscript version)

★:G in MS.

Ex. 7—*continued*

Ex. 7—*continued*

the print East rewrites the alto viol part to include another satement of the "cantate" figure, and also increases the melodic activity of the tenor viol (while eliminating parallel octaves with the treble viol in the process). At bar 13 he rewrites all the inner parts to eliminate parallel fifths between voice and treble viol and, more importantly, to create another Italian cadence, complete with suspended seventh on the downbeat.

The variation upon the opening "cantate" figure for bars 19-24 again induces the composer to rewrite the alto and tenor viol parts in an attempt to produce more imitative entries and to increase the movement in parallel thirds and sixths in these parts, which in the earlier version moved inelegantly in octaves by contrary motion. In addition, East expands the sequential repetition of the "cantate" point to include an entry on E, harmonized by a brief cadence on A, a harmonic area untouched in the original version. The opening of the succeeding "Ta na na na no" point is also altered slightly, which not only enhances the overlap between the soloists, but also enriches the harmony through several passing sevenths absent from the manuscript version.

The following section for full chorus comprises the most extensive difference between the two settings. In place of the original "Ta na na na no," a section of only eight bars, East introduces additional lines of text and some sixteen bars of music. "Now join we all together to welcome Sylvia hither" bears no musical relationship to the original. The chorus enters for the first time in the piece (and, indeed, for the first time in the *Third Set*), as the additional text specifically prescribes, and also leads to a clearly articulated cadence on the dominant of the dominant, a much needed improvement over the rather incessant tonic and dominant of the original. The succeeding "and sweetly sing" adopts the melodic shapes of the upper voices from the choral "cantate" of the original, but heightens their rhythmic activity and introduces a madrigalian interplay of upper and lower parts. The expanded choral "ta na na na no" also makes some use of a small group versus the full choir, and broadens out to the cadence with increased contrapuntal activity over a longer dominant pedal which prepares for the cadence more successfully than the rather cursory earlier treatment.

Part 2 shows fewer revisions, but the same musical goals. An additional bar at the opening enables the top three viols to enter separately rather than together as they had done in the Tenbury source (see ex. 8). At bar 5, the point where the voice originally entered, East introduces the bass viol, not as a simple harmonic support moving in fourths and fifths, but in imitation of the previous tenor viol line. Furthermore, the composer reorganizes the cadence over a dominant pedal to allow for expressive suspensions. Thus, as in part 1, the introduction takes on the greater expansiveness and contrapuntal activity of the older consort song, but up-dated through the Italianate cadence.

Ex. 8.   *Aye me, wherefore sighs*

(printed version)

(manuscript version)

The additional changes are minor ones. A few more passing notes are inserted in the viol parts so that the rising dotted figure from the bass and the quicker falling dotted figure from the alto viol in bar 17 find their way into other parts (see ex. 9). Later, in the viol interlude from bars 38 to 42, other small alternations are made to increase the number of appearances of a similar falling dotted figure and to allow its opening appearance (bar 38) more room in which to expand (see ex. 10). In bars 42-43, the treble viol is slightly changed, obviously after the realization that the pattern from bar 38 could thereby be given the status of a "point." Interestingly enough, in the cadence before "Eccho risoni" ("Echo sweetly sing") from the Tenbury manuscripts, we find its only use of the Morleian cadence with suspended seventh, which, of course, was preserved in *The Third Set.*

The 1610 setting of the brief text for part 3 admits few changes. As one might expect by now, the cadence in the viol introduction is up-dated to include the suspended seventh. In addition, the print expands the interlude before "And all the satyrs" by five quarter-notes, enough time for two additional entries in anticipation of the vocal line in tenor and bass (see ex. 11).

Ex. 9.   *Aye me, wherefore sighs*

(printed version)

(manuscript version)

★ ★ *passage omitted in MS*

The manuscript version ends very abruptly at this point. Perhaps East later felt it was too abrupt, for in the print he introduces a varied repetition of the opening "Sweet Muses" section. Rather than return to the opening quite literally, he uses a variation—in fact, the eight bars which originally opened the Tenbury version. The repetition then corresponds to the rewritten opening section until its last four bars, when another new, more imitative conclusion brings the piece to a close. Thus, East has tightened up the structure of the whole work through structural repetition. There had already been a certain amount of repetition: in the Italian version of part 1 the viol introduction returned for the choral "cantate," and in part 2 the earlier "Aye me" returned at bar 42. In addition, the "echo" section of part 2 recalled a similar, though not identical, passage from part 1. But through this return to the opening East gives the printed version of the work a clear ABCA′ structure.

Thus, East joins the growing group of English composers who made use of some sort of "structural repetition." Indeed, of the later "madrigalists," East employs the device as frequently as any, and is only surpassed in this respect by Thomas Weelkes, whose use of this technique has been treated as a relative

Ex. 10.   *Aye me, wherefore sighs*

(printed version)

(manuscript version)

novelty by David Brown.[16] After a solitary example in East's *First Set* (nos. 18-19, *My prime of youth/ The Spring is past),* such repetition crops up on three occasions in *The Second Set* (nos. 7-8, *In dolorous complaining/ Since teares would not obtain,* nos. 17-18, *Now Cloris laughs/ Forsaken Thyrsis,* and no. 22, *O metaphysical Tobacco*), once in *The Third Set* for *Sweet Muses,* and once in *The Fourth Set* (nos. 17-18, *Quick, quick away/ No haste, but good*). In every instance it is apparently motivated by the reappearance of a previous textual phrase later in the course of the poem.

If we have dwelt on this piece at length, it is because it illustrates so clearly the interaction of madrigalian and consort song aesthetics in the hands of this young Jacobean composer. Having initially drawn upon what seems to have been an original Italian text, and perhaps even an as yet unidentified Italian musical setting, East set it for the traditionally English combination of solo voices, viols and chorus. When he came to revise the work for publication he apparently felt it was not enough to translate the text, so he extensively reworked the composition, on the one hand, increasing the contrapuntal activity of the viol parts and introducing a reprise at the end after the manner of the verse idiom, and on the other, making his revision more Italianate through

Ex. 11.   *My peace and my pleasure*

(printed version)

(manuscript version)

devices such as antiphonal groupings of voices and especially through the
cadential forms associated with the madrigal. The resulting work is a charming
one, and perhaps East's most successful amalgamation of Italian and native
styles. Curiously, it represents the only such work by East to have survived.
East's other efforts in the expansive verse idiom all employ sacred texts, and
their combination of native and madrigalian features is never so convincing in
the more sober context.

The revisions of East's *When Israel came out of Egypt* are neither so
drastic nor so revealing as his reworkings of *Cantate Nimphe e pastori*. The
madrigalian exuberance of the "verse pastoral" had little place in the more
serious verse anthems, and their revisions concern themselves chiefly with
increasing the imitative activity of the viol parts. Thus, East extended the
introduction of *When Israel came out of Egypt* to almost double the original
length (see ex. 12). Initially the tenor and alto viol parts had entered with very
nondescript lines some four bars after the treble and bass viols had anticipated
the opening vocal phrase. This allowed very little time to prepare for the
entrance of the voice. For the reworking East simply tacked on five extra bars
to his original, during which the inner parts not only present the theme, but also

Ex. 12.   *When Israel came out of Egypt*

(printed version)

(manuscript version)

introduce harmonic variety by cadencing on the fifth, D, before the return to the final, G, at the first entrance of the bass. They then continue to weave new lines around the pre-existent treble and bass entries, filling out the harmony and enriching the harmonic color, as, for example, in the effective E-flat in the revised altus at bar 10.

A similar intensification of the imitative counterpoint appears in the first chorus, "And the house of Jacob, from among the strange children." The first version contained two entries in parallel thirds or sixths for the falling point "from among the strange children" (see ex. 13). By rethinking altus and bassus, the composer not only obtains two additional entries of the point, but also manages to overlap the previous phrase and to soften the cadence on D at bar 35. He appears not to have been especially bothered, however, by the fact that the additional entries were associated with the wrong textual phrase.

Just as East felt his original introduction was too brief, so he felt the final cadence to part 1 was much too cursory: in some parts the voices barely enter before the penultimate bar, if at all,[17] (see ex. 14). So for the print the composer inserted three more bars, which not only provide ample preparation for the final cadence, but also permit several entries of the spritely little point, "and the

Ex. 13.   *When Israel came out of Egypt*

(printed version)

(manuscript version)

little hills," which East manages to combine with the falling line, "like young sheep," into a primitive sort of double point, after the Italian manner. The final entry in the bass also picks up the rising sequential pattern of the two previous bass entries, driving the harmony more forcefully and logically toward the dominant of the penultimate bar.

The alterations in part 2 generally involve the insertion of additional imitative entries, often by merely tacking on extra bars. The original viol introduction to "And ye mountains that ye skipped like Rams," for instance, contained only a single anticipation of a figure related to the points for "that ye skipped" and "and ye little hills" (see ex. 15). For the revision East simply adds two bars at the beginning, during which the cantus and bassus present an additional entry of the point in thirds. The identical procedure reappears in the introduction to "Tremble, thou earth," this time involving another new entry of the point in the bass (see ex. 16).

Thus, in his revisions for *The Third Set,* Michael East concerned himself largely with small details, whether the elimination of parallel fifths and octaves, the insertion of extra imitative entries, or the "modernization" of cadential patterns. A comparison of the manuscript and 1618 printed versions of *O clap*

Ex. 14.   *When Israel came out of Egypt*

(printed version)

(manuscript version)

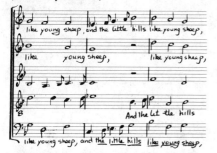 

your hands, on the other hand, seems to reveal a maturing of East's musical ideals. In terms of the amount of music in print, only William Byrd and Thomas Morley proved more prolific than Michael East—apparently never one to withold a piece from publication. Since *O clap your hands* does not appear in the *Third Set,* it is reasonable to assume that the first version was composed between 1610 and 1618. Before bringing *O clap your hands* to the printers he altered it much more extensively than either *Sweet Muses* or *When Israel came out of Egypt.* Hardly a bar fails to contain some change or other. By contrast with the rewritings in the previous works, East's alterations in *O clap your hands* are less concerned with surface details, and often involve quite extensive transformations of large sections, with more attention to their effect upon the work as a whole.

East's growth in maturity is especially clear when one compares the two versions of the second large section of part 1, beginning "He shall subdue the people"(see ex. 17). At first glance the comparison is puzzling, for what we call the "earlier version" seems to meet East's ideal better than the print. In the Tenbury manuscripts we find a nine-bar introduction in which the top three viols clearly anticipate the vocal line, whereas in the 1618 version the viols

Ex. 15.   *Ye mountains, that ye skipped*

(printed version)

(manuscript version)

appear much less closely related to the voice part. What would make Michael East reverse his artistic aims of 1610? Apparently a new-found concern with the development of the section as a whole, rather than an almost obsessive interest in rather self-conscious imitative entries.

The opening sixty-five bars of the anthem have centered around D, the "tonic" of the work as a whole, with brief excursions to F. The second half, in both versions, centers around g-minor. East's first conception plunges squarely into g, with a drop of a fifth from D to G in the quintus part, echoed at two-bar intervals by cantus and altus. The entry of bass and voice together in g, after a two-bar pedal, comes as no surprise, and simply provides more of what has gone before. In the later version, on the other hand, the flow of the viols toward the vocal entries seems much smoother, and certainly less square. After the previous cadence on a D-major chord, the quintus enters on F-natural, and, as each viol joins it, we seem to hover indeterminately until the half-cadence on D in bar 71 (compare the 2 plus 2 plus 2 of the earlier version). Then, after touching on a B-flat chord briefly in bar 73, D is reconfirmed with a strong

cadence, complete with 5-4-4-3 suspensions over an A-pedal, at which point a
                   7 6 5
                     3

Ex. 16.   *Tremble, thou earth*

(printed version)

(manuscript version)

voice enters, adding the F-sharp to the resolution. This first vocal phrase, not present in the original, then smoothly leads to g-minor, where the second voice (the first of the original!) enters. Even the shape of this vocal phrase has been altered. In the 1618 print, a smooth rise and fall, with a telling half-step at its apogee, replaces a more erratic line which changed direction at least five times in six bars. In both versions the music moves next to B-flat, but the transition in the later version is more logical, coming as the third member of a symmetrical grouping, and at the same time, smoother, since the falling line in the bass creates a chord of the sixth on the downbeat.

The alterations to the setting of "And the nations under us" are equally extensive. East's earlier attempt apparently set out to portray the subduing of the nations by frantic action. The imitative point once again moves very erratically, with a leap of a minor sixth to enhance its jagged contours, and tumbles into the texture from all sides like a pitched battle. This flurry of activity also extends to the harmony, where the preceding strong cadence on B-flat is immediately abandoned for movement to and fro between D and g. At the entrance of the bass voice one anticipates a possible turn to c-minor, but in the next bar D and g return. A B-natural four bars later again points toward c-minor, which then simply functions as a transition to a pedal-D with customary suspensions, and the inevitable cadence on G, which concludes the section.

Ex. 17.   *O clap your hands*

(printed version)

(manuscript version)

Ex. 17—*continued*

By 1618, however, East had apparently learned to marshall his forces in close order. The result is less a rout and more a well-ordered campaign. The old point is replaced by a new one which could hardly be more different: a line falling in half-notes through a fifth. Rather than try to heighten the tension by fussy, confused activity, the composer increases the intensity, first by shortening the gap between vocal entries, and later by changing from half-notes to quarters. After arriving at the dominant pedal, East twice throws the diminution of the subject ("under our feet") off the beat in alto and tenor, joined the second time in stretto by the top viol, who is followed almost immediately by another viol with a similar falling figure as they tumble down to the cadence.

The harmonic organization is likewise modified, preserving some of the gestures from the original, but using them more systematically, and articulating them more clearly. Thus, East does not leave the B-flat major from bar 88 quite so quickly in the later version, and when he does the pedal-D of bars 90-91 imparts a stronger sense of direction to the return to g-minor. As mentioned above, the original version had twice touched momentarily on c-minor. This move is restructured in the 1618 print. Instead of two brief gestures in that direction, we find a single emphasis on the tonal area of c-minor in bars 95-96. The repetition of the point in the tenor at bar 96, beginning on B-*flat* smoothly establishes the subsequent movement toward the cadence on G at bar 102. As a final touch, East replaces the stereotyped cadential pattern over the pedal-D by the sudden change to quarter-notes and rhythmic displacement, so that in place of the totally predictable, the cadence maintains a certain tension to the end of the section.

Originating from an age for which composers' sketches are practically non-existent, these earlier versions of works by Michael East provide a rare opportunity to observe the creative process in the mind of a Jacobean composer. Not only do they throw light upon the interaction of the older verse idiom and the more modern Italian madrigal in the developing aesthetic of one of the more prominent composers from the generation after Elizabeth, they also provide interesting insights into the maturation of his compositional technique.

As mentioned above, most of the other verse anthems from Tenbury 1162-7 also reveal the interaction of the verse idiom and the madrigalian aesthetic in the hands of other composers of East's generation. Thus, of the pieces which follow East's contributions to the source, eight can be attributed to Martin Peerson, one to Thomas Ravenscroft, and two to the mysterious William Simms on the basis of other manuscripts. Another eighteen, unique to this source, remain anonymous. This large corpus of pieces provides one of the most impressive witnesses to an abiding secular interest in the verse idiom after 1630.

The anonymous works in 1162-7 reveal the continued interaction between the madrigalian and the older native style, with a gradual infiltration of more and more modern elements. But the other works which follow East's in the source, and the anonymous ones in particular, all too frequently become bogged down in the complexities of imitative counterpoint of a rather simple-minded sort, and in details of madrigalian harmony or textual depiction. They lack the greater sense of overall shape which East managed at least occasionally to achieve in his mature works.

One of the most unusual features of the verse music of the Tenbury source involves a resurgence of interest in the virtually moribund consort song for solo voice or duet. In other sources from the second decade of the century (e.g., Myriell or Merro), there had been some residual interest in the old Elizabethan solo songs, *Abradad, Pandolpho,* etc. But by 1615 those songs had all but disappeared. In their place we found either larger verse anthems of a relatively contrapuntal character or lighter, much simpler pieces with largely homophonic accompaniment, and often very brief concluding choruses, of the sort printed in Thomas Ravenscroft's *Melismata* (1611) and *A Brief Discourse* (1614), or in Martin Peerson's *Private Music* (1620).

The dozen consort songs in 1162-7 appear strangely retrospective, for they have little in common with the lighter, up-to-date style of the 1620s. Instead, we find sober, religious texts, often based upon the Psalms (*O go not hence and leave us comfortless, O Lord let it be thy pleasure to deliver me* [Ps. 40:16], *Have mercy upon me O god* [Ps. 51:1], *My song shall be of mercy and judgment* [Ps. 101:1], etc.). In addition, nine of them employ the formal scheme involving a repetition of the final section, a favorite of the older consort song composers. Furthermore, their texture is consistently, almost incessantly, imitative. This group of consort songs thus seems to imitate quite consciously the external features of the old style whose primary exponent was William Byrd.

This time-honored mould is infused, however, with several new elements, in part derived from Italian practice, which create a much more modern flavor in these works, when judged from the frame of reference of the older consort song which they seem to emulate. This appears most prominently in the new harmonic style, which not only introduces rich and at times startling progressions, but also adds a measure of control to the contrapuntal lines which largely impedes their free flow, straight-jacketing them through increased dependence upon stereotyped chordal successions and cadential patterns of a sort that infiltrate the viol fantasia at roughly the same period. In addition, the vocal lines have sacrificed some of the gravity and deliberate delivery of the older consort song in favor of a more excited, fragmentary melodic style, emphasizing either word-painting or dramatic declamation of the text.

Number 86, *My song shall be of mercy and judgment,* is one of the more somber and superficially traditional examples in the set, preserving the old ABB form (see ex. 18). Movement is still largely in half-notes and whole-notes. The texture is fairly imitative, with a large number of anticipations of vocal phrases in the viols. The vocal line is also relatively grave. The details of the piece reveal, however, that *My song shall be of mercy* is nevertheless a modernized distortion of the older consort song. As one can see from the shape of the bass-line, which moves consistently by fourths, fifths, or octaves, the counterpoint is severely controlled by a tonal framework which seems strangely anachronistic in this context, moving squarely from bar to bar. In a vain effort to recapture the flow of the older consort song, the composer disguises the cadences, but always predictably. In the A-section, for example, virtually every evasion of the cadence involves a bass movement from the fifth to the sixth (e.g., bars 3, 9, 10, and 12), while in the B-section the composer has recourse to the cadence with a 7-6 suspension above a bass moving from the second to the first scale degree, which to his ears may have sounded archaic. It, too, loses its novelty through repeated hearings. The shapes of the imitative points, with their leaps by a third, fourth, and ubiquitous filled-in thirds, also betray the domination of harmonic concerns.

Ex. 18.   *My song shall be of mercy and judgment*

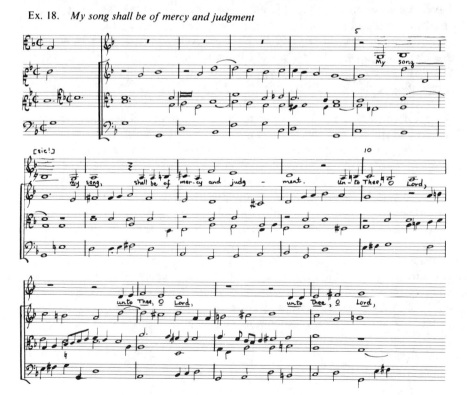

The vocal line, despite its many half-notes and whole-notes and frequent rests, is more at odds than in accord with the solo voices of Byrd's songs. Some gestures, such as the alteration of B-flat to B-natural on a held syllable (bars 5-6), are simply bizarre. Others, such as the line for "shall be of mercy and judgment" (bars 7-10), show how firmly harmonic concerns control the lines. The occasional leap of a sixth, a rarity in the melodic lines of the songs of Byrd and his age, is also readily explained by the composer's subjection of counterpoint to harmony (see ex. 19). This particular song may set out to recapture the gravity of the old consort song, but sacrifices all its means of contrapuntal and tonal variety—and much of its interest—in the process.

Ex. 19.   *My song shall be of mercy*

Number 89, *I cried unto thee, O Lord,* while preserving some of the sobriety of the vocal delivery of *My song shall be of mercy,* is even farther removed from the traditional consort song because of its infusion of "expressive" harmony. The general sentiments of the text are, of course, decidedly lugubrious, and perhaps seemed to provide the composer with the necessary excuse to indulge in a seemingly endless succession of suspensions, usually involving the madrigalian series, $\frac{7\ 6\ 5}{5\text{-}4\text{-}4\text{-}3}$. Often these take the normal

form, but more frequently the composer was not content with a simple statement of the formula, and therefore thwarts the expected resolution in order to produce still further examples, which redirect the tonal progressions abruptly after the fashion of *alla breve* passages in the madrigal (see ex. 20). An overabundance of cadential resolutions to the sixth degree (also common in *My song shall be of mercy*) likewise appears. Elsewhere in the piece additional suspensions are exploited in non-cadential situations. Perhaps the prime example appears at the beginning of the B-section, which includes four repetitions of the setting of "O deliver me" in the voice and a few others in the viols as well (see ex. 21). These range from the straightforward $\frac{6\ 5}{4\text{-}3}$ resolution to the more dramatic suspension involving a diminished fourth, to the most

abrasive combination of C, D, and E-flat over a G in the bass, which hearkens
back to more extreme madrigalian gestures.

Ex. 20.   *I cried unto thee, O Lord*

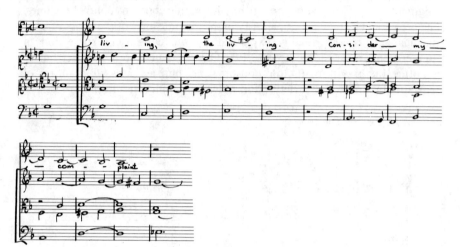

Ex. 21.   *I cried unto thee, O Lord*

Besides his obsession with suspensions, the composer makes very cautious chromatic experiments. Some simply involve the flattening of the sixth above the bass, which at bar 5 may seem very old-fashioned, but in the combination at bar 11 takes on a strangely "Neopolitan" flavor (see ex. 22). The only other attempts involve the consecutive chromatic inflections of a single note at bars 18 and 20. This fascination with "affective" harmony is probably another expression of the Caroline preoccupation with rich sonority. But such harmonic richness, like the earlier Jacobean composers' passion for the false relation of the Elizabethans, when divorced from specifically expressive contexts and employed with an essentially decorative intent, becomes cloying and tends to undermine any sense of long-range formal structure for the piece as a whole.

Ex. 22.   *I cried unto thee, O Lord*

Misdirected madrigalian rhetoric also lends a slightly comic air to these late blossoms. The vocal line of *I cried unto thee* offers such unusual moments as, for example, the setting of "for I am brought very low" (see ex. 23) which in both its rhythm and word-painting seems singularly at odds with the traditional consort song style, and yet is also a travesty of the later madrigal.

Another attempt to modernize the vocal style of the consort song appears in 73, *O Lord, let it by thy pleasure,* for SAT trio and viol accompaniment. Even the outward appearance of this song looks at odds with that of the older consort song, for, aside from the bass, whose role as simple harmonic support could hardly be more obvious—only the figures are missing—scarcely a whole-note or half-note even appears in the lines, whether instrumental or vocal (see ex. 24). The vocal lines move primarily in quarter-notes and eighth-notes, with

Ex. 23.   *I cried unto thee, O Lord*

no worry about allotting separate syllables to the shorter note values. Nor is there any particular concern about multiple repetitions of a single textual phrase. Rather than an interest in the literal word-painting of the madrigal, the emphasis has shifted to the dramatic declamation of the later Italian madrigal. Indeed, in contrast to the early consort song, where the vocal line stands apart from the instrumental parts because of its slower motion, in this later example exactly the reverse is true. The setting of the phrase, "let them be desolate and rewarded with shame," features *concitato*-like short repeated notes and some attention to matching duration with accent (though not without numerous slips). The setting of "fie upon thee" provides an even more drastic example. There was, of course, a precedent for attention to dramatic declamation closer to home in the works of the lutenist song writers and consort song writers as early as the second decade of the century. One well-known illustration from the repertory of verse anthems probably dates from before the turn of the century: Thomas Morley's *Out of the deep*. But the underlying sense of decorum of lute ayre and Elizabethan verse anthem would never have condoned the extremes found in this later work from Tenbury 1162-7.

Finally, the last of the consort songs, and probably one of the last works to be entered in Tenbury 1162-7, *O let thy mercy fall on me,* shows just how far the consort song departed from the models of its greatest Elizabethan and Jacobean exponent, William Byrd (see ex. 25). This, probably the oddest piece for voices and viols in the source, occupies only half a page at the very end of the five-part section. It still preserves the old ABB formal scheme, though the A-section breaks down into aa'a. The old extended instrumental introduction anticipating the vocal line, with some attempts at imitation, is also retained; but there the similarity ends. Movement is entirely in quarter-notes and eighth-notes, with four changes of harmony in each bar. The vocal line, whose opening phrase falls an octave in one-and-a-half bars, in naïve depiction of the text, normally changes syllables on every eighth-note, and frequently on sixteenth-notes. The movement of the parts is strictly controlled by the harmonic progressions, which fall into the patterns of functional harmony, such as the common I^6-II^6_5-v^7-I progressions at several cadences. The shape of the piece as a whole is clearly structured around a series of modulations, all closely related

Ex. 24. *O Lord, let it by thy pleasure*

to g-minor, and set off by a hiatus in all parts: I   III   I   ‖: V$^{\#3}$ I   :‖. The result seems more akin to a straightforward hymn-setting or perhaps to the lute song than to the traditional consort song.

Ex. 25.   *O let thy mercy fall on me*

The fourteen-odd unpublished verse anthems in the source, five of which remain anonymous, follow much the same stylistic pattern as that of the anthems of Michael East discussed in some detail above. They are closer still to the anonymous consort songs in their more extreme use of the expressive madrigalian gestures which East introduced into his verse anthems, but over which he exerted greater control. Interestingly enough, six of the verse anthems in 1162-7, including four of the anonymous anthems, adopt the consort song's common repetition of the final section. In general, they reveal the same tensionless, harmonically controlled counterpoint, spinning on with little striking articulation other than their stereotyped cadential patterns. The texts, like those of the anonymous consort songs, are excessively somber and frequently penitential, and are regularly the object of extensive madrigalian word-painting in their musical settings. But although the song settings rarely exceed a length of about fifty breves, the verse anthems grow to much larger dimensions.

Number 74, *He sent his word and healed them,* displays this greatly expanded scale. More than two hundred breves in length, it breaks down into six subsections:

(i)	*He sent his word*
(ii)	*O that man would therefore praise*
(iii)	*That they would offer unto him*
(iv)	*They that go down*
(v)	*For at his word the stormy wind ariseth*
(vi)	*They reel to and fro*

Works for voices and viols of this size are not without precedent from earlier in the century. Some of the "Cries" (including Richard Dering's *The City Cries* present in Tenbury 1162-7) are of roughly the same length. Some of the verse anthems of East and Peerson (such as the latter's *Fly ravished soul* in this source) also reach such dimensions. To sustain the interest in a work of this size some means of contrast, whether in texture, tonal area, or combination of voices, is necessary, not only to provide variety, but also to help impart some sort of perceptible structural organization to the whole. This is largely lacking from the present example, however, which, though it may attempt to exploit a different musical device (e.g., imitative counterpoint, word-painting, "expressive" harmony) in each section, introduces such a constant fluctuation of vocal scoring, with no readily apparent relationship to the structural articulation of the whole, that the piece seems disjointed. The harmonic organization, on the other hand, while readily betraying the composer's fascination with the stereotyped cadential patterns of an emerging tonal system, fails to realize the potential of the system, and presents instead a constant hovering between G and D. As a result, the anthem goes on too long, without creating enough harmonic space for itself to occupy.

The various sections of the work present many of the more extreme features of the consort songs, often in relative isolation. The opening section, for example, concentrates upon the same harmonically oriented, basically tensionless imitative counterpoint. The second section, on the other hand, exploits the newer affective harmony after the manner of "O deliver me" from *I cried unto thee,* discussed above (see ex. 26). It opens with twenty bars of suspensions, including most of those present in the other work, but with a special preference for the combination of the $\begin{smallmatrix} 7 & 6 & 5 \\ 5\text{-}4\text{-}4\text{-}3 \\ 3 \end{smallmatrix}$ suspension series with the old-fashioned, but still popular, false relation, which often makes it possible to wrench the harmony in new directions. Although the section may reflect that Jacobean and Caroline fascination with rich sonorities, which gives little thought to their textual justification, this example sounds even later, and seems a foreshadowing of English practice after mid-century.

Ex. 26.   *O that man would therefore praise*

The fourth section of the anthem is certainly the most madrigalian. "They that go down" (omitting the phrase "to the sea," incidentally) and "his wonders in the deep" provoke the inescapable falling points (see exx. 27 and 28). The exploitation of the bass voice, especially the murkier depths of its range, inevitably brings to mind Purcell's justly famous setting of the text. But Purcell knew the dangers of overemphasizing a relatively minor textual detail; not his predecessor, however, who is quite content to provide dozens of bars, all devoted to the same falling points.

Ex. 27. *They that go down*

Thus, there is not a great deal to distinguish between these later verse anthems and the consort songs of Tenbury 1162-7. Indeed, the introduction of duets and trios in the consort songs, and the less distinct differentiation between sections for a few soloists and the full chorus in the verse anthems, comes close to undermining the last basic difference between the two.

As pointed out above, a good percentage of the verse anthems in the Tenbury source remain anonymous. Given the scarcity of high quality works among them, it is perhaps not worth expending much effort in attempts to ascribe them. Their general features reflect the style of the generation of East, Peerson, Ravenscroft, and Simms, who all crop up in the source. East would seem an unlikely guess, if only because it is hard to imagine him leaving

Ex. 28.   *They that go down*

anything unprinted. Simms, on the other hand, was quite capable of writing music comparably uninspired and inelegant. Yet, while he may indulge occasionally in the Morleian cadential formula so common in these anonymous works, his counterpoint does not seem quite so strictly controlled by the harmonic system apparent in them. Rather than indulge in the chains of *alla breve* suspensions characteristic of several Tenbury pieces, Simms still remains addicted, instead, to the excessive use of the older false relation, which may betray a turn of mind slightly too old-fashioned for the anonymous works (see ex. 29).

Ex. 29.   *Away, fond thoughts*

What of Peerson or Ravenscroft? As other sources show (e.g., Hamond's collection), these two are often found together. The same is true in Tenury 1162-7, where the group on folios 64-79 begins with a work by Peerson and ends with one by Ravenscroft. It is significant that of these sixteen pieces, eight can be attributed to Peerson and one to Ravenscroft on the basis of other sources. Given the scribe's tendency to group pieces by composer it seems reasonable that others might also be by them, especially by Peerson. Several musical details strengthen this possibility. Peerson's *Praise the Lord* (fol. 64) and Ravenscroft's *O Lord, in thee is all my trust* both adopt the formal scheme, ABB, favored by the anonymous works. Furthermore, practically all of the verse compositions from Peerson's *Mottects or Grave Chamber Music* (1630)

(i.e., nos. 6, 7, 10, 11, 12, 14, 16, 20, and 23) employ this formal pattern. Several other features from Peerson's publication are also reflected in the anonymous pieces. They reveal the same flexibility of scoring, with a fondness for so many different voices in the verses that it becomes difficult to distinguish them from the full sections. Peerson's brand of imitative counterpoint shows the greatest similarity to that of Tenbury 1162-7 in its strict subservience to the harmonic organization, a fact made all the more obvious by the inclusion of a separate organ part, complete with figures, in the 1630 publication. Several passages also indulge in both the sonorous possibilities of the modern cadential patterns, extended to great lengths (see ex. 30), and in chains of suspensions for expressive purposes (see ex. 31). One commentator[18] has also remarked upon Peerson's idiosyncratic use of degree inflections of the sort which opened the vocal part of *My song shall be of mercy* (ex. 20) and which reappears in *I cried unto thee* (ex. 23). The manner of word-setting in the anonymous pieces also shows greatest similarity to Peerson's 1630 publication. We find the same policy of allotting syllables to quarter-notes, eighth-notes, or even to sixteenth-notes, the same attempts at dramatic declamation, and clear examples of extremes in vocal writing for descriptive purposes. One passage for bass solo from Peerson's *When thou has swept* exploits the depths of the vocal range in the same fashion apparent in *He sent his word* discussed above (see ex. 32).

There is therefore much to link Martin Peerson, the most prominent composer in Tenbury 1162-7, with the large body of anonymous works for voices and viols. But, though Peerson's works may not reveal a talent of the first rank,[19] one would hesitate to place them in the same category with these anonymous works, which seem to carry to further extremes those musical devices that they share with Peerson's pieces, especially in matters of "affective" dissonance and harmonically controlled counterpoint. Indeed, in many respects these anonymous works might well represent the not terribly competent efforts of a later composer trying to recapture the Jacobean style, perhaps as late as the 1640s.

It should be clear, in any event, that Tenbury 1162-7, rather than reflecting the musical taste of the last years of James I as previously believed, instead offers the clearest view of the verse idiom and its place in secular music-making during Charles's reign. Tenbury 1162-7 provides our clearest documentation for the transformation of the verse idiom through interaction with the madrigalian style. Its earlier versions of works by Michael East, when compared with the published texts, represent the most extensive and detailed witness to the manner in which a member of the younger generation responded to the possibilities of native versus Italian styles. Continuing with the works of the other "moderns" of the Jacobean period, Simms, Peerson, and Ravenscroft, Tenbury 1162-7 then extends still further to include works which may have been written, either under the influence of, or looking backwards toward the style apparent in, the later works of Martin Peerson. These anonymous consort songs and verse anthems represent one of the few surviving records of the state of the verse idiom in a secular context in the years between Peerson and Humphrey or Purcell.

Ex. 30.   *Cupid my pretty boy*

Ex. 31.   *And thou, Love*

Ex. 32.   *When thou hast swept*

page	Title	idiom	Composer	Prints
		(three-part pieces)		
1	A sea nymph sat upon the shore	f	[T. Wilkinson?]	
2	Farewell, disdainful	f	[T. Morley]	1593:10
4	Do you not know	f	[" "]	" :16
6	Now must I die	f	[" "]	" :13
8	As fair as morn	f	[J. Wilbye]	1609:5
10	Come shepherd swains	f	[" "]	" :1
12	O fly not, O take some pity	f	[T. Morley]	1593:11
14	Where art thou, wanton	f	[" "]	" :17
		(four-part pieces)		
16	O fairest maid	f		
17	Sweet Amarillis, o stay	f		
18	Danae, the fair	f		
19	When Cloris heard	f	[J. Wilbye]	1609:9
20	I love, alas! yet am not loved	f	[" "]	" :14
22	Happy streams, whose trembling fall	f	[" "]	" :10
		(five-part pieces)		
24	*I believe in God, the father almighty (i)*	v		
25	*He descended into Hell (ii)*	v		
26	I must depart all hapless	f	[L. Marenzio]	MT1588:22
27	Liquid and watery pearls	f	[" "]	" :31
28	My heart alas why dost thou love	f	[G. Conversi]	" :39
29	What doth my pretty darling	f	[L. Marenzio]	" :27
30	So gracious is thy sweet self	f	[G. Ferretti]	" :25
31	Cruel unkind my heart thou hast bereft	f	[" "]	" :26
32	O how fortunate they	f	[R. Ramsey]	
33	Cease now thy wailing (i)	f		
34	Stay then, and first behold (ii)	f		
35	So vain is all their pleasure	f		
36	O poor Amyntas	f		
38	O wretched Amyntas	f		
40	The white delightful swan	f	[H. Vecchi]	MT1597:1
41	Cynthia, thy song enchanting	f	[G. Croce]	" :4
42	So far, dear life	f	[G. Eremita]	" :3
43	Now turneth to former joy	f	[L. Marenzio]	
44	Sweet heart arise	f	[" "]	IM1590:14
45	When shall I cease lamenting	f	[N. Faignient]	MT1588:21
46	Within a greenwood	f	[G. Ferretti]	" :33
47	O help me soon	f		
48	Out alas, what should I say	f		
49	Nymphs and fairies	f	[T. Ravenscroft]	
50	Lure, faulkners, lure	f	[" "]	
51	With angel's face and brightness	f	[D. Norcomb]	1601:1
52	*Blow out the trumpet in Sion*	v	[M. Peerson]	
53	Behold now praise the Lord	f	[R. Alison]	1606:22
54	Hence stars, too dim of light	f	[M. East]	1601:unnum.
55	To pitch our toils	f		
56	*The Country Cry*	v	[R. Dering]	
57	*The City Cry*	v	[" "]	
58	*Now we have present made*	v		
59	*Cantate nymphe e pastori (i)*	v	[M. East]	1610:1
	Ahi me (ii)	v	[" "]	" :2
	Ma pace (iii)	v	[" "]	" :3
number				
60	*When Israel came out of Egypt (i)*	v	[" "]	" :4
61	*What aileth thee (ii)*	v	[" "]	" :5
62	*O clap your hands (i)*	v	[" "]	1618:10
63	*God is gone up (ii)*	v	[" "]	" :11
64	*Praise the Lord*	v	[M. Peerson]	
65	*O God, when thou wentest before*	v	[" "]	
66	*O go not hence*	ct		
67	*O come hither*	cs[1]		
68	*I am small*	v	[M. Peerson]	
69	*Thou hast brought me to great*	v		
70	*O deliver me*	cs		
71	*O go not from me*	v	[M. Peerson]	
72	*O do well unto thy servant*	cs		
73	*O Lord let it be thy pleasure*	ct		
74	*He sent his word and healed them*	v		
75	*Fly ravished soul (i)*	v	[M. Peerson]	
	Rest thee awhile (ii)	v	[" "]	
76	*Muse still thereon (iii)*	v	[" "]	
77	*Rain eyes (iv)*	v	[" "]	

---

1 This piece is classified as a full anthem in Daniels and Le Huray, *The Sources of English Church Music*, p. 70.

no.	Title	idiom	Composer	Prints
78	*I called upon the Lord (i)*	v	[M. Peerson]	
	All nations (ii)	v	[" "]	
	They kept me in on every side (iii)	v	[" "]	
	They came about me (iv)	v	[" "]	
79	*O Lord in thee is all my trust*	v	[T. Ravenscroft]	
80	*Rise, O my soul (i)*	v	[W. Simms]	
	And thou, my soul (ii)	v	[" "]	
	To thee, O Jesu (iii)	v	[" "]	
81	*Wherefore are men so loath to die*	v		
82	*O Lord consider my distress*	cs		
83	*Have mercy upon me (i)*	cd		
84	*Wash me throughly (ii)*	cd		
85	*Why standest thou so far off*	cs		
86	*My song shall be of mercy*	cs		
87	*I said I will take heed*	v		
88	*O magnify the Lord*	v		
89	*I cried unto the Lord*	cs		
90	*O let thy mercy fall on me*	cs		

(six-part pieces)

no.	Title	idiom	Composer	Prints
91	Shall I live so far distant	f	[L. Marenzio]	MT1597:20
92	Hard by a chrystal fountain	f	[G. Croce]	" :24
93	The Lady Oriana	f	[J. Wilbye]	1601:15
94	As Vesta was from Latmos hill	f	[T. Weelkes]	" :17
95	Dainty white pearl	f	[A. Bicci]	MT1597:23
96	Why dost thou shoot	f	[J. Wilbye]	1598:30
97	Lady when I behold	f	[" "]	" :24
98	Wilt thou, unkind, now leave me weeping	f	[R. Ramsey]	
99	Unkind, if you desire	f		
100	Unkind, O stay thy flying	f	[L. Marenzio]	IM1590:25
101	All ye nations of the world	f		
102	O Jonathan, woe is me for thee	f	[T. Weelkes]	
103	O my son Absalom	f	[" "]	
104	When David heard	f	[R. Ramsey]	
105	*Away fond thoughts*	v	[W. Simms]	
106	Laudate Dominus in sanctis (*a 8*)	f		
107	O sing unto the Lord (*a 9*)	f		

8

Conclusion

When historians of English music have turned their attention to the madrigal, they have found at their disposal an impressive corpus of sixteenth- and seventeenth-century published collections, more than forty in number, which represents the entire body of madrigal prints from the era. These madrigal books appeared in editions of hundreds of copies;[1] and their chances of survival were relatively great. Despite the vicissitudes of some 350 years, at least one complete copy of virtually every madrigal publication still remains.[2] An interpretation of the history of the English madrigal rests on the firm evidence of this collection.[3]

A mere two dozen manuscripts containing music for voices and viols might seem an unimpressive sampling by comparison with more than forty prints of "madrigals," and an equal number of lute ayre publications. Such figures are misleading, however, for, in contrast to the multiple copies of each edition of these other two genres, each of the twenty-four manuscript sources of the verse idiom is unique, and its chances of survival have been far less than those of the prints. Indeed, the chances of survival for one of the madrigal or lute ayre publications, by comparison with an individual manuscript source, might have been up to a thousand times as great, given the original number of copies initially available for circulation.

An elaborate set of manuscripts such as Myriell's *Tristitiae Remedium,* complete with engraved title page, elegant script, and fancy leather bindings, might stand to survive on the basis of its aesthetic appeal. But the less "aesthetically pleasing," and frequently downright ugly, sources such as Add. 37402-6 or Add. 29336-8, which must be representative of many manuscript sources in circulation during the first half of the seventeenth century, would have had no such appeal. An unmusical heir might at least hope to sell an elegant manuscript such as Myriell's, just as he might stand a good chance of selling one of Thomas East's prints, but he would very likely consign a plain manuscript to the fire. As Roger North wrote:

> And of these Fancys whole volumnes are left, scarce ever to be made use of but either in the ayre for kites or in the fire for singeing pullets.[4]

Only a few managed to endure long enough to become of interest to the curious antiquarians of the eighteenth and nineteenth centuries, the men who in a sense rescued these sources for posterity.

Thus, this handful of manuscripts of music for voices and viols must represent merely the "tip of the iceberg." If only eleven copies out of an edition of some 1,000 of Dowland's *Second Book of Songs* are still extant,[5] it seems reasonable that for every remaining secular manuscript source of consort songs or verse anthems, great numbers must have perished.

Though the number of surviving sources is small, they are widely spaced in both time and provenance. These manuscripts must represent as fair a sampling as many of today's opinion polls. In this light, it seems reasonable to give a certain amount of credence to the evidence of the manuscripts discussed in previous chapters as a guide to several aspects of the taste of the time, particularly since the sources frequently agree among themselves in these matters. There is, for example, great consistency in the attitudes of their compilers toward the madrigal, and this attitude would appear to reflect a change in musical taste from the middle of James I's reign. Joseph Kerman, in his discussion of the "serious" English madrigalist, John Ward, has commented upon the taste of Thomas Myriell:

> It is no surprise to find an earnest musical anthologist, the Reverend Thomas Myriell, selecting 13 madrigals by Ward for his *Tristitium Remediae* [*sic*] of 1616, together with 17 by Wilbye, 7 by Weelkes, as many as 25 from the anthologies, and only 3 by Thomas Morley.[6]

The table on the following pages shows, however, that there was nothing especially idiosyncratic about the taste of the "earnest" Thomas Myriell (see table 2). As a rule, the other manuscript compilers reveal the same preference for the Italian anthologies, as well as the best or more "serious" English prints. Thus, the 1588 *Musica Transalpina* served as a prominent source for virtually all the compilers, a distinction otherwise shared, interestingly enough, only by Michael East's *Third Set* of 1610 (which invariably provides pieces for voices and viols—not madrigals). Pieces from *Italian Madrigals Englished* and *Musica Transalpina II* also crop up consistently, but in smaller numbers. Of the English madrigalists, Wilbye and Weelkes appear most frequently. Myriell's interest in his friend, the "serious" Thomas Tomkins, was apparently shared by both Merro (certainly also an acquaintance of the Worcester organist) and Hamond. Hamond likewise maintained an interest in the "serious" John Ward.

Significantly enough, to judge by the table, Myriell was not alone in his basic lack of interest in Thomas Morley. The London clergyman might choose half-a-dozen works from the *Canzonets. Or Little Short Songs* (1593) for his lighter collection, Brussels II. 4109 (not known to Kerman, incidentally), and three from the 1595 *First Book of Ballets,* but otherwise Myriell ignores

Morley. Similarly, both Merro and Hamond pay even less attention to Morley, who only achieves any sort of prominence at all in the three-part section which opens the later source, Tenbury 1162-7.

For another aesthetic view, table 2 also includes the data from RCM 684, which, as indicated in the discussion of Hamond's manuscripts, is devoted almost exclusively to the madrigal. The verse idiom is represented there only by Gibbons's *Cries of London,* Dering's *Country Cry,* and Cobbold's *New Fashions.* Again, the scribe overwhelmingly favors the Italian anthologies, which provide well over half of the 130 works from the English madrigal prints in RCM 684. Otherwise, the most prominent collections are those of Firmage's neighbors, Wilbye and Kirbye (who, as we have seen, was an especially close friend). Thomas Morley, on the other hand, is represented by a scant six works, which puts him in the same category with the lesser figures in the collection.

Kerman, in speaking of later madrigal publications, may write of "a declining market which still finds profit in reprinting Morley's fresh compositions from the 1590's."[7] It appears that the publishers would have found little market for their Morley reprints among these manuscripts copyists. But perhaps these frequent reprints made manuscript copies unnecessary. As we have seen, however, scribes often had recourse to printed collections, including several such as *Musica Transalpina I,* Wilbye's *First Set,* Weelkes's *Ballets* of 1598, and Gibbons's three-part fantasias, which all ran to second, or even third, editions.[8] And both Hamond and Myriell readily copied large sections of John Dowland's *First Book of Ayres,* which ran to as many as four editions. Therefore the neglect of Morley in the manuscript sources may indeed reflect a lack of interest in his madrigals on the part of later Jacobeans.

One additional musical collector from outside this group may serve as a "control" by which to test this hypothesis, since he chose to buy music prints rather than to copy music himself. The Oxford benefactor, William Heather, included in his endowment of the music professorship over forty printed works,[9] the majority of which belong to the "English Madrigal School." As table 2 shows, Heather's taste was apparently broader than that of any of the manuscript anthologists under discussion. But, significantly, his taste seems to confirm what we saw in their collections: a strong interest in the Italian anthologists, the works of Weelkes and Wilbye, the "serious" later composers (Ward, Amner, and Tomkins)—and little interest in Morley. Heather may have bought up the earliest publications, the two sets by Byrd, as well as *Musica Transalpina* and *Italian Madrigals Englished,* but a gap appears in his collection, beginning with Morley's 1593 *Canzonets.* Like Myriell, he may have been interested in *The First Book of Ballets* of 1595, but otherwise he ignores all Morley's own works. Only Kirbye, Pilkington, Lichfield, Mundy, and Carlton were of less interest (as, indeed, they were for most of the manuscript compilers).

Table 2. Works from Printed Collections in Manuscripts

Print	V¹	Myriell T.R.	Brussels	Hamond	Merro	1162	Heather	684
MT1588		10		5	12	8	X	45
1588 Byrd		[4]²	22		[8] 1		X	
1589 Byrd		[2]		29			X	
IME 1590		3			6	2	X	17
1593 Morley			7	1		5		1
1594 Morley								3
1594 Mundy								
1595 Morley ballets		3	7				X	1
1595 Morley canzonets								
1597 Morley canzonets			7		2			
1597 Morley³			7		2	6	X	11
MT1597		10	7				X	14
1597 Kirbye		1						
1597 Weelkes		2					X	
1598 Morley		5		1				
1598 Wilbye		2			13	2	X	4
1598 Farnaby								
1598 Cavendish								
1598 Weelkes		6	8		14		X	2
1599 Farmer			4				X	
1599 Bennet								
1600 Weelkes	V							
1601 Carlton	V							
1601 Triumphs		1		1	7	4	X	1

Source	1	2	3	4	5	6		
1604 Greaves	V							
1604 Bateson	V	4	17				X	1
1604 East	V	10					X	
1606 Alison	V							1
1606 East	V		2				X	
1607 Jones	V	7	2					
1608 Weelkes			5				X	
1608 Youll								
1609 Wilbye	V	17	1		5		X	20
1610 East	V	[5]	[2]	1	[5]		X	1
1611 Byrd	V		[4]	1		[2]	X	
1612 Gibbons	V		16				X	
1613 Ward	V	13	13				X	
1613 Lichfield	V							2
1614 Leighton	V	15						
1615 Amner	V		[6]	7		[6] 11	X	
1618 Bateson	V	[2]	19				X	
1618 East 4th	V		[2]		[2]			
1618 East 5th	V							
1619 Vautor	V							
1620 Peerson	V							
1622 Tomkins		3						
1624 East	V		6			16 [3]	X	
1624 Pilkington	V		[6]				X	
1627 Hilton							X	
1630 Peerson	V							

1. A "V" in this column indicates some form of the phrase "for voices or viols" on the title page.
2. Numbers in brackets denote works in the verse idiom in the source.
3. Selected Canzonets.

Thus, one is left with the impression that Morley's kind of vocal confection, brilliant though it must have seemed to an earlier generation, did not entirely suit the taste of serious Jacobeans.[10] Morley did not outlive the queen whom he honored in his last collection, *The Triumphs of Oriana.* A decade after his death when he turns up in *Tristitiae Remedium,* it is more frequently as a composer of anthems or motets than of canzonets or ballets.

The "serious" attitude which Kerman attributes to Thomas Myriell seems to reflect a common Jacobean trend, characteristic of the other manuscript anthologists as well. Kerman has written that "In the 1580's it [interest in Italian music] was rather serious, adopting the European vogue for Marenzio; in the 1590's, under the influence of Morley, it became lighter and more popular, reflecting superficially the new trends in Italian music."[11] It appears that in some ways the reign of James I witnessed a return to the taste of the 1580s in Italian music—the madrigals of the Italian anthologies, "a large proportion of them... of a serious cast, as compared with native compositions,"[12] and especially the madrigals of Marenzio, by far the most popular Italian in the manuscript sources.

On the other hand, at the same time that a coarser musical taste began to find expression in collections such as Weelkes's *Aires or Fantastic Sprites* of 1608 or Ravenscroft's semipopular anthologies *(Deuteromelia, Pammelia, Melismata),* the better Jacobean composers, such as Wilbye, Ward, Gibbons, and Tomkins (who, as we have seen, were often of greatest interest to the manuscript compilers), seem to turn toward a more serious style. Thus, Wilbye's *Second Set* causes Kerman to remark upon the increase in the number of "individual abstract compositions" (which he links to the style of "Byrd and the old-fashioned composers"), a greater percentage of "moral poems of a native cast," and "the recession of the canzonet idiom."[13] The latecomer, John Ward, whose only madrigal set appeared in 1613, Kerman describes as "the most unilaterally serious musician of the English development."[14] Of course, Kerman, Jacquot, and Mellers have all called attention to the somber character of Gibbons's single set.[15]

But there may be another side to this apparent return to the taste of the 1580s, an especially significant one for the purpose of the present discussion—a resurgence of interest in the older native method for voices and viols. It was Kerman, following Dent's lead,[16] who first fully explored this native idiom. In doing so, he made clear the nature and extent of the madrigal in England in a way that Fellowes and his predecessors had never managed to do so. Indeed, the comparative method announced on Kerman's title page and applied in his study to the madrigalian idioms of England and Italy is perhaps even more fruitful when applied to native song and native madrigal. At the same time, in *The Elizabethan Madrigal* there is a certain assumption, emphasized by the frequent use of pejorative adjectives such as "old-fashioned," "antiquated," "abstract," "archaic," to describe the native idiom, that historical fact can be equated with critical judgment. At one point Kerman plainly states that "As for Byrd and Gibbons, of course, it is a real question whether they are more successful with the native style than Weelkes and Wilbye with the imported one";[17] but it is difficult to avoid the impression that they were irrationally stubborn to resist the Italian influence so strongly.[18]

To judge by the evidence of the manuscripts discussed above, the native style for voices and viols was not quite so moribund as Kerman implies. A few suggestions about its later development should make this clear, and perhaps also help to explain the demise of the madrigal.

Before summarizing the evidence of the manuscripts, one might turn one last time to the table of madrigals presented earlier (table 2). The first column in the list indicates which of the prints included the designation "apt for voices and viols," or some equivalent, on their title pages. The expression does not occur among the sixteenth-century prints. It turns up abruptly in 1600 on the title page of Weelkes's *Madrigals of 5. and 6. parts,* after which it is very rarely absent. Warwick Edwards, in an article on Elizabethan ensemble music, provides one possible explanation for this change at the turn of the century. In discussing the music of the 1580s he writes:

> The demand was for vocal music, like Byrd's *Psalmes, Sonets, and Songs* of 1588. Nicholas Yonge welcomed these songs, without actually naming them, in the dedication to his first volume of *Musica Transalpina* (1588), and complained, in connection with the musical gatherings which took place at his home, that "because they are not many in number, men delighted with varietie, have wished more of the same sort."[19]

The publications of the 1590s aimed to meet this demand for music to sing. But by 1600 there had been an obvious change in taste. Again, to quote Warwick Edwards:

> By the turn of the century the situation was altogether different. Several gentlemen or gentlemen-to-be, not to mention ladies, are known to have played the viol at this time, including the young William Cavendish in 1599, Philip Gawdy's sister-in-law in 1602, Anne Clifford aged about thirteen in 1603 and William Smith in his first quarter at Trinity College, Cambridge in 1605. Amateur viol players also appear in a number of plays which were first staged in the last few years of Elizabeth's reign: in Jonson's *Every Man out of his Humour* (1599) Fastidious "takes downe the violl, and playes"; characters in Marston's *Antonios Revenge* (1599) and Jonson's *Poetaster* (1601) accompany their own songs on the viol. It seems that Shakespeare's worthy knight Sir Andrew Aguecheek, "playes o'th Viol-de-gamboys" not only because he thinks it a desirable gentlemanly accomplishment, but also because it is the very latest fashion.[20]

Not only does the phrase "apt for voices or viols" on title pages attempt to appeal to this latest fashion, but the contents of the sets also begin to reflect the trend.

Michael East represents this musical transformation most clearly. After two sets of relatively orthodox madrigals, in 1610 he published a collection including aside from madrigals, also verse pastorals, verse anthems, and fantasias, all catering to the latest fashion, which for East was always a prime concern. In East's later volumes the trend is further reinforced by the constant inclusion of pieces for voices and viols, until in his *Sixth Set* of 1624 there is no longer any mention of madrigals at all.

Other composers also followed East's example. After he had published his first collection, *Pammelia,* in 1609, Thomas Ravenscroft included pieces for voices and viols, often with concluding choruses, in his *Deuteromelia* (1609), *Melismata* (1611), and *A Brief Discourse* (1614). In a more serious vein, Byrd's 1611 *Psalms, Songs, and Sonnets* included verse anthems, consort songs, and fantasias, in addition to strictly vocal pieces. For Byrd, such heterogeneous contents were, of course, a continuation of his own older practice, but even at the advanced age of 68 he may not have been above a conscious attempt to "corner the market." Sir William Leighton's *Tears or Lamentations* of 1614 (where the term "consort song" first appears) continues the serious trend, which is also reflected in Amner's *Sacred Hymns* of 1615. Works for voices and viols even turn up in Thomas Vautor's much lighter *Songs of Divers Airs and Natures* of 1619, where, for the laments on the death of Sir Thomas Beaumont and Prince Henry, the composer turns to the medium which, as we have seen, was traditionally associated with elegies. Finally, the verse idiom plays a very prominent role in both Martin Peerson's *Private Music* of 1620 and his *Motets or Grave Chamber Music* of 1630.

The more somber of these publications represent, as Joseph Kerman rightly points out, the nearest English equivalent to the Italian *lauda* or *madrigale spirtituale:*

> A solemn, unmadrigalesque native style was established in England for these "exhalations," primarily, it would appear, by a very popular publication by William Hunnis, ... *Seven Sobs of a Sorrowful Soul for Sin* ... The book was registered in 1581 and ten reprints are known from 1583 to 1629.[21]

The native idiom, then, was by long-standing tradition the accepted musical medium for sober or penitential sentiments. The notable revival of the verse idiom during the Jacobean era must be due at least in part to its appropriateness for the expression of the melancholy frame of mind so common early in the seventeenth century.

When they are viewed from something other than a madrigalian framework, the later printed collections confirm the pattern apparent in the manuscript sources discussed in previous chapters. London, the capital city, was obviously the center for what was fashionable and up-to-date. As Myriell's sources, the *Tristitiae Remedium* in particular, suggest, madrigals had become a secondary interest by 1616. Myriell shows a greater concern with the newer fashion—music for voices and viols, and with the contributions of the more fashionable composers, Michael East, Martin Peerson, William Simms, John Ward. Indeed, the London cleric goes so far as to append to his organ book (Christ Church MS 67, fol. iiiv) a list of purely vocal pieces from *Tristitiae Remedium* also "fit for vials and organ."[22]

The same preoccupation was also apparent in Add. 37402-6, probably dating from around 1610 or slightly later. In that source the scribes showed no interest in preserving the original integrity of madrigals, but transformed them into pieces for viols. The only vocal works which the scribe preserved in their original forms were those designed to delight both viol players and singers: the verse anthem and consort song. Add. 17786-91, the Wigthorpe manuscripts, also reveal a similar preoccupation and go one step further. Apart from viol fantasias, dances, and genuine consort songs, the scribe also includes a large number of ayres or continuo dialogues in full-dress arrangements for voices and viols, as though they were consort songs.

But aside from this apparent fascination with viol playing, other factors must have contributed to the decline of the madrigal and to the greater prominence of music for voices and viols after 1600. Again, Joseph Kerman has put forward a plausible hypothesis for the demise of the madrigal:

> The eclipse of the madrigal was hastened by another kind of music which proved its popularity in the little wave of music printing at the end of Byrd's monopoly. After the success of the first of Dowland's four books, a string of minor composers devoted themselves to lute-airs until the number of lute-air folios actually surpassed the number of madrigal-esque publications...At all events it seems clear that after the turn of the century the aesthetic basis of the madrigal seemed less attractive in England. The unelaborate song of the lutenists, and the abstract art of the virginalists and composers of fancies, were more to the taste of the time. Petrarchan poetry also ceded to a more native and more vigorous tradition allied to the music of the lute-air.[23]

The one musical form Kerman omits from the account is the older native combination of voices and viols, whose importance in the declining years of the madrigal this study has revealed. Not only does that form partake of "the abstract art" of the viol fantasias in vogue after 1600 (note how many of the younger verse anthem composers were as well-known as composers of fantasias as of verse anthems—or, indeed, of madrigals), but it also shares with the lute ayre the power to project its text relatively unencumbered, without the overabundance of sophisticated musical devices characteristic of the madrigal. Indeed, as some sources show (e.g., Add. 17786-91 and 17797), a significant portion of the later consort song repertory consisted of lute song arrangements or pieces by the lutenist-songwriters.[24] The growth of the verse idiom depended not only on its musical appeal but also upon the poetic values it enshrined, and upon its clear manner of presenting the text, both values which it shared with the lute ayre.

Therefore, when the development of English secular music is considered from another, perhaps a wider view, its course appears quite altered. The picture may be somewhat clearer if it is not seen as the "continual decline and breaking up of the madrigal ideal," whose "promise was only partially realized."[25] Indeed, such an attitude might have puzzled or surprised Jacobean musicians, with their renewed interest in music for viols, on the one hand, and an altered attitude toward poetic setting, on the other. But not only did the newer works for voices and viols cater to these trends, they also absorbed some madrigalian elements, such as "expressive" harmony or word-painting of a generally restrained variety. As we have seen in the earlier discussion of Michael East's revisions, this was precisely the sort of reconciliation that younger composers were attempting to achieve in the early years of the Jacobean age. The anthems or "verse pastorals" of East's *Third Set* of 1610 have been shown to reveal a heightened interest in the imitative counterpoint of the fantasia or older consort song, on the one hand, and a concern with madrigalian characteristics of expressive harmony, word-painting, or vocal scoring, on the other. This concern remained the main preoccupation of the other younger, more fashionable and contrapuntally minded composers, Martin Peerson, Thomas Ravenscroft, John Ward, William Simms.

Kerman writes:

> The style of the Baroque era breaks through the English madrigal sets as it had in Italy, though without the brilliant results that obtained there; thus the sets of Martin Peerson (1622 [sic] and 1630) and Walter Porter, a student of Monteverdi (1632).[26]

When one steps out of the strictly madrigalian framework, to view the development of Jacobean secular music in a broader context, the later sets represent, not only the "breakthrough of the baroque era," but also the logical outcome of the process of creating newer forms by reconciling "fashionable" trends with an older, long-familiar idiom. Thus, while the light, brief pieces for solo voice, viols, and chorus in Peerson's *Private Music* of 1620 represent the adaptation of elements from the lute ayre, the large-scale, expansive and flexible works from his *Motets or Grave Chamber Music* (1630) stand in the tradition of the full-fledged Jacobean verse anthem, which had been infused with various madrigalian elements. The inclusion of a separate keyboard part (essentially the treble and bass lines plus some figures) in the later volume may give it the air of the "stile nuovo." As we have seen (especially in the discussion of Tenbury 1162-7), however, these works reveal no abrupt or startling stylistic transformation, but have roots solidly embedded in an old and long-standing tradition, known in England before the madrigal had made its appearance.

The discussion in previous chapters has emphasized the manner in which various musical enthusiasts reacted to the verse idiom, and also the transformations it underwent during the first decades of the seventeenth century. As table 3 shows, the scribes have many interests in common. Obviously, the most prominent figures are members of the younger generation of composers, East and Peerson, who find their way into almost every source from the earliest, Add. 37402-6, to the latest, Tenbury 1162-7, possibly compiled at a distance of almost forty years. The obscure William Simms, of whom next to nothing is known, and who has left us but three verse anthems, inevitably turns up in almost every manuscript. These composers are the overwhelming favorites in the London sources of Thomas Myriell in particular. As we have seen, the London manuscripts tend to reflect most clearly the latest developments, what was most fashionable during the second half of the reign of James I. Thus, the sources from the capital also show a special interest in Ravenscroft and John Ward, whose works for voices and viols follow to some extent the more exuberant models of East and Peerson.

The manuscripts from the eastern counties, on the other hand, reveal that the musical preferences of the capital were also particularly important in the Cambridge area. Indeed, in the absence of definite external evidence, it is not impossible that some sources assigned here to the east might derive from London. Thomas Hamond's manuscripts, whose provenance can be established beyond question, reveal that taste in the eastern counties still followed the model of Jacobean London quite closely during the reign of Charles I, affording prominent places to Peerson, Ravenscroft, East, et al. Add. 29366-8, though strong in the works of Cambridge figures such as Ramsey and Wilkinson, still provide an important place for Peerson, Simms, and East. Still later the same figures, East, Peerson, Ravenscroft, and Simms, continue to predominate in Tenbury 1162-7, which shows some ties with the Cambridge area, though it probably derives in fact from London, and may reflect musical taste from nearer mid-century. Thus, there appears to have been an especially strong link between London and the eastern counties, which both share an enthusiasm for the more exuberant verse anthems, with their variable textures, expressive harmony, and occasional word-painting, an interest that was preserved extraordinarily late by the eastern scribes.

But according to John Merro's manuscripts, quite the opposite was the case in the west country. The more extrovert members of the younger generation had made only small inroads into Gloucestershire by 1630, to judge by Drexel 4180-5 and Add. 17792-6. We find only four verse anthems by East, and the inescapable *Rise O my soul* by Simms (misattributed, however, to East), and a solitary verse anthem by Martin Peerson (misattributed to a "Mr Palmer"). Merro seems to have preferred the more traditional stylists of the Jacobean period: Amner, Tomkins, and Gibbons. Significantly, he still gives

Table 3. Verse Anthems or Consort Songs in Manuscript[1]

Composer	29372	56	807	Hamond	29366	Merro	Oxford	37402[2]	1162
Amner		2		5		6			
Batten									
Bull	1	2	1				1	2	
Byrd	5	3		4		13		3	7
East	7	1		10	2	5		2	
Gibbons	3	1				3			
Hooper		2							
M. Jeffreys	1	3	3						
Nicolson							6	1	
Peerson	21	1		12	1	1	1	3	13
Ravenscroft	3	3		8					1
Simms	1	2			3	1			2
Tomkins	2						1	1	
Ward	3	6						1	
Weelkes	1							1	
Wigthorpe					10		5		
Wilkinson	3	3	1	0	0			1	
anon.	0	0		0		7	11		20
Total no. in the source:	65	36	5	42	22	39	39	35	47

1. Individual parts of anthems or consort songs are counted separately.
2. For 37402 the totals include the "arrangements" of the 5-part "Orianas" as consort duets.

pride of place to William Byrd, who had been largely eclipsed by Peerson and his followers in the London and Cambridge manuscripts.

Oxford, on the other hand, betrays links to Gloucester and the West. Not only does Richard Nicolson of Magdalen turn up in John Merro's manuscripts, but some of Merro's manuscripts (e.g., Bodl. MSS Mus. Sch. D245-247) ultimately found their way to Oxford. To judge by consort songs and verse anthems in the surviving manuscripts, that university town may have been as much a backwater as Gloucester. Of nearly fifty consort songs or verse anthems, only three are by better-known composers of the time. Of the others, the vast majority were composed by local figures, chiefly William Wigthorpe of New College or Richard Nicolson of Magdalen. Furthermore, a large percentage were consort songs, either Elizabethan works by Robert Parsons, Nathaniel Patrick, or others of their generation, or lighter, more contemporary examples, modeled largely upon the lute ayre, and chiefly by Wigthorpe or Nicolson. A good number seem to be stage songs, which may once have found a place in the many dramatic productions at the University. The few verse anthems largely reflect the pattern of Merro's sources, following the somewhat more traditional, restrained style of Gibbons or Tomkins rather than the more ebullient, extrovert example of Peerson or East. If, as has been suggested, the Oxford manuscripts were tools for music teaching or choir training, the preponderance of consort songs and the inclusion of the more sober verse anthems could as easily reflect a concern with didactic usefulness as a traditional, old-fashioned aesthetic outlook.

One has frequently had occasion to remark upon the scribes' surprising lack of interest in William Byrd, undoubtedly the finest practitioner of the verse idiom. Of all the scribes, only the provincial John Merro affords him a place of honor. Otherwise his consort songs and verse anthems appear only rarely, if at all, and are far outnumbered by the contributions of East and his school. Inevitably Byrd is represented either by *Lullaby/Be still my blessed babe,* simply too popular and well-loved to be ignored, or by *Christ rising/Christ is risen,* which at least in its scoring (with two sopranos in every verse and no fewer than eight choral interjections) anticipates the more variegated timbres of the Jacobean age.

In the light of what we now know of the more "fashionable" verse idiom of East, Peerson, and their generation, it becomes more apparent why sources so strongly concerned with music for voices and viols should neglect the works of William Byrd. A look at any of the consort songs or verse anthems from Byrd's latest publication, the 1611 *Psalms, Songs, and Sonnets,* roughly contemporary with East's *Third Set,* reveals a musical conception quite foreign to the taste of the Jacobean scribes. Indeed, Byrd's style must have seemed odder still to the Caroline secular anthologists, and perhaps incomprehensible to the scribe of Tenbury 1162-7, where Byrd is totally ignored. But Byrd's works have a richness of sonority to match the purpler passages increasingly common in the more extreme Jacobean works, as shown particularly by *Ah silly soul* from the 1611 publication (see the two extracts in ex. 1). The verse anthems of East, Peerson, and their generation have little to equal the richness of the "Amen" of *O God that guides* from the same collection (see ex. 2). But in Byrd the harmonic richness derives from the free interaction of the independent contrapuntal lines, unfettered by harmonic successions which would become increasingly stereotyped in other Jacobean works. The truth of this readily emerges from any attempt to describe them in conventional figured bass notation, which can be applied with some success to the later anthems and consort songs of Byrd's successors. Only very rarely do the pieces for voices and viols reveal the Italianate cadential progression with suspended seventh, which Peerson and his generation adopted from Morley.

Ex. 1.   *Ah silly soul*

Ex. 2.   *O God that guides*

A search through the later consort songs recently recovered from manuscript and ascribed to Byrd by Philip Brett[27] turns up less than half-a-dozen examples of that cadence, and in virtually all of them the independent movements of the parts still refuse to conform to the stereotyped patterns.[28] The most extreme example, *Wretched Albinus,* a setting of verses upon the fall of the Earl of Essex, contains several such moments (see ex. 3). Significantly, Philip Brett, in pointing out its exaggerated character, has suggested that "from the opening plunge of its first vocal phrase to the progressively diminishing repeats of its last, the song quietly and affectionately parodies not only the old 'death-song' but also Byrd's own elegiac manner."[29] One is tempted to see in it as well a parody of the new directions in which the consort song was heading in its adoption of many gestures proper to the madrigal, but undoubtedly indecorous to Byrd's way of thinking.

The same might also be true of the charming *My mistress had a little dog,* which Brett assigns to the period 1596 to 1605.[30] This expansive work, some eighty breves in length, with a three-fold repetition of its strophic opening section and a repetition of the concluding portion as well, reaches the dimensions of some Jacobean verse anthems or verse pastorals. Throughout its length, Byrd constantly adopts, with tongue-in-cheek, many of the devices that become so common in Jacobean works for voices and viols: the frequent movement in quarter-notes and even eighth-notes, repetition of vocal phrases, examples of naïve word-painting (including for "a tumbler fine" the Italianate roulade so common in Wilbye's madrigals and which in fact opens East's *Sweet Muses*), "expressive" suspensions (still treated with reserve, however) with a change to movement in half-notes for "But out, alas," and even a reference to the "Cries" at "Oyez! Oyez! Ye hounds and beagles all." Thus, for this light-hearted and amusing text Byrd composes a consort song that seems to parody the more ebullient gestures of the Jacobean verse idiom, just as *Wretched Albinus* seems to mimic its more pathetic features.

Ex. 3. *Wretched Albinus*

Given the probable dates of composition for these works, one may be endowing Byrd with extraordinary powers of foresight by this suggestion. But, as Dent has pointed out,[31] he would parody the chromaticism of the madrigal in *Come woeful Orpheus* from the 1611 set. The string of evaded and redirected progressions from *Wretched Albinus* quoted above certainly foreshadow the favorite devices of Martin Peerson and Michael East. Indeed, the abrupt and unexpected tonal shift at line 5 of that song mirrors exactly what we have seen in Peerson, and especially in the later works from Tenbury 1162-7.

Whether or not Byrd in fact intended the parody to extend so far, the style of these two consort songs was for him certainly exceptional. Therefore his contributions to the genre, by comparison with those of Peerson and his generation, must soon have seemed outdated. For a time the old favorites such as *Lullaby* and *Christ rising* might hold their own through long-standing familiarity. But by the time the scribe of the London source, Christ Church 56-60, or the scribe of the very late Tenbury 1162-7, put pen to paper it was too late, even for these works.

It is in a way ironic that just as William Byrd, who doggedly pursued his own personal style, gradually declined in popularity, so the composer who most represents the lighter madrigal style, Thomas Morley, fell so quickly from favor after 1600. But the older native style for voices and viols, on the other hand, having survived the glamorous flurries around the lighter Elizabethan madrigal, found a new lease on life during the reign of James I. By a process of adaptation, through which it absorbed elements from both the moribund madrigal and the more modern lute ayre, and also by its appeal to the new fascination with viol playing, the old, long-familiar English verse idiom seems to have gathered to itself a wide following, to judge by the surviving prints and manuscripts. In 1601 the sober Richard Carlton must have felt somewhat alone when he penned the preface to his *Madrigals to Five Voices,* which appeared concurrently with *The Triumphs of Oriana,* when the madrigal seemed to be at the height of popularity. But fifteen years later the picture had altered, and for the rest of the reign of James I and long into that of his son, many composers would perhaps have shared the sentiments which Carlton had expressed in the last years of the Elizabethan age:

I have laboured somewhat to imitate the *Italian,* they being in these dayes (with the most) in high request, yet may *I* not nor cannot forget that *I* am an Englishman.

Notes

Preface

1. For example, Thomas Weelkes's *O my son Absalom,* part 2 of *When David heard,* appears on its own in eight different pre-Restoration sources.

2. Edmund H. Fellowes, *English Madrigal Verse,* revised by F.W. Sternfeld and David Greer, 3d edition (Oxford, 1967).

Chapter 1

1. John Morehen, "The Sources of English Cathedral Music, 1617-1644," unpublished Ph.D. dissertation (Cambridge University, 1969).

2. Warwick Edwards, "The Sources of Elizabethan Consort Music," unpublished Ph.D. dissertation (Cambridge University, 1974).

3. Peter le Huray, "Towards a Definitive Study of Pre-Restoration Anglican Service Music," *MD., XIV* (1960), 168.

4. Augustus Hughes-Hughes, *Catalogue of Manuscript Music in the British Museum,* 3 vols. (London, 1906).

5. E.H. Fellowes, *The Catalogue of the Manuscripts in the Library of St. Michael's College, Tenbury* (Paris, 1934).

6. F. Madan's *A Summary Catalogue of Western Manuscripts in the Bodleian Library at Oxford* (Oxford, 1895-1953) includes only cursory descriptions of the music manuscripts. In G.E.P. Arkwright's *Catalogue of Music in the Library of Christ Church Oxford,* 2 vols. (London, 1915), volume I contains an index of all pieces, ordered by composer, while volume II includes incipits of anonymous vocal works. There are no inventories of entire manuscripts. "The Catalogue of the Manuscripts in the Library of the Royal College of Music" prepared by W.B. Squire and R. Erlebach contains detailed inventories of the manuscripts, but is only available in typescript at the RCM and the British Library. A very cursory article on the collection of the New York Public Library (including numerous errors) appeared in *Sammelbände der Internationalen Musik-Gesellschaft,* IV (1903), 738-50.

7. The use of viols, however, is never specified in the sources, and rests to a certain extent upon outside evidence and tradition.

8. In *The Principles of Musik* (London, 1636), Charles Butler writes: "But because *Entata* are often out of tune, (which sometimes happens in the midst of the Music, when it is neither good

to continue, nor to correct the fault) therefore, to avoid all offence, (where the least should not be given) in our Choir-solemnities only the Wind-instruments (whose Notes are constant) be in use" (p. 103; spelling and punctuation modernized). Peter le Huray discovered only two specific references to the use of viols in church during this period. See *Music and the Reformation in England* (London, 1967), p. 128.

9. Richard Nicolson's *O Lord consider my distress* seems to be a viol arrangement of an older anthem by Edward Smith of Durham (this piece is treated extensively in the discussion of Bodl. MSS Mus. Sch. D 212-216 in chap. 5). But Smith's original Elizabethan conception might even have included viols. One post-Restoration manuscript, Christ Church MS 21, among the most important sources for Orlando Gibbon's verse anthems, shows the sort of complications this arrangement process could create for later scholars. To quote David Wulstan, "There are indications, seen when comparing the versions in Ch Ch MS 21 with those of other manuscripts, that in some instances, if not the majority, the string parts preserved are arrangements of organ scores which in turn are redactions of pre-existing string parts." *Orlando Gibbons: Verse Anthems*, in *EECM*, III (London, 1964), p. viii. The problem receives further consideration in John Morehen, "The English Consort and Verse Anthems," *EMu*, VI (1978), 381-85.

10. F. Ll. Harrison, for example, in discussing the music of Byrd's three song collections (1588, 1589, 1611), emphasizes that it "is historically important for its maintenance of a line of development which led from the court and domestic music of Henry VIII's time to the Jacobean verse-anthem and ayre." See "Church Music in England," *NOHM*, IV (London, 1968), p. 504.

11. Philip Brett, "The Songs of William Byrd," unpublished Ph.D. dissertation (Cambridge University, 1965). On the Paston sources, see also Brett's "Edward Paston (1550-1630): a Norfolk Gentleman and his Musical Collection," *Transactions of the Cambridge Bibliographical Society*, IV (1964), 51-69.

12. Sometime near the end of James I's reign, but perhaps even as early as 1615, some anthems probably were conceived originally with organ. Thomas Weelkes, for example, has left not a single verse anthem with viol accompaniment. Even *Give ear O Lord,* Weelkes's sole contribution to Myriell's *Tristitiae Remedium* in this genre, requires an organ for its performance.

13. Some sources now in American libraries would still be in British ones but for Rimbault's not entirely ethical techniques of enlarging his private collection, subsequently dispersed at his death. See W.G. Hiscock. *Christ Church Miscellaney* (Oxford, 1946), pp. 127-33.

14. See Pamela Willetts, "The Identity of Thomas Myriell," *ML*, LIII (1972), 431-33.

Chapter 2

1. See Denis Stevens, *Thomas Tomkins* (New York, 1967), p. 43; Thurston Dart, "Music and Musicians at Chichester Cathedral," *ML*, XLII (1961), 224; Craig Monson, "Thomas Weelkes: a new fa-la," *MT*, CXIII (1972), 133.

2. Pamela Willetts, "Musical Connections of Thomas Myriell," *ML*, XLIX (1968), 36-42. Miss Willetts identified Myriell's hand in Christ Church MSS 44, 61-66, 67, and 459-62, as well as in British Library Additional MS 29427 and Brussels, Bibliothèque Royale MS II.4109 (Fétis 3095). John Aplin, on the other hand, attempted to link two of the Christ Church sets, 61-66 and 67, to Christ Church 56-60 and has suggested that all derive from the household of Sir Henry Fanshawe. His arguments were considerably weakened, however, by his unfamiliarity

with Pamela Willetts's earlier discoveries. See his "Sir Henry Fanshawe and two Sets of Early Seventeenth-Century Part-books at Christ Church, Oxford," *ML,* LVII (1976), 11-24; see also "Correspondence," *ML,* LVII (1976), 343-44.

3. Pamela Willetts, "The Identity of Thomas Myriell," *ML,* LIII (1972), 431-33.

4. The following system of abbreviations will be used to distinguish the various Myriell MSS discussed in this chapter:

B.L. Add. 29372-7	29372	Christ Church 61-66	61
B.L. Add. 29427	29427	Christ Church 67	67
Brussels MS II. 4109	4109	Christ Church 459-62	459
Christ Church MS 44	44		

5. Willetts, "Musical Connections," p. 39.

6. Willetts, "The Identity," pp. 431-33.

7. The poem is also of Cambridge origin. See Philip Brett, *Consort Songs,* in *MB,* XXII (London, 1967), p. 179, for a discussion of the connection between John Tomkins and the Cambridge poet, Phineas Fletcher, probable author of the text of the song.

8. See chap. 3, following.

9. See David Scott, "Nicholas Yonge and his Transalpine Music," *MT,* CXVI (1975), 875.

10. David Scott, *The Music of St. Paul's Cathedral* (London, 1972), p. 15.

11. The records of St. Stephen's attest to at least one meeting between Milton and Myriell— Myriell officiated at the wedding of Milton's daughter on Nov. 22, 1623. See William Parker, "Thomas Myriell," *Notes and Queries,* CLXXXVIII (1945), 103.

12. On Martin Peerson, see Marc Eccles, "Martin Peerson and the Blackfriars," *Shakespeare Survey,* XI (1958), 100-106.

13. See David Mateer, "Ravenscroft, Thomas," *Grove 6,* XV,p. 623.

14. For a discussion of Ravenscroft's theatrical songs, see Andrew Sabol, "Ravenscroft's 'Melismata' and the Children of Paul's," *Renaissance News,* XII (1959), 3-9; also W.J. Lawrence, "Thomas Ravenscroft's Theatrical Associations," *Modern Language Review,* XIX (1924), 418-423.

15. Richard Marlowe, ed., *Giles and Richard Farnaby: Keyboard Music,* in *MB,* XXIV (London, 1965), pp. xxi-xxii.

16. For a discussion of this distinctive category of Jacobean music, see Vincent Duckles, "The English Musical Elegy of the late Renaissance," *Aspects of Medieval and Renaissance Music,* ed. Jan LaRue (New York, 1966), pp. 134-53. Duckles points to Prince Henry's death as the inspiration for many pieces, especially those treating the Absalom text. See also Thurston Dart, "Two English Musicians in Heidelberg in 1613," *MT,* CXI (1970), 29. It should be pointed out, however, that none of the Absalom or Jonathan pieces is specifically linked to Prince Henry's death by an annotation such as "Passion on the death of Prince Henry."

17. Number 17, *O give me the comfort,* part 2 of *Turn thy face,* does not appear in 29427. A comparison of the musical texts in 29427 with those in *The Third Set* makes it clear that the scribe was copying from the print.

18. Willetts, "Musical Connections," pp. 40-41.

19. Stevens, *Thomas Tomkins,* p. 99. See also Pamela Willetts, "Musical Connections," p. 38: "It is a valuable early, and occasionally unique, source for anthems and songs by Tomkins, Peerson, Ward and Nathaniel Gyles, all of whom were active in London before 1616, when 'Tristitiae Remedium' was completed."

20. Notari's original title page is reproduced in Gottfried Fraenkel, *Decorative Music Title Pages* (New York, 1968), Pl. 65.

21. See Joseph Kerman, *The Elizabethan Madrigal, A Comparative Study* (New York, 1962), pp. 243-45.

22. John Merro, the provincial scribe from Gloucester, whose major set of partbooks (Drexel 4180-5) is even larger than *Tristitiae Remedium,* fared somewhat better, chiefly by drawing upon the simpler sacred works from John Day's generation. With the possible exception of Thomas Hamond, whose taste seems somewhat broader and less discriminating, collectors at all interested in music for voices and viols rarely concerned themselves with music in less than five parts.

23. Myriell did not have access to Byrd's original version, which appears in Bodl. MS Mus. Sch. E 423, and Christ Church MSS 984-88, and which has been published in volume XVI of *The Byrd Edition,* ed. Philip Brett (London, 1975); see pp. 138-43.

24. See *Michael East: Fourth Set of Books (1618),* in *EM,* XXXIb (revised by Philip Brett and Thurston Dart), (London, 1962), especially pp. 87, 98, and 102.

25. George Hennessy, *Novum Repertorium Ecclesiasticum Parochiale Londinense* (London, 1898), pp. 67 and 320-21.

26. I should like to thank Mr. Robert Ford for calling my attention to Stubb's connection with St. Gregory's and for providing his burial record.

27. Page numbers from *Thomas Tomkins Songs of 3, 4, 5, and 6 parts (1622),* in *EM,* XVIII (revised by Thurston Dart), (London, 1960).

28. Peter le Huray in *Music and the Reformation in England,* p. 330, mistakenly lists the several parts as individual anthems. Nor does he distinguish between Ward's three-part and six-part settings of *Praise the Lord.* Le Huray's more recent *The Sources of English Church Music 1549-1660,* in *EECM,* suppl. vol. I (London, 1972), pp. 151-52, continues to classify the various sections of the three-part work as different anthems.

29. But not so late as le Huray's suggested 1625: *Music and the Reformation,* p. 100.

30. The records of Canterbury Cathedral include some fourteen references to the Pysings, father and son, between 1635 and 1707. See Robert Hovendon, *The Register Booke of Christeninges, Marriages, and Burialls within the Precinct of the Cathedrall and Metropolitical Church of Christe of Canterburie,* in *The Publications of the Harleian Society.* Registers. II (London, 1878).

31. See J. Bunker Clark, "Adrian Batten and John Barnard: Colleagues and Collaborators," *MD,* XXII (1968), 207-29. A catch, *Come, follow me,* appears in Playford's *Catch that Catch Can* (1685). See Andrew Ashbee, "Pysing [Pising (e)], William," *Grove 6,* XV, p. 485.

32. Norman Josephs, "Ives [Ive, Ivy], Simon (i)," *Grove 6,* IX, p. 429.

33. The Christ Church Library also contains another organ part for these two Ward anthems (MS 1215 [3]). It has been preserved in the following form (foliation added by the present writer):

Praise the Lo: 103 psalme	1
The Lord executeth righteousness	1ᵛ
(leaf cut; stub remains)	
The Lord hath prepared his seat in heaven	2
Have mercy upon me O God 51 psalm	2ᵛ
Behold I was shapen in wickedness	3
Turn thy face	3ᵛ
Deliver me from bloodguiltiness	4
(fol. 4v blank and very dirty)	
For look how high	5
The days of man	5

Originally fols. 1 and 5 and 2 and 3 must have formed separate gatherings within a separate sheet, consisting of the missing folio after fol. 1 and its other half, fol. 4. This would explain the mix-up in the sequence of pieces as it now stands, and why fol. 4ᵛ is so dirty. Thus, this little manuscript closely resembles the insertions which occur in 61 and 67, and one must ask if it could have been the rough copy for 67. The texts are remarkably close (differences in three accidentals provide the only discrepancies on the first page of *Behold I was shapen*), even down to details such as tied notes and the repetition of accidentals. The hands also happen to be similar in a general way.

34. See David Pinto, "William Lawes' music for viol consort," *EMu,* VI (1978), 22. Pinto further suggests that "This hand may be a later example of that found in British Library Add. 17786-91," which, however, seems highly unlikely. See chap. 5.

35. David Pinto, "William Lawes' Suites for the viols and the autograph Sources," *Chelys,* IV (1972), 11.

36. First pointed out by Willetts in "Musical Connections," p. 36.

37. Ibid., p. 37.

38. Ibid.

39. Stevens, *Thomas Tomkins,* p. 36: "Of this mode [the Lydian] is that passionate lamentation of the musical king for the death of his son *Absalom,* composed in five parts by Mr. Thomas Tomkins, now organist of His Majesty's chapel. The melodious harmony of which, when I heard it in the Music-School (Oxon), whether I should more admire the sweet well-governed voices, with consonant instruments, of the singers, or the exquisite invention, wit, and art of the composer, it was hard to determine."

40. Willetts, "Musical Connections," p. 41.

41. Pamela Willetts, *Handlist of Music MSS acquired 1908-1967* (London, 1970), p. 8. See also Miss Willetts's "Sir Nicholas Le Strange and John Jenkins," *ML,* XLII (1961), 30-43.

42. Some such comparisons, though with no clear connection to Myriell's collection, appear in Andrew Ashbee, "A Further Look at Some of the Le Strange Manuscripts," *Chelys,* V (1973-74), 24-41.

43. Willetts, "Musical Connections," p. 39.

44. The manuscripts are Royal College of Music MSS 1045-51; British Library Add. 29289; and St. Michael's College, Tenbury MS 791. See J. Bunker Clark, "Adrian Batten and John Barnard," pp. 207-29.

45. Jean Jacquot, "Lyrisme et sentiment tragique dans les madrigaux d'Orlando Gibbons," *Musique et poésie au XVIe siècle* (Paris, 1954), 139-51; Wilfred Mellers, "La Mélancholie au début du XVIIe siècle et le madrigal anglais," ibid., 153-68.

46. Philip van Wilder's *Blessed art thou that fearest God* is an exception to this rule. The anthem was very popular, however, with both the Elizabethan and Jacobeans.

47. To judge from the extant sources, *Come tread the paths* was copied for the last time in 29427. For *Abradad,* Egerton MS 3665 and Drexel 4180-5 could be slightly later.

48. See Frank Ll. Harrison, "Church Music in England," *NOHM,* IV (1968), 505-14. See also Aplin, "Sir Henry Fanshawe and two Sets of Early Seventeenth-Century Part-books."

49. Peter le Huray, "Towards a Definitive Study of Pre-Restoration Anglican Church Music," *MD,* XIV (1960), 193.

50. Pamela Willetts's omission of 56-60 from "Musical Connections," tacitly rejects le Huray's view. But compare with John Aplin, "Sir Henry Fanshawe and two Sets of Early Seventeenth-Century Part-books."

51. Compare, for example, the groups of pieces from Add. 29427 in 29372, or those from Drexel 4180-5 in Add. 17792-6.

52. For further discussion of Ravenscroft's St. Paul's associations, see Sabol, "Ravenscroft's 'Melismata' and the Children of Paul's."

53. Daniel and le Huray failed to notice it in the latter source. See *Sources of English Church Music,* p. 116.

54. See Philip Brett, "The Two Musical Personalities of Thomas Weelkes," *ML,* LIII (1972), 371-72. Compare Gibbons's *O all true faithful hearts:* "O all true faithful hearts with one accord, United in one hand sing to the Lord, For he our David from the snares of death hath freed.'

55. On the Clark Library source, see Richard Charteris, "A Rediscovered Source of English Consort Music," *Chelys,* V (1973-74), 3-6.

56. Thurston Dart, "The Repertory of the Royal Wind Music," *Galpin Society Journal,* XI (1958), 70-77.

57. Robert Ford, "Some Court-Related Manuscripts," as yet unpublished.

58. Three hands appear in Simms's *Rise O my soul,* Ravenscroft's *In Thee, O Lord,* Amner's *Consider all ye passers-by,* and Weelkes's *Gloria in excelsis deo, sing my soul,* for example.

59. Ward's *This is a joyful, happy holiday,* Bull's *Almighty God, who by the leading of a star,* and Tye's *Christ rising,* for example.

60. Aplin, "Sir Henry Fanshawe and two Sets of Early Seventeenth-Century Part-books."

61. The same version reappears in John Merro's MSS, Drexel 4180-5 and Add. 17792-6. See chap. 4, following.

62. Harrison, "Church Music in England," p. 512 and note.

63. Brett, "The Two Musical Personalities of Thomas Weelkes," pp. 371-72.

64. Examples quoted by Harrison in "Church Music in England," pp. 506-13.

65. The piece, which is anonymous here and attributed to "Mr Coste" in Myriell, is among the earliest and most dubious anthems bearing Byrd's name. See Craig Monson, "Authenticity and Chronology in Byrd's Church Anthems," *JAMS,* XXXV (1982), in press.

66. See Philip Brett, "Edward Paston (1550-1630): a Norfolk Gentleman and His Musical Collection." *Transactions of the Cambridge Bibliographical Society,* IV (1964), pp. 51-69.

67. Philippe Oboussier, "Parsons, William," *Grove 6,* XIV, pp. 249-50.

68. *My song shall be of mercy* survives only in RCM 1045-51; *Praise the Lord* appears in Tenbury 791 (related to 1045-51), and in the Oxford sources, Christ Church MSS 1220-24 and St. John's College MS 180.

69. Peter le Huray, "Jeffreys, Matthew," *Grove 6,* IX, p. 586.

70. Four anthems survive only in sacred manuscripts, four appear only in secular sources, and four in both.

71. An incomplete *Praise the Lord, O ye servants* and the First and Second Service survive in post-Restoration additions to a copy of Barnard's *First Book of Selected Church Musick* at Gloucester Cathedral. The popular full anthem, *Rejoice in the Lord, O ye righteous* appears in Drexel MSS 4180-5 and B.L. Add. 17792-6, both copied by John Merro of Gloucester (see chap. 4).

72. The text underlay for the two sources is not identical, however.

73. The popular *Star Anthem* also appears in the Oxford source, Bodl. MSS Mus. Sch. D 212-216 and in John Baldwin's Commonplace Book (Royal Music Library MS 24.D.2); an incomplete *I am feeble* survives only in Royal Music Library 24.D.2. These are the only two anthems to appear in secular sources outside the capital.

74. See David Brown, *Thomas Weelkes* (London, 1969), p. 154.

75. Willibald Nagel reproduces the following reference from the court records: "Randall paradyso deceased the 16th day of Jan 1569 in the paryshe of saint oliver in hartstreet besyde the croched fryers in london, and was buryed the 17th day of the same moneth in the same parysh in the churchyard, as yt ys to be seen in the boke of the same paryshe of buryelles according to the ordyer...By me *Thos. Whalley.*" See Nagel, "Annalen der englischen Hofmusik von der Zeit Heinrich's VIII. bis zum Tode Karl's I. (1509-1649)," *Monatsheft für Musik-Geschichte,* XXVI (1894), 28-29.

73. The second half had appeared much earlier on p. 234, apparently copied from 29427.

Chapter 3

1. British Library, Add. MSS 18936-9, for example, which belonged to Stephen Aldhouse of Matlask, near Town Barningham in Norfolk. For a discussion of this source see Philip Brett, "Edward Paston (1550-1630): a Norfolk Gentleman and his Musical Collection, *Transactions of the Cambridge Bibliographical Society,* IV (1964), 51-69; also Craig Monson, "Thomas Weelkes: a new fa-la," *MT,* CXIII (1972), 133-35. Another source, Paris, Bibliothèque de la Conservatoire MS Rés. 1186, was apparently compiled by Robert Creighton in Cambridge during the 1630s, to judge by the dates appended to several works in that source.

2. Margaret Crum, "A Seventeenth-Century Collection of Music Belonging to Thomas Hamond, a Suffolk Landowner," *Bodleian Library Record,* VI (1957), 373-86. See also A. Hyatt King, *Some British Collectors of Music c. 1600-1960* (Cambridge, 1963).

3. Crum, "A Seventeenth-Century Collection of Music," 373-74.

4. These are not all from the popular sixteenth-century prints of "Englished" foreign works, however (see catalogue).

5. See Emil Vogel, Alfred Einstein, Francois Lesure, Claudio Sartori, *Bibliografia della Musica Italiana Vocale Profana Pubblicata dal 1500 al 1700,* I (Pomezia, 1977), p. 237.

6. I should like to thank Professor Jane Bernstein for pointing out to me the facts of Firmage's Cambridge career and the existence of his will.

7. The will is printed in full in Joseph J. Muskett, *Suffolk Manorial Families,* I (London, 1897), p. 292.

8. Not, as G.E.P. Arkwright suggested, "towards the middle of the seventeenth century." *Old English Edition,* no. 3 (London, 1891), p. 5.

9. From the inscription on the covers of Add. MSS 30480-4 (a facsimile appears in A. Hyatt King, *Some British Collectors of Music*), we know that Hamond's musical interests go back at least to 1615, so it is quite possible that he had begun copying music during the second decade of the century.

10. Pamela Willetts, "Sir Nicholas Le Strange and John Jenkins," *ML,* XLII (1961), 39.

11. Ibid.

12. The will is printed in Joseph J. Muskett, *Suffolk Manorial Families,* I, p. 259.

13. Crum, "A Seventeenth-Century Collection of Music," p. 374.

14. John Venn and John A. Venn, *Alumni Cantabrigiensis,* part 1, II (Cambridge, 1922), pp. 293-95. By an interesting coincidence, a Thomas Hamond was listed as a lay-clerk at King's College in 1602, when he received payments for copying a set of chapel choirbooks. See John Morehen, "The Sources of English Cathedral Music, c. 1617-c. 1644," unpublished Ph.D. dissertation (Cambridge University, 1969), p. 212.

15. Daniel and le Huray apparently overlooked the piece in Hamond's books, for they simply list it as anonymous and in the Peterhouse sources. *The Sources of English Church Music, 1549-1660, EECM,* supplementary volume I (London, 1972), p. 72.

16. Ibid., p. 83.

17. For a discussion of Ravenscroft's theatrical songs, see A.J. Sabol, "Ravenscroft's 'Melismata' and the Children of Paul's," *Renaissance News,* XII (1959), 3-9; also W.J. Lawrence, "Thomas Ravanscroft's Theatrical Associations," *Modern Language Review,* XIX (1924), 418-23.

18. David Mateer, "Ravenscroft, Thomas," *Grove 6,* XV, p. 623.

19. See Marc Eccles, "Martin Peerson and the Blackfriars," *Shakespeare Survey,* XI (1958), 100-106.

20. Kirbye's place in the history of the English madrigal is discussed more fully in Craig Monson, "George Kirbye and the English Madrigal," *ML,* LIX (1978), 290-315. The article borrows and refines several ideas presented here, and includes the texts of all the unpublished works.

21. Joseph Kerman, *The Elizabethan Madrigal, A Comparative Study* (New York, 1962), p. 221.

22. In addition to the opening line, the poet seems to have borrowed and adapted "The floods forsaking their delightful swelling" and "Their wonted storms and every blast rebelling." Line 7 also sounds remarkably like "At liberty against the cage rebelling" from Lassus's *The nightingale so pleasant and so gay* from *Musica Transalpina,* and the anacreontic theme of the madrigal is rather like that of Byrd's sonnet, *Upon a summer's day love went to swim* from his 1589 publication.

23. Kerman, *The Elizabethan Madrigal*, p. 15.

24. Further confirmation of Kirbye's somewhat elevated and atypical literary aspirations appear in the *First Set* in the form of a lament, *Up then Melpomene,* from Spenser's *Shepherd's Calendar*—the only attempt by a genuine English madrigalist to set Spenser's verse. The only other Spenser settings occur in the works of composers in the native tradition of secular song: Richard Carlton, once again, and Orlando Gibbons.

25. Philip Brett, "Word-Setting in the Songs of Byrd," *PRMA*, XCVIII (1971-1972), 52.

26. Manuscript copyists very rarely copied additional stanzas, even when they had appeared in their printed sources.

27. Jean Jacquot, "Lyrisme et sentiment tragique dans les madrigaux d'Orlando Gibbons," *Musique et Poésie au xvie Siècle* (Paris, 1954), 139-51; and Wilfred Mellers, "La Mélancholie au début du XVIIe siècle et le madrigal anglais," ibid., 153-68.

28. It is interesting to note that Carlton's *Madrigals to Five Voices* also contains an elegy in memory of Sir John Shelton of Norfolk *(Sound saddest notes),* whose brother married one of the Jermyns of Rushbrooke Hall, where Kirbye was employed. See *Richard Carlton Madrigals to Five Voices (1601),* in *EM,* XXVII (revised by Thurston Dart), (London, 1960), xi.

29. Arkwright, *Old English Edition,* no. 3, p. 6. This suggestion occurs in a discusssion of the Firmage MSS. It appears that Arkwright was at that time unaware of the unpublished works in F 16-19 and F 2-24, which he mentions only in *Old English Edition,* no. 5 (London, 1892), pp. 4-5.

30. Arkwright, *Old English Edition,* no. 3, p. 6.

31. Kerman, *The Elizabethan Madrigal*, p. 222.

32. Ibid.

33. Ibid.

34. A similar clash occurs at "and die I shall" in *Flora fair nymph* by John Ward, one of the more contrapuntally oriented madrigalists.

35. Kerman, *The Elizabethan Madrigal*, p. 222.

36. Brett, "Word-Setting in the Songs of Byrd," p. 52.

37. Kerman, *The Elizabethan Madrigal*, pp. 221-23.

38. David Brown, *Thomas Weelkes* (London, 1969).

39. Kerman, *The Elizabethan Madrigal*, p. 222. No. 18 in fact freely varies both its first and second sections. Another freely varied opening appears in no. 21. Kirbye shows less interest in ballet or canzonet forms than in the ABB form, so prominent in the consort song repertory. Eleven of the twenty-four pieces from the 1597 collection and eleven of the unpublished works repeat their final sections.

40. Brown, *Thomas Weelkes.* Brown tends to over-emphasize Weelkes's unique position in the use of the technique, however. Although structural repetition may not have been common before the turn of the century (there are isolated examples in Wilbye's and John Bennet's 1598 collections and even a case or two in Morley), a rash of examples appears after 1600 in the works of Michael East (1604: 18-19; 1606: 7-8, 17-18, 22; 1610: 1-3), Henry Lichfield (1613: 13-14), Thomas Tomkins (1622: 7-8), Thomas Vautor (1619: 4 and 19), John Ward (1613: 1-

2), and John Wilbye (1609: 1, 3, 31). Other instances can also be found in the works of the lutenist song writers, John Danyel, and John Dowland and Robert Jones. It may be significant that of the madrigalists, Bennet, Ward, and especially East are also known for their interest in the native tradition as expressed in consort song and verse anthem, while others (East, Lichfield, Vautor, and Ward) are linked to the lutenist song writers, however tenuously, by an interest in some of the same texts—see Edward Doughtie, *Lyrics from English Ayres 1596-1622* (Cambridge, Mass., 1970), pp. 472, 483 (East), 529 (Lichfield), 472, 543, 549 (Vautor), 478, 585 (Ward). Thus, this sort of repetition seems primarily associated with genres that share the power to project the words of the text and its form unobscured rather than to express individual images in madrigalian fashion: the lute ayre, consort song, and verse anthem. Perhaps the appearance of text-oriented musical repetition in the works of these later madrigalists indicates that after 1600 even the madrigal itself became subject, on occasion, to this older aesthetic outlook.

41. Phillip Brett, "The Two Musical Personalities of Thomas Weelkes," *ML,* LIII (1972), 375-76.

42. Crum, "A Seventeenth-Century Collection of Music," p. 382.

43. Bennet's four-part version is printed in *John Bennet Madrigals to Four Voices (1599),* in *EM,* XXIII (revised by Davitt Moroney), (London, 1979), pp. 124-28.

44. Aside from *Tristitiae Remedium,* which includes an isolated motet by Ravenscroft, Hamond's books seem to be the only pre-Restoration collection to preserve motets by these composers.

45. C. Stainer, "Fabritius (Fabricus), Albinus," *Grove 5,* III, pp. 2-3. The writer of the article was apparently unaware that Fabritio's work was known in England during the seventeenth century, as was the author of the article in the more recent *Grove*—see Walter Blankenburg, "Fabritius [Fabricus], Albinus," *Grove 6,* VI, p. 349.

46. The ascription apparently escaped Daniel and le Huray, who list the work as anonymous in *The Sources of English Church Music,* p. 71.

47. It is quite possible, of course, that they appeared in a set of books no longer extant.

48. Daniel and le Huray failed to notice that Hamond includes *How vain the toils* in F 20-24 *(The Sources of English Church Music,* p. 85).

49. Also notably absent in Byrd's ever-popular *Lullaby.*

50. See the discussions of Add. MSS 29366-8, Add. MSS 37402-6, Christ Church MSS 56-60, and especially Tenbury MSS 1162-7, which reveal that prepublication copies of East's anthems remained in circulation for decades.

51. Crum, "A Seventeenth-Century Collection of Music," p. 379.

52. For further discussion of this point see the chapter on Tenbury MSS 1162-7.

53. Augustus Hughes-Hughes, *Catalogue of Manuscript Music in the British Museum,* I, p. 5.

54. Edward Thompson, *Robert Ramsey: Sacred Music,* in *EECM,* VII (1967), p. ix.

55. Philip Brett, ed., *Consort Songs, M.B,* XXII (London, 1967), p. 173.

56. Myriell's early altus book, Add. 29427, contains *When David heard* by Ramsey among its many laments for Prince Henry; but Myriell never included it in *Tristitiae Remedium;* Myriell, of course, began his career in Cambridge. Tenbury 1162-7 contains a number of Ramsey works, but reveals both London and Cambridge repertory (see chap. 7).

57. The work occurs in Add. 29427, but was rejected from *Tristitiae Remedium.*

58. Aside from these two manuscripts, the only other source is Myriell's *Tristitiae Remedium.*

59. Jeffrey Mark, "Wilkinson, Thomas," *Grove 5,* IX, p. 299.

60. Robert Creighton (1593-1672), who received his M.A. from Trinity College, Cambridge in 1621, served as professor of Greek from 1625 until 1639, and as public orator from 1627 until 1639. He was for a time chaplain to Charles I and also dean of Wells. After the Restoration he became bishop of Bath and Wells (1670-72). His son, Robert Creighton (c. 1639-1734) followed a very similar career. He became a fellow of Trinity in 1662 and served as professor of Greek from 1662 until 1674. In that year he became a canon and precentor of Wells. (*DNB,* XIII, pp. 69-70)

61. Morehen, "Sources."

62. Peter le Huray, "Wilkinson (first name unknown)," *Grove 6,* XX, p. 420.

63. Compare the (correct) ascription of *Cruel unkind, adieu* to Pallavicino, although it is anonymous in the surviving partbooks.

64. The alto part reappears anonymously in Myriell's Add. 29427, transposed down a fourth. It was not recopied into *Tristitiae Remedium.*

65. The setting is especially long-winded in its manifold repetitions of some points (see the opening "I am the resurrection"). It reveals a tendency to repeat the same two parts in (not necessarily invertible) counterpoint in different voices rather frequently and to return to the same melodic shapes later in the course of the piece. See *Orlando Gibbons: Full Anthems, Hymns and Fragmentary Verse Anthems,* in *EECM,* XXI (ed. by David Wulstan), (London, 1978), pp. 24-31 for a reconstructed version. One cannot rule out the possibility of misattribution by the scribe. The authenticity of the anthem has been questioned by Paul Vining—see "English Church Music Sources," *MT,* CXIV (1973), 257-58.

66. E.H. Fellowes, *Orlando Gibbons,* 2nd ed. (London, 1951), pp. 34-35.

67. Morehen, "Sources," p. 136.

68. Denis Stevens, *Thomas Tomkins* (New York, 1967), pp. 72-73.

69. "It is not inconceivable that some of the boys [i.e., choristers] were pluralists, using their talents possibly in King's College Chapel and/or Trinity College Chapel also. Although Cosin's harsh criticisms of the Trinity and King's choristers argues against this theory, it must be noted that the university waits (as opposed to the town waits) served both Trinity and Peterhouse at this period." Morehen, "Sources," p. 136.

70. Quoted in E.H. Fellowes, *The English Madrigal Composers* (Oxford, 1948), p. 272.

71. The list of partbooks in the collection of one such group from Oxford, which used the "Carlisle Partbooks" (JAC 58), includes more than a dozen different sets of printed books. See James Walter Brown, "An Elizabethan Song-Cycle," *The Cornhill Magazine,* XLVIII (1920), 573.

72. Bearsley is one of the few composers in the source occasionally described as "Mr."

73. John Morehen, "The Southwell Minster Tenor Part-Book in the Library of St. Michael's College Tenbury (MS. 1382)," *ML,* L (1969), 363.

74. Denis Stevens, on the other hand, suggests that the twelve-part *O praise the Lord* might have been written for the degree. See *Thomas Tomkins,* p. 84.

75. Daniel and le Huray apparently were unaware of the source for the former, and mistakenly describe *Cantai mentre* as a motet. See *The Sources of English Church Music, 1549-1660*, pp. 73 and 132.

76. Edward Thompson, "Robert Ramsey," *MQ,* XLIX (1963), 212.

77. East served for a time as a lay-clerk at Ely—see Philip Brett, "East (Easte, Est, Este), Michael," *Grove 6,* V, p. 801. Peerson was born in Cambridgeshire.

78. Susi Jeans, "Simmes," *Grove 5,* supplementary volume, p. 410.

79. A William Symmes matriculated at Emanuel College, Cambridge in 1619, graduated AB in 1622 and A.M. in 1626 (Venn, *University of Cambridge Matriculations and Degrees, 1544-1659,* p. 609); it seems unlikely, however, that this was the composer.

80. This and the following information from Wilburn B. Newcomb, "Warwick, Thomas," *MGG,* XIV, cols. 262-63.

Chapter 4

1. Pamela Willetts, "Music from the Circle of Anthony Wood at Oxford," *British Museum Quarterly,* XXIV (1961), 71-75.

2. Philip Brett, ed., *Consort Songs, MB,* XXII (London, 1967), p. 173. I shall have occasion to modify or correct this description in the following pages.

3. Andrew Ashbee, in "Lowe, Jenkins and Merro," *ML,* XLVIII (1967), 311, gives Merro's death date as 23 March 1636. Elsewhere Ashbee has given the year of death as 1639. See "Instrumental Music from the Library of John Browne (1608-1691), Clerk of the Parliaments," *ML,* LVIII (1977), 49.

4. These and subsequent numberings are taken from MS 4180 (see catalogue).

5. All books except 4180 begin this group with *Lullaby.* In 4180 the section begins with *Constant Penelope,* which perhaps was subsequently entered on a blank folio before *Lullaby* in that book.

6. E.H. Fellowes, "Bateson, Thomas," *Grove 5,* I, p. 498.

7. Willetts, "Music from the Circle of Anthony Wood," p. 74.

8. Hugh Davies appears in the Gloucester bassus book, in Christ Church 544-53 (The Hereford copy of Barnard), and also in Bodleian MS Mus. D 162 (from New College), and in the Barnard sources, Royal College of Music 1045-51 and Tenbury 791. "Smith of Salop" only reappears in Ludlow SRO 356, MS 3.

9. John Morehen, "The Sources of English Cathedral Music, c. 1617-c. 1644," unpublished Ph.D. dissertation (Cambridge University), 1969, pp. 345-46.

10. The few annotations in 4180, chiefly supplying attributions to the instrumental works at the close of the partbooks, seem to be the work of a modern librarian, especially since they provide the fantasias with the appropriate numbers from Meyer's catalogue.

11. See W.G. Hiscock, *Christ Church Miscellaney* (Oxford, 1946), pp. 127-33.

12. Edward F. Rimbault, *A Collection of Anthems by composers of the Madrigalian Era* (London, c. 1846), p. 1. This publication also contains several anthems by East which do not appear in 4180; they were probably transcribed from East's *Third Set* (1610) or his *Sixth Set* (1624).

13. I should like to thank Mr. John Wing, Assistant Librarian of Christ Church, for checking the early lists for me, and also for searching the *Catalogus Evelynianus.*

14. I am indebted to Ms. Susan Sommer for attempting to find the Evelyn press mark, or references to it, at the New York Public Library.

15. *Catalogue of the Valuable Library of the Late Edward Francis Rimbault* (London, 1877), p. 86.

16. One might also point out the absence of the laments for Prince Henry which appear repeatedly in many of the other sources, particularly those from London and the Cambridge area.

17. Merro had witnessed the will of Ann Tomkins of Gloucester, stepmother to the composer. See Ashbee, "Lowe, Jenkins and Merro," p. 311.

18. See Emil Vogel, *Bibliothek der Gedruckten Weltlichen Vocalmusik Italiens,* II, pp. 448-49, 452-54, 458-59.

19. It is interesting to note that Byrd's *O God give ear,* the only one of the ten Psalms from the 1588 print to lack the designation "first singing part," and therefore the only one which may have been conceived without voices and viols in mind, is the only Psalm from Byrd's 1588 set which Merro chooses for inclusion in his section of five-part *full* anthems, which it opens.

20. The song and its attribution are fully discussed by Philip Brett in "The Songs of William Byrd," unpublished Ph.D. dissertation (Cambridge University), 1965, pp. 135-43.

21. See Brett, *Consort Songs,* p. 185, for a discussion of this question and a listing of the variants.

22. In Add. 37402-6 we find "she hath but one eye, and that is almost out, and a hole in her hip or there about," which RCM 2059 softens to the relatively innocuous "with a hole in her ear and a slit in her nose"!

23. Described by Philip Brett in an unpublished paper delivered to the national meeting of the American Musicological Society, 1970, to appear in a revised version in *Source Materials and the Interpretation of Music: a Memorial Volume to Thurston Dart* (in press).

24. It is also possible that Merro might have acquired the piece from Thomas Tomkins, another likely link to the Chapel Royal.

25. Philip Brett, "The Songs of William Byrd," p. 238.

26. William Byrd, *Consort Songs,* in *Byrd Ed,* XV (edited by Philip Brett), (London, 1970), p. 179. The song is printed on pp. 158-60 of that volume.

27. See *Ye Sacred Muses* (opening), *Thou poets' friend* (opening), *Content is rich* (transition to the final repeated section), *As Caesar wept* (transition to the final repeated section). Only *Triumph with pleasant melody* (opening of part 2) offers a roughly comparable use of the point. Significantly, Brett finds this last work unlike Byrd: "The claims of Thomas [Byrd as the possible composer] might be dismissed more easily if the piece did not itself cast doubts on William's authorship. It is crude and unlovely. Yet it is not so removed from the composer's mature style as the more beautiful 'The day delayed' or 'My little sweet darling,' and I believe it must be accepted as a very early, and rather ambitious attempt at the form." Ibid., p. 171. All the other songs cited above also appear in the same volume.

28. Though not so late as the other additions in paler ink (e.g., Lugge's *Short Service,* the section of consort songs, etc.).

29. One further source, British Library Additional MS 29481, shows certain scribal similarities to Merro's MSS (formation of clefs, custos, long note stems, "jagged" barring of eighth-notes). Pamela Willetts, though recognizing its similarity to 4180 and 17792, ultimately concluded that the hand was not the same (personal communication).

Chapter 5

1. John Ward, "*Joan qd John* and other fragments at Western Reserve University," *Aspects of Medieval and Renaissance Music,* edited by John La Rue (New York, 1966), pp. 832-55.

2. Gordon Spearritt, "Richard Nicholson and the 'Joane, quoth John' Songs," *Studies in Music,* II (1968), 33-42; also by the same author, "The Consort Songs and Madrigals of Richard Nicholson," *Musicology,* II (1965/67), 42-67. See also Jeffrey Mark, "The Song-cycle in England: Some Early 17th-century Examples," *MT,* LXVI (1925), 325-28.

3. "Superius" (17786), "Medius" (17787), "Contratenor" (17788), "Tenor" (17789), "Sextus" (17790), and "Bassus" (17791).

4. David Pinto has suggested that the subsidiary hand in Christ Church MS 67, also responsible for fol. 36 of Christ Church MS 62, "may be a later example of that found in British Library Add. 17786-91." See Pinto, "William Lawes' Music for Viol Consort," *EMu,* VI (1978), 22. Though the hands are not without similarities, it is difficult to agree with Pinto's suggestion that they are identical (cf. pls. 8 and 17).

5. Philip Brett, ed., *Consort Songs, MB,* XXII (1967), p. 178.

6. See E.H. Fellowes, *William Byrd* (London, 1936), pp. 162-63.

7. Philip Brett, "The Songs of William Byrd," unpublished Ph.D. dissertation (Cambridge University), 1965, pp. 126-28.

8. See the separate catalogue provided for Add. 17790.

9. Gordon Spearritt's hypothesis that the scribe forgot to copy the words of *Joan quoth John* into the medius book (17787) shows how easily the scholar can arrive at false conclusions by taking one piece out of the context of the whole manuscript. See his "Richard Nicholson and the 'Joane, quoth John' Songs," pp. 36-37.

10. *Fitzwilliam Virginal Book,* II, p. 12, arranged by Farnaby; Paris, Rés. 1186, fol. 55^v; and the Camphuysen MS all contain it in keyboard versions.

11. The piece has been published with words added to the cantus part in Brett, *Consort Songs,* p. 98.

12. The closest parallel would be Isaiah 51:6—"Lift up your eyes to the heavens and look at the earth beneath."

13. Claude M. Simpson, *The British Broadside Ballad and its Music* (New Brunswick, 1966).

14. Sternfield and Greer, *English Madrigal Verse.*

15. G.E.P. Arkwright, "Early Elizabethan Stage Music," *The Musical Antiquary,* I (1909/10), 34.

16. See Brett, *Consort Songs,* p. 183. The song is printed on p. 90.

17. This possibility was suggested by Philip Brett on the basis of 17786-91 in *Consort Songs,* p. xix. An illustration of vocal lines being doubled by viols could be provided by a detail from

the portrait of Sir Henry Unton in the National Portrait Gallery, London. It appears that all five performers are playing viols, and some may be singing was well. One should point out, however, that the painting has also been interpreted as a depiction of a boy (with his back to the viewer) singing to the accompaniment of four viols. See Philip Brett and Thurston Dart, "Songs by William Byrd in manuscripts at Harvard," *Harvard Library Bulletin,* XIV (1960), 343.

18.   For an alternative hypothesis, see *Orlando Gibbons: Verse Anthems,* in *EECM,* III (edited by David Wolstan), (London, 1962), pp. viii and 221. The question is discussed in Craig Monson, "Consort Song and Verse Anthem: a Few Performance Problems," *Journal of the Viola da Gamba Society of America,* XIII (1976), 4-11.

19.   All three are printed in *Six English Tunes,* edited by Peter Warlock.

20.   David Fuller, "The Jonsonian Masque and its Music, *ML,* LIV (1973), 449.

21.   Brett, *Consort Songs,* p. 175.

22.   James Pruett, "Charles Butler—Musician, Grammarian, Apiarist," *MQ,* XLIX (1963), 498-509, contains a facsimile of the *Bees' Madrigal* and a transcription of certain sections of the piece. Butler's ear for bee's music, already apparent from the first edition of *The Feminine Monarchie* (1609), only appears fully developed in the 1634 edition, rather late for a connection with 17786-91.

23.   Alfred Harbage, *Annals of English Drama* (Philadelphia, 1964), pp. 54-55.

24.   John Ward, "Music for *A Handeful of Pleasant Delites,*" *JAMS,* X (1957), 171n.

25.   Brett, *Consort Songs,* pp. 183-84.

26.   That is:

27.   Sidney Beck, ed., *The First Book of Consort Lessons Collected by Thomas Morley* (New York, 1959), pp. 29-30. The "James" is James Harding (ca. 1560-1626), who from 1581 until 1625 served as flutist of the King's Musick.

28.   I should like to thank Professor Alan Curtis for pointing out the existence of these last three versions to me.

29.   In nos. 36 and 37 circular patterns are inserted for the first time to fill up the unused portions of the staves, while other staves are left blank, a practice entirely absent from earlier folios of the manuscripts, where pieces were entered close upon one another. Because both nos. 38 and 39 are attributed to Nathaniel Patrick (d. 1594/5), one would expect them to have appeared in the group of older songs, nos. 7-12, where Patrick's *Climb not too high* occurs. The scribe must have discovered them later and inserted them, together with nos. 36-7, on the blank folios before no. 40. Patterns of circular penwork again are used to fill blank staves, creating the impression that the copyist was trying to fill more space than really necessary. Furthermore, in several of the partbooks both pieces are unnumbered, while in the "sextus" book *Send forth thy sighs* was originally numbered "36": the top half of the "6" has been erased and a tail added to form a lopsided "9".

30. See David Brown, Walter Collins, and Peter le Huray, *Thomas Weelkes Collected Anthems,* in *MB,* XXIII (London, 1966), p. xviii.

31. J. Foster, *Alumni Oxoniensis* (Oxford, 1891), p. 1422.

32. Anthony a Wood, *Fasti Oxonienses,* I (London, 1721), p. 203.

33. Edward Darcy, dedicatee of Weelkes's *Ballets and Madrigals to 5 voices* (1595) and George Brooke, dedicatee of the *Madrigals of 6 parts* (1600) were prominent members of Raleigh's circle, and also strengthen Weelkes's link to the Mermaid Tavern. See G.A. Philipps, "Patronage in the Career of Thomas Weelkes," *MQ,* LXII (1976), 46-57.

34. Wyn K. Ford, "The Life and Works of John Okeover (or Oker)," *PRMA,* LXXXIV (1957-1958), 71-80.

35. Wood, *Fasti Oxonienses,* I, p. 256.

36. A music inventory from Thorndon Hall, Essex, main residence of the Petre family, bears an annotation dated June 1616 stating that music books had been "delivered into the charge of John Oker." See John Bennet and Pamela Willetts, "Richard Mico," *Chelys,* VII (1977), 24-46.

37. See Peter Platt, "Dering's Life and Training," *ML,* XXXIII (1952), 41-49.

38. Joseph Kerman, "Byrd's Motets: Chronology and Canon," *JAMS,* XIV (1961), 361n.

39. David Brown, *Thomas Weelkes,* (London, 1969), pp. 155-56.

40. John Morehen, "The Southwell Minster Tenor Part-Book in the Library of St. Michael's College Tenbury (MS. 1382)," *ML,* L (1969), 352-64.

41. This hypothesis was originally suggested by Philip Brett, *Consort Songs,* p. xxi.

42. J. Bunker Clark and Maurice Bevan, "New biographical facts about Adrian Batten," *JAMS,* XXIII (1970), 332.

43. For this information I am indebted to Francis W. Steer, editor of *The Catalogue of Archives of New College, Oxford.*

44. Philip Brett, "The Two Musical Personalities of Thomas Weelkes," *ML,* LIII (1972), 369-76.

45. The other notable exception being Christ Church MSS 56-60.

46. Tenbury MS 1382, on the other hand, contains a large number of contrafacta of Byrd motets and also a contrafactum of the verse anthem, *Behold O God,* which gets a new text, *Now Israel may say.* The verse anthem is otherwise known only from Bodleian MS Mus D 162—a New College manuscript.

47. David Fuller, "The Jonsonian Masque and its Music," *ML,* LIV (1973), 449. Printed in Andrew J. Sabol, *Four Hundred Songs and Dances from the Stuart Masque* (Providence, 1978), pp. 333-34.

48. Tenbury 1382 likewise contains three anthems by Patrick which do not reappear elsewhere.

49. There are records to show that two such provincial imitations of courtly fashions were attempted at Lincoln by John Hilton in 1593, and Arkwright has suggested that Patrick's dramatic songs were perhaps originally intended for similar dramatic productions at Worcester. See G.E.P. Arkwright, "Elizabethan Choirboy Plays and their Music," *PRMA,* XL (1913/14), 131-32. For additional consideration of the possible use of these songs for university drama, see the discussion of Add. 17797.

50. Wigthorpe's treatment of *To plead my faith* by Daniel Bachelor, which also appeared in *A Musical Banquet* (1610), differs somewhat from this pattern. In addition to a few minor textual changes, both the melody and especially the bass-line reveal a number of differences from the published text, which would seem to indicate that Wigthorpe was working from an alternative to Robert Dowland's printed version. For a further discussion of the two consort song settings of Dowland's *Sorrow stay,* see chap. 6.

51. See Andrew J. Sabol, "Two Songs with Accompaniment for an Elizabethan Choirboy Play," *Studies in the Renaissance,* V (1958), 155.

52. Mary Chan, "*Cynthia's Revels* and Music for a Choir School: Christ Church Manuscript 439," *Studies in the Renaissance,* XVIII (1971), 149.

53. Brett, *Consort Songs,* p. 183.

54. The anonymous *Come, Charon, Come* in Drexel 4180-5 does involve a dialogue between Charon and a soul, perhaps the earliest extant setting of this popular Elizabethan and Jacobean subject (see Brett, *Consort Songs,* pp. 53 and 181). There is nothing, however, to connect it with a specific play.

55. For example, Robert Jones's *Ultimum Vale* (1605), *Fourth Book* (1609); Bartlet's *Book of Ayres* (1606); Coperario's *Funeral Tears* (1606); Ferrabosco's *Ayres* (1609), etc.

56. See *Byrd Ed,* XV, nos. 1, 2, 4, 5. Arkwright provides evidence of choral sections in Elizabethan play songs; see his "Elizabethan Choirboy Plays and their Music," p. 125.

57. Brett, *Consort Songs,* p. 182.

58. John Bergsagel, "The Date and provenance of the Forrest-Heyther Collection of Tudor Masses," *ML,* XLIV (1963), 246.

59. In the manuscripts outside this Oxford circle where we find examples of Nicolson's work, such abbreviations do not occur (e.g., Drexel 4180-5; RCM 1145).

60. Philip Brett logically suggests that this consort song arrangement may be the work of the copyist rather than the composer's conception; *Consort Songs,* p. 183.

61. Both versions appear in Brett, *Consort Songs,* pp. 87-88.

62. *The Catalogue of Manuscript Music in the British Museum,* vol. I, p. 7.

63. Peter le Huray, *Music and the Reformation in England* (London, 1967), p. 320.

64. Sleeve notes to *Music at Magdalen: Record I The xvii Century,* (Argo ZRG 693), 1972.

65. Brett, *Consort Songs,* p. 173.

66. Gordon Spearritt, on the other hand, apparently failed to notice any stylistic difference between this song and Nicolson's others for voice and viols: "The style of writing is similar to that of the consort songs discussed earlier, and so to that of Nicholson's madrigals." Spearritt, "The Consort Songs and madrigals of Richard Nicholson." p. 46.

67. Joseph Kerman, *The Elizabethan Madrigal, A Comparative Study* (New York, 1962), p. 99. Nicolson's works could hardly be considered "clear precursors of Byrd's 'Pastorals'," as Kerman suggests (p. 105n), given the relative ages of the composers.

68. Gordon Spearritt reached this conclusion in his article cited above (n. 66). While his conclusions are probably correct, he fails to produce any especially convincing stylistic criteria to substantiate them. John Morehen includes the anonymous madrigals in *Richard*

Nicolson Collected Madrigals, in *EM,* XXXVII (London, 1976), where all Nicolson's madrigals can be found. For another discussion of the madrigals, see Craig Monson, "Richard Nicolson: madrigals from Jacobean Oxford," *E Mu,* VI (1978), 429-35.

69. Printed in *The Triumphs of Oriana (1601),* in *EM,* XXXII (revised by Thurston Dart), (London, 1962), pp. 88-101. See also *Richard Nicolson, Collected Madrigals,* in *EM,* XXXVII (edited by John Morehen), (London, 1976), pp. 58-74.

70. Ibid., p. 1.

71. Ibid., pp. 20-21.

72. Ibid., pp. 29-37.

73. Ibid., p. 2-5.

74. Ibid., p. 47.

75. Ibid., pp. 27-28, bar 64 onward.

76. Frederick Boas, *University Drama in the Tudor Age* (New York, 1971), p. 348.

77. Alfred Harbage, *Annals of English Drama* (Philadelphia, 1964), pp. 12-13.

78. Boas, *University Drama,* p. 385.

79. *Ajax Flagellifer* (1605), *Julius et Gonzaga* and *Spurius* (both 1617), *Andronicus Comnenus* (1618), *Phocus* (1619), *Doublet, Breeches, and Shirt* (1620), *Fuimus Troes* (1625); Harbage, *Annals of English Drama,* pp. 90-121.

80. The anthem is printed in William Byrd, *The English Anthems,* in *Byrd Ed,* XI, (edited by Craig Monson), (London, in press). Its authenticity is discussed more fully in that volume.

81. For further discussion of this source and its unreliability, see Philip Brett, "Edward Paston (1550-1630): a Norfolk Gentleman and his Musical Collection," *Transactions of the Cambridge Bibliographical Society,* IV (1964), especially p. 60; Joseph Kerman, review of Byrd *CW* in *JAMS,* III (1950), 276; Kerman, "Byrd's Motets: Chronology and Canon," pp. 374, 381-82; and Craig Monson, "Thomas Weelkes: a new fa-la," *MT,* CXIII (1972), 133-35.

82. The other anthem by Stonnard, *Hearken all ye people,* is published by Concordia Publishing House, no. 98-1856, (St. Louis, 1966), in an edition by John Morehen.

83. Margaret Crum, "Early Lists of the Oxford Music School Collection," *ML,* XLVIII (1967), 23.

84. Ibid., p. 30.

85. Bergsagel, "The Date and Provenance of the Forrest-Heyther Collection of Tudor Masses," pp. 245-46.

86. John Morehen, "The Sources of English Cathedral Music, c. 1617-c. 1644," unpublished Ph.D. dissertation (Cambridge University, 1969), p. 65.

87. Crum, "Early Lists of the Oxford Music School Collection," p. 23.

88. *Thomas Tomkins, Musica Deo Sacra II,* in *EECM,* IX (edited by Bernard Rose), (London, 1968), p. 164.

89. Foster, *Alumni Oxoniensis,* II, p. 474.

90. Willa McClung Evans, *Henry Lawes Musician and Friend of Poets* (London, 1941), p. 134. It is puzzling that Evelyn, who matriculated in 1637, here describes a play with music performed

before King Charles at Christ Church in late August 1636. Perhaps he had paid an earlier visit to the University the previous year.

91. At least one later musician recognized the inappropriateness of these designations, for they have been crossed out in D 213, where they had been used to distinguish between the two parts of a "gimmel" in Mundy's *O give thanks unto the Lord.*

92. John Morehen, "The Southwell Minster Tenor Part-Book," p. 363.

93. The other two are also verse anthems: the incomplete *Bow down thine ear* survives in the Peterhouse Caroline partbooks, while *I will magnify thee* occurs at Durham, and in the secular sources Add. 29366-8 and Christ Church 61-66.

94. Crum, "Early Lists of the Oxford Music School Collection," p. 26.

95. The anthem survives in manuscript additions to three of the volumes from Barnard's *First Book of Selected Church Music.* In this light it is interesting to note that the Oxford source, Tenbury 1382 ultimately found its way to Lichfield as part of the collection of John Alcock, organist at Lichfield from 1750 until 1760.

96. David Wulstan was apparently unaware of the alternative attribution to Edward Smith. See the sleeve notes to *Music at Magdalen I* (Argo ZRG 698), which includes performances of both Nicolson's verse anthems. Morehen likewise fails to remark upon the extensive differences between the two settings, though he does point out the concordance with the Durham manuscripts; see his "Sources," p. 415.

97. Ibid., pp. 12 and 24.

98. Ibid., pp. 59-71. Brooking came from Bristol to Durham in 1620.

99. Ibid., p. 97. Morehen writes that the Durham sources "must be regarded as a prime source for the not inconsiderable corpus of music by Durham composers Edward Smith, Elias Smith, William Smith, John Foster, John Greers and Henry Palmer."

100. Only one mean part survives in the Durham set of partbooks containing Smith's anthem. It transmits the mean solo in verse 3 and one of those in verse 4, as well as the top part for all the choruses. My knowledge of Smith's anthem is based upon the photostats of the Durham MSS in the Senate House Library, London, which do not include the folios on which the first contratenor part might be found.

101. In addition, the Durham organ part contains no "cues" for these missing solos.

102. One wonders if perhaps it was the text of this final section, reminiscent of Nicolson's full anthem, *O pray for the peace of Jerusalem,* which originally inspired him to rework Edward Smith's version.

103. Printed in *TCM Octavo Edition,* no. 48, (edited by S.T. Warner), (Oxford, n.d.).

104. Brown, *Thomas Weelkes.*

105. See, for example, *Almighty God which by thy son* ("and commandest him earnestly to feed thy flock"); *Behold Thou hast made my days* ("and verily every man living...", "and now, Lord, what is my hope," "O spare me a little"); *Blessed are all they* ("For thou shalt eat the labour of thy hands," "Lo, thus shall the man be blessed"); *Glorious and powerful God* ("Thou dwell'st not in stone temples," "O down on us..."); *Grant O Holy Trinity* ("And everlasting reward"), etc.

106. One exception, Nathaniel Giles, possibly a clerk at Magdalen College Chapel in 1577, later served as Master of the Choristers at Windsor and as Organist of the Chapel Royal, and was

involved in some of the London choirboy plays. He seems, however, to have abandoned Magdalen after only a single year there.

Chapter 6

1. Number 54, *Non vi bastava* by Masnelli seems to be latest; see Augustus Hughes-Hughes, *Catalogue of Manuscript Music in the British Museum,* III (London, 1906-1909), p. 223. Number 50, *Tra la dolcezza* by Luzzaschi bears the date "1599" in the British Library catalogue. Although the madrigal appears in volumes dated 1592 *(La Gloria musicale di diversi Eccelentissimi Auttori a cinque voci),* 1594 *(Quarto Libro),* and 1613 *(Seconda Scelta della madrigali a cinque voci),* I find no record of a publication in 1599. See A.G. Spiro, "The Five-Part Madrigals of Luzzasco Luzzaschi," unpublished Ph.D. dissertation (Boston University, 1961).

2. Yonge's dedicatory letter from *Musica Transalpina* is reprinted in full in Alfredo Obertello, *Madrigali Italiani in Inghilterra* (Milan, 1949), pp. 209-11.

3. Warwick Edwards, "The Performance of Ensemble Music in Elizabethan England," *PRMA,* XCVII (1970-1971), 113-23.

4. Wolfgang Boetticher, *Orlando di Lasso und seine Zeit* (Kassel, 1958), p. 202.

5. Hughes-Hughes, *Catalogue of MS Music in the B.M.,* III, p. 224.

6. Paul Doe questions the attribution to Tallis; *Tallis,* 2d ed. (London, 1976), p. 62n. Apparently the text was reasonably popular with the Elizabethans, for two other settings, ascribed to Shepherd, appear in Drexel 4180-5.

7. Joseph Kerman, "Byrd's Motets: Chronology and Canon," *JAMS,* XIV (1961), 365 and 377.

8. In addition to Dow, Tenbury 341-4 ("Mr. Roose"), Essex Record Office D/DP.Z 6/1 (anon.), Drexel 4180-5 ("Mr. Tallis"—a confusion with Tallis's motet of that title?), and Add. 17792-96.

9. The version in 37402-6 was apparently overlooked by Robert Weidner in his edition of Tye's instrumental music (Christopher Tye, *The Instrumental Music. Recent Researches in the Music of the Renaissance,* III, New Haven, 1967).

10. Warwick Edwards, "The Sources of Elizabethan Consort Music," unpublished Ph.D. dissertation (Cambridge University), 1974, p. 24.

11. Joseph Kerman, *The Elizabethan Madrigal, A Comparative Study* (New York, 1962), pp. 119-20.

12. Printed in *Richard Carlton, Madrigals to Five Voices (1601),* in *EM,* XVII (revised by Thurston Dart), (London, 1960), pp. 93-99.

13. See William Byrd, *Madrigals, Songs and Canons,* in *Byrd Ed,* XVI, (edited by Philip Brett), (London, 1976).

14. Philip Brett, "Edward Paston (1550-1630): a Norfolk Gentleman and his Musical Collection," *Transactions of the Cambridge Bibliographical Society,* IV (1964), 51-69.

15. Philip Brett questions the authenticity of this repetition in *Byrd Ed.,* XVI, p. 126.

16. Philip Brett, ed., *Consort Songs, MB,* XXII (London, 1967), p. 126.

17. Brett, *Consort Songs,* p. 181. Brett unfortunately fails to notice the attribution to Mundy.

18. Printed in Brett, *Consort Songs,* pp. 100-101. It was discussed briefly in the previous chapter dealing with the Oxford sources.

19. George Kirbye's madrigal has the title from the first edition, *Bright Phoebus;* the MSS also transmit printing errors from that edition.

20. This practice is not unknown from other sources. See, for example, Nicolson's *Sweet they say such virtue lies* in Brett, *Consort Songs,* no. 53. See also *Byrd Ed.,* XV, nos. 18, 29, 34-36, 41, though in these cases the practice usually involves the conversion of consort solos into duets or trios.

21. These folios are missing from 37404.

22. The prepublication version of East's anthem is discussed extensively in chap. 7.

23. Printed in Brett, *Consort Songs,* p. 64.

24. A few isolated examples in this format are bound into the Peterhouse Caroline partbooks.

25. Compare the setting of Byrd's *Great Service Te Deum* in Add. 17792-6.

26. Before his *Third Set,* East had not experimented with such heterogeneous contents, mixing madrigals, fantasias, consort songs, and verse anthems. Therefore, some of the nonmadrigalian pieces might have been composed before the *Second Set,* but failed to find a place there because of the more normal, homogeneous contents of the composer's first two books.

Chapter 7

1. See *A Catalogue of the very Valuable and Celebrated Library of Music Books, late the property of James Bartleman Esq... This collection will be sold by auction by Mr. White... London, 1822.*

2. E.H. Fellowes, *The Catalogue of the Manuscripts in the Library of St. Michael's College Tenbury,* (Paris, 1934), p. 249; *Robert Ramsey, English Sacred Music,* in *EECM,* VII, (edited by Edward Thompson), (London, 1967), p. 142; Ralph T. Daniel and Peter le Huray, *The Sources of English Church Music, EECM,* supplementary volume I (London, 1972), p. 6.

3. Philip Brett, ed., *Consort Songs, MB,* XXII (London, 1967), p. 174.

4. Personal communication. In the original version of this chapter, a scribal concordance between 1162 and 2033 was suggested. After subsequent discussion with Robert Ford and Pamela Willetts, the hypothesis was rejected.

5. Other sources which Ford suggests are in the same hand (RCM 2034, Drexel 4300, London, Gresham College VI.3.43-44) likewise contain the work of a later generation of composers: John Jenkins (1592-1678), Matthew Locke (1621/2-1677), William Young (d. 1662).

6. I should like to thank Mr. Ford for freely sharing his findings with me. The concordance between Christ Church 430 and the "Layton Ring MS" was also observed by Ashbee in "Instrumental music from the Library of John Browne (1608-1691), Clerk of the Parliaments," *ML,* LVIII (1977), p. 53.

7. David Pinto, "William Lawes' music for viol consort," *EMu,* VI (1978), 14-15.

8. See Andrew Ashbee, "Instrumental Music from the Library of John Browne (1608-1691)"; see also Pinto, "William Lawes' music for viol consort"; a further article by Nigel Fortune and Iain Fenlon, "Music Manuscripts of John Browne (1608-1691) and from Stanford Hall, Leicestershire," will appear in *Source Materials and the Interpretation of Music: a Memorial Volume to Thurston Dart.*

9. Pinto, "William Lawes' music for viol consort," p. 14.

10. Daniel and le Huray overlooked the Paris manuscript in *Sources of English Church Music*, p. 72.

11. Edward Thompson, "Robert Ramsey," *MQ,* XLIX (1963), 218-20.

12. Ibid., p. 220.

13. Ibid., p. 212.

14. Joseph Kerman, *The Elizabethan Madrigal, A Comparative Study* (New York, 1962), p. 253n. The fifth neapolitan is borrowed from Weelkes.

15. Compare Marenzio's very similar figure for the opening of his *Cantate Ninfe leggiadrette:*

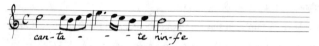

16. David Brown, *Thomas Weelkes* (London, 1969).

17. There is considerable variation in the underlay in the various manuscript versions of this section. The musical example follows that in Tenbury 1162-7.

18. Audrey Jones, "Peerson, Martin," *Grove 6,* XIV, p. 335.

19. It is difficult to agree with Marylin Wailes's enthusiastic description of Peerson as "one of her [England's] greatest composers"; "Martin Peerson," *PRMA,* LXXX (1953-1954), 59.

Chapter 8

1. We know, for example, that a thousand copies of Dowland's *Second Book of Songs* were printed—see Margaret Dowling, "The Printing of John Dowland's *Second Booke of Songes or Ayres," The Library,* Ser. 4, XII (1932), 365-82. But this number was certainly exceptional. Furthermore, as Philip Brett points out ("The Songs of William Byrd," unpublished Ph.D. dissertation, Cambridge University, 1965, pp. 213-14), a set of madrigal partbooks required many more sheets of paper than the single volume in folio for a book of lute ayres. Brett suggests 250-300 copies as a reasonable number for a set of madrigals *a* 5.

2. There is a single exception, Robert Jones's *First Set of Madrigals,* 1607, for which only the cantus and bassus survive in print. Interestingly enough, thanks to Myriell, nos. 7-10 and 22 can be reconstructed, since he copied them into Brussels MS II.4109. In addition, Thomas Hamond preserves the complete musical text for nos. 25 and 26.

3. Joseph Kerman's excellent book, *The Elizabethan Madrigal, A Comparative Study* (New York, 1962), was indeed written from the printed sources as edited by Fellowes. Information on manuscript sources is incidental and forms no great part of his work. One wonders how his conclusions would have differed had the manuscripts come under his scrutiny.

4. John Wilson, *Roger North on Music* (London, 1959), p. 290.

5. Diana Poulton, *John Dowland, His Life and Music* (London, 1972), p. 490.

6. Kerman, *The Elizabethan Madrigal,* p. 244.

7. Ibid., p. 253.

8. Lists of English musical reprints and re-issues can be found in Kerman, ibid., p. 264, and in Brett, "The Songs of William Byrd," p. 215, which amplifies and corrects Kerman.

9. The list is printed in Margaret Crum, "Early Lists of the Oxford Music School Collection," *ML,* XLVIII (1967), 24-26.

10. It appears that Morley likewise failed to appeal to eighteenth-century taste. The "list of scores" of the Madrigal Society in its early years shows that Morley was less well-known and less frequently sung than madrigalists such as Bennet and Wilbye—the clear favorite. See Percy Lovell, "'Ancient Music' in Eighteenth-Century England," *ML,* LX (1979), 401-15.

11. Kerman, *The Elizabethan Madrigal,* p. 70.

12. Ibid., p. 71.

13. Ibid., pp. 238-39. ·

14. Ibid., p. 243.

15. Ibid., pp. 34, 122-27; Jean Jacquot, "Lyrisme et sentiment tragique dans les madrigaux d'Orlando Gibbons," *Musique et Poésie au XVIIe Siècle* (Paris, 1954), pp. 139-51; Wilfred Mellers, "La Mélancholie au début du xviie siècle et le madrigal anglais," ibid., pp. 153-68.

16. Edward J. Dent, "William Byrd and the Madrigal," *Festschrift für Johannes Wolf* (Berlin, 1929), pp. 24-30.

17. Kerman, *The Elizabethan Madrigal,* p. 254.

18. Philip Brett has argued a rational basis for their decision in "Word-Setting in the Songs of Byrd," *PRMA,* XCVIII (1971-1972), 47-64.

19. Warwick Edwards, "The Performance of Ensemble Music in Elizabethan England," *PRMA,* XCVII (1970-1971), 119.

20. Ibid., p. 122.

21. Kerman, *The Elizabethan Madrigal,* p. 6.

22. This intriguing list was discussed in chap. 2, above.

23. Kerman, *The Elizabethan Madrigal,* p. 252.

24. David Greer has also argued that the serious lute ayre was an offshoot of the consort song which preceded it, and that lute ayres and part songs may have been sung as solos with viol accompaniment. See Greer, "The Part-Songs of the English Lutenists," *PRMA,* XCIV (1967-68), 97-110.

25. Kerman, *The Elizabethan Madrigal,* pp. 153 and 250, respectively.

26. Ibid., p. 254.

27. William Byrd, *Consort Songs, in Byrd Ed,* XV (edited by Philip Brett), (London, 1970).

28. See, for example, *An aged dame,* bars 45 and 49; *He that all earthly pleasure scorns,* bar 22; *Quis me statim,* bar 8; *Wretched Albinus,* passim.

29. Brett "Word-Setting in the Songs of Byrd," p. 58.

30. In *Byrd Ed,* XV, p. 177. The piece is printed on pp. 131-43 of that volume.

31. Dent, "William Byrd and the Madrigal," p. 30.

Bibliography

Books and Articles

Aplin, John. "Sir Henry Fanshawe and Two Sets of early Seventeenth-Century Part-books at Christ Church, Oxford," *ML*, LVII (1976), 11-24.

Arkwright, G.E.P. "Early Elizabethan Stage Music," *The Musical Antiquary*, I (1909-1910), 30-40.

_____. "Elizabethan Choirboy Plays and their Music," *PRMA*, XL (1913-1914), 117-38.

Ashbee, Andrew. "A Further Look at Some of the Le Strange Manuscripts," *Chelys*, V (1973-1974), 24-41.

_____. "Instrumental Music from the Library of John Browne (1608-1691), Clerk of the Parliaments," *ML*, LVIII (1977), 43-59.

_____. "Lowe, Jenkins and Merro," *ML*, XLVIII (1967), 310-11.

_____. "Pysing [Pising(e)], William," *Grove 6*, XV, p. 485.

Beeks, Graydon, "A Discussion of Tenbury MSS 1162-7," unpublished seminar paper, University of California at Berkeley, 1970.

Bennet, John, and Willetts, Pamela. "Richard Mico," *Chelys*, VII (1977), 24-46.

Bergsagel, John. "The Date and Provenance of the Forrest-Heyther Collection of Tudor Masses," *ML*, XLIV (1963), 240-48.

Bernstein, Jane. "The Chanson in England, 1530-1640: A Study of Sources and Styles," unpublished Ph.D. dissertation, University of California at Berkeley, 1974.

Blankenburg, Walter. "Fabritius [Fabricius], Albinus," *Grove 6*, VI, p. 349.

Blezzard, Judith. "The Lumley books," *MT*, CXII (1971), 128-30.

Boas, Frederick. *University Drama in the Tudor Age*. New York, 1971.

Boetticher, Wolfgang. *Orlando di Lasso und seine Zeit*. Kassel and Basel, 1958.

Botstiber, Hugo. "Musicalia in der New York Public Library," *SIMG*, IV (1903), 738-50.

Boyd, Morrison C. *Elizabethan Music and Musical Criticism*. Philadelphia, 1940.

Brennecke, Ernst. *John Milton the Elder and his Music*. New York, 1938.

Brett, Philip. "East (Easte, Est, Este), Michael," *Grove 6*, V, pp. 801-2.

_____. "Edward Paston (1550-1630): a Norfolk Gentleman and his Musical Collection," *Transactions of the Cambridge Bibliographical Society*, IV (1964), 51-69.

_____. "The English Consort Song," *PRMA*, LXXXVIII (1961-1962), 73-88.

_____, and Dart, Thurston. "Songs by William Byrd in manuscripts at Harvard," *Harvard Library Bulletin*, XIV (1960), 343-65.

_____. "The Songs of William Byrd," unpublished Ph.D. dissertation, Cambridge University, 1965.

_____. "The Two Musical Personalities of Thomas Weelkes," *ML*, LIII (1972), 369-376.

_____. "Word-Setting in the Songs of Byrd," *PRMA*, XCVIII (1971-1972), 47-64.

Brown, David. *Thomas Weelkes*. London, 1969.

Brown, Howard. *Music in the Renaissance.* Englewood Cliffs, 1976.

Browne, James. "An Elizabethan Song-Cycle," *The Cornhill Magazine,* XLVIII (1920), 572-79.

Butler, Charles. *The Principles of Musik.* London. 1636.

Buxton, John. *Elizabethan Taste.* London, 1963.

Chan, Mary. "Cynthia's Revels and Music for a Choir School: Christ Church Manuscript Mus 439," *Studies in the Renaissance,* XVIII (1971), 134-72.

Charteris, Richard. "Autographs of John Coprario," *ML,* LVI (1975), 41-46.

_____. "Consort Music Manuscripts in Archbishop Marsh's Library Dublin," *R.M.A. Chronicle,* XIII (1977), 27-63.

_____. "Four Caroline Part-books," *ML,* LIX (1978), 49-51.

_____. *John Coprario: a thematic catalogue of his Music.* New York, 1977.

_____. "John Coprario's Five- and Six-Part Pieces: Instrumental or Vocal?" *ML,* LVII (1976), 370-78.

_____. "A Rediscovered Source of English Consort Music," *Chelys,* V (1973-1974), 3-6.

Clark, Andrew. *Register of the University of Oxford.* Oxford, 1887-1889.

Clark, J. Bunker, "Adrian Batten and John Barnard: Colleagues and Collaborators," *MD,* XXII (1968), 207-29.

_____, and Bevan, Maurice. "New biographical facts about Adrian Batten," *JAMS,* XXIII (1970), 331-33.

Crum, Margaret. "A Seventeenth-Century Collection of Music Belonging to Thomas Hamond, a Suffolk Landowner," *Bodleian Library Record,* VI (1957), 373-86.

_____. "Early Lists of the Oxford Music School Collection," *ML,* XLVIII (1967), 23-34.

Daniel, Ralph T., and le Huray, Peter. *The Sources of English Church Music 1549-1660. EECM,* supplementary volume I. London, 1972.

Dart, Thurston. "Music and Musicians at Chichester Cathedral," *ML,* XLII (1961), 221-26.

_____. "Two English Musicians in Heidelberg in 1613," *MT,* CXI (1970), 29-32.

_____. "The Repertory of the Royal Wind Music," *The Galpin Society Journal,* XI (1958), 70-77.

Dent, Edward J. "William Byrd and the Madrigal," *Festschrift für Johannes Wolf.* Berlin, 1929. Pp. 24-30.

Dictionary of National Biography. Edited by Sir Sidney Lee. 63 volumes, 3 supplementary volumes. London, 1920.

Doe, Paul. *Tallis,* 2d edition. London, 1976.

Doughtie, Edward. *Lyrics from English Ayres 1596-1622.* Cambridge, Mass., 1970.

Dowling, Margaret, "The Printing of John Dowland's *Second Booke of Songs or Ayres,*" *The Library,* Ser. 4, XII (1932), 365-82.

Duckles, Vincent. "The English Elegy of the Late Renaissance," *Aspects of Medieval and Renaissance Music.* Edited by Jan La Rue. New York, 1966. Pp. 134-53.

Eccles, Mark. "Martin Peerson and the Blackfriars," *Shakespeare Survey,* XI (1958), 100-106.

Edwards, Warwick. "The Performance of Ensemble Music in Elizabethan England," *PRMA,* XCVII (1970-1971), 113-23.

_____. "The Sources of Elizabethan Consort Music," unpublished Ph.D. dissertation, Cambridge
University, 1974.

Evans, Willa McClung. *Henry Lawes Musician and Friend of Poets.* London, 1941.

Fellowes, Edmund H. "Bateson, Thomas," *Grove 5,* I, 497-99.

_____. *English Madrigal Verse.* Revised and enlarged by F.W. Sternfeld and David Greer, 3d edition. Oxford, 1967.

_____. *Orlando Gibbons.* 2nd edition. London, 1951.

_____. *The Catalogue of the Manuscripts in the Library of St. Michael's College Tenbury.* Paris, 1934.

_____. *The English Madrigal Composers.* London, 1948.

_____. *William Byrd.* London, 1936.

Ford, Wyn. K., "An English Liturgical Partbook of the 17th Century," *JAMS,* XII (1959), 144-60.

_____. "The Life and Works of John Okeover (or Oker)," *PRMA,* LXXXIV (1957-1958), 71-80.

Foster, J. *Alumni Oxoniensis.* 4 vols. Oxford, 1891.

Fraenkel, Gottfried. *Decorative Music Title Pages,* New York, 1968.

Fuller, David. "The Jonsonian Masque and its Music," *ML,* LIV (1973), 440-52.

Greer, David. "The Part-Songs of the English Lutenists," *PRMA,* XCIV (1967-1968), 97-110.

Harbage, Alfred. *Annals of English Drama.* Philadelphia, 1964.

Harrison, Frank Ll. "Church Music in England," *NOHM,* IV. London, 1968. Pp. 465-519.

Hennessy, George. *Novum Repertorium Ecclesiasticum Parochiale Londinense.* London, 1898.

Hiscock, W.G. *Christ Church Miscellaney.* Oxford, 1946.

Hovendon, Robert. *The Register Booke of Christeninges, Marriages, and Burialls within the Precinct of the Cathedrall and Metropoliticall Church of Christe of Canterburie. The Publications of the Harleian Society. Registers.* Vol. 2. London, 1878.

Hughes-Hughes, Augustus. *Catalogue of Manuscript Music in the British Museum.* 4 volumes. London, 1906-1909.

Jacquot, Jean. "Lyrisme et sentiment tragique dans les madrigaux d'Orlando Gibbons," *Musique et Poésie au xvie Siècle.* Edited by Jean Jacquot. Paris, 1954, Pp. 139-52.

Jeans, Susi. "Simmes," *Grove 5,* supplementary volume, p. 410.

Jones, Audrey. "Peerson [Pearson], Martin," *Grove 6,* XIV, pp. 334-35.

Josephs, Norman. "Ives [Ive, Ivy], Simon (i)," *Grove 6,* IX, pp. 429-430.

Kerman, Joseph. "Byrd's Motets: Chronology and Canon," *JAMS,* XIV (1961), 359-82.

_____. Review of Byrd *CW,* vols. X-XVII. *JAMS,* III (1950), 273-77.

_____. *The Elizabethan Madrigal, A Comparative Study.* New York, 1962.

King, A. Hyatt. *Some British Collectors of Music c. 1600-1960.* Cambridge, 1963.

Lafontaine, Henry C. de. *The King's Musick.* London, 1909.

Lawrence, W.J. "Thomas Ravenscroft's Theatrical Associations," *Modern Language Review,* XIX (1924), 418-23.

le Huray, Peter. *Music and the Reformation in England.* London, 1967.

_____. "Towards a Definitive Study of Pre-Restoration Anglican Church Music," *MD,* XIV (1960), 167-95.

_____. "Wilkinson, (first name unknown)," *Grove 6,* XX, p. 420.

Lovell, Percy. " 'Ancient' Music in Eighteenth-Century England," *ML,* LX (1979), 401-15.

Lumsden, David. "The Sources of English Lute Music (1540-1620)," unpublished Ph.D. dissertation, Cambridge University, 1955.

Mace, Thomas. *Musick's Monument.* London, 1676.

Madan, F. *A Summary Catalogue of Western Manuscripts in the Bodleian Library at Oxford.* Oxford, 1895-1953.

Mark, Jeffrey. "Ramsey, Robert," *Grove 5,* VII, p. 41.

_____. "The Song-Cycle in England: Some Early 17th-century Examples," *MT,* LXVI (1925), 325-28.

_____. "Wilkinson, Thomas," *Grove 5,* IX, 299.

Mellers, Wilfred. "La Mélancholie au début du xviie siècle et le madrigal anglais," *Musique et Poésie au xvie Siècle.* Edited by Jean Jacquot. Paris, 1954. Pp. 153-68.

Meyer, Ernst H. *English Chamber Music.* London, 1946.

_____. *Die Mehrstimmige Spielmusik des 17. Jahrhunderts in Nord- und Mittel-Europa.* Kassel, 1934.

Monson, Craig A. "Authenticity and Chronology in Byrd's Church Anthems," *JAMS* (in press).

_____. "Consort Song and Verse Anthem: a Few Performance Problems," *Journal of the Viola da Gamba Society of America,* XIII (1976), 4-11.

_____. "George Kirbye and the English Madrigal," *ML*, LIX (1978), 290-315.

_____. "Richard Nicolson: madrigals from Jacobean Oxford," *Early Music*, VI (1978), 429-35.

_____. "Thomas Myriell's Manuscript Collection: one View of Musical Taste in Jacobean London," *JAMS*, XXX (1977), 419-65.

_____. "Thomas Weelkes: a new fa-la," *MT*, CXIII (1972), 133-35.

Morehen, John. "The English Consort and Verse Anthems," *Early Music*, VI (1978), 381-85.

_____. "The Sources of English Cathedral Music, c. 1617-c. 1644," unpublished Ph.D. dissertation, Cambridge University, 1969.

_____. "The Southwell Minster Tenor Part-Book in the Library of St. Michael's College Tenbury (MS. 1382)," *ML*, L (1969), 352-64.

Muskett, Joseph J. *Suffolk Manorial Families*. I. London, 1897.

Nagel, Willibald, "Annalen der englischen Hofmusik von der Zeit Heinrich's VIII. bis zum Tode Karl's I. (1509-1649)," *Monatsheft für Musik-Geschichte*, XXVI (1894).

Neighbour, Oliver. *The Consort and Keyboard Music of William Byrd*. London, 1978.

_____. "New Consort Music by Byrd," *MT*, CVIII (1967), 506-8.

Newcomb, Wilburn W. "Warwick, Thomas," *MGG*, XIV, cols. 262-63.

Obertello, Alfredo. *Madrigali Italiani in Inghilterra*. Milan, 1949.

Parker, William. "Thomas Myriell," *Notes and Queries*, CLXXXVIII (1945), 103.

Parrott, Andrew. "Grett and solompne singing," *Early Music*, VI (1978), 182-87.

Pattison, Bruce. *Music and Poetry of the English Renaissance*. London, 1948.

Peacham, Henry. *Complete Gentleman*. London, 1622.

Philipps. G.A. "Patronage in the Career of Thomas Weelkes," *MQ*, LXII (1976), 46-57.

Pinto, David. "William Lawes' Consort Suites for the Viols and the Autograph Sources," *Chelys*, IV (1972), 11-16.

_____. "William Lawes' Music for Viol Consort," *Early Music*, VI (1978), 12-24.

Poulton, Diana. *John Dowland, His Life and Works*. London, 1972.

Pruett, James. "Charles Butler—Musician, Grammarian, Apiarist," *MQ*, XLIX (1963), 498-509.

Ravenscroft, Thomas. *A briefe discourse*. London, 1614. Reprinted New York, 1971.

Rimbault, Edward F., ed. *The Old Cheque-book of the Chapel Royal. Camden Society*. London, 1872. Reprinted New York, 1966.

Sabol, Andrew J. *Four Hundred Songs and Dances from the Stuart Masque*. Providence, R.I., 1978.

_____. "Ravenscroft's 'Melismata' and the Children of Paul's," *Renaissance News*, XII (1959), 3-9.

_____. "Two Songs with Accompaniment for an Elizabethan Choirboy Play," *Studies in the Renaissance*, V (1958), 145-59.

Schofield, Bertram, and Dart, Thurston. "Tregian's Anthology," *ML*, XXXII (1951), 205-16.

Scott, David. "Nicholas Yonge and his transalpine music," *MT*, CXVI (1975), 875-76.

_____. *The Music of St. Paul's Cathedral*. London, 1972.

Simpson, Claude M. *The British Broadside Ballad and its Music*. New Brunswick, 1966.

Spearritt, Gordon. "Richard Nicholson and the 'Joane, quoth John' Songs," *Studies in Music*, II (1968), 33-42.

_____. "The Consort Songs and Madrigals of Richard Nicholson," *Musicology*, II (1965/1967), 42-67.

Spiro, A.G. "The Five-Part Madrigals of Luzzasco Luzzaschi," unpublished Ph.D. dissertation, Boston University, 1961.

Squire, W.B., and Erlebach, R. "The Catalogue of the Manuscripts in the Library of the Royal College of Music," unpublished typescript.

Stainer, Charles. "Fabritius [Fabricius], Albinus," *Grove 5*, III, 2-3.

Stevens, Denis. *Thomas Tomkins*. New York, 1967.

Stevens, John. *Music and poetry in the early Tudor court*. London, 1961.

Thompson, Edward. "Robert Ramsey," *MQ,* XLIX (1963), 210-24.

Venn, John, and Venn, John A. *Alumni Cantabrigiensis.* Cambridge, 1922-1954.

_____. *University of Cambridge Matriculations and Degrees, 1544-1659.* Cambridge, 1913.

Vining, Paul. "English Church Music Sources," *MT,* CXIV (1973), 257-58.

_____. "Orlando Gibbons: an Index of the Full and Verse Anthems," *Early Music,* III (1975), 379-81.

_____. "Orlando Gibbons: the Incomplete Verse Anthems," *ML,* LV (1974), 70-76.

Vogel, Emil, and Einstein, Alfred, Lesure, Francois, Sartori, Claudio. *Bibliografia della Musica Italiana Vocale Profana Pubblicata dal 1500 al 1700.* Pomezia, 1977.

Wailes, Marylin. "Martin Peerson," *PRMA,* LXXX (1953-1954), 59-71.

Ward, John. "*Joan qd John* and other fragments at Western Reserve University," *Aspects of Medieval and Renaissance Music.* Edited by Jan La Rue. New York, 1966. Pp. 832-55.

_____. "Music for *A Handefull of Pleasant Delites,"JAMS,* X (1957), 151-80.

Willetts, Pamela. *Handlist of Music Manuscripts acquired 1908-1967.* London, 1967.

_____. "John Lilly, musician and music copyist," *Bodleian Library Record,* VII (1967), 307-11.

_____. "Musical Connections of Thomas Myriell," *ML,* XLIX (1968), 36-42.

_____. "Music from the Circle of Anthony Wood at Oxford," *British Museum Quarterly,* XXIV (1961), 71-75.

_____. "Sir Nicholas Le Strange and John Jenkins," *ML,* XLII (1961), 30-43.

_____. "The Identity of Thomas Myriell," *ML,* LIII (1972), 431-33.

Wilson, John. *Roger North on Music.* London, 1959.

Wood, Anthony à. *Fasti Oxonienses.* London, 1721.

Woodfill, Walter L. *Musicians in English Society from Elizabeth to Charles I.* Princeton, 1953.

Wulstan, David. Sleeve notes to *Music at Magdalen: the xvii Century.* (Argo ZRG 693), 1972.

Music Consulted

Amner, John. *Sacred Hymns.* London, 1615.

Arkwright, G.E.P., ed. *Six Madrigals to Four Voices by George Kirbye. Old English Edition,* III. London, 1891.

_____. *Six Madrigals to Six Voices by George Kirbye. Old English Edition,* V. London, 1892.

Barclay Squire, W., and Maitland, J.A. Fuller, eds. *The Fitzwilliam Virginal Book,* 2 vols. Leipzig, 1899. Reprinted New York, 1963.

Beck, Sidney, ed. *The First Book of Consort Lessons Collected by Thomas Morley.* New York, 1959.

Brett, Philip, ed. *Consort Songs. MB,* XXII. London, 1967.

Byrd, William. *The Collected Works of William Byrd.* 20 vols. Edited by Edmund H. Fellowes. London, 1937-1950.

_____. *The Collected Works of William Byrd.* Edited by E.H. Fellowes and revised under the direction of Thurston Dart. Vols. 2, 3, 12, 13, 14.

_____. *Consort Songs. The Byrd Edition,* XV. Edited by Philip Brett. London, 1970.

_____. *The English Anthems. The Byrd Edition,* XI. Edited by Craig Monson. London (in press).

_____. *Madrigals, Songs and Canons. The Byrd Edition,* XVI. Edited by Philip Brett. London, 1976.

Carlton, Richard. *Madrigals to Five Voices (1601). The English Madrigalists,* XXVII. Edited by E.H. Fellowes, revised by Thurston Dart. London, 1960.

Croce, Giovanni. *Musica Sacra.* London, 1608.

Damon, William. *The Second Book of the Musicke of M. William Damon.* London, 1591.

Dowland, John. *Lachrimae, or Seaven Teares* [1605]. Facsimile edition with commentary by Warwick Edwards. Leeds, 1974.

————. *Second Book of Songs (1600). The English Lute-Songs,* V and VI. Edited by E.H. Fellowes, revised by Thurston Dart. London, 1969.

Dowland, Robert. *A Musicall Banquet (1610). The English Lute-Songs,* XX. Edited by Peter Stroud. London, 1968.

East, Michael. *First Set of Madrigals to 3, 4, and 5 parts (1604). The English Madrigalists,* XXIX. Edited by E.H. Fellowes, revised by Thurston Dart. London, 1960.

————. *Fourth Set of Books. The English Madrigalists,* XXXIb. Revised by Philip Brett and Thurston Dart. London, 1962.

————. *Third Set of Books. The English Madrigalists,* XXXIa. Revised by Thurston Dart, Philip Brett, and Alexis Vlasto. London, 1962.

Gibbons, Orlando. *Do not repine fair sun.* Edited by Philip Brett. London, 1961.

————. *First Set of Madrigals and Motets (1612). The English Madrigalists,* V. Edited by E.H. Fellowes, revised by Thurston Dart. London, 1964.

————. *Full Anthems, Hymns and Fragmentary Verse Anthems. Early English Church Music,* XXI. Edited by David Wulstan. London, 1978.

————. *Verse Anthems. Early English Church Music,* III. Edited by David Wulstan. London, 1962.

Guami, Giuseppe. *Canzoni da Sonare a quattro, cinque e otto voci con basso continuo.* Edited by Treneo Fuser and Oscar Mischiati. Florence, 1968.

Jones, Robert. *First Set of Madrigals (1607). The English Madrigalists,* XXXVa. Edited by E.H. Fellowes, revised by Thurston Dart. London, 1961.

Kirbye, George (See also Arkwright, G.E.P.)

————. *First Set of Madrigals (1597). The English Madrigalists,* XXIV. Edited by E.H. Fellowes, revised by Thurston Dart; associate editor, Philip Brett. London, 1960.

Leighton, William. *The Tears or Lamentations of a Sorrowful Soul. Early English Church Music,* XI. Edited by Cecil Hill. London, 1970.

Marlowe, Richard, ed. *Giles and Richard Farnaby: Keyboard Music. Musica Britannica,* XXIV. London, 1965.

Morley, Thomas. *Canzonets or Little Short Songs (1593). The English Madrigalists,* I. Edited by E.H. Fellowes, revised by Thurston Dart. London, 1956.

————. *Canzonets to Five and Six Voices (1597). The English Madrigalists,* III. Edited by E.H. Fellowes, revised by Sally Dunkley. London, 1977.

————. *First Book of Ballets (1595). The English Madrigalists,* IV. Edited by E.H. Fellowes, revised by Thurston Dart. London, 1965.

————. *First Book of Madrigals (1594). The English Madrigalists,* II. Edited by E.H. Fellowes, revised by Thurston Dart. London, 1963.

————. *The Triumphs of Oriana. The English Madrigalists,* XXXII. Edited by E.H. Fellowes, revised by Thurston Dart. London, 1962.

Nicolson, Richard. *Collected Madrigals. The English Madrigalists,* XXXVII. Edited by John Morehen. London, 1976.

————. *When Jesus sat at Meat. Tudor Church Music Octavo Edition.* Edited by S.T. Warner. Oxford, n.d.

Peerson, Martin. *Mottects or Grave Chamber Music.* London, 1630.

————. *Private Music.* London, 1620.

Ramsey, Robert. *English Sacred Music. Early English Church Music,* VII. Edited by Edward Thompson.
London, 1967.

Ravenscroft, Thomas. *Pammelia; Deuteromelia; Melismata.* Edited by MacEdward Leach. Philadelphia, 1961.

Sabol, Andrew J. *Four Hundred Songs and Dances from the Stuart Masque.* Providence, R.I., 1978.

Stonnard, William. *Hearken all ye people.* Edited by John Morehen. St. Louis, 1966.

Tomkins, Thomas. *Musica Deo Sacra, I, II, and III. Early English Church Music,* V, IX, and XIV. Edited by Bernard Rose. London, 1965, 1968, and 1973.

_____. *Songs of 3, 4, 5, and 6 Parts (1622). The English Madrigalists,* XVIII. Revised by Thurston Dart. London, 1960.

Tye, Christopher. *The Instrumental Music. Recent Researches in the Music of the Renaissance,* III. Edited by Robert Weidner. New Haven, 1967.

Vautor, Thomas. *Songs of Divers Airs and Natures (1619). The English Madrigalists,* XXXIV. Edited by E.H. Fellowes, revised by Thurston Dart. London, 1958.

Ward, John. *Madrigals to 3. 4. 5. and 6. Parts (1613). The English Madrigalists,* XIX. Edited by E.H. Fellowes, revised by Thurston Dart. London, 1968.

Watson, Thomas. *Italian Madrigals Englished.* London, 1590.

Weelkes, Thomas. *Airs or Fantastic Spirites (1608). The English Madrigalists,* XIII. Edited by E.H. Fellowes, revised by Thurston Dart. London, 1965.

_____. *Ballets and Madrigals to Five Voices (1598). The English Madrigalists,* X. Edited by E.H. Fellowes, revised by Thurston Dart. London, 1968.

_____. *Collected Anthems. Musica Britannica,* XXIII. Edited by David Brown, Walter Collins, and Peter le Huray. London, 1966.

_____. *Madrigals of Five and Six Parts (1600). The English Madrigalists,* XI and XII. Edited by E.H. Fellowes, revised by Thurston Dart. London, 1968.

_____. *Madrigals to 3, 4, 5 and 6 Voices (1597). The English Madrigalists,* IX. Edited by E.H. Fellowes, revised by Thurston Dart. London, 1967.

Wilbye, John. *First Set of Madrigals (1598). The English Madrigalists,* VI. Edited by E.H. Fellowes, revised by Thurston Dart. London, 1966.

_____. *Second Set of Madrigals (1609). The English Madrigalists,* VII. Edited by E.H. Fellowes, revised by Thurston Dart. London, 1966.

Yonge, Nicholas. *Musica Transalpina I, 1588.* Facsimile Edition. New York, 1972.

_____. *Musica Transalpina II.* London, 1597.

Index

Manuscript Index

Title Index for Vocal Works

Works appearing in the MSS inventoried above include citations of the relevant MS numbers in parentheses. Page numbers in italic indicate the location of these inventories in the text.